T0330569

State Competence and Economic Growth in Japan

In economics, few issues are more central than the role of the state in the economy; in Japanese studies, few are more central than the role that the Japanese government has played in postwar economic growth.

With exquisite attention to theory and meticulous attention to detail, this book focuses on both these topics with startling results. Yoshiro Miwa asks whether a state can correct market failures, and in particular he critically analyses the performance of the Japanese economy as a result of state intervention in it. In order to examine the capacity of the state to promote growth, Miwa examines the Japanese machine tool industry, the government's role in promoting this sector and government efforts to achieve growth in small and medium-sized enterprises in Japan.

Despite the huge interest worldwide in Japan's economic history and industrial performance, there is no other book that has approached this important topic in such a theoretically rigorous and incisive manner.

Yoshiro Miwa is Professor of Economics at the University of Tokyo.

Routledge Studies in the Growth Economies of Asia

State Competence and Economic Growth in Japan

Yoshiro Miwa

LONDON AND NEW YORK

First published 1998 in Japanese by
Yuki-Kaku Publishing Co., Ltd.Address 2-17,
Kanda Jimbo-cho, Chiyoda-ku, Tokyo 101-0051, Japan

This edition published 2004
by RoutledgeCurzon

Published 2013 by
Routledge
2 Park Square, Milton Park, Abingdon, Oxon, OX14 4RN

Simultaneously published in the USA and Canada
by Routledge
711 Third Avenue, New York, NY 10017

Routledge is an imprint of the Taylor & Francis Group, an informa business

© 1998, 2004 Yoshiro Miwa

Typeset in Perpetua by Taylor & Francis Books Ltd

British Library Cataloguing in Publication Data
A catalogue record for this book is available from the
British Library

Library of Congress Cataloging-in-Publication Data
A catalog record for this book has been requested

ISBN 978-0-415-32875-3 (hbk)

To my wife, Kazuko

Contents

List of Illustrations

Figures

Tables

List of abbreviations

ARC	Administrative Reform Committee
DS	Deregulation Subcommittee (of ARC)
EPA	Economic Planning Agency
FILP	Fiscal investment and loan program
FTC	Fair Trade Commission
IBJ	Industrial Bank of Japan
JDB	Japan Development Bank
JFIUSP	Japanese Federation of Industrial Unions of Steel Products
JMTBA	Japan Machine Tool Builders Association
JNCA	Japan Newspaper Companies Association
LDP	Liberal Democratic Party
MIPA	Machinery Industries Promotion Act
MITI	Ministry of International Trade and Industry
MoF	Ministry of Finance
MTBA	Machine Tool Building Act
NGMA	National General Mobilization Act
PTCA	Precision Tool Control Association
SCA	Shipbuilding Control Association
SMEA	Small and Medium-sized Enterprise Agency

Preface

I

The legislature, were it possible that its deliberations could be always directed, not by the clamorous importunity of partial interest but by an extensive view of the general good, ought upon this very account, perhaps, to be particularly careful neither to establish any new monopolies of this kind, nor to extend further those which are already established. Every such regulation introduces some degree of real disorder into the constitution of the state, which it will be difficult afterwards to cure without occasioning another disorder.

To expect, indeed, that freedom of trade should ever be entirely restored in Great Britain, is as absurd as to expect that an Oceana or Utopia should ever be established in it. Not only the prejudices of the public, but what is much more unconquerable, the private interests of many individuals, irresistibly oppose it. ... The member of parliament who supports every proposal for strengthening this monopoly, is sure to acquire not only the reputation of understanding trade, but great popularity and influence with an order of men whose numbers and wealth render them of great importance. If he opposes them, on the contrary, and still more if he has authority enough to be able to thwart them, neither the most acknowledged probity, nor the highest rank, nor the greatest public services, can protect him from the most infamous abuse and detection, from personal insults, nor sometimes from real danger, arising from the insolent outrage of furious and disappointed monopolists.

(Adam Smith 1776: pp.437–8)

This statement, with which Adam Smith expressed his view of the state more than 200 years ago, has stronger public support in contemporary Japan than in Smith's time. In modern Japan, 'administrative reform and deregulation' have become the slogans of the day. The same is true of many other economies as well. Across the globe, voters in democratic economies stand united in their hope for a less regulated world.

As George Stigler pointed out in his 1964 presidential address to the American Economic Association (Stigler 1965), Smith distrusted not the competence of the state but its motives. As Stigler read him, Smith believed that in most cases the state could efficiently achieve what it wanted, including mistaken ends. As a result, Smith makes little of inept or inefficient governmental conduct – but he also offers no evidence that the state can achieve its goals.

Smith's intellectual heirs did little to advance this state other than endlessly to repeat his claims. Smith himself never showed that the principal problem with regulation was the goals that the state selected. Instead, it fell to Stigler 200 years later to begin the empirical enterprise we so desperately needed. It was Stigler who noted that we lacked a usable theory of social and political control of economic activity. It was Stigler who explained that lack by showing how hard it was to create a theory of public policy. And it was Stigler who, by both exhortation and example, urged us to study state intervention in economic activity empirically. To do all this when so many scholars and voters seem to support 'big government' took extraordinary intellectual courage, but this was a courage typical of Stigler.

Empirical studies on the competence of the state remain primitive. We are still at the trial-and-error stage, searching for a common research ground. What are the right issues to research? How should we investigate them? What sectors should we study? Upon what aspects of economic life should we focus? What data should we use? What data might we need? In the book that follows, I conduct a preliminary study of state competence by focusing upon the competence of the state in wartime and postwar Japan.

As an institution, the state supplies goods and services to various groups within the public. The voting public elects the legislators. The legislators then – purportedly as agents of the voting public – decide when, where, what, at whose expense, and for whom the goods and services should be supplied. Necessarily, these legislators delegate much of the job to professional bureaucracies.

The result is a process with dynamics that differ fundamentally from those in economic markets. In the latter, a consumer reveals his preference for goods and services directly to sellers. If several sellers will provide the goods he wants at a price he will pay, he chooses the combination of quality and price that maximizes his utility. If he demands too high a quality at too low a price he will find his demands unfilled. Through this market process, the optimal allocation of resources ensues.

As Smith argues, although the state places orders for goods and services on behalf of the public, it does so in a way that tends to be guided by the clamorous importunity of partial interests. And yet, as in private markets, if it orders a given product at too low a price no one will sell. If it ordered 50,000 cars that were capable of going at 500km/hour, to be delivered in five months, Toyota would not fill the order. Neither would GE, Sony, IBM, Honda, or BMW. Much the same would occur if it ordered the elixir of eternal youth. Nor would anything change if a Stalinesque autocrat simply ordered a firm to fulfill its order. The state is not almighty and does not have Aladdin's lamp.

Like individuals and firms, the state incurs costs in what it does. Since it has but limited competence (and since that competence varies across sectors), it does some tasks better than others. In turn, it can promote the public good through its intervention only when it can achieve an objective more efficiently than private actors.

Unfortunately, the state lacks many of the incentives to avoid inefficient (or simply unfeasible) projects that individuals and firms face. A firm that cannot produce cost-effectively will simply disappear. Not so with the state and its component agencies. Indeed, perverse as it may seem, because high costs tend to lead to larger budgets and increased personnel – agencies sometimes have exactly the wrong incentives.

Myriad empirical questions follow. When can the state competently fill a public order? How does a given agency behave when it receives an order that it cannot competently fill? Will it refuse to supply it or try to dissuade legislators from demanding it? When might an agency pretend to fill an order that it understands to be impossible but report a success several years later on the theory that most people have long forgotten the order? Will the public in fact have forgotten? When will it remember? More broadly, when and how will voters monitor the state?

These issues touch crucially on fundamental questions about the role of the state in postwar Japan. For example, observers often claim that 'industrial policy' contributed to Japan's postwar industrial success. Yet what basis do they have for that view? What evidence? Indeed, what do they mean by 'industrial policy'? Who demanded the policy, and who implemented it? Suppose the legislature dictated the policy. Did it give bureaucrats sufficient resources to achieve it? Were those bureaucrats able to do what was asked? If so, how were they able to do what bureaucrats under far more powerful socialist regimes could not do?

At least by 1970, most people no longer claimed that industrial policy was effective. What had occurred? Where had the competence of the state gone? Most people now also recognize that state intervention into sectors outside manufacturing, such as financial services, agriculture, distribution, transportation, and healthcare, has rarely succeeded. Was the Japanese government able to overcome what similar governments could not? If so, why?

In this book, I study the competence of the state by focusing on state intervention in specific industries during specific periods. As competence is not directly observable, I instead focus on the state's behavior – something that is both observable and a function of state competence. As an economist interested in national (i.e., consumer) economic welfare, my ultimate concern is the proper function and performance of the state in market economies. In studying specific industries during specific periods, I have tried to keep in mind the general questions above about state competence. By doing so, I hope I have produced a study with lessons that – given appropriate caveats – will apply more broadly to other industries, other times, and other economies.

II

This book consists of three parts. Part I focuses on the machine tool industry under wartime controls and Part II on the same industry under postwar regulation. If ever there were circumstances that would have given regulators the resources they needed to implement national policy, they were there in the early years of the war. Under the exigencies of military need, regulators in those early years enjoyed massive public support, largely compliant legislators, and enormous government resources.

It is that military exigency that makes the early wartime years the ideal laboratory of state competence. To measure the force of gravity, we need to observe falling objects in a vacuum, where air resistance will not slow the acceleration toward the Earth. To measure the theoretical competence of the state, we need to observe its behavior under favorable government control, where neither public resistance, inadequate funding, nor inappropriate statutes will dampen its effectiveness.

If instead we studied a state's competence under conditions where it faced public opposition, inappropriate legislation, or trivial funding, we would learn nothing about its potential competence. After all, even a brilliantly effective organization could not have performed under those conditions. On the other hand, if even under ideal conditions the state acts incompetently, we should be skeptical about broad claims on behalf of the state's contribution. What we need to know, then, is the net contribution that state regulators can make under the most favorable conditions available.

In order to promote industrial development effectively, regulators need legal authority and generous resources. As Part I illustrates, during the 1930s the Japanese government tried hard to promote the production of military aircraft, vessels, weapons, and other equipment. Machine tools were a pivotal part of this need, for some machine tools were themselves important military production equipment, while others were necessary to produce other equipment. Accordingly, the government gave the expansion and improvement of the machine tool industry the highest priority. Consistent with that priority, it gave regulators a clear policy mandate, strong legal authority, and preferential access to all the resources that mattered – whether production materials, foreign currency, or the labor force. If ever there was a world in which the state could reveal its competence, this was it.

Upon studying this industry in Part I, I conclude that wartime intervention largely failed. Despite all the advantages that the regulators had, they were unable to implement their policies. Whether during the expansionist late 1930s or the desperate early 1940s, they seldom affected industry performance. Even during the last stages of the war, they could not obtain what they wanted from the industry. Ultimately, the state was simply incompetent.

III

In Part II, I study the performance of the machinery industries under the 1956 Machinery Industry Promotion Act (MIPA).[1] Typically, observers characterize Japan's postwar industrial success through the performance of machinery industries like automobile manufacturing and shipbuilding. Many argue that the industries (like the machine tool industry) designated by the MIPA as targets for policy promotion played a key role in Japan's industrial success. For fifteen years – from the start of the explosive growth in the machinery industries to the time when Japan's industrial success caught the world's attention – this Act was the central weapon of industrial policy in these industries.

According to conventional wisdom, the MIPA contributed much to the growth of these machinery industries. The claim is important for, if true, this experience could inform both developing economies and the former socialist economies. These countries are now struggling to 'marketize' a centralized command economy and to develop their own machinery industries. If true, the claim would seem to justify selective government intervention. On the other hand, if the claim is false, such intervention would at best lead to a waste of time and energy and cause massive policy confusion. At worst, it could lead to profound economic stagnation.

Accordingly, I end Part II by asking the general question: under what conditions will 'industrial policy' be effective and desirable? I conclude that the answer is seldom, if ever. In the process, I confirm the increasingly widespread view that more conventional observers have grossly exaggerated the effectiveness of Japan's postwar industrial policy.

Around 1960 the Japanese government carried out a series of 'liberalizations,' including the ostensible abolition of most non-tariff trade restrictions. This change removed many of the tools that regulators had still enjoyed at the time of enactment of the MIPA. Even in 1956, however, they were under far stricter restrictions than had been the case during wartime, whether in making or in enforcing policy. Moreover, the objective of the 1956 Act was never as clear as the regulatory mandates had been during the war. Neither did the 1956 program have the high governmental priority that promotion of the machinery industry enjoyed during wartime.

Part II concludes that the MIPA and its associated policies ultimately accomplished very little. At the core, the policies involved loans at preferential rates from the Japan Development Bank and the Small Business Finance Corporation. No other unusual policies were actively used. The loans themselves came with terms that varied little from market rates and were used at levels close to the debt levels that would have prevailed in their absence. Ultimately, the Act did little to promote the development of any of the industries designated under it.

IV

Part III, comprising two chapters, focuses on the competence of the state and its relation to the behavior and function of the state in the context of small business regulation. Chapter 3 investigates how regulators behave when they receive and fill too demanding an order, far beyond their competence. Since the turn of the century, Japanese policies for small businesses have received strong support from the public and accordingly from all political parties. With the political slogan of 'destroying and eliminating the dual structure' of the economy, the state greatly expanded and strengthened its small business policies after 1960. More than any other legislation, the 1963 Small Business Basic Act symbolized this commitment.

The notion that the Japanese economy had a 'dual structure' ultimately turned on Marxist assumptions about the ability of 'monopoly capital' to exploit systematically the general public, the *petit bourgeoisie*. As such, it had as much validity as the rest of the Marxist canon – which is to say, none. Consequently, small business policy during this period faced a hard task on dual grounds: the incompetence of the state and the downright incoherence of the objective.

Like most conventional claims about Japan's industrial policy generally, most of the conventional claims about Japan's small business policies are false. Taking small business policies as an example, Chapter 3 provides detailed information about a variety of issues: what polices were actually adopted, how they were implemented, why they were ineffective, and why ineffective policies were adopted.

Chapter 4 asks who determines the substance of policy and explores the issue through the recent efforts of the Japan Newspaper Companies Association to retain its resale price maintenance (RPM) scheme. The immediate issue was whether to revoke the industry's antitrust exemption from the RPM ban. The resulting dispute became one of the hottest political issues of 1995. Through this example, I ask who actually determines the substance of policy, what that 'policy' actually is, when and in what situations a person becomes identified as a 'decision maker,' where the boundary of the state lies, and who should be regarded as its members.

For several years in the mid-1990s, I served on two deregulation committees: the Deregulation Subcommittee of the Administrative Reform Committee, and the Deregulation Committee of the Government Headquarters for Administrative Reform. This opportunity to participate in the political decision-making process gave me a chance to do what I had never done before: to study, at the shortest possible range, how political issues are selected for discussion and settlement, how individual issues are actually treated and processed, how and why some issues become politically hot, who is seemingly and actually influential, and how individual players on the political stage behave and what roles they play.

Moreover, as a committee member directly in charge of the newspaper RPM issue, I was heavily involved in the ensuing 'disorder.' Indeed, for three years I served as the newspaper trade association's target of choice in its campaign to maintain its antitrust exemption. Using this experience and the information that I was able to collect through the dispute, I outline the contours of the controversy and trace its implications: how an issue becomes highly political, how it takes the form that it does, and how the final settlement emerges.

V

I wrote this book primarily for two groups of people. The first consists of those scholars and students interested in industrial organization or economic theory. For them, I hope the book raises important issues in the theory of the firm, in market analysis, in political economy, and in public policy – including institutional choice in transitional economies. The second group consists of comparativists interested in Japan. For them, I hope the book challenges many of the key assumptions about modern Japanese economic history.

In this volume, I argue that there has been nothing peculiar about Japanese economic growth. Even under the wartime controls, markets dominated the Japanese economy, and the state had a limited function. During the rapid economic growth of the 1950s and 1960s, this limited governmental role continued. Most accounts claim otherwise, but in the book that follows I show that their accounts of Japanese economic growth are either false or grossly exaggerated.

In an earlier work (Miwa 1996a), I characterized the conventional view of the Japanese economy as including two basic assumptions: (1) that factors peculiar to Japan played a critical role in economic development; and (2) that, by carrying out its 'industrial policy' and intervening heavily in (or guiding and leading) the private sector, the Japanese government promoted economic growth. In Part III of that work I concluded that the industrial policy was ineffective and thus contributed little to industrial success. However, that conclusion has not been widely accepted, and in the 1990s many scholars began to urge on transitional economies what they called a Japanese model. Through this model (often characterized by the phrase '(East) Asian miracle'), they urged the governments of the transitional economies to learn from Japan. And the lessons they proposed to teach from Japan were those of government intervention.

Perhaps many readers will be surprised by the views, information, and conclusions in this book. If they have followed the literature on Japan, this is only natural. They will bring to the book the belief that, at least before the 1970s, the Japanese government powerfully intervened in the economy and led the private sector forward. The immediate acceptance of and enthusiastic support for Professor Chalmers Johnson's *MITI and the Japanese Miracle: The Growth of Industrial Policy, 1925–1975* (Johnson 1982) and its Japanese translation in 1982 – with its emphasis on the role of the 'developmental state' in the Japanese economic miracle – epitomize the effect of this conventional wisdom.

Even prominent economists have accepted this view of Japanese economic regulation. Paul Krugman (1997: p.140), for example, writes that 'There is no question that before the early 1970s the Japanese system was heavily directed from the top, with MITI and the Ministry of Finance influencing the allocation of credit and foreign exchange in an effort to push the economy where they liked.'[2] Along this line, many observers believe that the Japanese system was heavily directed from the top in the 1950s and 1960s, and yet more strongly directed under wartime controls. Even after the recent recession and the many revelations of regulatory incompetence, this belief persists.

However, once readers begin to ask how the Japanese government could do what it is alleged to have done, they will inevitably turn to the critical question of state competence: could bureaucrats have achieved what they are said to have achieved? Even with unlimited power, could they have played the role attributed to them? To date, I am aware of no one who has seriously asked this question about the Japanese government.

'Correlation does not imply causation,'[3] even when the facts are true. In the context of Japan, observers have drawn causal conclusions from toy facts. They accurately begin with Japan's remarkable economic development since the mid-nineteenth century. However, they couple that with anecdotes about a strong, competent, and heavily interventionist state. They then conclude that the latter caused the former. Not just lay people but even academics firmly believe that a competent state led the Japanese economy to today's wealth, and it thereby serves as a counterexample to the now dominant view that only through the free market can we prosper.

Readers will learn that this Japan-based view has no ground. Nobody has ever tested either the competence of the Japanese state or its active intervention and its contribution to development. As shown in this book, the state was not competent enough to do such a job and actually did not even try. Ultimately, it was the market that played by far the greater role in the achievement. The notion that the Japanese government fostered economic growth through its intervention is instead a fable, a story we collectively tell and retell because we so badly wish it were true.

Everyone loves a good story. So do economists love fables to illustrate or even support fundamental economic theory. Although some of these fables are factually inaccurate, their appeal to economists continues undiminished, being recited in countless classrooms, textbooks, and academic seminars. Besides providing entertainment, telling stories conveys information, creates social bonds, and passes along moral values. Because the oral and written traditions of academics, particularly of economists, eventually affect public policy, it is imperative to set the record straight (Spulber 2002: p.1). Unfortunately, many economists remain enslaved to fables, and the fable of the growth-promoting Japanese government is a fable with many adherents.

VI

At least on the surface, the wartime Japanese government seems to have had extremely strong authority and power. Notwithstanding that power, however, it did not perform more effectively than its Western counterparts or intervene in the private sector more successfully. Instead, the wartime government regulated the economy about as well as Western governments have done (which is not very well) – and exactly as standard economic theory predicts.

Like my earlier book (Miwa 1996a), this volume may arouse strong reactions. Many misgivings, I suspect, stem from the fact that only recently have many scholars began to study the Japanese economy using standard economics principles (Miwa 1999: pp.1250–3). To avoid confusion, let me begin with a few rejoinders.

No doubt some readers will suggest that where there is smoke, there must be fire. Let me counter with a Japanese proverb that comes originally from China: 'If one dog barks at his shadow, a hundred dogs bark at his voice' (an approximate equivalent in English may be 'much ado about nothing'). Has anyone actually seen the fire? What proves that the fire has ever actually existed? What actually was the alleged fire? Many scholars begin their study of the Japanese economy by assuming that Japan is fundamentally different. Yet because they do so, their conclusions become close to religious faith. In turn, testing the conventional views of the Japanese economy begins to resemble research into evidence of UFOs.

Perhaps readers will reply by asking 'if you're right, why is there so much discussion about Japan's industrial policy or about the government's contribution to economic growth?' My answer is in three parts. First, many ignore the *post hoc, ergo propter hoc* fallacy. Many observers note that the economy has grown, note that bureaucrats purported to promote growth, and they then conclude that those bureaucrats must have caused the growth. Second, demand for this literature is strong among politicians, government officials, journalists, and academics, particularly in the former socialist economies. Naturally, Japanese politicians and government officials are happy to support this belief in the effectiveness of their programs.

Third, as is so often the case with academics, books beget books, and as they do a fad can metamorphose into an apparent subfield. With the respectability that large numbers create, scholars have effectively created their own industries – 'Japan's industrial policy literature industry,' for example, and the 'main bank literature industry.'

It is a touchstone of accepted economics that all explanations must run in terms of the actions and reactions of individuals. It is my purpose in this book, as in Miwa 1996a, to demonstrate that Japan has long been 'a world of exchange by agreement rather than by coercion [where] the costs and benefits of agreement determine its scope' (Stigler 1992: p.456). Because Japan has been a world of exchange, the standard principles of economics explain the dominant patterns of both economic and political phenomena.[4] These principles are not those that anyone invented to explain Japan. Indeed, they were not invented to explain any particular society, and nowhere in this volume do I argue that Japan is different from other societies.

I wish to deal only with Japan, and only with basic contours of government behavior and market function, which I consider challenge enough. But this is not a monograph in 'area studies.' Although every country has its peculiarities (as does every government, firm, or group of firms), the focus in social science should not be on peculiarity as such. Rather, the focus should be on the development of comparable studies for a wide variety of economies in a way that facilitates comparison and generalization. Through that comparative work, I hope that we will be able to understand better the competence of governments and to plan their economic role more sensibly. If the Japanese economy is distinctive enough to merit closer investigation, so are the economies in other countries.

Since the thirteenth century, when the descriptions of Cipango or Zipangu in Marco Polo's book *Il Milione* set a definite goal for Columbus in his journey, Japan has been a rich source of enthusiasm, imagination and myth for Westerners. Enthusiasm is fine; but imagination and myth can be counterproductive – as the recent literature using Japan to encourage the governments of transitional economies to regulate with a heavy hand illustrates. I hope that this book will push us toward a fuller, more accurate understanding of the Japanese government and economy.

VII

Basically, this book is the English version of my Japanese book, *Seifu no noryoku* (*The Competence of the State*), which was published in 1998 by Yuhikaku (Miwa 1998c). Chapters 1 and 2 are revised and expanded versions of the papers 'The competence, behavior, the function of the state,' parts 1 and 2, which are published in *Keizaigaku ronshu* (Economic Review) of the University of Tokyo (Miwa 1996b, 1997a). Chapter 3 is based on the paper for a World Bank research project (Miwa 1995) and Chapter 4 on the paper published in *Keizaigaku ronshu* (Miwa 1997b). I choose 'State Competence and Economic Growth in Japan' as a title to explicate the intention and focus of this book further.

The origin of the research for the book may be traced back to the beginning of the 1980s, when I published a series of papers arguing that Japan's industrial policy had been far less effective than was widely believed. The research started with such naïve questions as the following: why do so many, both in Japan and elsewhere, believe that 'industrial policy' has been effective in Japan? Why are so many people enthusiastic about such ineffective policies? Can we improve the effectiveness of industrial policy by changing the policy measures? And what is the nature of the system for decision making and implementation?

With a shift in my research focus toward organizational behavior, particularly decision-making processes in large firms, my interest in those questions deepened further. In the 1990s, along with a persistent and steady trend in Japan toward administrative reform and deregulation, I developed a strong interest in the function and the appropriate role of the state. Needless to say, my experiences on the committees described earlier decisively contributed to my research. The chaos of government policy looks different from the inside than from the outside. Watching a process that had long mystified me unfold with me as a participant, I often said to myself simply: 'Aha, so that's the reason!'

Soon after completing the Japanese version of the book, I began a collaborative effort with Professor J. Mark Ramseyer of the Harvard Law School. This work has resulted in fifteen papers and three books, some of which (e.g., Miwa and Ramseyer 2000a, 2001a, 2002b, 2002e, 2002f, 2003a, 2003b, 2003e, 2004a, 2004b) are closely related to the focus of this volume. Obviously this book has profited greatly both from the collaborative effort itself and from its products, including those now in process. I hope that interested readers will proceed to our joint products, *Fable of the Keiretsu and Other Tales from Japan We Wish Were True* (Miwa and Ramseyer 2004b), for instance.

A long time has elapsed since the original idea for this book began to grow. Over that period, many friends in many institutions have shared their ideas with me, both in conversation and through their gracious comments on my drafts. Those who were particularly generous with their time and thoughts include Eisuke Daito, Akira Hara, Naohiko Jinno, Hideki Kanda, Yoshitsugu Kanemoto, Ryutaro Komiya, Motonari Kurasawa, Toshihiro Matsumura, Katsuji Nakagane, Tetsuji Okazaki, Haruhito Takeda, Toshimasa Tsuruta, Masu Uekusa, Noriyuki Yanagawa, and Kazuo Wada. Above all, Professor J. Mark Ramseyer of the Harvard Law School both as the co-author of a series of joint works and as an English editor made a tremendous contribution to the substance and readability of this book. In addition, I received many helpful comments from participants in numerous conferences and workshops. I could not have completed this work without the assistance of many people in industry and within the state (both politicians and bureaucrats). I particularly learned from the participants on the Deregulation Subcommittee of the Administration Reform Committee, who were generous with their time and frank in expressing their views.

I gratefully acknowledge the permission of Yuhikaku to produce this English version of my earlier work, and also the permission of publishers Keizaigaku ronshu and the Clarendon Press, to revise and include original papers on which the Japanese version was based. I received financial support from the University of Tokyo Research Fund Grant of the Economics Department, the Sloan

Foundation, and the East Asian Legal Studies Program of the Harvard Law School. My secretary, Nobuko Kubo, contributed much in completing both this and the Japanese edition, and Lionel Meehan did great work in editing my English. I am happy to thank them all.

Last, but by no means least, I thank my wife, Kazuko, for her understanding and forgiveness through the many evenings and weekends lost while writing this book. It is to her that I affectionately dedicate this book.

Yoshiro Miwa
Tokyo
July 2003

Notes

1 The Act on Temporary Measures for the Promotion of the Machinery Industries (*Kikai kogyo shinko renji sochi ho*).
2 As shown in Part II, many Japanese certainly share this view, such as Okazaki and Okuno-Fujiwara (1999).
3 As Heckman (2000) notes, the phrase is generally attributed to Karl Pearson. In this book, a more general statement – 'association does not imply causation' – may fit better.
4 In this book, I go back to the period of wartime control, but the same applies even to the late nineteenth century, as shown in Miwa and Ramseyer (2000a, 2000b, 2002b, 2002c, 2004b).

Part I

Wartime control

1 The machine tool industry under wartime control

1.1 THE ISSUES

1.1.1 Introduction

'We have a list, a long list, of market failures,' wrote Stigler (1975: p.112), and they form the premise for any argument that the government should intervene in the private sector. As Stigler saw it (*ibid*.: p.112), there were 'only two alternatives to the market: the state, and prayer,' but sometimes our reliance on the former seems predicated on a good dose of the latter. For all too often we take for granted the ability of the government to improve on the market. Remember 'the imperfectibility of the political system,' Stigler (*ibid*.: p.112) reminds us, and stay aware 'of its susceptibility to the well-placed minority, of its tardiness in adopting new technologies, of the bureaus that are forgotten islands of indolence, of the carelessness (or worse) of the public's rights by eminent politicians in advancing their private fortunes.' While that cynicism may not form much of a basis for policy recommendations, neither will any 'unreasoning optimism' about the state as 'an institution of noble goals and irresistible means' (*ibid*.: p.112). Unless we know something about the competence with which the state will intervene, market failure will not warrant government intervention. 'We may tell the society to jump out the market frying pan,' concluded Stigler (*ibid*.: p.113), 'but we have no basis for predicting whether it will land in the fire or a luxurious bed.'

Although most economists agree that government intervention into private-sector activities, be it regulation, industrial policy or social policy, can be justified only when it is in response to market failure, at that point agreement ends. Views differ on the precise definition of market failure; under what conditions it occurs; the appropriate governmental policy to address that market failure; who ought to determine that policy; who ought to control the behavior of government, and how; the calculation of policy cost and policy cost components; and which market failures justify government intervention (after taking policy cost into consideration)? Obviously, these issues have to be addressed in context, and conclusions may differ from case to case. However, the trend towards deregulation and re-evaluating regulation in industrialized market economies since the mid-1970s, and the collapse of centralized economic systems in former socialist countries towards the end of the 1980s, invites two observations. First, it is quite often dangerous to ask the government to respond to market failures. Second, the conventional view of the state or the government's competence tends to be too optimistic.

Major points for consideration

Despite the obvious relevance of state competence to questions of policy, we have a paucity of knowledge about the issue. And before studying that competence, several preliminary issues arise. Fortunately, many (although not all) of these more preliminary questions have been the subject of extensive theoretical and empirical research during the past twenty years in public choice and modern political economy, and I rely on that literature when relevant. These issues include the following. Who decides the role of the government and defines government policy? How independent is the executive from the legislature? When and how do legislators monitor the executive branch, and when and how do voters monitor the legislators? When do legislators delegate discretion to the executive branch, and how broad a discretion do they delegate? When the legislators restrict executive discretion, how do they do so? Many regulatory models posit bureaucratic competence (even expertise) in the executive branch, but how much competence or expertise do bureaucrats actually possess, and on what issues? In turn, this issue of bureaucratic competence and expertise magnifies the importance of the monitoring questions: given that bureaucrats are more competent in some areas than in others, how does that comparative competence affect the discretion that legislators delegate to bureaucrats and the monitoring that they undertake? And how does all this affect the discretion that voters delegate to legislators and the monitoring that they in turn undertake?

The government cannot and does not become competent in doing everything

The view of the state that sees it as an enterprise, born as a rational organization designed for achieving given objectives, invites careful consideration of the above points. The state's role and character grows and changes according to the particular constraints on its activities and the voters and various interest groups with which it interacts. At each moment, the state exists as an organization with distinctive competence in such factors as personnel, know-how, and external relationships. The state's competence is the product of past decisions and activity, both long-term planned activity and accumulated everyday experience. Any enterprise, including the state (when intervening in the private sector), has a comparative advantage both in selecting business fields in which to grow and in responding to the changing environment. Only those enterprises with a comparative advantage in a particular market are enthusiastic about participating and growing in that market. Thus the competence of an enterprise (potentially including the state) will strongly influence its behavior. Following from this, the actual function of the executive branch of government will depend on its competence. Consequently, even when the legislature possesses the ability to control the behavior of the executive, its ability to obtain the performance it wants from the executive will be circumscribed by the competence that the executive branch brings to the project.

In short, the government cannot and does not become competent in doing everything, both because of the constraints under which it operates and because of the cost–performance calculation. Even an enterprise of the highest caliber will not succeed in every industrial sector. Likewise, the government will not and cannot succeed on every political issue. Thus, in Part I, viewing the government as an organization-like enterprise, I investigate the competence, behavior and function of the government under wartime controls. Despite the widespread consensus about the high competence of the Japanese state,[1] there have been few detailed empirical studies of factual cases. To this end, I use evidence from the machine tool manufacturing industry to address these issues of state competence. I focus on the wartime controls on the machine tool industry in Part I and on regulation of the machinery and machine tool industries since the mid-1950s under the Act on Temporary Measures for the Promotion of the Machinery Industries in Part II (*Kikai kogyo shinko rinji sochi-ho* or *Kishin-ho*; hereafter the MIPA).

1.1.2   Why the machine tool industry?

As introduced above, any investigation into the competence of the state is necessarily a context-specific investigation. That is, the various factors that constrain the state's activity must be taken into account when assessing the state's ability to achieve a given policy objective. Some of these factors include the conditions within the particular industrial sector targeted by the state's policy, the time of implementation of the policy, the anticipated policy objective, the general public sentiment towards the government, and the public evaluation of a particular policy.

Four reasons for focusing on the machine tool industry

I focus on the machine tool industry for four reasons:

1   The machine tool industry was of strategic importance to Japan's industrial success and high economic growth.

2   An examination of the machine tool industry is essential to an understanding of the factors supporting the postwar growth of the overall Japanese economy. The industry is therefore an important object of research.
3   An examination of the machine tool industry serves as an important case study of the effectiveness and efficiency of policy in general and of policies for promoting the development of particular industries in particular.
4   A large portion of the economic role expected of the government in Japan is understood to be that of the development of industry-promoting policies.

This case study of the machine tool industry can thus serve as a stepping stone toward more generalized research on the function the government has played in Japan.

The machinery and machine tool industries were not just crucial to the economy; they both involve complicated non-standardized goods and have been badly understudied. Many of the extant studies of industry-promoting policies have focused on industries producing standardized 'basic materials or products,' such as coal mining, petroleum refining, electricity, steel, and ocean shipping. Compared with these industries, the manufacturing of machine tools involves the production of radically non-standardized products that are subject to ongoing innovation – innovation that tracks both wide swings in demand and sometimes rapid changes in the underlying technology. Yet notwithstanding its importance and these manufacturing issues, few scholars have studied the role that government policy played in the industry.

Many have argued that the effectiveness of Japan's industrial policy fell during the 1970s as the government lost its coercive powers in the wake of the trade liberalization it had implemented. According to this conventional view, during the heyday of Japanese industrial policy in the 1950s and 1960s, that policy was extremely effective due to the tremendous power that the government could and did use to enforce its promotional policies. To test this assumption, in the first two parts of this book I focus on the period before the government lost this alleged power. Also, especially during the wartime control period I study in Part I, the whole economy is alleged to have been strictly controlled by the government. In this 'effective industrial policy environment,' the expansion of machine tool manufacturing and the improvement in performance and quality of machine tool products (particularly for aircraft production) was a policy objective of the highest priority. This study of Japanese government machine tool industry-promoting policies will serve to test the consensus that industrial policy was effective in Japan until the 1970s.

1.1.3   Why the machine tool industry under wartime control?

Part I focuses on the machine tool industry during the wartime control period, from the second half of the 1930s to the end of World War II in 1945. Part II focuses on the promotional policies, particularly those for machinery industries like the machine tool industry, adopted after 1956. The explanation of why I choose these periods requires a brief description of the history of the industry.

A history of the industry

The value of Japan's machine tool production surpassed that of West Germany in 1981 and that of the USA to become world leader in 1982. In 1992, the relative production of these three countries can be illustrated by taking the Japanese figure as a base with a nominal value of 100. By comparison, German production was 70, while the USA brought up the rear with a mere 30. Also, Japan's machine tool export ratio was above 30 percent that year (Japanese Machine Tool Builders Association (hereafter JMTBA) 1992).

This situation was strikingly different a decade after the end of World War II. In 1955, when the government was debating the MIPA, which would commence the following year, Japan's machine tool imports (¥4.04 billion) exceeded its total production (¥3.68 billion,[2] including ¥720 million for export). Furthermore, the machine tools in most industries were 'extremely superannuated and obsolete, left unattended with inadequate replacement during the postwar transition period.' The same commentator notes that 'Japan's machine tool industry suffered from stagnation for ten years since the collapse of the wartime economy. ... The biggest problem facing the industry was increasing competition from continuously improving and innovative imported machines.'[3]

Automobile manufacturing necessarily relies heavily on machine tools, yet during the several decades since 1955 Japanese automobile firms rapidly increased both the quality of their cars and the productivity of their manufacturing process (see Miwa 1996a: ch. 4). This dramatic expansion in car production could occur only with commensurate quality improvements and productivity gains in areas ranging from stamping and machining to the production of tyres, bearings, glass, steel, and machine tools. In 1955, the Toyota Motor Corporation began large-scale passenger car production with its Crown model (still in production, but not exported to the USA). The total number of passenger cars produced in Japan that year was 20,000, but within ten years, the number had risen to 696,000, 100,000 of which were exported, and within twenty years to 4,568,000, 40 percent of which were exported. A car is composed of over 5,000 generic varieties of component and about 20,000 actual components. The joint effort of a huge number of firms underlies successful vehicle production. In the seven years from 1955, machine tool production grew thirty-fold to over ¥100 billion. Simultaneously, imports of machine tools grew twelve-fold to over ¥47 billion. These fabrication and assembly industries (of which automobile production is a classic example) have been the highlight of Japan's industrial success and economic development. The development of machine tools thus lies at the heart of Japan's industrial success.

Two reasons for beginning with the industry under wartime control

The relevance of prewar growth to postwar development

The development of machine tool and automobile parts production was fundamental to the 1956 MIPA. However, the government had pursued policies of the same general character prior to the enactment of this law since about 1952. Therefore, the content and role of government policy in the machine tool industry and its effectiveness during the ten years since Japan's independence in 1952 are subjects of our keen concern, but this is the objective of Part II.

In Part I, I focus on the ten years since the second half of the 1930s. There are two reasons for this, the first being that during this period the machine tool industry exhibited extraordinarily rapid expansion and growth, which strongly influenced the development of the industry after the war. Figure 1.1 shows Japan's total machine tool production over the six and half decades from 1930 to 1994. It gives both the number of machines produced and their aggregate weight,[4] and it suggests observations about Japanese machine tool production. First, and most obvious, the industry grew rapidly in the years after 1931. During the seven years from 1931 to 1938, the number of machines produced expanded thirty-fold and their aggregate weight fifty-fold.

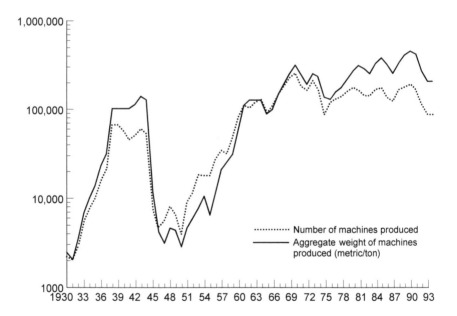

Figure 1.1 Machine tool production in Japan, 1930–94

Source: JMTBA 1969: p.74, extended over the period 1969–94.

Second, by 1955 the industry had shrunk dramatically. That year, production stood at 27 percent (by quantity) and 5 percent (by weight) of their earlier peaks (1938 in terms of quantity and 1943 by weight). Only in 1960 and 1967, respectively, did production pass those prewar peaks.

Third, the Japanese economy experienced a historically unprecedented boom in the second half of the 1950s. During this period, the industry expanded production rapidly owing to an explosion in capacity investment that swept through the Japanese economy. This investment, together with investment in technological skills and know-how and the accumulated stock of prewar machine tools, provided the platform for the growth in the second half of the 1950s. Fourth, most of the machine tool producers that played major roles during the postwar boom were born during the prewar growth period.[5]

Thus, as the third and last points show, the prewar growth process in the industry is of high relevance to postwar development, and an investigation of the prewar situation is fundamental to an understanding of the postwar machine tool industry.

Wartime government powers

The second reason is that the wartime government was able to pursue its policy of industrial development far more freely. The government exercised strong regulative powers with only loose constraints during the war. Accordingly, we are able to observe the behavior of the government empowered to intervene (or allowed to allocate subsidies) in the private sector under purer conditions, analogous to an experiment in a laboratory. During the 1950s (and especially after the 1960s liberalizations) the government was subject to far stronger constraints.

Examining the decision-making process of government agencies during the war generates some surprising conclusions. For instance, concerning the machine tool industry under wartime controls, each individual government agency in charge of an industry was requested to fully devote itself to the well-defined national target of promoting the industry, and was delegated virtually unconstrained authority to intervene in the industry to achieve this objective. However, the task was difficult, and the government did not use all the authority legally allowed it. For example, because of the scarcity of metals and foreign exchange during the war, the government had the authority to order factories to scrap their production equipment and channel the resulting raw material into the production of more urgently needed machines. It was a power that the government hesitated to use. Both the Precision Tool Section of the Ministry of Commerce and Industry supervising the industry and the affiliated Precision Tool Control Association (PTCA) were extremely reluctant to promote more efficient or higher-quality production systems through such measures as preferential access to precious resources like scrapped steel. This scenario suggests that even with wide discretion in law to intervene in the private sector, a government may be reluctant to actually do so.

One can restate this issue more generally. The prewar industry is not just important for its comparative value – to enable us to compare it with the postwar regime and to evaluate more meaningfully the postwar regulatory framework – although it clearly is important for that purpose. It is also important as a study of the competence of the state itself. For to study state competence more generally, one must examine the competence that the state acquires when it has the greatest leeway to obtain whatever competence it needs. The wartime Japanese government had enormous leeway. Given the political environment of the second half of the twentieth century, the postwar government had very little.

1.1.4   Basic issues

The expansion of munitions industries became a national policy of the highest priority after the Sino-Japanese War began in 1937. Accordingly, increasing production and improving quality in the machine tool industry, and promoting domestic production of machine tools to safeguard against any import interruption, became policies of extreme importance. Interestingly, though, the government neither actively tried to reorganize the industry in line with this national policy nor played an important role in influencing industry performance. Why?

In Part I, I explore that question through seven questions.

1   What generally could the government have done to improve industry performance?
2   More specifically, what else could the government actually have done other than allocate preferentially to the industry such 'basic materials' as foreign currency, production materials like steel and energy, labor, and funds?
3   Were these policy measures sufficiently effective in achieving the policy objective?
4   If the government failed to achieve the desired policy objective (in fact it did not), what were the basic reasons for this?
5   Would more powerful and wide-ranging government intervention have helped?
6   If so, why did the government not give itself that power and authority?
7   Although the government did give itself some interventionist powers, why did it introduce those powers only gradually? What restrained it?

Related principal–agent questions

These issues can be reorganized into a series of questions based on a standard principal–agent regulation model (Laffont and Tirole 1993; Armstrong *et al.* 1994) in which the government is the principal and machine tool manufacturers are the agents. What were the critical conditions restraining the government's decision making? Did a unity of will exist in the government that was strong enough to apply a model of optimizing behavior under an explicit objective function? Was this condition maintained throughout the period? More particularly, did government bureaucrats agree about the relative priority of such goals as the expansion of machine tool production in general and individual machine tools, the substitution of domestic for imported machines, improvements in the quality of existing machines, technological innovation in the industry, and flexibility in application? When it came to using the machines for production, did bureaucrats in the government agree about the relative priorities of airplane construction, shipbuilding, and other military production? If not (and they did not agree), how did the lack of consensus affect decision making?

On those issues where government personnel did agree, did they have the competence to specify and implement their policy goals? Did they have the power to enforce their preferences on the firms? Beyond manipulating prices, what tools did they use? For example, did they try to intervene in the trades that firms made? Did they try to direct the decision-making processes within individual firms?

Why did the government give itself the powers that it did when it did? For example, why were a series of institutional arrangements aimed at achieving stronger control implemented only gradually? Conversely, why were they even implemented at all? Did the government make such decisions on a cost–benefit basis? If it did, what factors influenced the calculations? For example, how important were the following four issues: (1) the resistance to giving the government stronger enforcement powers; (2) the level of the objectives that the government hoped to achieve; (3) changes in the level of the objectives that the government hoped to achieve and in the price of achieving those objectives; and (4) changes in the political power of the militarists in the government.

1.1.5   The basic view of the book and two related points

Like arrangements within and between firms, the relations within a government and with the firms it potentially regulates occur in a world of privately skewed incentives and asymmetric information. A government may nominally have the authority to control a firm or its component members, but it is not almighty. It does not possess all the information that it needs to govern. Seldom if ever will it have the information it needs to control firms or promote their growth or profitability.

The essence of the government's problems is most clearly illustrated in the following statement from Hayek (1945: pp.524–5):

> If we can agree that the economic problem of society is mainly one of rapid adaptation to changes in the particular circumstances of time and place, it would seem to follow that the ultimate decisions must be left to the people

who are familiar with these circumstances, who know directly of the relevant changes and of the resources immediately available to meet them. ... We must solve it by some form of decentralization. But this answers only part of our problem. We need decentralization because only thus can we ensure that the knowledge of the particular circumstances of time and place will be promptly used. But the 'man on the spot' cannot decide solely on the basis of his limited but intimate knowledge of the facts of his immediate surroundings. There still remains the problem of communicating to him such further information as he needs to fit his decisions into the whole pattern of changes of the larger economic system.

Two related points

Two related points are essential to Part I. First, even if it is empowered to intervene in the decision making of every individual agent, the government would not necessarily be able to achieve its objective and may not even be able to promote its objectives at all. Not infrequently, individuals respond to a government in ways that offset its intervention. In the end (as the socialist governments all too soon discovered), the government will find itself with a less efficient economy and no closer to its policy objectives.

Second, the level of difficulty that a government faces greatly differs across cases, depending on the issue to which it must respond. When an issue is well defined and wide agreement exists among relevant economic agents, the associated difficulty might be small. This is sometimes the case, for instance, when the issue is one of allocating a given amount of material between agents. However, the difficulty is much greater when the issue is not just the simple allocation but the achievement of specific goals by manipulating the allocation of materials. In such a situation, the government may try to allocate resources to favor firms that most effectively promote the government's goals. To do so, however, it must be able to evaluate the effectiveness of each feasible allocation in the choice set. Its task is even harder when it must consider not just the incumbent firms but also the actions of firms that can potentially enter the industry.[6]

1.1.6   The structure and conclusions of Part I

The discussion below is divided into a main body and a conclusion. The main body consists of two further sections, 1.2 and 1.3. Section 1.2 focuses on the period after the establishment of the PTCA in January 1942 under the 1941 Imperial Order for Key Industry Associations. Section 1.3 focuses on the legislative and regulatory framework of the period before the establishment, and Section 1.4 concludes.

Why I begin with the PTCA

I begin the study of the competence, behavior, and function of the government concerning the machine tool industry under wartime control by studying the function of the PTCA. I do so to place the wartime regulatory framework in historical perspective. The association represents 'Japan's wartime control at its most well-organized stage' (JMTBA 1962: p.131). Yet it is a stage that the government reached only slowly and gradually. Prior to the setting up of the association, the industry had been subject to little government regulation. By starting with the PTCA itself, I bring out that historical context and illustrate the way in which the industry had earlier been under very lax control.

Section 1.2

The basic conclusion is that the state was incompetent, and that such incompetence continued until the end of the war. The government's role in the industry was far from active or critical, even at this most well-organized stage of control via a control association. During this period, the last three and half years of imperial Japan before the end of World War II, the government, led by the military, made every effort to achieve their objectives. But their 'innumerable regulatory actions are conclusive proof, not of effective regulation, but of the desire to regulate' (Stigler and Friedland 1962: p.1). If the government failed so thoroughly even under these circumstances, it could not have played an important role in the period preceding the establishment of the control association.

Sections 1.3 and 1.4

Section 1.3 focuses upon two specific aspects of the government's wartime control. Those are the 1938 Machine Tool Building Act and a series of other regulations empowering the government to subsidize machine tool builders for the purpose of the trial production of new machine tool models. Examples of the latter regulations include the 1938 Rules Concerning the Subsidies for Trial Production of Machine Tools and the 1939 Imperial Order for General Mobilization Experiments and Research. I investigate these policies in Section 1.3, although the period when many manufacturers conducted trials with government subsidies overlaps heavily with the period of operation of the PTCA. The concluding section, Section 1.4, is a summary of Part I.

The conclusion of Part I

Concerning the impact of government policy on the machine tool manufacturing industry under wartime control, the evidence in Part I yields the following conclusions. First, despite strong requests from the military, the enforcement of government policy in the industry was neither active nor powerful. Second, the 'promotion policies' that the government did actually implement neither could nor did have much impact on industry performance.

Third, compared with the situation at the start of the war, by 1945 the economy had made remarkable progress in the accumulation of machine tools and in the ability to develop and produce new products. Yet most of the progress resulted from voluntary supplier responses to high demand, not to the government's industry-promotion policy.

To be sure, the government's preferential allocation policies – including the allocation of foreign currency, production materials, finance, and workers – did help to drive the increase in supply. If one calls this 'promotion policy,' then government policy did increase supply. Crucially, however, this is the only effective promotional policy that the government adopted.

What is more, the increased supply that the government induced through its preferential allocation policies was not a cost-justified supply increase. Over time, the cost the government paid for preferentially allocating foreign currency and basic materials increased dramatically. Because of this, even if the stock of production equipment at the end of the war was of great value, it was not value that covered production costs. As rational economic policy, even the preferential allocation policy was not cost-justified.

1.2   THE PRECISION TOOL CONTROL ASSOCIATION AND THE MACHINE TOOL INDUSTRY

1.2.1   Introduction

Some may criticize the methodology of Part I, that is, investigating the state's competence and its relation to the state's behavior and function by examining state intervention in the machine tool industry under wartime control. Criticism may run something like this: wartime control was during an emergency too extreme to provide any real insight into the basic character of the state, and it will not provide insight regarding postwar industrial policies like those for the machine tool industry. However, it was during this period that the state enjoyed great authority and power under relatively few constraints. Such a situation enables us to investigate and observe the state's competence, and the related behavior and function of the state. Fewer factors clouded the state's actions during this period, and the corollary is that we are therefore better able to evaluate its fundamental competence.

I assume that the same economic principles that govern market responses to state intervention apply as much during wartime as during peacetime. The nature of the regulation itself may or may not change, but the nature of the cost–benefit analysis that the regulated firms undertake remains the same, whatever the political constraints on the government. As a simple example, take government responses to rice shortages in Japan during wartime (1939–40) (see Nakamura 1974: p.87) and peacetime (1994). In 1939, rice shortages were serious due to a drought, and the government, worrying about a repeat of the rice riots that had plagued it in earlier years, issued the Rice Control Rule in October 1940. In this rice rationing, the government purchased and distributed all rice harvested and ordered all sellers to sell only rice that blended foreign and domestic varieties. Novelist Kafu Nagai recorded this in his diary entry for 14 January 1941:

> A man from the rice shop delivered the bag of rice I ordered last evening together with a much smaller bag. By government regulation the rice mix was ordered to be 20% foreign rice with 80% domestic rice. However, he brought them separately (unmixed), and asked me to give his regards to any policeman who happened to drop by for investigation. Foreign rice came from Thailand, he explained.

The government issued a similar order during the 1994 shortage, and the market responded almost identically.

Illustration: the case of the bearing industry

Let us begin with a description of the state of the bearing industry at the end of World War II. The industry supplied basic components: together with cogs and screws, bearings were among the most basic and common components in the machinery and machine tool industries. Consider this quote from the Japan Bearing Industry Association (1965: p.27):

> During the war, though imprudent, the bearing industry achieved several remarkable results. First, with users' cooperation, the industry could fill almost all kinds of bearing demand from automobile manufacturers. This was achieved by a company called Fujikoshi Co. specializing in supplying master gauges, and each producer then specializing in individual models. Second, the industry could satisfy almost all the bearing demand from machine tool builders as well. Though there still remained noise problems, the products could for the most part satisfy the requirements in size and precision. Third, bearing producers also succeeded in the domestic production of various high-precision bearings like those for aircraft production, and thus they made notable progress in manufacturing technology. Without a state of national emergency [the war], Japan's bearing industry could not have achieved such remarkable technical progress or such accumulation of stocks in technology and production equipment.

Four points for discussion

Keeping in mind that similar evaluations of other sectors of the wartime machine tool industry have been made, one can make the following four points about the above quotation:

1   Although the state of the industry at the end of the war was greatly different from that at the beginning, it is not clear whether industry progress was attributable to state policies for the industry. In order to evaluate the effectiveness of bearing industry policy, we must first define clearly the precise content of state policy and then examine whether that policy operated successfully to promote industry development and to stimulate domestic production of designated products. The outbreak of war meant that imports were interrupted, and hence military demand for bearing production shifted totally to the domestic bearing industry, which accordingly stimulated domestic production. Was it this turn of events or was it state policy for the industry that we have to thank for such enormous development in the bearing industry? The answer is not altogether clear, but it is of critical importance in evaluating policy effectiveness.

2   Was the alleged policy actually adopted? Every policy is more or less a political performance. Those who promote a policy tend to overstate its importance, and what they allegedly did often greatly differs from what they actually did. Focus must be placed upon the actual impact of actual policies.

3   If a policy was implemented differently to the policies adopted, did the difference matter? If implementing the policy as adopted would have produced little difference in the state of the industry, then we can say that the policy actually adopted would have had little impact.

4   A desirable policy is one with benefits that are larger than its costs. How should we evaluate the benefits and costs of technical progress achieved during the war, and how should we evaluate the stocks in technology and production equipment remaining at the end of the war? Because the stocks remaining at the war's end tended to be for military production, they did not always have a civilian use. Even if domestic production was greatly promoted in this industry, that by itself is of no value. Furthermore, policy costs are a function of the quantities of resource inputs and their prices. The input prices of basic materials and resources such as production facilities, foreign currency, finance, and labor were much higher during the war than in normal times. During the war, these resources were under total and strict state control, and preferential allocation of those resources to specific sectors resulted in big sacrifices in other industrial activities and also in people's lives. The fundamental question is whether state policy created a net national economic benefit beyond its cost.

1.2.2   A historical timeline[7]

The following timeline is intended to provide a very brief, general overview of important events during the periods that Part I examines. It is hoped that it will help readers to reach a more holistic view of matters examined in this part and serve as a reference for readers while reading through this part. An asterisk suggests a direct reference to the machine tool industry.

1932.1   The Shanghai Incident. Despite its nominal non-aggression policy, the Japanese government had dispatched troops to Shanghai; these troops then clashed with Chinese troops near Shanghai and began the gradually escalating conflict between China and Japan.

1937.7   The Lukouch'iao Incident. A clash on the outskirts of Beijing that led to the Sino-Japanese conflict.

    .9   The Temporary Import–Export Grading Act (*Yushutsu-nyu hin tou rinji sochi-ho*), the Temporary Funds Coordination Act (*Rinji shikin chosei-ho*), the Act to Apply the 1918 Military Industry Mobilization Act (*Gunju kogyo doin-ho*), and the Temporary Act for Ship Control (*Rinji senpaku kanri-ho*) took effect. Establishment of the (government-run) Machinery Laboratory.*

10 Establishment of the Planning Office. The Materials Mobilization Plan for October–December 1937 (the first plan).

1938.1 The Materials Mobilization Plan for 1938 (revised in June).

3 Promulgation of the Machine Tool Building Act (MTBA).* Establishment of the National General Mobilization Act (*Kokka sodoin-ho*) and the Electricity State Control Act (promulgated in April and effective in May).

3–6 Introduction of rationing for cotton thread, gasoline, animal feed, ammonium sulfate, and steel.

7 Designation of six companies, including Ohkuma and Ikegai, as licensed makers of machine tools under the MTBA.* Opening by Planning Office of S-model machine tools.* Promulgation and enforcement of Rules Concerning Machine Tool Supply Controls.*

8 Promulgation of Rules Concerning Subsidies for Trial Production of Machine Tools.*

10 Designation of four additional companies, including Kokusan Seiki and Shibaura Machine Tools, as licensed makers of machine tools (by May 1941, designated firms would number twenty-one).* Establishment of the Committee on Machine Tool Building.*

1939.1 Cabinet decision on the Production Capacity Expansion Plan.

8 Promulgation of General Mobilization Experiment and Research Order (*Sodoin shiken kenkyu-rei*).*

9 Promulgation of Rules Concerning Machinery Equipment Control.*

10 Promulgation of the Price Control Order (the order prohibited the raising of prices, wages, land and housing rent, and other items above the level of 18 September 1939).

12 Establishment of Toyokawa Naval Arsenal. Establishment of the First Machine Tool Industrial Union.*

1940.6 US machine tool embargo.*

7 Establishment of the Military Ordnance Industry Association.* US adoption of an export license system for scrap iron and petroleum. Beginning of controversy over Economic New Order. Break-up of labor unions.

12 Cabinet decision on the Economic New Order Plan.

1941.3 Strengthening revision of the National General Mobilization Act.

8 Promulgation of Imperial Order for Key Industry Associations,* upon which twelve control associations were established, beginning with the Steel Control Association in October.

12 The outbreak of Pacific War. Promulgation of financial policies for emergency. Promulgation of the Corporation Approval Order and the Materials Control Order.

1942.1 Establishment of the Precision Tool Control Association (PTCA).*

2 Establishment of the Wartime Finance Corporation. Revision of the Bank of Japan Act. Promulgation of the Special Subsidy Act for Arms Manufacturing Plants.

3 Cabinet decision to promote corporate reorganization and job conversion of small businesses.

4 Promulgation of the Finance Control Associations Order. Establishment of finance control associations.

5 Promulgation of the Corporation Reorganization Order and the Financial Business Reorganization Order.

8 Establishment of the Machine Tool Components Manufacturers Union.* Promulgation of Rules Concerning the Certificate of Excellent Machine Tools.*

11 Opening of the National Machine Tools Exhibition.*

1943.3 Promulgation of the Act for Exceptional Wartime Administration Concerning Procedure and Jurisdiction (this Act gave the prime minister the authority to control production in five key industries: steel, coal, light metals, shipbuilding, and aircraft).

10 Promulgation of the Munitions Company Act.

11 Establishment of the Ministry of Munitions. First designation of 150 companies as munitions companies (the second designation of 422 companies came in April 1944, and a third designation of 109 occurred in December 1944).

1944.1 Establishment of the Airforce Manufacturing Industry Association. Production of Wartime-model Machine Tools.* Start of the financial institution designation system to munitions companies.

2 Announcement of policy to reorganize machinery industries.*

1945.4 Promulgation of the munitions arsenal system and designation of Nakajima Aircraft as the first munitions arsenal and Kawanishi Aircraft as the second.

8 End of World War II.

1.2.3   The PTCA: an outline from official statements

The efficient allocation of resources through effective government control is always hard, and wartime Japan was no exception. The system for control and materials allocation was not only huge but also extremely complicated. Largely, it did not work.

Government control was reinforced step by step

As can be seen from the historical timeline, particularly the period from 1937 to 1945 saw extremely strict government economic controls, with government control of the overall economy reinforced step by step. Since 1937, when it became clear that the war in China would be protracted, the controls grew broader in coverage and the system became stronger. Nakamura (1983: p.290) summarizes the logic of the system in a step-by-step process as follows:

1   Limited funds had to be preferentially channeled towards the industries necessary for military expansion. Thus, control over funds became unavoidable.
2   An import control system was necessary to ensure stable importation of goods for direct military manufacturing and of facilities for key industries supporting military production.
3   These imports had to be paid for within the limits of foreign currency resources derived from exports, non-merchandise receipts, gold shipments, sales of foreign bonds, and other emergency measures.
4   The most important foreign currency earning exports were cotton textiles and other light manufactures, so there was a need to ensure imports of the raw materials for these industries.
5   The import capacity available for privately used goods was only the amount left over after military import needs and export-industry raw material needs were subtracted from total import capacity. Toward this end, the Materials Mobilization Plan was an imperative (and here too the government needed control over funds).
6   Production of ordinary consumer goods for consumption had to be reduced, and therefore price controls were imperative.
7   An organization for the control of distribution became necessary.
8   Since the labor force had already been reduced by conscription, the maintenance of production required a new class of workers. To this end, 'labor mobilization' and 'national conscription' became necessary.

The starting point of analysis: the establishment of the PTCA

In investigating the impact of government intervention in the private sector with particular emphasis on policy effectiveness, it is useful to first choose a point in time and analyse the government–industry interaction that occurred. Then, using that period as a benchmark, analyse the interaction during the periods directly before and after the chosen time.

I choose as the starting point of analysis the establishment of the Precision Tool Control Association (PTCA) in January 1942. The PTCA was established by the Imperial Order for Key Industry Associations of July 1941, which in turn was based on section 18 of the National General Mobilization Act. That Act provides: 'in wartime, if necessary for general mobilization, the government may by Imperial Order order the owners of enterprises considered relevant for general mobilization to establish an association for controlling their business. ... The government may force compliance with any such government order in any way necessary.' The government order is illustrative of the highest stage of Japan's wartime control, decreeing the establishment of control associations to manage the key wartime industries (JMTBA 1962: p.131). Section 4 stipulated that 'the primary objective of control associations is to assume total control of an industry and to carry out national policy within an industry in order to maximize the national economic potential.'

The PTCA

Under section 5 of the statute, the Minister of Commerce and Industry (hereafter, the Commerce Ministry) designated firms to be members of the PTCA. As of 1 December 1941, the list of members included 318 producers of machine tools, forty of general tools, nineteen of bearings, and four of precision tools. The minister appointed the president of Osaka Kiko Co. as the first chairman of the PTCA.

The primary task of the PTCA was to supplement the administrative competence of the Precision Tool Section of the Machinery Bureau in the Commerce Ministry. During 1940–1, wartime control became much stronger and far-reaching, consequently making the task of industry control much more complicated. This led to a call for simpler and more efficient and competent administration, and the government attempted to answer this call with the establishment of powerful control associations by industry members (*ibid.*: p.132). The PTCA was in charge of a wide variety of products called 'precision tools,' including machine tools, tools, bearings, measuring machinery, optical machinery, and experimental machinery, simply because those products were all under the jurisdiction of the Precision Tool Section. The association itself was a private organization and relied fully on membership fees for its operation. However, its objective was to plan and implement national policy.

Section 1 of the statute stipulated:

> The primary objective of the Association is to cooperate with the government in managing total control of the industry and in planning and implementing national policy for the industry, thereby promoting the manufacturing and distribution of precision tools in Japan, and so completing the High-Level National Security System.

The PTCA made efforts to restructure the industry and coordinate both the demand for and the supply and price of products. To this end, the association participated in the government's planning regarding the production and distribution of machine tools, the supply of and demand for production materials, equipment, finance, labor, fuel, and energy, and related issues concerning the industry. The task and sphere of authority of the association was further detailed in the Control Rule of the PTCA, which stipulated that individual members of the association had to obey fully the guidance and instructions of the association. The association's role as an effective extension of the Precision Tool Section of the Commerce Ministry became clearer with the Imperial Order for the Delegation of Government Authority, promulgated in 1943. This order clarified the bounds of the government authority delegated to control associations. The authority delegated to the PTCA was so wide as to establish the association as a fully functioning control execution organization under the wartime economic system (*ibid.*: pp.132–3).

The Commerce Ministry delegated a variety of powers to the control associations (e.g., authority to grant permission under the Foundry Use Restriction Rule or the Machinery Use Restriction Rule, and analogous authority under the Scrap Iron Distribution Control Rule and the Carbide Distribution Control Rule). The procedure for submitting necessary documents under the above rules was changed from a direct submission to the relevant ministries to a submission through the association. Furthermore, the documentation required under a variety of regulations was also required to be submitted through the PTCA: the Machine Tool Building Act, the Imperial Order for Implementing the MTBA, the Rule for Implementing the MTBA, the Subsidy Granting Rule for Trial Production of New Machine Tools, the Rule for Authorizing Superior Machine Tools, the Key Machines Manufacturing Act, the Imperial Order for Implementing this Act, the Rule for Implementing this Act, the Subsidy Granting Rule for Trial Production of New Key Machines, and the Imperial Order for Controlling Corporate Accounting (*ibid.*: p.133).

The production instruction system

The association's goal was to expand the production of precision tools, including machine tools, for military production. This task was to be accomplished by strategically allocating materials throughout the industry in accordance with the Materials Mobilization Plan. In this regard, the association intervened in all aspects of individual members' plant management, except for funds for capacity investment. Furthermore, the military and banks made preferential loans to them (*ibid.*: p.133). Toward this end, the association adopted the production instruction system and a materials rationing system.

Under the production instruction system, each factory reported its quarterly production plans for each model, based upon capacity and the volume of orders received. The association then controlled the process of production by examining these plans, particularly the suitability of the orders and the feasibility of the stated production capacity. The association made every effort to facilitate the full production outlined in the plans it examined and tried to allocate the resources needed so that member firms could devote themselves to maximizing their production capacity. Yet military demand increased explosively as the war progressed and soon far exceeded the aggregate capacity of all plants. The association was then faced with the task of rationing resources preferentially to sectors (those sectors making products whose demand priority was the highest) designated by the government.

At this stage, reports to the association from factories divided demand into five categories: from the Army Ordnance Department; from the Army Air Services Department; from the Naval Technical Department; from the Department of Naval Aeronautics; and general demand from both the government and the private sector. For each category, the reports described the details of the model and the size of machines, and the volume of orders. The association then organized production meetings with representatives from the various groups and discussed production plans and the rationing required (*ibid.*: p.134). In coordinating private and military demand, the machinery industries were unusual. According to the JMTBA (*ibid.*: p.134):

> Other control associations based on the National General Mobilization Act covered only private demand and not military demand. It is worthy of special mention that production control and the rationing of global demand [that is, demand from the military, the government, and the private sector] was carried out only regarding machine tools.

Materials rationing system

The Materials Department of the PTCA calculated the quantities of materials needed to produce each model at each individual plant by determining the unit material requirements. Every effort was then made for their full supply. The association issued certificates for materials rationing to members, with which they purchased the materials they needed from sellers in the Steel Control Association.[8]

Even for a standardized material like steel, the system for control and materials allocation constituted a large pyramid. The Japanese Federation of Industrial Unions of Steel Products (JFIUSP) and its 1,000-plus component unions organized under the Act on Industrial Unions constituted the key control institutions in the machinery manufacturing sector. The federation literally controlled chains of associations in each prefecture or each industry. Among this chain of associations was the Japanese Federation of Machinery Manufacturers Unions, which was comprised of industrial unions of Japan's representative manufacturers from the heavy machinery industry. Also in this chain were federations of steel products industrial unions from each of forty-seven prefectures, federations of sixteen additional industrial unions from various industries, federations of thirty-three trans-prefectural industrial unions, and federations of thirteen federations of industrial unions in new industries. Steel, a fundamental material for machinery manufacturing, was allocated throughout the machinery manufacturing industries through this huge pyramidal system of control.

In the machine tool industry, the producers designated under the Machine Tool Building Act together organized the Japan Machine Tool Builders Union. Non-designated producers organized their own unions in seven prefectures and formed the Industrial Federation of Industrial Unions of Machine Tool Builders as their national association. Previously, machine tool makers organized unions in such prefectures as Tokyo, Osaka, Aichi, Hyogo, and Shizuoka and then gained membership in the JFIUSP by becoming affiliated with other JFIUSP-affiliated unions in their prefecture. According to the general machinery section chief of the Machinery Bureau in the Commerce Ministry:

> prefectural federations had in the past adopted industrial performance of indi-vidual plants as the standard by which materials allocation was determined, which was not considered consistent with the requirements of this situation. Accordingly in July 1939, we reorganized producers that met our threshold standards in the machinery manufacturing sectors … for expanding industrial production, into prefectural industrial unions in each sector.
>
> (Hashii 1940a: p.125)

The system for control and materials allocation was not only a large pyramid but also extremely complicated. Often a company, particularly a large company, would belong to more than one control organization. On 10 May 1944, Toshiba, for instance, belonged to eight military control associations, including the Naval Electric Industry Association, the Naval Shipbuilding Industry Association, the Naval Machine Tool Industry Association, the Airforce Industry Association, and the Military Ordnance Industry Association; to five other control associations, including the Electric Machinery Control Association, the Precision Tool Control Association, and the Steel Control Association; and to thirty-three industrial unions (Toshiba 1963: p.178).

Troubles with the supply of materials

The smooth production of machine tools required the provision of the needed materials in proper quantities, of proper quality, and in step with the buyer's production schedule. However, with worsening supply conditions, material supplies tended to be delayed, which forced buyers to turn to materials of lesser quality. Because production plans then deviated from the actual rationing that occurred, the certificates could not always be honored.

In July 1939, the unions under the Japanese Federation of Machinery Manufacturers Unions unanimously adopted a card system to regulate the rationing of steel, and the Japan Machine Tool Builders Union adopted the system at the same time. After that period, each producer was required to fill in the details of orders for production received on a card of the prescribed form, which included the type and model of tool ordered, the purpose of its use, the quantity of materials needed, the time of delivery, the production schedule, and so forth. This card would be presented to the union for assessment, and the union control committee then examined the order of steel represented by the submitted card to determine whether it accorded with the circumstances at the time. If it approved the order, the union issued a ticket for steel rationing of the endorsed quantity. Materials were not allocated to unapproved orders. Although matters became more routine inside the union with the introduction of the card system (*ibid.*: p.127), even by May 1941 only twenty-two machine tool makers had been designated under the Act and had joined the union, and they did not dominate the machine tool industry. According to Hashii (*ibid.*):

> Machine tool industrial unions in each prefecture also conducted the practice of allocating materials preferentially by approval to fill orders. In addition, they too adopted in October a card system whereby after examining the details of submitted cards they allocated materials. Their card system was however much simpler than that of the Japan Machine Tool Builders Union.

Note that it was in November 1943 that the Ministry of Munitions was established and 150 enterprises were designated as munitions companies. The procurement of materials was not easy even before this stage. Steel, as the core material for machine tool production, had been subject to rationing through tickets since July 1937, including all materials from non-ferrous metals to bearings and electrical/electronic components. Although materials were preferentially rationed to machine tool production for military use, military factories received far less than they demanded. About the process, Toyo Machines (later Mitsubishi Machine Tools) complained in March 1941:

> (1) Iron and steel are of such bad quality that we are always uneasy about using them. (2) It is extremely difficult to procure high speed steel for tools and non-ferrous metals. (3) It is impossible to procure electric wires even with rationing tickets, and we find none in the market. (4) We have been allocated no rations of imported bearings, and the quality of domestic bearings is unsatisfactorily low.
>
> (Mitsubishi Heavy Industries 1964: pp.50–1)

The association's actual task changed with the progress of the war. Doing away with the submission of plans by producers for examination by the association, it accepted orders directly from users and then allocated production to association members. With this change, the struggle for first-class makers' products became even keener. In principle, military production was treated preferentially, especially aircraft production, and only second- and third-class machine tools remained for the production of goods for civilian use (JMTBA 1962: p.137). In any event, shortages of raw materials continued to grow, and by 1944 supply problems threatened the very survival of machine tool production (*ibid.*: p.136).

1.2.4   Evaluation of the PTCA's function: (1) introduction of the mainstream view

Identifying and rigorously evaluating the actual function of an organization like the PTCA is seldom easy. Evaluating the effect of a policy or the impact of an event presupposes its identification. In this case, we have to identify any likely deviations between the actual state of affairs and the hypothetical state without the association. First, let us introduce the view generally accepted by commentators in this area.

Nakamura and Hara's overall appraisal of the control association system

Despite its popular image as 'wartime control at its peak or ultimate,' mainstream evaluation of the actual function of the PTCA is not very flattering. Nakamura and Hara (1972: pp.72, 120–1) provide the following overall appraisal of the industry control system based on control associations like the PTCA:

> The contribution of 'control associations' to production increase was not great. Government authorities were seldom delegated as planned to 'control associations.' Above all, the material shortages simply cannot be resolved by merely reorganizing institutions. Moreover, the major industry figures that were anticipated to head control associations did not move from their original industry positions. Hence association posts were taken by retired veterans. … The associations were expected to complete the four tasks of planning and research, production control, technical guidance, and management guidance. … What associations actually performed was far from the role expected of them, that is making every effort toward realizing production increases by improving efficiency through industry-wide collaboration with government. Rather, all they actually did were routine works for industry control as a body subordinate to the controlling government section, 'coordinating' tasks in

prompting the preferential allocation of production materials to large firms, and further 'reorganizing' small businesses within the industry.

The delegation of government authority to associations did not proceed as planned, as this next passage describes:

> The control associations, far from achieving the regulation of the industries that was expected of them, were accused of inefficiency and bureaucratization. With the progress of war, requests for military production expansion became increasingly urgent, and the control association system was criticized as obsolete and ineffective for controlling industries. … Some argued that production should be reorganized to a system completely controlled by the state, like the corporation system or steering committee system. Others argued that the state should buy up during the war all the key industries and operate them as privately owned–state managed enterprises. When authority was actually delegated to the associations, well over a year after their establishment and on a far more restricted basis than was planned at the start, the associations were no longer recognized as principal agents for wartime production expansion. The control association system was abandoned as a failure, with insufficient time to use the limited authority delegated to them. The role expected of control systems shifted to the state controlled enterprises designated under the Munitions Company Act since November 1943.

Three points from Nakamura and Hara on the control association system

Although the standard by which they judge the control associations is unclear, Nakamura and Hara (*ibid.*) summarize their function with the following three points, with which I agree.

First, unable to operate effectively, the associations had no substantial impact on the behavior of individual firms or on aggregate industry supply. As I discuss below, most control associations were formed by restructuring established cartels. I do not argue that control associations did absolutely nothing. Rather, I argue that the restructuring of the cartels into control associations had no substantial impact on the industry. Moreover, in the precision tool manufacturing sector, including the machine tool industry, the Precision Tool Section by itself performed no substantial 'coordinating' role.

Second, there was tremendous resistance to the establishment of the control associations both from industry and within the government at every step in their establishment and operation. For instance, there was resistance to the enactment of the Imperial Order for Key Industry Associations, under which the control associations were established, to the very establishment of the associations and to their operating process, which involved the delegation of government control to the associations to strengthen and expand their roles. Because of this resistance, even if the government could have had stronger legal powers, their effective operation would have been far from easy.

An issue that has been hotly debated since the publication of the Basic Plan for Establishing the Economic New Order at the beginning of December 1940 was the organizational structure of the control associations: whether several control associations should be established, one in each sector of the machinery industry, or simply one all-governing machinery control association. In December 1941, it was finally agreed that industry-specific control associations were desirable, and control associations were established in the precision tools, industrial machinery, electrical and electronics machinery, automobiles, and locomotive industries. The Machinery Industry Council was assigned the voluntary task of coordinating these five associations (Kawasaki 1943: p.299).

A quotation from Kawasaki, in which a journalist appointed to the Commerce Ministry described the administration of machinery production, is illustrative:

> It is well known that tradition, the nature of the present system of administration, and on extreme occasions even the breakdown of interpersonal relationships, caused conflicts, miscommunication, and a lack of coordination among concerned government sections or ministries, giving rise to much trouble. This applies particularly to the machinery industries, where so wide a variety of materials are necessary for production. The lack of coordination among concerned government sections still remains today as it did before. The improvement of the coordination of players and policies within the several industries which comprise the machinery industry ought to be fundamental to economic planning for the machinery industry. It has now been agreed to establish a control association in each individual industry; unfortunately this leaves the present system of uncoordinated administration untouched. Accordingly, a central coordinating organization, having the power to swiftly and appropriately solve the troubles between those control associations and conflicts among concerned government sections is necessary. After all, efficient machinery production together with expansions in machinery production requires a close relationship among these individual industries.
>
> (*ibid.*: p.306)

Third, the widespread resistance to control associations declined when expanding production in key industries such as aircraft manufacturing became a high priority. At least then we can observe a unity of purpose within the government. With this, direct state control of industry under the above-mentioned state-controlled enterprises designated under the Munitions Company Act became at least theoretically possible.

Under this system, the state appointed directors to private firms, and those directors then relayed government production instructions to the production managers at their companies and monitored their compliance. The state also had the right to both discipline and dismiss company directors and production managers for non-compliance, and further had authority to order the alteration of corporate charters as necessary. This effectively put private enterprises under army-like organization, but whether it effectively expanded production is another question (which I discuss in Section 1.2.12). Short-term impact aside, such a move seldom raises production and virtually never improves efficiency.

However, I do not argue that persons directly in charge of this change did not understand the ramifications of it. Saburo Endo, the first air ordnance bureau chief of the Munitions Ministry, stated in his interview that 'I knew that the public-owned enterprise was essentially inefficient. ... If this system were to live long, managers and employees would grow listless, akin to public servants' (Ando 1966: p.307).

The situation was not improved even in aircraft production in the later stages

The second and the third points mentioned above are well illustrated by the following scenario of actual events. In the autumn of 1943, with the military request to produce 55,000 aircraft per year for the Top-Level National Security Zone, the government adopted a production target of 40,000 aircraft. It adopted a wide variety of policies to achieve this target, even before it merged the Planning Office with the military production-related sections of the Commerce Ministry to form the Ministry of Munitions. For instance, in March 1943 the prime minister's authority was much strengthened with the Act on Exceptional Wartime Administration concerning Procedure and Jurisdiction. With this newly delegated authority, the prime minister designated five industries as industries of ultimate importance – steel, coal, light metals, shipbuilding, and aircraft manufacturing – and was empowered to give orders for expansion of production in these industries. At the same time, the government organized the Conference on the Wartime Economy and under the Administration Inspection Rule established the Administration Inspector Body. It appointed seven cabinet counselors to the body for the purpose of investigating potential for expansion of production in individual industries. In the same month, 541 factories in eight industries were designated for investigation of machine production expansion. It carried out first-round inspections in May. However, the course of the war had already aggravated the situation. The battle of Guadalcanal caused the government to draft many ships from the private sector, and that in turn disrupted the supply of basic materials like steel (Hara 1989: pp.89, 91). To tackle this situation, the government then organized the Temporary Commission on Production Expansion at the end of November 1942.

These policies for expanding military aircraft production suggest three points: (1) by strengthening the prime minister's authority, the government did try to facilitate cooperation and policy coherence across agency lines; (2) it tried to foster that cooperation and coherence only in relation to expansion of production in the five listed industries; (3) it did not organize a group to inspect industry until May 1943. Kawasaki (1943: pp.278–9) described the administration for machinery production in 1943 as follows:

> What I require first of control associations is for them to fully observe and understand the present state of their own industry. It is obvious that we should not fill orders, without exactly understanding the present state and the competence of their own factories. Likewise, we should not take the responsibility of filling the orders, without fully understanding the competence, efficiency, state of operation and labor management, and material availability of individual factories, and accordingly the state of the industry. Thus, above all, a control association should study precisely the state of the industry and association members. It is not too much to emphasize this point. ... Once this request is filled, it may safely be said that the control association would achieve more than half of the objective. An impatient demand only for the delegation of authority to control associations suggests a failure in fully understanding this point.

1.2.5   Evaluation of the PTCA's function: (2) background to the establishment of control associations

As the war effort deteriorated in 1943, the prime minister's authority was strengthened and government intervention in production increased, as mentioned above. And it is at this stage that we see the government taking the step of enacting the Munitions Company Act. More precisely, it was *only* at this last stage and under such urgent circumstances that the government took such action. This Act codifies the basic function and actual roles of control associations. Understanding that function and those roles requires an investigation of the background of the establishment of the associations.

The New Economic Order and the Imperial Order for Key Industry Associations

The Imperial Order for Key Industry Associations (by which the control associations were established) was made public in August 1941. This was almost a year after the New Economic Order as a component of 'Konoe New Order' became a critical political issue, which was in the autumn of 1940.

In June 1940, Konoe Ayamaro, strongly advocating the 'New Order,' resigned as chairman of the Privy Council, a political-legal body separate from the parliamentary government. The Army responded to his resignation by withholding the war minister, and the Yonai Cabinet duly collapsed. Konoe then formed his second cabinet and began to implement his New Order – albeit still without clarifying what he meant by it. He organized the Imperial Rule Assistance Association and became its first president, but this organization soon changed character and became an organization subordinate to the Ministry of the Interior. The dream of the 'Political New Order' crumbled rapidly (Nakamura and Hara 1972: pp.71, 88).

The political debate centered on two issues. The first was economic. With the Sino-Japanese War in progress since 1937, military expenditure had increased drastically, and the Japanese international balance of payments had fallen into huge deficit. The economy had become extremely difficult to manage, and this led to strong calls for the establishment of direct control over both materials and finance. The second was ideological, namely that both the political Right (by the Army) and the Socialist Popular Party (also connected with the Army) argued strongly for reform of the capitalist system (*ibid.*: p.71).

With the onset of the 'New Order' debate, the Planning Office rapidly began to draft various basic plans, such as the Economic System Reorganization Plan, the Corporate Finance and Accounting Control Plan, and the Industry Rationalization Plan. The Economic New Order Plan declared its basic objectives with four points: (1) establishing a national economic ideology that would support and contribute to the nation's security; (2) reforming the free enterprise system; (3) organizing the national economy into a totally planned production organ; and (4) constructing a national security system to implement the nation's objectives. Readers will realize that what the Planning Office produced here was the conceptual foundation to wartime controls and therefore to the control associations.

The private sector was, not surprisingly, fundamentally opposed to radical plans for reorganizing the economic system. Instead, firms in the private sector proposed that they themselves should reorganize the system of economic control because they best understood the real economy. For instance, the National Congress for Cooperation over Price Control, attended by representatives of most nationwide economic associations, argued as follows on 19 July 1940:

> Self-regulation is a key to effective economic control. The controlling body and the controlled body ought to be part of one unit. In the past, a private economic enterprise has simply been a profit pursuing institution (the controlled), with the government intervening into its activities to control it (the controller). In such a situation it is extremely hard even for the strongest power to achieve the overall goal without very well organized government– business cooperation. We should immediately reorganize and strengthen our industry unions and associations and appoint industry leaders as the chairmen.

We, the private sector, should participate in economic planning and control, using this organizational structure as the foundations for effective implementation of this our self-governing goal.

(*Yearbook of the National Congress for Cooperation over Price Control*, June 1941, pp.139–40)

The New Economic Order debate

The Planning Office had almost determined the outline of the new basic plan at the end of September 1940, when details of the plan leaked to newspapers. The papers then reported that the plan would adopt the separation of management from ownership model. The business community reacted negatively, and the New Economic Order debate ensued and continued until November. 'It was more serious than any other government–business debate that had occurred since the start of direct control. The so-called business offensive reached its peak in November when even cabinet members became involved' (Nakamura and Hara 1972: p.96). On 12 November, a meeting of economic ministers was held, and discussion commenced about the basic plan for establishing the Economic New Order. However, the meeting was unable to reach a conclusion, even after convening not just one but several meetings, due to tremendous resistance to the plan. A modified version of the plan, adopted on 1 December, in fact closely reflected the proposals of the business community in many areas. However, the business community remained dissatisfied with the plan, and the cabinet finally adopted a further revised version on 7 December.

Being a compromise between 'reform' bureaucrats, who advocated stronger state control of the economy, and the business community, which advocated the opposite, the plan as eventually adopted remained ambiguous. That ambiguity, in turn, would generate continuing disagreements between private-sector firms and the government for the rest of the war.

From the cabinet decision to the control associations

From the initial development of the plan to the establishment of the Imperial Order for Key Industry Associations and the control associations, the private sector and the bureaucracy struggled over interpretations of the plan and the policies to implement it. Each worked to shift the policies to its private advantage (*ibid.*: pp.100, 102), and more than a year passed before the PTCA began operations.

The Tokyo Chamber of Commerce (1941: p.2), at the beginning of its survey report on the progress of small business mergers at the end of 1940, described business mergers as the central objective of industrial reorganization policy: 'Business mergers are inevitable. It is the only way of survival for businesses. On this point, however, the government has not yet clearly indicated their stance, that is, whether they will promote mergers or not. Business, suffering from disorder, strongly demanded the swift determination of government policy on mergers.' Stating that there were clamorous arguments for and against the issue, the survey report introduced four main points against any potential merger policy: (1) independently managed firms seemed to be more profitable than merged firms; (2) business mergers were fine as an ideal but difficult to realize in practice; (3) the question of what business would do if in the future the economic system reverted to a free enterprise system; and (4) that business mergers would deprive the country of many traditional family-owned and -operated firms. These four elements of opposition to business mergers consistently posed large obstacles to government wartime control.

The publication of the Imperial Order for Key Industry Associations was delayed until 30 August 1941. The most serious cause of the delay was the conflict of opinion among government institutions, particularly the Commerce Ministry and the Planning Office. The former was backed by the business community and the latter by 'reform' bureaucrats (Nakamura and Hara 1972: pp.113–14).

Parallel to the cabinet decision regarding the basic plan, the bureaucracy intended to propose to the Diet a law, the Industrial Organization Act, with which it would restructure industry associations. The General Affairs Bureau of the Commerce Ministry finalized the draft bill for this law in December 1940. However, 'because of tremendous political complications surrounding the draft law, particularly due to strong opposition both from the ideological right wing and bureaucrats of the Interior Ministry and from "the business offensive," a total change of character was forced upon the Konoe New Order in general, including the Political New Order' (*ibid.*: p.107). In the end, the Commerce Ministry abandoned its bill and resorted instead to a Key Industry Associations Order.

Furthermore, the cabinet order for designating key industries, expected to appear within two weeks of the imperial order, was also delayed. Nakamura and Hara describe two reasons for the delay:

> First, the Commerce Ministry strongly insisted that the chairman of control associations should be full-time. In opposition to this the business sector argued that making the post of chairman full-time would mean that the chairman would have to leave his own business, which of course people were reluctant to do. Thus, having a full-time chairman would potentially exclude quality candidates from consideration. Second, there was a heated struggle among ministries for jurisdiction over control associations.
>
> (*ibid.*: p.115)

Nakamura and Hara also give examples of such struggles. For instance, after much conflict between bureaucratic agencies, the agencies reached a temporary compromise on 14 October that detailed the following four points of agreement: (1) the designation of industries to control associations would proceed gradually, step by step; (2) the ministries having jurisdiction over a control association could give the association instructions even if they did not directly control it; (3) the ministry in charge of a control association would communicate with the ministry in charge of demand sectors concerning supply–demand control and price controls for that sector; and (4) the chairman of a control association should come from a private firm and be in principle full-time, and comprehensive government authority should be delegated to the control associations (*ibid.*: p.115).

The first designation of members for twelve associations in nine industries was made public on 30 October.

Two faces of the control associations

A control association, thus finally established, had two faces: first, that of a trade association for private firms; and, second, that of a government institution to influence those private firms. Because of their character as private trade associations, there was no assurance that an association's control function would be used to improve the 'public interest,' even though it had been restructured from private cartels into national control institutions. Yet the new governmental aspect of the associations necessitated a tremendous administrative expansion – an expansion far beyond the administrative scale of the associations' former cartel headquarters.

An association also suffered from coordination of jurisdiction with its supervising government agency, the bureaucratization of its own organization, and efficiency declines due to jurisdictional disputes with rival associations. As mentioned above, the delegation of government authority to control associations was finally settled on 17 November 1942, which was a whole year after the commencement of the control associations (*ibid.*: p.119).

In 1943, Kawasaki (1943: p.319) made the following comment on the control associations in general, including the PTCA. If his comment in any way reflects the true state of affairs, it is only natural that the machinery control associations did not achieve remarkable success by the end of the war in 1945. His comment was that:

> We had to make every effort in establishing a planned production system suitable for the war, taking well into account the vices of the past control system. Only a half year has passed since the start of the control associations, and it is too early to expect them to have fully flourished. We had to concede the next one or two years at least as a preparatory stage. Rome was not built in a day. Problems to be overcome to make the control associations effective are large and serious, and we need long time.

1.2.6   Evaluation of the PTCA's function:
(3) potential effectiveness of a policy

Let us now examine the potential effectiveness of a policy like establishing control associations for implementing policy objectives. The level of effectiveness of any policy should be evaluated by the extent to which any predetermined objective was realized (I ignore unintentional policy impacts) and accordingly those policy objectives must at the outset be clearly defined.

Control associations were the product of great compromise, with strong resistance and heated controversy surrounding their establishment. Therefore the precise role expected of control associations was somewhat unclear. Neither was it apparent whose expectations were reflected in the policies finally adopted; nor was there serious discussion on improving policy details.

In this complicated situation, I take here a simple path. First, I assume that the government could foresee all the potential economic effects of its policies and all the potential ways through which it might implement those policies. Second, assuming the correctness of the predicted policy effects, I then compare the projected policy effect with its probable costs to calculate the maximum net value and ultimate desirability of the policy. I will then discount that value by taking into consideration the constraints that conditioned the policy, such as the procedure for designing and implementing policy. The final figure reached will represent an estimate of policy effectiveness.

Even the most competent government could not effectively achieve policy goals if there were no potential effects of the policy to start with, if there were no potential paths by which to implement those potential effects, or if policy costs were tremendously high. As shown below, in the machine tool industry under wartime control, the potential effect of the policies was limited, and control association options for their implementation were limited by many strong constraints.

The basic model for discussion

Let us suppose that the government has both a strong will and a well-defined objective when it implements an industry promotion policy. Suppose also that new entry into the targeted industry is prohibited, which assures that the industry members, the subject of the policy, are given. Now assume that each firm in the industry maximizes its profits subject to the existing constraints, which obviously include those constraints that are the subject of government policy. Such a situation, or close to it, existed under the Materials Mobilization Plans, which began in the last quarter of 1937. Basic production materials like steel were strictly rationed by the government. Thus the extremely limited availability of materials to be allocated to each industry to achieve national policy became one of the key constraints for relevant government agencies in implementing that policy.

Let us add four simplifying assumptions to the above scenario:

1   The range of feasible products for each firm is fixed. Given this, new product development is not a policy issue, and the government has no interest in each firm's competence in product development.
2   The quality and performance of a product are given. Therefore the government has no interest in each firm's competence in improving product quality and performance.
3   The production cost of an item is given. The government therefore has no interest in each firm's competence in cost reduction.
4   The government has precise and relevant information about each target firm's product range, product quality and performance, and production costs.

In the above scenario, the optimal paths of policy implementation for the government to achieve policy objectives are obvious. First, it will select the best mix of products from the available range among producers in the industry. Second, it will send its orders to the most efficient manufacturers of the products at prices equal to production costs. Third, it will allocate to those chosen efficient manufacturers the minimum necessary amount of materials.[9] The fact of wartime control has no significance.

The government in the above scenario faces essentially the same issue as managers in procurement sections of the contemporary Japanese government, or managers in the purchasing sections of automobile manufacturers under long-term trade relationships with parts suppliers. In the latter cases, a purchasing agent neither welcomes collusive behavior among suppliers nor forces them to form a cartel or control association. Thus, in the above-stated scenario, establishing control associations seems unlikely to be a rational policy.[10] Production control is unnecessary and irrelevant and would contribute no potential benefit to the government yet generate substantial policy implementation costs.

The effect of relaxing assumptions

Now let us relax some of the assumptions in the above scenario. Suppose we eliminate the fourth assumption, that the government has precise relevant information regarding each firm's product range, product quality and performance, and production costs. This assumption is unrealistic anyway, and it would only have been satisfied in circumstances where individual firms had small product ranges, with small variations in product quality and performance, and further where there were only small differences in manufacturing costs between rival enterprises (presumably based upon well-established production technology). In the machinery industries, including the machine tool industry, there are typically a large number of firms with a wide range of products in their catalogs. Nor would the assumption hold in the situations that managers face both in the procurement sections of today's Japanese government and in the purchasing sections of car manufacturers. Yet even without such information, the government has no reason to establish control associations. A car maker solves the problem by using competitive pressures between suppliers through bidding requirements, and the government could do the same (see Miwa 1996a: ch. 4; Miwa and Ramseyer 2000c).

If a control association were to cooperate with the government, each member firm would likely be uncooperative with the association in providing information regarding products anyway. An association that was uncooperative with government, on the other hand, would have the necessary product information but would probably not cooperate with government to the government's best advantage. Thus, even had it wanted to gather the information, the government could have gained little by establishing control associations in the machinery industries.

The same argument applies to each of the other three additional assumptions in the above scenario. Suppose we eliminate, for instance, the third assumption, meaning that the competence level of individual firms in the target industry differs regarding reducing manufacturing costs, and further that the government lacks precise knowledge of the competence of each firm. This situation again represents the reality faced by managers both in the procurement sections of contemporary Japanese government and in the purchasing sections of car makers trading with parts suppliers. Yet such buyers find no reason to force suppliers to organize a cartel or to establish a control association. Without precise knowledge, establishing a control association would contribute nothing to improving government control. Instead, they allocate their orders through competitive bidding. Ultimately, whether or not the four assumptions hold, control associations seem unlikely to be a rational policy.

The elimination of the underlying assumption that new entry into the target industry is prohibited only strengthens the above conclusion. Fixing the industry members by prohibiting new entry does have the benefit of cutting the cost of collecting information, making control easier. Accordingly, unless this assumption is satisfied, organizing an efficient centralized supply system, taking every potential entrant well into account, becomes more difficult. However, managers in the government's procurement sections and in automobile manufacturers' purchasing sections actually welcome new entrants with products that offer better cost performance, both directly for cost reduction and indirectly to increase competitive pressure on incumbent suppliers. Although the wartime control associations did prohibit industry entry, the government could not rationally have imposed that requirement to decrease its costs.

Kawasaki (1943: pp.298–9) concluded that the success of overall planning in the machinery industry totally depended on the effective and efficient mobilization plan for machinery products, and on close coordination between purchasers and suppliers, functioning as one mind and one body towards achieving the mobilization plan. The mobilization of domestic production was difficult because of the following three factors: (1) a detailed classification of all machinery was necessary; (2) each manufacturer made so wide a variety of products that it was almost impossible to estimate the production capacity for all individual products; and (3) when both the number of suppliers was small and demand forecasts were simple, it was relatively easy to make and carry out consistent demand–supply plans. Otherwise, however, making such plans was very difficult. These reasons suggest that the government, or at least some people in it, clearly and correctly recognized that the machine tool industry was one of the sectors most unsuited for machinery mobilization, and that planning was unlikely to promote its own best interests.

Was establishing control associations a rational economic policy?

Assuming that the government is competent, one struggles to think of any further plausible scenarios where the establishment of control associations could have been a rational policy. If so, then the control associations and the Munitions Company Act would not have represented rational ways to increase production and productivity, even under the circumstances of the time. Underlying the argument and support for strict industry control was an ideology critical of a free economic system, upon which the Economic New Order debate flourished, encompassing such issues as the separation of management from ownership, dividend restrictions, the public role of directors, leader discipline, and the reward system.

1.2.7 Evaluation of the PTCA's function: (4) comparison with shipbuilding control

Onozuka Ichiro

As mentioned above, the government established the Administrative Inspection Body to investigate the potential for expanding production in individual industries, and this body carried out the first round of inspections in May 1943. The very fact of these inspections suggests that, through its own institutions or through alternative organizations, the government did not collect detailed information on industries, or on enterprises within individual industries. Partly because of this, seldom do we find either formal documents or description of the policy history of the government, or studies based on such materials. As a memoir of a person in the Naval Technical Department directly in charge of shipbuilding control and planned shipbuilding, however, Onozuka's work (1962) is an exception.

Onozuka Ichiro belonged to the merchant marine subsection of the Fourth Section. Although finally published in 1962, this memoir was written during 1946–51, shortly after the events described. According to historian Teratani (1993: p.35), 'His career is really valuable, because he stayed at the center of the planned shipbuilding section over the period. It is not too much to say that only through his record of experience we could reach a detailed understanding of planned shipbuilding.'

A nationwide investigation in the shipbuilding industry

In order to investigate the causes of the bad performance of the first-ranked ship-yards and also to provide technical instructions to individual shipyards for drastic expansion in future shipbuilding, the Naval Technical Department organized a team headed by technical Vice-admiral Niwata that carried out a nationwide investigation of all first-ranked shipyards during October–December 1942. This investigation enabled the Navy to understand precisely the competence and tech-nical level of individual shipyards (Onozuka 1962: pp.49–50). Their instructions were primarily concerned with (1) the enforcement of work plans and scientific plant control methods related to them; (2) material management control methods; (3) practices for mass-production technology; and (4) detailed advice for the expansion and improvement of production facilities. Emphasizing the fruits of the tour, Onozuka (*ibid.*: p.49) concluded that it was not too much to say that with this tour most shipyards in Japan understood for the first time what planned shipbuilding was and understood mass production in practice. The government designated those shipyards that were building and repairing mainly naval vessels or steel ships over 50 meters long as first-ranked, to be controlled by the Naval Technical Department. Others, called second-ranked, were under the control of the Communications Ministry. At the start about thirty plants were first-ranked, but the number increased later to almost fifty. As explained below, the majority of arms manufacturing industries were originally under the direct control of the War Ministry (i.e., the Army) and the Navy Ministry, and in most cases they remained outside the jurisdiction of the control associations. However, with the establishment of the Shipbuilding Control Association, partial control over shipbuilding, which had been under the jurisdiction of the Communications Ministry, was transferred to the Navy Ministry, meaning that the building and repairing of all steel ships now fell under the administration of the Navy Ministry.

'The war headquarters aimed to rebuild military strength through increasing naval transportation capacity, and aimed to do this by directing the whole of the nation's power into the sector.' To this end, they carried out the sixth administra-tive inspection focusing on first-ranked shipyards between December 1943 and February 1944. 'The objective was to estimate the technological boundaries of Japan's shipbuilding capacity … and to propose concrete plans for shipbuilding at maximum (volume and technologies) capacity. The tour team included as accompanying members influential men from ministries like the Navy Ministry and associations in the private sector' (*ibid.*: p.63).

The Shipbuilding Control Association

We have no detailed information on the role and function of the Precision Tool Section of the Machinery Bureau in the Commerce Ministry, which was in charge of the Precision Tool Control Association. On 16 June 1939, the Commerce Ministry was totally reorganized in order to strengthen the government's control over industry. The ministry was reorganized into bureaus corresponding to individual industrial sectors, at the head of which was the Minister's Secretariat. As a result, the Machinery Bureau and under its control the Precision Tool Section, were established. However, at the time that the Sino-Japanese conflict accelerated in 1937, the precision tool industry, including the machine tool industry, among other industries, as controlled by the Manufacturing Administration Section of the Manufacturing Administration Bureau. The Manufacturing Administration Bureau was in charge of 'administration for manufacturing' in general and was distinguished both from the Control Bureau in charge of 'administration concerning industry control and industrial rationalization' and from the Occupational Change Policy Division, which was in charge of 'emergent administration of industry maintenance and restructuring' (JMTBA 1962: p.131; MITI 1962: pp.233–47).

We therefore have only to study the Shipbuilding Control Association (hereafter, the SCA), assuming that its characteristics were at least similar to the PTCA, and then draw conclusions regarding the PTCA by inference. I have chosen the shipbuilding industry as a comparative reference, primarily due to the outstanding importance and performance of shipbuilding during the war, and to the fact that shipbuilding is a machinery industry that shares technological similarity with the machine tool industry. As Takushiro Hattori, the strategy section chief of the Imperial Headquarters of the Military Department at the outbreak of the Pacific War, later argued, 'the strength of the nation totally depended on the amount of ships we possessed. The volume of ships was indeed of critical importance to the war effort' (Hattori 1965: p.156).

The SCA began with fourteen members, mostly large shipbuilders. Additional designations eventually increased membership to twenty-three domestic shipbuilders, three offshore shipbuilders, three shipbuilding machine manufacturers, and eight shipbuilders' control unions (Onozuka 1962: p.16). A simple comparison of this number of members with the PTCA's 318 members strongly suggests that the controller's burden must have been greater by far in the case of the PTCA, that is if they had intended to be effective.

The SCA was established around the Shipbuilders Federation, an incorporated association, by restructuring the then-voluntary association of large shipbuilders into a compulsory association. All shipbuilders and enterprises of related works joined the association, with small shipbuilders and manufacturers of supplementary machinery forming associations in order to join (*ibid.*: p.16).

Two points to note

Two points are worth noting here. First, the government had kept a keen eye on the development of this industry since long before the SCA's establishment. The government had prepared the legal foundation for active intervention in the sector through supervising shipping and providing subsidies to shipbuilders 'for the smooth transportation of basic materials' (*ibid.*: p.11). The Five-Year Plan for Key Industries dated June 1937 paid special attention to the shipbuilding industry and planned to expand Japan's current production capacity of 500,000 tons to 860,000 tons in the 1941 financial year (Nakamura 1983: pp.276–85). The National General Mobilization Act of April 1938 designated ships as a mobilization material and ship production and repair as a mobilization activity. Also, the Factories and Workplaces Control Order, which was made under the National General Mobilization Act in 1939, placed most major shipyards under government control. Furthermore, the Shipbuilding Industry Act was enacted in April (and took effect in December) 1939. Under this Act, the Shipbuilders Federation, which had been established in July 1937 by fourteen major shipbuilders, changed its name to the Shipbuilders Unions Federation and was supposed to control the whole industry.

However, the second and more important point is that despite the breadth of legal authority available to the government to intervene in the industry, 'the government had not put those plans into action, presumably because the time was not ripe' (Onozuka 1962: p.11). 'It is appropriate to say that they did nothing at all' (*ibid.*: p.8). As he described it, although enacted during semi-wartime, this Act was basically of a peacetime character, intended to promote the supply of good ships at lower prices, and to secure the shipbuilders' management rather than to prepare for industry control. However, due to both the rapid development of the wartime economy and the very busy situation, almost nothing could be achieved under the Act.

Direct government control over the shipbuilding industry began in September 1939 with the Shipbuilding Approval System, which was established under the New Shipping Control approved by the cabinet in August. Under this system, the Communications Ministry examined (according to given standards) and either approved or disapproved all plans for the production of ships over 50 meters long. The urgency of the need for any given ship was considered when approving or not approving any ship under examination. An examination institution was also established, the Shipbuilding Coordination Council, as a subordinate organization of the Ship Management Committee. Chaired by the chief of the Shipping Bureau of the Communications Ministry, this institution consisted of the following members: the department or section chief from the War Ministry, the Navy Ministry, the Planning Office, the Finance Ministry, and the Commerce Ministry, together with section chiefs of the Shipping Bureau of the Communications Ministry, a representative in charge of funding coordination at the Bank of Japan, and representatives of both the Shippers Association and the Shipbuilders Association. However, the standards adopted and applied were quite loose (*ibid.*: pp.9–10).

Control shifted to a license system in February 1940 with the Shipping Control Order, established under the National General Mobilization Act. Again, however, 'in practice, no remarkable change occurred.'

The shipbuilding and machine tool industries
before the establishment of control associations

It is convenient to compare here the state of affairs in the shipbuilding industry leading up to the establishment of the SCA with the situation in the machine tool industry leading up to the establishment of the PTCA. I will periodically make comparisons between the machine tool and shipbuilding industries from this point. In the machine tool industry, the Japanese Machine Tool Builders Union had been established by the five major machine tool builders, dubbed the 'Five Majors,'[11] in 1934. Later, the Machine Tool Building Act, enacted in March and taking effect in July 1938, was expected to expand the production of the Five Majors and to raise the production technology levels of the other major builders to that of the Five Majors. At the beginning, only six builders were designated as targets of policy under the Act, but this was increased to twenty-one in May 1941. However, this represented only a small fraction of the 318 machine tool builders that would eventually become members of the PTCA.

Thus the initial state of government control in the machine tool industry, which is the background to the PTCA, was different from that in the shipbuilding industry. That is, the SCA was in essence the old Shipbuilders Federation, established by literally changing the name of the Shipbuilders Federation to the Shipbuilding Control Association. Furthermore, the Shipbuilders Federation, which included all major shipbuilders, was a powerful association, representing almost 90 percent of Japan's total shipbuilding capacity. As can be seen from the figures above, the total number of all machine tool makers designated by the Machine Tool Building Act (the MTBA) accounted for a much smaller share of the machine tool industry.

Together with enacting control association laws, the government put into effect a Four-Year Plan for Expanding Production Capacity (a cabinet decision in January 1939). As part of this plan, in addition to the establishment of the Japanese Machine Tool Builders Association for members designated under the

MTBA, the First Machine Tool Industrial Union was organized in major individual prefectures and consisted of selected top-class small machine tool makers. Furthermore, the National Machine Tool Industrial Union was organized in coordination with the prefectural unions, and boasted 296 members at its commencement in July 1939 and 403 in August 1940. In addition, the remaining one thousand, several hundred small manufacturers were organized into unions and placed under the control of the Federation of Prefectural Regional Industrial Unions (JMTBA 1962: p.127). However, the fact remained that at the end of the 1939 financial year, the association's and the unions' shares of production were 27.2 and 72.8 percent, respectively, by value and 13.8 and 86.2 percent in terms of the number of machines produced. Thus the market share of the makers designated under the Act as their policy targets was extremely small compared with the industry total.[12]

The arms manufacturing industry remained outside the jurisdiction of control associations

As Nakamura and Hara (1972: p.120) describe, the industry of the highest importance to the wartime economy was arms manufacturing, and it was designated by the Factories and Workplaces Control Act to come under the direct control of the War Ministry and the Navy Ministry. The arms manufacturing industry therefore remained outside the jurisdiction of control associations. Even the arms manufacturing divisions of enterprises that were members of control associations had no connection with those associations at all. Such arms divisions of association members were separated from the jurisdiction of control associations and organized into the Army Ordnance Association and the Navy Ordnance Association, which were associations with no legal foundation.

Private arms factories strongly hoped to be designated by the military as members of these ordnance associations because being a plant directly managed by the military or under military control was far more advantageous in terms of materials procurement and advance payment than waiting for materials rationing through control associations of the Commerce Ministry (or the Munitions Ministry). Thus the most critical sector of the wartime economy remained outside the jurisdiction of control associations.

The SCA was supposed to perform a more crucial role, but...

However, the situation was different in the shipbuilding industry, and the SCA was supposed to perform a more crucial role. The fact that approximately 30 percent of private-sector shipbuilding capacity had been devoted to military vessels meant that building commercial ships smoothly as scheduled required coordination with the building of military vessels. For this purpose, the government centralized the administration of and responsibility for shipbuilding in major private plants in the Navy, hoping that private shipbuilding would benefit from the military's immense power in the wartime economy.

However, the Naval Technical Department was too busy building and repairing its own vessels to focus on commercial shipbuilding. This department was not interested in controlling the shipbuilding industry or even in studying marine transportation capacity. It intended to avoid troublesome tasks like inspection and therefore limited its own jurisdiction regarding commercial shipbuilding to ships over 50 meters long. Therefore, from the beginning of the Naval Technical Department's undertaking of the administration of commercial shipbuilding, the department intended to be just an executive organ, simply overseeing shipbuilding from plans drawn up by the communications minister. In fact, however, as nothing concrete had been determined regarding commercial shipbuilding, whether it be policy, drawings for standardized ships to be built, or the production plans for individual shipyards, the Naval Technical Department headquarters had no choice but to make concrete plans by itself. The result was its eventual total commitment to commercial shipbuilding (Onozuka 1962: pp.38–9). In short, the Navy had to accept this request for the administration of commercial shipbuilding, even though it had neither the competence nor the preparation time to implement effective industry control in the commercial shipbuilding industry.

The character of industry supervision and intervention conducted by the civilian and military ministries was fundamentally different. A technical officer (administrator) of a ministry like the Commerce Ministry (civilian) supervised only those industries within the jurisdiction of the ministry to which he belonged. Communication with the technical officer's ministry would be limited to those issues concerning defects or points to be improved. A military administrator, on the other hand, was different. As a promoter of production representing the ministry on the demand side, he would supervise and coordinate the whole process of production and imports, dealing with such points as quantity, quality, and delivery times for items ordered. He could also make every effort to eliminate obstacles to production objectives by communicating with other ministries (Nakamura and Hara 1972: p.120). As shown above, even after the centralization of administration and responsibility for shipbuilding in the Navy, the government found effective control of shipbuilding difficult to realize. How then could the PTCA, without such intervention ability or centralization, achieve the goal of effective industry control?

Industry control in the machine tool industry

The war headquarters organized the Military Ordnance Industry Association, the Navy Ordnance Industry Association, and the Airforce Manufacturing Industry

Association. Each association had its own Machine Tool Section, which cooperated with other sections of the association to achieve military production by providing the machine tool equipment demanded.

As mentioned in Section 1.2.3, soon after its establishment, the PTCA's task expanded to include the rationing of products and materials. The association received reports from individual plants on their orders received classified into five categories, four of which were orders from the military, for instance from the Naval Technical Department. The association held production meetings at which these reports were discussed. Production meetings were attended by representatives from all demand sectors, such as the military, other sectors of government, and private firms. Thus, in this industry, 'all the parties concerned, the military, the government, and the private, united and cooperated with the Association in controlling production and distribution' (JMTBA 1962: p.135). This was probably different from the situation in other control associations, where the parties concerned could not say a word concerning military demand.[13]

Whether the control was effective is another question, even in the machine tool industry. Although we have no explicit statement regarding their effectiveness, it is plausible that the following description of the latter stages of the industry under PTCA control more or less applies to the preceding stages: 'With time the struggle for products from first grade builders grew more intense. High priority was accorded to military demand, particularly demand for aircraft production, which left machine tools of only second or third grade builders for civil demand' (*ibid.*: p.137). In short, an obvious function of the control of the machine tool industry was to exclude private demand in the name of military demand.

The same occurred in the bearing industry. The allocation of materials under the Materials Mobilization Plan to the PTCA controlling the bearing manufacturing industry (nineteen members) was decided at the Third Division of the Temporary Materials Coordination Bureau, with further allocation between the Army, the Navy, and the private sector being determined at an allocation meeting organized by the PTCA. Following the determination of materials allocation between demand sectors, the War, Navy, and Commerce Ministries sent orders to individual bearing manufacturers in accordance with their allocations. Products of the 'Big Five' like NSK and NTN (Toyo Bearings) were almost exclusively dedicated for military use, and only other manufacturers' products were allocated to the private sector. Furthermore, as the war intensified, even the products of these other producers went to the military (Japan Bearing Industry Association 1965: p.25).

Articles 51 and 52 of the Key Industry Associations Order provided for discussions between the minister in charge of any control association and the war and navy ministers. Such discussions were held, and the government, at least on the surface, declared a policy to transfer plant management step by step from the military to control associations. However, this policy was not realized, and instead the military used the ability to hold discussions regarding control associations under articles 51 and 52 to intervene in the operation of control associations, far from transferring management to them (Nakamura and Hara 1972: p.120). Thus neither the commerce minister nor the Precision Tool Section of the Commerce Ministry in charge of the PTCA had any active role in industry control.

Incentives for investment in capacity

The war headquarters planned to increase military strength by increasing the national capacity of marine transportation, which had suffered badly due to many ships being lost in the war effort. This was to be done gradually with newly built ships and also with captured ships, which were intended to more than replace the volume of ships lost. However, the war did not proceed as expected. The volume of lost ships was far larger than expected, and hence marine transportation capacity decreased. Coupled with the naval blockade, the collapse of marine transportation capacity was a decisive factor in the eventual defeat (Onozuka 1962: p.34). Despite strong demand for rapid new shipbuilding and higher shipbuilding targets, the shipbuilding industry continuously missed deadlines, and this resulted in a policy of planned shipbuilding during the period from December 1942 to April 1944. Furthermore, this policy placed emphasis purely on 'volume-oriented production' (*ibid.*: pp.36, 46).

Revising the Industrial Equipment Corporation Act, the government designated ships as target equipment under this Act in addition to the aircraft and liquid fuel industries. Moreover, by inserting the phrase 'building ships according to government standards and instructions' into the Act, the government directed the corporation to order ships in bulk. The government also adopted measures for making loans for purchasing ships thus ordered (law amendment, 3 June 1942; Onozuka 1962: pp.24–6).

In industries like shipbuilding and machine tool manufacturing, investment in capacity is a long-term commitment requiring a long time both to make the investment and to recover the investment cost through effective use. Because of this, private companies asked the government for a profit guarantee to enable them to expand production capacity to fill government orders. Coupled with the unstable and unpredictable character of military demand and the colorful past relations between the military and shipbuilders, the smooth operation of planned shipbuilding must have been accompanied with incentives for suppliers.

With the progress of the war, war-related expenditure expanded explosively and changed dramatically in constitution (see Murakami 1994: pp.156–7, table 1). Regarding the expansion of military expenditure, Murakami states that with the outbreak of the Sino-Japanese War military production increased dramatically, which suppressed any possible expansion in production capacity in response to civilian demand. On the other hand, in terms of the constitution of that military demand and expenditure, the focus of military demand soon shifted from arms for killing and wounding to mobile arms, and from ground-use to aircraft and anti-aircraft armaments. Accordingly, military orders were not based on a consistent long-term plan.

For instance, Japan Steel Works, the largest private arms manufacturer, was ordered to build a tank factory in November 1938; after the devotion of much effort in the project, it launched its first product in July 1942. In August of the same year, however, it received an abrupt order from the military to transform the plant for aircraft and anti-aircraft arms production. The factory was duly reorganized for the production of guns and cannons. The machine tools in the former tank plant were also ordered to be offered to the Military Air Services Department, and they were eventually transferred to aircraft production plants owned by Mitsubishi Heavy Industries. The company history described these events as, 'startled ... a great surprise ... of grave embarrassment beyond words,' and described themselves as 'a victim of national policy for centralized aircraft production.' Likewise, Kobe Steel decided not to introduce project-specific equipment. 'Thus, the biggest concerns of private companies in taking part in arms production were unexpected changes in production items due to changes in the war situation, together with the future need to cope with the post-war situation, particularly remaining plant equipment too project-specific to convert to other uses. Another obstacle for those companies was the fact that the military budgetary unit was a mere one year, therefore they had no guarantee of a long-run production schedule' (*ibid.*: pp.159–60).

I have not been able to find any such incentives in the machine tool industry. Major machine tool makers had bitter memories of the Navy's 'Eight–Eight' Fleet Plan, whereby the Hara Cabinet (September 1918 to November 1921) had planned to increase Japan's naval power by eight battleships and eight battle cruisers in the wake of World War I. However, the Washington Naval Conference in December 1921 imposed a ten-year moratorium on the construction of capital ships and armaments and fortifications. As a result, the government canceled all orders for large warships and ordered all unfinished vessels to be destroyed. This resulted in huge orders for machine tools being canceled (JMTBA 1962: pp.65–9). After this experience, machine tool makers were reluctant to expand production and make relevant investment in capacity, even in the second half of the 1930s, partly because of their difficult history with the military, but the lack of incentives must also have strongly conditioned the effectiveness of policy in this industry.

The situation of legal regulation in the shipbuilding industry

With the centralization of the administration and responsibility for shipbuilding in the Navy Ministry, and also the shifting of the management of planned shipbuilding from the Communication Ministry to the Navy Ministry, shipbuilding control was thought to be perfect. However, although the shipbuilding control structure might have been perfect, many legal constraints on the management of individual ship-yards remained. The government attempted to sidestep these constraints by delegating all the authority and responsibility for building first-grade ships, which lay scattered between several ministries, to an official appointed by the navy minister. In most cases, the navy minister appointed the chief naval inspector of the Naval Technical Department for this purpose, and this was mostly realized during April–June 1943 as an extraordinary measure under the above-mentioned (see Section 1.2.4) Act for Exceptional Wartime Administration concerning Procedure and Jurisdiction (Onozuka 1962: p. 30).

However, despite these efforts to sidestep direct legal constraints on the regu-lation of shipbuilding, 'in addition to laws and ordinances directly concerning shipbuilding and shipping, shipbuilding under national control was also regulated indirectly by many laws.' Among the laws indirectly regulating the shipbuilding industry, of main concern were the Order Regarding Ships for Air Defense, the Rule for Air Defense by Ships, the Act for Ship Protection, and the Implementation Rule for Ship Protection. The following regulations were also relevant: the Munitions Company Act (October 1943), the Order to Corporations for Sufficient Military Supply (January 1945), the Factories and Workplaces Control Order (May 1938), the Order to Facilities for National General Mobilization Tasks, the Special Subsidy Act for Arms Manufacturing Plants, the Temporary Funds Coordination Act, the Workforce Coordination Order, and the Materials Control Order (*ibid.*: p. 32).

The situation of legal regulation in the machine tool industry

The legal regulation in the machine tool industry was at best equivalent to that in the shipbuilding industry but probably much weaker. Furthermore, while the authority for shipbuilding control was centralized in the Navy, the Precision Tool Section of the Commerce Ministry was independent of the War Ministry and the Navy Ministry. Accordingly, the section and its affiliate, the PTCA, must have faced much greater difficulties in controlling machine tool manufacturing because of this decentralized control.

In addition, the shipbuilding industry was designated as one of the five key industries by the Exceptional Wartime Administration Act for Procedure and Jurisdiction only after April 1943. The prime minister used the authority granted by this Act to effectively control the industry and further centralize control, but this applied only to the second half of the life of the SCA. When one compares this situation with that of the machine tool industry, which remained outside these five key industries, one realizes how decentralized, and therefore ineffec-tive, control must have been in the machine tool industry.

1.2.8 Evaluation of the PTCA's function:
(5) conflict between the Army and the Navy

Conflict between the Army and the Navy

Conflict between the Army and the Navy was so fierce that many say that it was the conflict between the Airforces in the Army and the Navy, rather than the conflict with the USA and the UK, that destroyed Japan. Indeed, although Nakajima Aircraft and Mitsubishi Heavy Industries dominated aircraft and aircraft engine production,[14] they manufactured their planes for the Army and the Navy in separate factories (Murakami 1994: pp.164–76). As the managing director of Mitsubishi Heavy Industries and head of the Nagoya engine factory recalled:

> Like all other aircraft manufacturing plants, Nakajima's engine plants for the Army were separated from those for the Navy. It was obvious, however, that the joint production of engines for the Army and the Navy, and reorganizing the working process on models, would contribute much to production expansion, and only Mitsubishi Engines unified production. Troubled by keen competition between the Army and the Navy regarding their quota, however, we decided to construct new plants in Shizuoka for the Army and in Kyoto for the Navy in a public-ownership–private-management form.
>
> (Fukao 1979: p.130)

This rivalry reached beyond production to design. According to its managing director, Mitsubishi Aircraft completed an ideal basic engine model, the Venus 40 (*ibid.*: p.110). The Navy liked it and placed an unprecedented volume of orders. As it had the same characteristics as the Navy's A4 model in fundamental areas like cylinder diameter, it was dubbed the Venus 3. Offended by this, the Army refused to adopt the model, choosing instead Nakajima's HA-5 model. Even when Mitsubishi remodeled and reconstructed a specialized Venus 40 for the Army, it refused to adopt it. Fukao describes the Venus 40 thus: '[it] contributed much to the overseas bombing in the Sino-Japanese conflict as far inland as Chongqing, powering the core mid-size bombers. However, the KI-21 bombers of the Army with the HA-5 engine could not succeed in bombing Chongqing even from Yuncheng in Shanxi province.'

As Saburo Endo, the first chief of the Air Ordnance Bureau of the Munitions Ministry, later described it, for reasons of secrecy engineers involved in aircraft production for the Army were not allowed to communicate with engineers in the same enterprise engaged in aircraft development for the Navy. Mutual storage of Army and Navy materials and components for aircraft production was not permitted either (Ando 1966: p.302). Endo explains (*ibid.*: p.303) that the military could justify as much funding as it pleased as 'temporary military expenditure.' As a result, the military ignored cost and budget constraints when ordering air weapons. The Army and Navy also strongly opposed each other in recruiting and training personnel.

Some unification of Army and Navy production was achieved with the birth of the Munitions Ministry in November 1943 as part of a huge administrative restructuring. Even then, though, only the production of airplanes was unified. A proposal to unify engineering research was rejected by both the Army and the Navy on the grounds that they could not delegate such matters to Munitions Ministry officials.

Endo continued (*ibid.*):

> The Munitions Ministry was established by combining all sections of the Commerce Ministry (other than sections for commerce administration) and the aircraft industry administrative inspection sections of both the War and the Navy Ministry. The Air Ordnance Bureau was established for the administration of the aircraft industry. All officials appointed to this Bureau were originally active soldiers or civilians attached to the Army.

The Materials Mobilization Plans and the Army–Navy conflict

Under the 1918 Military Industry Mobilization Act (which actually came into force in 1937 with the Act Concerning Implementation of the Military Industry Mobilization Act; see Ando 1966: pp.187–94 for legal detail) and also under the National General Mobilization Act of 1938, many munitions plants were appointed as 'designated plants' by either the Army or the Navy, but there was never any overlap. Moreover, the Army and the Navy often contested fiercely for allocation of materials rations under the Materials Mobilization Plans. Such unrest often delayed the planning schedule. As a result, planned supply quantities were often artificially inflated simply to achieve political compromise, despite the lack of realistic supply potential (Nakamura 1974: p.131).

The Materials Mobilization Plan commenced with the establishment of the Planning Office, which was to implement the mobilization plan. The Planning Office was established by extending the authority and role of the Planning Agency and then renaming it. The first plan was that for the last quarter of 1937. However, the Planning Office was in essence established as an organization for coordinating the economic policies of the cabinet and was unsuited to conducting the unified management of planning and control. Some argued for a 'product mobilization plan' as the ideal management and control structure. For such reasons as basic shortage of information, the rapidly changing political situation, and lack of coordination in the government, even in 1940 when the system was well established the plan covered only 350 raw material items.

The Planning Office itself had no authority to execute the plans; it fell instead to individual ministries like the Commerce Ministry to administer those aspects of a plan that fell within their own jurisdictions. For instance, it was the Army and Navy Ministries that formulated policies for the production of arms, aircraft, and ships. Even after the birth of the Munitions Ministry in November 1943, the Army and the Navy Ministries did not respect the authority of the Munitions Ministry. On many occasions, the munitions minister was forced to arbitrate between the army and navy ministers (US Strategic Bombing Survey 1946: pp.45–6).

In 1943, the demand for expansion of aircraft production became intense, causing severe conflict between the Army and the Navy over the steel quotas determined in the 1943 Materials Mobilization Plan. The Planning Office was forced to massage the steel supply capacity figures to give the appearance of an extra 1 million tons of capacity, raising 'total capacity' to 5.04 million tons, just to satisfy the Army and the Navy and achieve finalization of the plan (Nakamura 1977: p.131).

In 1944, the bottleneck in the shipbuilding sector not only of steel but also of supplementary materials such as fuel, electricity, oxygen, and carbide was severe, meaning that these materials were not being successfully allocated according to the quotas determined under the plan. Furthermore, even quotas of cement and wood detailed under the plan could not have been realized without preferential treatment in transportation (Onozuka 1962: p.66). Onozuka further writes that 'quotas for repairs included those for damaged ships. As usual, the number was tremendously over-estimated with the Plan having a quota of 100 thousand tons, but we estimated the necessary amount to be 40 thousand tons' (*ibid.*: p.51).

Ayakoto Okazaki was for two years the officer in the Commerce Ministry in charge of the materials rationing implementation plan for each quarter. Following that, he became section chief of the Second Section, in charge of the Materials Mobilization Plan and the War Industries Mobilization Plan of the Munitions Bureau in the Navy Ministry from October 1941 to June 1943. Describing the situation as being one that 'despite his every effort, the Navy could acquire less than half of their minimum requirement,' Okazaki commented that 'the first plan was by far the best and most organized' (Ando 1966: pp.284, 289).

Thus the Army–Navy conflict seriously damaged not only the aircraft industry but also all the other industries under wartime control. In effect, the members of the PTCA faced circumstances where 'production plans deviated from the actual rationing of materials to realize that production, meaning that certificates could not always be honored' (JMTBA 1962: p.136).

The conflict remained serious even in shipbuilding

The conflict remained serious in shipbuilding even after the centralization of administration and responsibility for building and repairing steel ships in the Navy. The Naval Technical Department, directly in charge, was extremely eager to gain control over the plants the Army had cultivated. The Army strongly resisted the Navy's plans, arguing that the Army's armament needs would be unreasonably suppressed, and insisted on equal treatment for Army and Navy vessels. Also, in the Navy, the Military Affairs Bureau and the Munitions Bureau did not in fact abandon the 'capital ships first' principle, and the coordination of the rivalry between naval vessel production and planned shipbuilding was not easy. Formal Navy doctrine had already shifted to a priority for aircraft carriers (Onozuka 1962: pp.46–9).

The situation for the PTCA could not have been any better than the situation of planned shipbuilding, which enjoyed centralized administration. The PTCA directed meetings with representatives from each demand group – the military, the government, and the private sector – regarding all facets of precision tool production (JMTBA 1962: p.134). However, the effectiveness of the PTCA was extremely limited. As the US Strategic Bombing Survey (1946: pp.36, 46) described, during the first year of the war no institution existed that bore unified responsibility for the implementation of economic mobilization plans, and even in later years, an effective centralized system for materials rationing was never established (see also Nakahara 1981, especially chs 10 and 17).

Hattori (1965: pp.141, 143) expresses a similar view:

> every nation has its own national defense, and the national defense cannot do without planning. … Today the plan, covering politics, economy, and military affairs, must be a synthesis of politics and strategy. … In Japan, however, partly due to the customs associated with the national governance structure, no such synthesized planning for national defense ever existed.
>
> The three major powers, the Army, the Navy, and the government, opposed one another, and the true picture of war leadership was one of compromise between the three. Consequently, policy and strategy often suffered from lack of uniformity of ideas and from lack of timeliness and consistency in decision making.

The final decision regarding materials allocations was on many occasions based on the result of scuffling where the loudest voice won, rather than on careful consideration. Under such circumstances, there was no room for the PTCA to play an active role.

1.2.9   Evaluation of the PTCA's function: (6) the production management competence of the Army and Navy

*Why focus on the production management competence
of the Army and Navy?*

Suppose that the following factors seriously conditioned the task of the control associations: the conflict between the Army and Navy, internal conflicts within the Army and Navy, inter-ministry conflicts of interest and opinion, and jurisdictional divisions within the government more generally. At this point, the Hayek problem mentioned above emerges: the problem of communicating to 'the man on the spot' such further information as he needs to fit his decisions into the whole pattern of changes occurring in the larger economic system.

If 'the man on the spot' was each PTCA member, did the controlling principal, that is the Precision Tool Section and the PTCA, possess the will and competence to solve the Hayek problem in the wartime machine tool industry? The answer is clearly 'No,' and it seems to be of little value to pursue this issue further regarding the Precision Tool Section and the PTCA. I therefore now focus on the will and competence of the Army and the Navy in controlling and managing the production process.

The weapons procurement section

The weapons procurement section was, as a management unit, a monopsony isolated from the competitive pressures of the market, and it almost always suffered from such evils of monopoly as inefficiency and a lack of progressiveness. As a government office, it must also have suffered from the disadvantages of bureaucracy, like inflexibility. Moreover, being a part of the military, it tended to neglect efficiency, with the following two results: insufficient personnel sufficiently competent in production management and having relevant know-how; and an inappropriate allocation of talent to tasks like control and production management.

When Ayakoto Okazaki became involved in the mobilization plan, he visited the Munitions Ministry to explain the resource constraints to Navy leaders. But the reaction of the people from the Navy Ministry and the Naval General Staff when shown the figures and statistics was totally cynical and bantering. At that time, he says, the military was so wrapped up in the idea of the Japanese spirit (*yamoto-damashii*) and the military spirit that they were totally uninterested in figures relating to available resources (Ando 1966: p.286). How much they believed what they said is unclear, but at least one, an engineer drafted from Nakajima Aircraft to the Tokyo Artillery Arsenal as a technical lieutenant, describes a similar atmosphere (Maekawa 1996: p.86): 'there were soldiers insisting that "we will shoot down enemy planes with the Japanese spirit".'

The inferior state of arsenals

It is now almost common knowledge that throughout World War II the Army and the Navy fully revealed their poor competence in managing and operating weapons production. I cite here an example that illustrates just how difficult it was for weapons manufacturers to keep pace with production technology independently.

At the end of the 1930s, the Navy established arsenals for the production of small arms and shells, and the Army expanded these arsenals. In April 1938, the chief of the Army Central Arsenal sent an instruction to the head of Nagoya Army Arsenal to study methods and equipment for the mass production of small arms. The latter organized a study group with members from Army arsenals as well as the private sector. As chairman, he spoke as follows at the first meeting, emphasizing three points: (1) that the current production system in Army arsenals was obsolete; (2) that this was almost inevitable for arsenals; and (3) that they clearly recognized that to achieve effective reform they needed advice from various parties, including the private sector.

> We began small arms production on a large scale in this arsenal in 1900. We have always made efforts in improving production methods in accordance with technical progress. However, because of various budgetary constraints, we have not been able to carry out fundamental reorganization, but merely partial modifications. Accordingly, the basic production method is truly obsolete. In normal times, low workload has inhibited our ability to thoroughly study the mass-production method. With the recent military incident in China the Army needed armament expansion, particularly the speedy mass-production of small arms. Thus ... we have an urgent need to drastically improve ... production methods and equipment, in order to expand production capacity.
>
> (quoted in JMTBA 1962: p.103)

The report of the study group stated, for instance:

> the recent trends in the industry are of mechanization, high-speed operation, electrification, replacement of hand works by machine, and conversions to special machine tools, which in total were aimed towards improving efficiency. It is needless to say that today's small-scale, traditional man-power based system of arms production should be revolutionized into mechanized production systems as much and speedily as possible.
>
> (quoted in *ibid.*: pp.103–4)

The Toriimatsu plant of the Nagoya Arsenal, which was newly built in 1939 based on the study report, boasted state-of-the-art machinery and equipment rivaling that of any Army arsenal (*ibid.*: p.103). Again, however, the JMTBA (*ibid.*: pp.101, 104) tells a different story. The Toyokawa Naval Arsenal, built in 1939 for the mass production of machine-guns and ammunition, did actually introduce mechanized tools. However, they were used only to make holes and for cutting for ammunition production; after the cutting stage, machining processes were conducted as before, with many single-purpose lathes.

The state's incompetence in managing weapons production

The inferior state of the arsenals, which were owned and directly managed either by the Army or by the Navy, provokes much doubt about the state's competence in production management. Weapons were produced mainly by private companies and not by state-owned arsenals. Private companies produced 76 percent of military weapons (1937–45) and 67 percent of naval weapons, but 97 percent of the Army's and 95 percent of the Navy's airplanes were produced by private companies (Murakami 1994: p.162, table 3). The minority role of the state- or military-owned arsenals in Japan was similar to that in other countries, which in turn suggests that the military's recognition of the better performance of private-sector management and production was common among countries.

Many also criticized the delays experienced in modernizing the arsenals' production systems and their low productivity. For instance, in January 1945, the chief engineer of Ikegai Metalworks pointed out:

> The aircraft industry, being of prime importance in planning the war strategy, was preferentially treated in machinery equipment rationing. Not only imported machines but also many domestically produced new models were equipped in aircraft manufacturing plants. Those machines, however, were in many cases improperly used. For instance, high-capacity lathes such as turret lathes, multi-bit lathes, and automatic lathes were furnished with insufficient tools, most of which moreover were used for a single purpose, thus exhibiting inferior performance to engine lathes. In those cases, with a careful process analysis, we have to achieve their most effective use with proper tools.
>
> (Hayasaka 1964: p.192; see also Okumura 1977: part II)

As the JMTBA (1962: p.148) describes it:

> During World War II Japan produced aircraft and weapons with equipment and machine tools and by methods which were technologically obsolete. Europe and the U.S. intended to decrease the number of workers engaged in weapons production as much as possible both by integrating processes and by introducing high-capacity automated and specific-purpose machines. In Japan, the procedural fragmentation prevalent during World War I was maintained, and the number of equipped machine tools simply increased, which was a blatant waste of labor force.

Underdevelopment in mass-production industries like automobile manufacturing, with its accompanying lack of tools and jig precision, the unsystematic use of machines, and a lack of standardization and convertibility of components, was a primary cause of low productivity. The state's incompetence in managing weapons production, and a lack of comprehension about the urgency of the problem, was also a basic cause of low productivity.

Illustration of the difficulty in solving Hayek's problem

It is seldom easy to solve Hayek's problem, which is how to communicate to 'the man on the spot' such further information as he needs to fit his decisions into the whole pattern of changes in the larger economic system. As with private-sector firms, this principle also applies to principals (the government) during wartime, particularly when they insist on solving problems by intervening directly in the details of each agent firm's management, or even when they try to convey information and instructions to firm managers in order to facilitate coordination.[15]

Plant performance in machinery industries like the machine tool industry critically depends upon the behavior of skilled workers and their expertise and discretionary working customs. A principal faces great difficulty in changing such working customs when it introduces new machines and restructures overall production, since the new machinery and processes may reduce the value of a worker's skills. The following episode, where skilled workers in Ikegai Metalworks[16] ignored the instructions of Kishiro Ikegai, a brother of the company founder and a leading engineer, typifies the difficulty that the Japanese government faced. If the government had had relevant detailed information about the plant, it probably could have overcome such resistance. Apparently, it did not.

> Intending to avoid excessive dependence upon workers' skills, Kishiro preferred turret lathes to engine lathes. He suggested that workers use prefabricated chasing tools as a standard bit at the finishing stage of threading operations with engine lathes. Workers, however, did not actually follow this suggestion. When workers found Kishiro personally conducting workplace inspections, they often furnished chasing tool on the tool rest for a while until Kishiro had left.
>
> (Hayasaka 1964: p.440)

Summing up

It is unlikely that the government (as the controlling principal) possessed sufficient competence in the machine tool industry to manage the internal running of individual manufacturing enterprises efficiently. A comparison of the shipbuilding industry with the machine tool industry reveals two reasons for this. First, as mentioned above, the Navy only precisely understood the competence and technical level of individual shipyards for the first time through the inspection tour conducted during October–December 1942. Before this, it had almost no relevant information. Second, compared with shipbuilding, it is much harder to manage and control production in the machine tool industry due to such factors as the larger number of enterprises, the larger number and wider variety of items produced, and tremendous differences in the technological levels of enterprises.

As the JMTBA (1962: p.147) described it: 'producing weapons with automated machines or specific-purpose machine tools of high efficiency and high performance never occurred to the national leaders.' Moreover, as the following tale suggests, the government actually hindered active trials of more efficient machines by private firms. The story goes that the Toyokawa Naval Arsenal used many single-purpose machine tools in making machine-gun ammunition, but private companies like Dai-nippon Heiki and Aichi Tokei adopted multi-head automated machines.

> In Japan at that time, however, the production of ammunition using automated machines was considered ludicrous. The war headquarters thought that machine-gun bullets and shells should be manufactured with the bare hands of the loyal Japanese worker, arguing that production with automated machines was inadequate for mobilizing people's minds.
>
> (*ibid.*: p.146)

1.2.10   Evaluation of the PTCA's function: (7) standardization

Calls for the standardization of shipbuilding

Most ships are custom-made, and it takes a long time to arrange a huge variety of materials and components when designing and building a ship according to an order with detailed specifications. And it takes at least six months (usually a full year) after commencement to complete a ship (Teratani 1993: p.7). The government adopted promotional policies like subsidies for the shipbuilding industry around the time of the Manchurian conflict in September 1931. After the outbreak of the Sino-Japanese War in the late 1930s, however, the government emphasized the shortage of shipbuilding capacity and demanded an expansion in that capacity. Calls for the standardization of shipbuilding increased as well, since the mass production of standardized ships would not only shorten construction time but also reduce costs.

This process led to the organization of the Society for Ship Improvement in June 1937, which tackled the issues of capacity expansion and standardization in shipbuilding. This society, which included members from both the government and the private sector, published its conclusion in April 1939, recommending the adoption of six standardized models of tramp cargo ship.

Unfortunately, though, the society's work by itself did not make any contribution to shipbuilding control, as Onozuka (1962: p.6) describes:

The quality and performance of these adopted models were higher than the typical tramp cargo ships of the time. These models represent the fruit of a government–private sector joint research project, but the adoption of these models was not enforced at all. Moreover, only the outline and measurements of the adopted models were specified, with all other details remaining unspecified. Further, concrete descriptions of auxiliary equipment and components were totally lacking.

'Planned shipbuilding' and standardized ship models

At the first stage of 'planned shipbuilding,' while urging the transition to building standardized ships, the government adhered to the principle that the standardized models adopted should be of high quality, as inferior ships might harm the postwar shipping industry. The full-scale construction of standardized ships began at the end of 1942, when the Industrial Equipment Corporation Act was revised to enable that corporation to support shipbuilding. Most ships scheduled for completion during 1942 were those planned by private ship owners and already under preparation or construction in shipyards before the outbreak of war.

Also around the end of 1942, the government started research into simplifying ship construction in order to shorten the manufacturing process and conserve production materials. The government focused particularly on models suitable for mass production by adopting welded structures. Its concern for the postwar shipping industry disappeared as Japan's position in the war deteriorated, and by the time it had started to design the second wave of wartime standardized ship models in November 1942, it placed stronger emphasis on the conservation of materials and mass production. Construction of some of these models started in June 1943, and others started in October of the same year. Soon after this, however, shipbuilding fell below capacity because of a materials shortage, and the volume of ships lost greatly exceeded the number of those newly produced. In the second half of 1944, despite imminent defeat, the government, 'turning their eyes away from reality, continued to produce shipbuilding plans' (Onozuka 1962: pp. 23–72).

'Standardization' in the machine tool industry

'Standardization' will often entail circumstances where relevant parties are allowed to adopt policies or methods as common rules to mutually confine part or the whole of each relevant party's choice set. Individual parties will often form groups of various sizes and types and immediately begin inter-party and inter-group negotiations. Negotiations will likely center on such points as the definition of each party's choice set, the optimal choices between alternatives, the enforcement of choices made, the coordination of individual reactions to post-choice environmental changes, the question of who will assume leadership roles, and the like. In the negotiation process, if it is allowed, some parties might withdraw cooperation. Like a cartel agreement, such group actions can sometimes generate socially harmful results, regardless of any government participation.

Many in the machine tool industry had advocated 'standardization' since the early days. However, the effectiveness of standardization as a cost reduction policy and in achieving shorter lead times would have depended on the characteristics of each individual firm. The reaction of individual firms in the machine tool industry to policies varied tremendously, occasionally resulting in no remarkable policy achievement. For instance, the Office of Resources released S-model machine tools, together with specifications and designs, to the public in April 1938. The Planning Office recommended them as standardized machine tools for small machine tool makers in July 1938. However, they were not widely accepted (JMTBA 1962: p.112).

The next quotation, from Mr Hayasaka's speech at the end of 1942, is suggestive of three points: (1) as in shipbuilding, standardization was feasible in some sectors of the industry but not in every one; (2) even where standardization was feasible, it did not necessarily succeed; and (3) failure to act quickly to address the situation would generate high costs.

> Because of the basic varied character of demand, the variety of machine tool models expands exponentially. When builders choose models freely as they do in Japan, the number of models even for the same purpose increases tremendously, by far exceeding any reasonable level of necessity. During wartime model variety tends to expand even more. Contemporary machine tool builders are forced to accept orders to manufacture quite a wide variety of machine tool models. This is so as demand increases for single-purpose machines and specific-purpose machines both for naval vessel construction and for aircraft production, and also as the mass-production method is increasingly adopted at the request of the Machine Tool Builders Association. … In fields like engine lathes and milling machines, we should reduce the number of models and build machines as efficiently as possible in a mass-production method. … We have to make consistent plans regarding model selection and production of machine tools, around which plants, equipment, and related personnel should be developed and trained.
>
> (Hayasaka 1964: pp.347–8)

Policies adopted for standardization in the machine tool industry

We do observe some standardization policies in the machine tool industry, despite such difficulties as the large number of manufacturers, the tremendous variety of products, and the virtual incompetence of control organizations symbolically revealed by the conflicts between the Army and the Navy, and within the Navy between the Naval Aeronautics Department and the Naval Technical Department.

For instance, in 1942, at the instigation of the Naval Technical Department, the Machine Tool Division of the Naval Industries Association established the Naval Machine Tool Model Select Committee, which selected machine tool models for the Naval Technical Department. Because of the 'aircraft first' principle at the time, machine tool production capacity was devoted principally to machine tools for aircraft production. Therefore the Naval Technical Department had to make efforts to ensure that as many machine tools as possible were actually reserved for its purpose. It did this by requesting concentrated production from makers (JMTBA 1962: p.140).

The Commerce Ministry intended to reduce the number of machine tools to achieve more concentrated production. The ministry selected thirty-five engine lathe models from the 160 existing models and fifty-two models of milling machine from 180 to be the subject of concentrated production. The PTCA exhibited these selected models in Tokyo in May 1943, supported by three ministries, the Commerce, the War, and the Navy. The Commerce Ministry also appointed 'leader enterprises' from among the firms producing selected machines and intended to enforce the joint production of machine tools between these leader firms and the others. By this time, however, because of the materials shortages and the strong demand for shorter lead times in production, the manufacturers had no choice but to cut production of standard model machine tools (JMTBA 1962: pp.136–7).

The production of standard wartime models began in the machine tool industry at approximately the same time as the second wave of planning and building standardized ships in the shipbuilding industry. Standard model production was encouraged by the stronger requests for mass production but delayed by the materials and labor shortages. The result, as Onozuka (1962: p.52) put it, was 'in a word, ships of low quality and low speed.' The government similarly encouraged the production of standard machine tools by designating some plants as 'models' and ordering the others to form production groups around them.

1.2.11   Evaluation of the PTCA's function: (8) organizing production

Industrial reorganization policy

The government adopted a number of measures to reorganize industry and increase production capacity. On 11 December 1941, it promulgated the Corporation Approval Order (Imperial Order No. 1084, based on section 16 of the General Mobilization Act), which established the need for government approval for new corporations. The Pacific War had broken out three days before as a part of World War II. In addition, the government promulgated the Corporation Reorganization Order (Imperial Order No. 503) on 13 May 1942.

In 1942, Masataka Toyoda, the Corporation Bureau chief of the Commerce Ministry, explained the need for corporate reorganization, shift work, and stability. 'It would never happen,' he declared, 'that with the Corporation Reorganization Order all the businesses smaller than some determined scale would be ordered to shut down':

> As before, we first make the corporation reorganization policy for each industry, with which reorganization will proceed step by step under the government–private cooperation. The Order was established as the legal foundation to take a definitive action to such a situation that some industry members would pull persistently in a different direction from the will of the majority.
>
> (Toyoda 1942: p.97)

To promote war-related production, on 1 June 1943 the cabinet formulated the Basic Policy on Corporate Reorganization for Strengthening War Potential. A variety of corporate reorganizations followed, transforming the character of industry from being autonomous to being government-driven. The policy classified industrial sectors into three groups. The first group, which included the textile industry, was characterized as sectors from which the government could divert part of the workforce, manufacturing equipment, and metal to 'more urgent needs.' The sectors in the second group, which included the five key industries together with the machinery and the petroleum industries, were the recipients of equipment and labor diverted from the first group and were asked to reorganize urgently to expand production capacity.

Furthermore, on 28 September 1943, the cabinet decided to establish the Munitions Ministry as a unified administrative body for aircraft production. The Air Ordnance Bureau, established to control aircraft production for both the Army and the Navy and ranking with the General Mobilization Bureau, took over most of the functions of the Planning Office in addition to various controlling functions.

However, as described above, organizational reform was ineffective in mitigating the Army–Navy conflict, and 'the fierce Army–Navy struggle over converted plants continued till the end of the war' (MITI 1964: pp.562–72). 'Corporation reorganization' actually contributed to some industrial progress in the first group and may also have contributed to the growth of a third group, which included industries producing daily necessities.[17] However, in the second group, the government seems merely to have tried – unsuccessfully – to reorganize the overall production system to expand capacity and improve productivity.

Wartime machine tool models and corporate groups for their production

With the cabinet decision of 31 August 1943 on Emergency Measures Concerning Machine Tools Necessary for Expanding Aircraft Production, the government determined wartime machine tool models and organized corporate groups for their production. The government adopted these policies for two reasons. First, most general-purpose machine tools in aircraft production plants were actually used as if they were single-purpose machine tools. Therefore single-purpose machines would more than suffice. Second, shortages in materials and labor became much more severe despite stronger demand for increased production, meaning that it became critical to economize on materials consumed. Wartime models for lathes and milling machines were determined, and twenty-two corporate groups were organized, eleven for each category. Aircraft manufacturers provided the original specifications and designs of these machine tools, but the engineering drawings were in fact finalized after taking into consideration the capability and equipment of machine tool makers. 'Organizing corporate groups was a trial the PTCA adopted to achieve production expansion. Such groups were primarily based on regional connections, also taking into consideration specific factors concerning inter-plant relationships' (JMTBA 1962: p.150). Lead factories were appointed for each corporate group and were called the 'responsible plant'; the other group members were called 'cooperative plants.'

This story from the company history of the largest machine tool maker of the time, Hitachi Seiki Co., gives us some idea of the ineffectiveness of the industry reorganization policy. Hitachi Seiki received a government order through the PTCA to produce milling machines for the military. The company completed the engineering drawings and experimental production in a very short time. In February 1944, a corporate group (the First Tokyo Group) was organized with eleven cooperative plants. The firms discussed the division of labor and method of coordination, but by August they could no longer procure the necessary raw materials. Inevitably, that shortage caused the 'cooperative' plants to turn uncooperative toward government policies, and production could not proceed (Hitachi Seiki 1963: pp.102–3).

The JMTBA (1962: p.151) puts these industry reorganization policies in a more positive light, but the tale becomes less plausible in view of the Hitachi Seiki experience. The account also hints at the remoteness of the government from individual firms, even under wartime control.

> The greatest benefit of organizing corporate groups was that for the first time effective control over the production of individual plants was secured. Under the precision tool control system, however eagerly a correspondent tried to influence production through control of materials, it was individual plants that decided the actual production schedule. Under this corporate group system, an

individual plant was part of a group, and there was no choice but to follow the head plant's production program. A head plant, receiving materials rationing for member plants in bulk and also controlling labor allocation between plants, could control production in affiliated plants extremely effectively.

We find nothing about corporate groups in the company history of Mitsubishi Machine Tool Co. (formerly Toyo Machines) (Mitsubishi Heavy Industries 1964), which was the responsible plant for the Third Osaka Corporate Group for production of wartime lathe models. We also have to question whether there were sufficient incentives for a responsible plant to 'control production in cooperative plants with considerable force.' Group production covered only part of aircraft machine tool demand, and aircraft machine tool demand represented only part of machine tool demand.

The corporate group structure was not specific to the machine tool industry and was adopted widely. With the enactment of the Munitions Company Act, the government determined in February 1944 the 'Basic Policy for Reorganizing Machinery Industries' in order to reorganize the second industry group, including the five key industries. The government designated the core plants that would receive government orders and asked those plants to organize their teams of cooperative plants. The Kawasaki branch of Toshiba, for instance, organized more than 300 plants (see Toshiba 1963: pp.140–1).

Wartime models of machine tools were seldom highly valued

Wartime machine tool models were seldom highly valued. In addition to the fact that the range of potential applications of such single-purpose machines was strictly limited, they suffered from low quality, rapid deterioration in precision, and a lack of durability due both to the shortage and to the low quality of the raw materials used to produce them. Furthermore, the adoption of wartime models saved many component materials, but 'the conservation of special steel and copper alloy served only to impair heavy machinability at high production speeds, which was the trend of technological development at the time. These machine tools, which suffered from expanded quantity at the cost of quality, naturally could not meet with standards required for aircraft production, the cream of modern technology. At this moment, Japan's war potential had already [been] exhausted' (Mitsubishi Heavy Industries 1964: pp.85–6).

Thus the observation that the PTCA functioned as an operating principal for producing wartime models and organizing corporate groups is hardly evidence of it serving any important role. Even when wartime models were produced on a large scale, the reality of the situation was that it was the mass production of low-quality machines and therefore could hardly be highly regarded as positively contributing to the machine tool industry (*ibid.*: p.82).

1.2.12   Evaluation of the PTCA's function: (9) the Munitions Company Act

With the establishment of the Munitions Ministry, the Precision Tool Section of the Machinery Bureau (the Commerce Ministry) in charge of the PTCA was moved under the control of the Munitions Ministry, but it retained its original form. In September 1944, the machine tool industry was ordered to divert production totally toward manufacturing aircraft parts. In addition, the government ordered production sites to be relocated to rural areas, together with aircraft manufacturing, to avoid air raids.

The company history of Mitsubishi Machine Tool Co. described the relocations as a total waste. Regarding the main Mitsubishi factory in Hiroshima, construction of both an underground plant and a mountain plant began, the intention being to create areas away from the danger of air raids and so enable uninterrupted production. During the construction of these factories, gasoline shortages rendered trucks useless, so cow and horse carriages were used instead. Production at these new factories had hardly begun when the war ended (*ibid.*: pp.91–2).

However, this move seriously dislocated the industry, and the PTCA cut its administrative operations and by 1945 had stopped functioning entirely. Nonetheless, it remained a nominal control association under the Key Industry Associations Order until the end of the war.

The Munitions Company Act, and the privately owned–state-managed system

In line with the establishment of the Munitions Ministry, the Munitions Company Act took effect in December 1943. This Act applied to any munitions company, which it defined as 'a company designated by the government from among companies doing business in producing and repairing military supplies such as weapons, aircraft, vessels, and other key munitions' (section 2 of the Act). At its outset in January 1944, 150 companies were designated, and by April 1944 424 had been designated. Eventually, the number of designated munitions companies amounted to about 700 (MITI 1962: p.318).

A designated munitions company had to appoint 'a person responsible for production, or for simplicity a production supervisor,' who represented the company and was responsible to the government for production. A production supervisor could appoint an agent called 'a production manager' in each plant. A munitions company could not dismiss a production supervisor without government approval, but the government could dismiss a production supervisor if it judged him to be unsuited to the position.[18]

> By introducing a military-style organizational structure into the industry, the government intended to place companies under a command–obedience

relationship. In this way, it intended to expand production while maintaining a capitalist system but without radically reforming the system of corporate management. Within this industrial structure, the government adopted various preferential treatment measures, such as preferential rationing of materials, labor, and finance, loss compensation schemes, and subsidies

(Nakamura 1977: p.141).

In April 1945, the so-called 'privately owned–state-managed' system was introduced in the aircraft manufacturing industry, and Nakajima Aircraft Co. and Kawanishi Aircraft Co. were assigned to the First and the Second Munitions Arsenals, respectively.

Endo, the first chief of the Ordnance Bureau of the Munitions Ministry, claimed to encounter strong resistance to this scheme within the Army, with some Army officers even arguing that 'Endo was red.' He accepted the advice of Koyata Iwasaki, the leader of Mitsubishi *zaibatsu*, that he did not understand the business, and abandoned his plans to designate Mitsubishi Heavy Industries, the other large aircraft manufacturer, to an arsenal (Ando 1966: pp.305–6).

In June 1934, Mitsubishi Shipbuilding Co. and Mitsubishi Aircraft Co. merged into Mitsubishi Heavy Industries. Fukao (1979: p.140), managing director of the new company and the head of the First Nagoya Engine Manufacturing Plant, describes plans to place Mitsubishi's factories related to aircraft production under public control. These plans were apparently abandoned when Koshiro Shiba, former chairman of Mitsubishi Aircraft, severely criticized the inefficiency of public management. Fukao also reports a secret story that the chief of the Military Affairs Bureau of the Army Ministry, Major-General Kenryo Sato, asked Mitsubishi if it would accept a proposal to transfer the nationwide management of aircraft-related production to Mitsubishi. Mitsubishi immediately declined. Fukao notes that the 'Ordnance Bureau of the Munitions Ministry was in charge of aircraft production.' Fukao reasons that such 'a request from this person simply reveals how deeply irritated they were with the situation' (*ibid.*).

Policy effect

We have little information as to the actual effects of these government policies and actions. What we do have though are company records. According to Mitsubishi Heavy Industries (1964: pp.87–8), when Mitsubishi Machine Tool Co. was designated as a munitions company in January 1944, a soldier and a sailor in active service came to the factory in military uniform as supervising officers, and roared at anybody, even at the president and the plant head. They also report that, when the demand for production expansion intensified yet materials shortages worsened, a group of soldiers came to the office and, rattling sabers, pressured the plant head to expand production until two or three o'clock in the morning.

Both the military and the Munitions Ministry were incompetent in production management. Moreover, because of the unavailability of raw materials, their active intervention in production did virtually nothing to expand production. Given that the military could not even produce efficiently at its own arsenals, it is unimaginable that by placing private factories under military control they would have been able to expand production to levels that had previously been out of reach.

In my view, most people involved probably realized these dynamics, particularly those who were involved in the control and management of the firms involved. There were two possible groups of exceptions though: the enthusiastic supporters of the Economic New Order and the groups of ideologically driven officers and bureaucrats opposed to 'liberal economic thinking.'

Fukao (1979: pp.140–1), for instance, describes how 'the president of Nihon Tokushu Togyo (NGP Spark Plugs) was forced to resign from his office by a captain from the Navy Supervising Office because production expansion was not fulfilled as was demanded. Many supervising officers [of the military] believed that simply pressuring production supervisors would result in effective production expansion, and consequently they were hated by business people.'

Business leaders resisted the idea symbolically embodied in the Munitions Company Act both explicitly and implicitly (see, for example, MITI 1964: p.598). What the government feared most in enacting the Act was 'the possibility that it might be self-defeating and impede the very goals intended to be achieved under the Act, namely productivity gains and production expansion, through fundamental review of the basic character of enterprises destabilizing the total economic system' (Kitano 1944: p.43).

However, the following quotes from Moriya and Nishihori suggest that the military did not intervene in all critical production spots. Moriya states that 'The Naval Arsenals were very technologically advanced, and so intervened in the operations of private companies in the area of technology. Alternatively the Army was very anti-interventionist and left most things to the companies. They rarely intervened in management or production.' Nishihori explains that 'it was fortunate that the Army never intervened in production.' Furthermore, Moriya continues that 'the Army said nothing about production' (Mitsubishi Heavy Industries 1988: p.51). At the time that these passages were made public in 1988, Gakuji Moriya was counsel to Mitsubishi Heavy Industries, and Setsuzo Nishihori was managing director. Both men had worked in the Army Production Department of Mitsubishi Heavy Industries' aircraft factory in Nagoya. According to Nishihori, 'the quality of pre-war Navy aircraft was outstanding, whereas most pre-war Army aircraft were of lesser quality than those of the Navy. What was interesting though was that from the point of view of aircraft production technology, the Navy's production method and technology remained unchanged, undergoing no changes at all' (*ibid.*: p.49).

The government intended to unify the administration for munitions procurement and thereby improve performance, particularly in aircraft production. It conducted a series of institutional reforms, including the establishment of the Munitions Ministry, to this end. However, as MITI (1962: p.291) later describes:

> the principal element of munitions administration remained with the Army and the Navy. Even where the Munitions Ministry did have jurisdiction, control was paralyzed due to the Army–Navy struggles over plants and materials. The success of reforms was thus close to zero.

Conclusion

Since mid-1944, the 'greatest headache of a "control manager" when faced with planning shipbuilding was that defeat seemed almost inevitable, whether they took all relevant information on the war situation into consideration or otherwise.' Just when 'Japan could have achieved plentiful gains in production capacity, materials supplies decreased drastically, peaking-out in the first quarter of 1944. Japan faced a shipbuilding capacity surplus even before the end of the War' (Onozuka 1962: pp.72, 85).

Here we arrive at a conclusion that none of the following factors had a strong impact on the machine tool industry. Institutional reforms like establishing the Munitions Ministry, enacting the Munitions Company Act, and designating munitions companies under the Act had no remarkable impact on the industry. And neither did the assignment of Nakajima Aircraft and Kawanishi Aircraft to munitions arsenals.

'By the time of the sea battle off Midway Island people in Japan gradually began to recognize that Japan had been seriously weakened, and the possibility of recovery was grim. This realization aroused anxiety and confusion both among the military and the public,' argues Fukao (1979: pp.140–1). Concerning the situation at the time, Fukao recounts several episodes that 'he now understands to be the consequence of people's devastating impatience' and comments that 'people everywhere were in great haste to put their casual ideas into effect, indicating that they had lost their presence of mind.' Examples include plans by civilians to develop long-distance bombers capable of reaching the USA or to extract oil from pine-tree roots for use as aircraft fuel. Furthermore, the military's plans to dig tunnels was accompanied by great anxiety and confusion.

Concerning the effectiveness of the administration inspector, who investigated the potential for expanding production in various industries (see Section 1.2.5), Fukao (1956: p.79) writes:

> In September 1943 Ginjiro Fujiwara, the Administration Inspector, came to Nagoya and visited the Nagoya Aircraft Plant on his first day here, and the Nagoya Engine Plant on his second. Prior to the visit, people from the Munitions Ministry asked me to take great care when discussing anything with the Inspector, emphasizing that the Inspector represented the Emperor. This appeared to suggest to me that I should not give my open and frank

opinions. On that day, without instruction from this old and prudent Inspector, a ceremony was held just to impress upon us the military's production expansion demands. The military stated that they would not return until we agreed to undertake and fulfill their demands for production expansion.

1.2.13   Evaluation of the PTCA's function: (10) product innovation and new product development

In the preceding sections, we investigated the actual functions and roles of the various players involved in wartime machine tool control, such as the PTCA, the PT Section of the Commerce Ministry in direct charge of the association, and the Army and the Navy. Throughout our investigation, we took the range of products to be produced as given. We addressed the development of new models only as a digression. Let us turn briefly, then, to innovation and product development under wartime controls.

Inducing innovation in machine tools is a harder objective to achieve

Generally speaking, it is harder to use raw materials allocation policy to improve production efficiency than it is to use the policy to minimize complaints. It is still harder to use the policy to create incentives toward innovation and new product development. Innovation in machine tools could have improved aircraft production efficiency greatly. However, as shown above, the government apparently lacked both the will and the competence to raise production efficiency in the machine tool industry. Even less could it have fostered innovation.

In the machine tool industry, a new model or type of machine tends to be created for a specific production process. This state of affairs resulted in a long list of product items that could not be substituted for each other. Because of this, most innovative machine tools were born as single-purpose machines, some of which were then developed into general-purpose machine tools (Hayasaka 1964: p.663).

Engine lathes and milling machines were typically the most widely used machines. As shown above, the government promoted mass production of standardized wartime models of these machines. Even regarding these well-established machine tools, the military ordered experimental production, for which Hitachi Seiki, for instance, had to complete engineering drawings and experimental production in a very short time. The JMTBA (1962: p.150) states that an aircraft producer would present an outline of a design and an engineering drawing, but the engineering drawing was finalized by the manufacturer, taking the manufacturer's equipment into consideration.

The war headquarters organized the Military Ordnance Industry Association, the Navy Ordnance Industry Association, and the Airforce Manufacturing Industry Association. It was through these associations that discussions were held about the models needed to produce weapons, ships, aircraft, and other equipment. Each association incorporated a machine tools division, which produced machine tools at the request of other divisions in the association. In the process, the domestic production of machine tools was promoted, and with it military supply (*ibid.*: p.138).

Obviously, though, the military did not play an active role in establishing this system of cooperative production. For instance, the Tank Division of the Military Ordnance Industry Association sent five requests to the Machine Tool Division in 1940, the first of which was to complete as soon as possible the thirty-five models they listed. Following other requests concerning capacity, precision, and tools, the last request concerned the time of delivery. The Machine Tool Division complained of the long lead times and demanded more prompt delivery. However, all the Association could do was to ask individual producers 'to make their best efforts not to cause serious delays in producing previously ordered machines by manufacturing new machines' (*ibid.*).

Policies and product innovation in the machine tool industry

In September 1939, the government issued the Imperial Order for General Mobilization Experiment, which was based on section 25 of the General Mobilization Act. As a result of this order, much experimental production of machine tools began, most of which continued during the life of the PTCA and some of which remained unfinished at the end of the war.

Of particular significance here are two famous special machine tool manufacturing groups for aircraft engine production, namely the Homare Group and the Atsuta Group. At the beginning of the war, Japanese aircraft were produced in small batches using general-purpose machine tools. During the latter stages of the war, however, aircraft engines were mass produced, based upon highly efficient special machine tools of various kinds. In 1943, production batches reached the level of hundreds per month, so the basic conditions necessary for transition to mass production with special machine tools were satisfied.

Nakajima Aircraft started developing supplementary components and special machine tools for use in the production of its 'Homare' engine. It sought cooperation from machine tool makers in the form of engineering drawings and the manufacture of special machine tools. Machine tool makers, including Hitachi Seiki and Ikegai Metalworks, formed the Homare Group, and each member was delegated responsibility for making particular special machine tools. Most planned models were high-performance electrically, mechanically, or hydraulically controlled machine tools, but only half of the models were completed by the end of the war.

This movement was born voluntarily in answer to the technological requirements that appeared with expanded production rather than in response to strong government requests or orders. The Atsuta Group was organized by such firms as Kawasaki Aircraft and Aichi Aircraft to develop special machine tools. However, with their late start – even later than the Homare Group – they did not accomplish much by the end of the war (JMTBA 1962: p.156). However, no precise information is available to enable any estimate of the actual effect of the activities of the Atsuta Group regarding aircraft production.

The company history of Hitachi Seiki, then the country's largest machine tool maker and a member of the Homare Group, simply reports that production of engineering drawings had begun in the spring of 1944, and a machine (based on a plan almost the same as today's transfer machine) was completed, but it experienced many problems in machining precision and was bombed soon after being installed (Hitachi Seiki 1963: pp.113–14). The company history of Mitsubishi Machine Tools (Mitsubishi Heavy Industries 1964) contains no reference to the Atsuta Group, despite Mitsubishi Machine Tools being a member of the group. Mitsubishi Machine Tools was the successor of the former Toyo Kikai, which later inherited the machine tool production business from the Nagoya plant of Mitsubishi Electric. In May 1945, the company merged with Mitsubishi Heavy Industries on military request.

Mitsubishi Heavy Industries, with its fully competent machine tool division producing manufacturing equipment, had already completed special machine tools for aircraft engine production in 1943. Its was the first Japanese transfer machine, with about thirty machining units, under electric and hydraulic control (JMTBA 1962: p.156).

According to Fukao (1979: pp.116–17, 125, 132), managers of the Nagoya plant of Mitsubishi Aircraft thought it desirable to adopt a mass-production system for engine manufacturing even at the stage of small-lot production. To do so, they established an independent organization, the production equipment section, to design and manufacture special machine tools. A new factory for manufacturing engines, the Daiko plant, with technically advanced equipment and a drawing office, was duly completed, and the Nagoya factory became an independent organization. The production engineering section was expanded into a division, and the large plant (encompassing 16,500 square meters and 500 sets of machine tools) contributed much to engine production by manufacturing special machine tools. Other manufacturers of aircraft engines relied entirely on general-purpose machine tools from machine tool makers, but Mitsubishi produced special machine tools for its own use and finally developed even transfer machines.

> Special machine tools made it possible even for unskilled workers to do high-level work otherwise possible only for the skilled. Allocating a small number of skilled workers to special machine tool production allowed us mass production of engines with high precision by large numbers of the unskilled.

Consequently we could accomplish the production expansion six times over, increasing employees, mostly the unskilled and students, from 4,468 at the time of independence to 85,000 in six years.

(Fukao 1979: p.125)

If the military or other aircraft producers had been sufficiently strong-willed and had the competence to make rational decisions, they would have made the transition to condensed-use production systems that utilized simultaneously the many special machine tools then available much more swiftly.

1.2.14   Summary of Section 1.2

Section 1.2, focusing on the machine tool industry, has studied the competence, behavior, and function of the state during the operation of the control associations in achieving their ultimate objective of winning the war. The basic conclusion is that the state was incompetent and that such incompetence continued until the end of the war. Although this period has been described as 'the highest stage of Japan's wartime control,' at least in the machine tool industry, any authority delegated was rarely utilized, and government policy had only a minor impact on ultimate production quantities.

This conclusion can be detailed as the following five points:

1   During the last three and half years of the war, the government led by the military did what it could to win the war. Many laws and ordinances for Japanese wartime control were enacted, and a huge organizational apparatus for control was created and strengthened step by step. Alas for the military, its 'innumerable regulatory actions are conclusive proof, not of effective regulation, but of the desire to regulate' (Stigler and Friedland 1962: p.1).

2   Various factors conditioned the government's free use of the authority and power delegated to it, and even with the control associations every step the government took to strengthen its control generated resistance both within and outside the government. Even inside the military, the Army and the Navy were locked in a fierce rivalry, and internal conflicts plagued even these military branches.

3   The control associations quickly showed their own ineffectiveness. The control apparatus then shifted to the munitions companies and to a 'privately owned–state-managed' system. But no tactic allowed the government to influence the behavior of individual firms substantially.

4   The PTCA survived until the end of the war as an affiliate of the PT Section of the Commerce Ministry. Although it thus operated as an affiliate of a government control section, it was composed entirely of private companies and had no coercive powers. Faced with government dissatisfaction with

industry members, it could do no more than ask individual makers to try not to cause serious delays in producing machines that had been ordered.

5   The government demanded that firms expand production and improve product quality, and it tried to produce such results through its control efforts and industry reorganization plans. But the results were lackluster at best. Ironically enough, because of the inactive government, it was primarily the voluntary participation of private companies and market forces that generated production increases.

Note that the period of strong government control was short. It had three and half years from the creation of control associations to the end of the war in August 1945, and less then two years from the promulgation of the Munitions Company Act. Moreover, already in 1944 at the latest people in Japan were gradually beginning to recognize that the possibility of recovery was grim, which aroused anxiety and confusion among both the military and the public. Imperial Japan during this period is a spectacular exhibition of trial and error (and failure) toward the effective and efficient operation of a command economy.

1.3   THE BEHAVIOR AND FUNCTION OF THE STATE BEFORE THE PRECISION TOOL CONTROL ASSOCIATION

1.3.1   Introduction

The period of operation of the control associations, which were established under the Imperial Order for Key Industry Associations, has been described as 'the highest stage of Japan's wartime control' (JMTBA 1962: p.137). Yet the function of the Precision Tool Control Association (PTCA) was, as shown above, very limited. The Imperial Order for Key Industry Associations was established under the National General Mobilization Act (NGMA). This Act 'delegated to the government sweeping authority, virtually a blank check, empowering it to intervene in every sector of the economy.' The Act simply provided a general legal basis for authority to be delegated and left the details of specific delegations of authority to be concluded by imperial orders, which the Act provided for (Nakamura 1974: p.58).

However, in the machine tool industry at least, even after the outbreak of war the authority actually delegated was very rarely used, and any influence the government actually had on individual companies and on the industry in general was in most cases trivial. This suggests two things. First, that various factors conditioned the government's free use of authority and power delegated to it, and that similar inhibiting factors must also have existed in the period preceding the war. Taking the analysis one step further, in the period preceding the war, when the government enjoyed much less authority yet still faced various factors that inhibited the use of authority, government intervention must have been less active and its influence much less than during the war. Second, Stigler and Friedland's (1962: p.1) general comment on government regulation, that 'the innumerable regulatory actions [of government] are conclusive proof, not of effective regulation, but of the desire to regulate,' also applies to Japan's wartime situation, where many laws and ordinances for wartime control were enacted. This holds true first for the NGMA. The government had this enacted using the strong political force of the Army. The Diet, especially the Minsei-to Party and the Seiyukai Party, was highly critical of this law.[19] It also holds particularly true for a series of wartime control laws that the government managed to have enacted against strong opposition, which delegated blanket authority to it with no mechanism for subsequent review.

As shown in the timeline in Section 1.2, the state enacted a myriad of control laws prior to the establishment of the twelve control associations in 1941. It can probably be said that the economy was under wartime control even before the period of the control associations. In this section, I investigate the effect of government policies in the machine tool industry during the period prior to the PTCA, focusing on these control laws, on what the state intended to achieve with them, and on what the state actually could and did achieve. In particular, I focus upon two control laws. These are the Machine Tool Building Act of September 1938 and the Order for Machine Tool Experiment Production of January 1941. The latter was established under the General Mobilization Experiment and Research Order, which was in turn established under section 25 of the NGMA of 1938.

As the previous section also demonstrated, the impact of industry control during the PTCA period was strictly limited. Moreover, the government does not appear to have intended to achieve greater effects. This is true even of the periods of the Munitions Ministry and the Munitions Companies Control, which coincide with the second half of the PTCA period. However, what of the period before the control associations, that is the period of the control laws that this section focuses on? If control associations represented 'the highest stage of Japan's wartime control' and even then government policy had little effect, we can infer that the impact of government policy and control in this industry prior to the control associations was more limited than during the control associations period. It was probably also more limited than during the Munitions Ministry and Munitions Companies period.

Three points to note as background information

Before I begin the analysis, it is useful to note three points as background information:

1   As illustrated in Figure 1.1 and Table 1.1, the prewar peak for machine tool output in terms of the number of units produced was reached in 1938. The peak in terms of the aggregate weight of the machines was reached in 1943, with the 1938 level standing at about 70 percent of that 1943 peak.
2   Output began to increase dramatically after the Shanghai Incident in 1932. Output was over thirty times higher than the 1932 level in 1938 in terms of the number of units produced and almost fifty times higher in aggregate weight of machines produced.
3   Production increases accompanied tremendous increases in machine tool imports. The value of imported machine tools in 1939 was twenty-six times greater than in 1932, with imports representing over 57 percent of the value of machines produced domestically.

Table 1.1 Production and sale of machine tools, 1909–68

Year	Production Quantity (number of machines)	Production Weight (tons)	Production Value (Yen million) (A)	Exports (B)	Imports (C)	Domestic demand (D) = (A) - (B) + (C)	Export ratio (B)/(A) (%)	Import dependence ratio (D)/(C) (%)
1909	–	–	0	–	3	3.10	–	96.77
1914	–	–	0	–	2	2.00	–	100.00
1915	–	–	1	0.3	0.9	1.60	30.00	56.25
1916	–	–	8	1	2	9.00	12.50	22.22
1917	–	–	12	0.8	3	14.20	6.70	21.13
1918	–	–	18	1	7	24.00	5.60	29.17
1919	–	–	6	0.9	11	16.10	15.00	68.32
1920	–	–	11	–	14	25.00	–	56.00
1921	–	–	9	0.4	11	19.60	4.40	56.12
1922	–	–	7	0.4	7	13.60	5.70	51.47
1923	–	–	5	0.2	4	8.80	4.00	45.45
1924	–	–	9	0.6	8	16.40	6.70	48.78
1925	–	–	6	0.3	6	11.70	5.00	51.28
1926	–	–	7	0.3	3	9.70	4.30	30.93
1927	–	–	8	0.7	5	12.30	8.80	40.65
1928	–	–	8	0.5	4	11.50	6.30	34.78
1929	–	–	6	0.4	6	11.60	6.70	51.72
1930	2,250	2,385	4	0.3	5	8.70	7.50	57.47
1931	2,100	2,100	4	0.2	3	6.80	5.00	44.12

Table 1.1 Contd.

| Year | Production | | | Exports | Imports | Domestic demand | Export ratio | Import dependence ratio |
| | Quantity | Weight | Value | (B) | (C) | (D) = (A) - (B) + (C) | (B)/(A) (%) | (D)/(C) (%) |
	(number of machines)	(tons)	(Yen million) (A)					
1932	3,000	3,470	8	0.2	6	13.80	2.50	43.48
1933	5,618	6,970	11	0.3	11	21.70	2.70	50.69
1934	7,747	10,150	17	0.4	14	30.60	2.40	45.75
1935	10,054	14,000	19	0.4	10	28.60	2.10	34.97
1936	16,227	23,600	31	1	15	45.00	3.20	33.33
1937	21,888	32,450	50	2	41	89.00	4.00	46.07
1938	67,260	100,800	240	4	92	328.00	1.70	28.05
1939	66,830	102,240	275	11	157	421.00	4.00	37.29
1940	58,088	101,700	312	13	79	378.00	4.20	20.90
1941	46,058	103,100	318	10	26	334.00	3.10	7.78
1942	50,833	114,036	428	11	9	426.00	2.60	2.11
1943	60,134	140,753	603	11	8	600.00	1.80	1.33
1944	53,844	128,728	723	12	0	711.05	1.70	0.01
1945	7,316	11,810	130	0	0	129.94	0.10	0.03
1946	4,791	4,289	106	0	–	106.00	0	–
1947	5,544	3,228	150	1	–	149.10	0.60	–
1948	8,051	4,690	500	1	–	499.00	0.20	–
1949	6,680	4,473	871	51	42	862.00	5.90	4.87

1949	6,680	4,473	871	51	42	862.00	5.90	4.87
1950	4,039	2,948	566	214	133	485.00	37.80	27.42
1951	9,139	4,714	1,066	286	134	914.00	26.80	14.66
1952	11,587	5,946	1,707	352	848	2,203.00	20.60	38.49
1953	18,722	7,747	3,738	411	2,254	5,581.00	11.00	40.39
1954	18,124	10,541	5,385	549	5,229	10,065.00	10.20	51.95
1955	18,147	6,591	3,680	715	4,042	7,007.00	19.40	57.69
1956	28,068	11,626	7,174	527	2,523	9,170.00	7.30	27.51
1957	34,824	21,406	15,549	724	12,201	27,026.00	4.70	45.15
1958	32,652	26,290	21,113	479	13,777	34,411.00	2.30	40.04
1959	47,830	31,443	24,318	497	10,449	34,270.00	2.00	30.49
1960	80,143	59,619	45,169	1,624	19,701	63,246.00	3.60	31.15
1961	114,959	110,102	81,882	2,434	38,899	118,347.00	3.00	32.87
1962	104,701	127,105	100,892	2,587	47,581	145,886.00	2.60	32.62
1963	120,541	126,558	95,132	4,295	22,796	113,633.00	4.50	20.06
1964	131,053	121,538	90,906	6,509	21,319	105,716.00	7.20	20.17
1965	90,356	89,242	70,349	8,943	13,963	75,369.00	12.70	18.53
1966	107,969	98,373	76,553	14,611	7,586	69,528.00	19.10	10.91
1967	153,949	149,685	126,041	17,642	12,839	121,238.00	14.10	10.59
1968	184,260	194,984	175,986	18,584	34,176	191,578.00	10.60	17.84

Source: JMTBA 1969: p. 74.

1.3.2   The environment at the beginning of the policy

The market for machine tools in prewar Japan

Machine tool production increased tremendously with the outbreak of war and shrank dramatically with its end. Prior to World War II, machinery industries using mass production, like the sewing machine and automobile industries, had not yet been developed in Japan, and hence the only market for machine tools of significant size were the munitions and related industries. Accordingly, the machine tool industry depended completely upon military demand, which fluctuated wildly in volume, components, and quality with the beginning and end of the many military campaigns that Japan conducted. Faced with such volatile demand, machine tool makers had to hedge their bets just to survive. Makers of machine tools were wary and untrusting of the Jack-in-the-box unreliability of government and military demand, and the government was thus forced to tread carefully when requesting rapid expansion of production or product development. This acted as a seriously binding constraint upon government intervention in the industry.

The machine tool industry was greatly stimulated during the Russo-Japanese War (1904–5) by orders from military arsenals, which could no longer secure machine tool imports due to the war. With the end of the war, however, military demand decreased sharply, and makers were unable to survive on machine tool production alone (JMTBA 1962: pp.53–5). According to Hayasaka (1964: p.476), after the Russo-Japanese War 'people in Japan did not recognize the importance of machine tools. They thought it better to import them … arguing that Japan, with its undeveloped machine tool industry, should import them from the US.'

World War I and the subsequent armaments expansion program (symbolized by the Navy's Eight–Eight Fleet Plan, referred to in Section 1.2.7) caused a repeat of the feast-or-famine demand cycle for machine tools, but on a much larger scale. The value of domestic machine tool production in 1918 was twelve times larger than that in 1915. Imports also increased dramatically, over seven times during the same period (although the value of imports in 1918 was merely double the average of the three years preceding the war). The average import ratio (value of imports to value of domestic demand) during 1916–18 was only about 25 percent (JMTBA 1962: p.59, table 14).

Japan's modern machinery industries, including military arsenals, began production totally dependent upon products and technology from Europe and the USA. Then, when no longer able to import machine tools satisfactorily due to the war, the government was forced to meet the explosive increase in demand predominantly using domestic machine tools. Even the military arsenals ordered basic machine tools from Japanese producers (see JMTBA 1962: pp.59–65, which includes a list of tools made).

World War I ended in November 1918, but the Hara Cabinet (formed in September) started a fourteen-year armaments expansion program for the 'perfection of national defense.' In 1920, the first fiscal year of the program, national defense expenditure accounted for 48 percent of the national budget. The machine tool industry became optimistic about its future despite the war's end, and companies accordingly carried out active expansion programs of their own accord. The Navy's Eight–Eight Fleet Plan was based on a 'big ship, big cannon' (or 'capital ship first') principle, reorganizing Japan's Navy with eight battleships, like the *Nagato* and the *Mutsu*, and eight battle cruisers, like the *Amagi* and the *Akagi*. The Army's focus was on organizing mechanized troops and an airforce (*ibid.*: pp.65–9).

However, with the ten-year moratorium on the construction of capital ships and limits on armaments and fortifications reached at the Washington Naval Conference in December 1921, all orders for large warships were canceled, and all unfinished vessels were destroyed. Thus the machine tool industry, which expanded explosively after the outbreak of the war, was stripped of its most important market. Coupled with the depression in the economy that began in spring 1920, 'it is not too much to say that the machine tool industry, with huge excess capacity, lost all direction' (*ibid.*: p.69).

It was only after the Shanghai Incident in January 1932 that military demand for machine tools revived on any noticeable scale. However, Japan's machine tool makers had by that stage 'fallen into a deep hibernation' with the disarmament, forced to scramble for survival over ten years. The peak value of machine tool production during the war was ¥18 million in 1916. Since 1921, that value consistently remained below ¥10 million until 1932, with a trough of ¥3.94 million in 1931 (MITI 1976: p.446, table 136).

The state of the machine tool industry at the time of the Shanghai Incident

Military production did not increase remarkably immediately after the Shanghai Incident; the only increase in demand was for supplementary supplies. However, the focus of military production gradually shifted to that for armaments expansion, with which demand for machine tools increased sharply. Unfortunately, only a small number of machine tool makers survived the decade of depression.

The state of the machine tool industry in the early 1930s can be summed up in four points:

1   The major machine tool makers were the Big Five: Ikegai Metalworks, Niigata Metalworks, Ohkuma Metalworks, Karatsu Metalworks, and Tokyo Gas–Electric Industries (see JMTBA 1962: p.64, table 15 for a list of makers).

2   Makers of machine tools had developed characteristics that reflected their history. A good example was their tendency to copy imported machine tools during peaks in demand. This continued at least until the end of World War II and heavily restricted the behavior of producers under wartime control. That is, they could produce general-purpose machines only, and their machining technology, due to the characteristics of military demand, was always one step behind the frontier. Therefore, although military demand for domestic machine tool production may have developed machine manufacturing technology, it did little to foster the ability of domestic makers to develop their original ideas into commodities (*ibid.*: pp.76–7).

3   During 'the deep ten-year hibernation,' the technological levels of Japan's machine tool makers had fallen well behind the world frontier. During this decade, the international machine tool industry experienced at least two major developments with which international producers moved one step ahead of Japan. The first was that tungsten carbide tools were invented in Germany in 1926. Because of their high tolerance for heat, the tools facilitated high-speed cutting. However, the fragility of these tools necessitated revolutionary changes in the design and structure of machine tools to avoid vibration and shock. Second, single-purpose machine tools, collect-type machine tools, and mechanized machine tools were developed with the expansion of mass production in industries like the US automobile industry. However, Japan's producers, far from being able to follow these developments, were eager to produce a wide variety of machines simply to survive the depression. Each maker therefore produced a wide variety of machines, whereas in other countries there was specialization in production between industry members. Because each Japanese maker was willing to produce virtually any machine ordered, none invented original products (Hayasaka 1964: pp.495–6).

4   Machine tool makers were cautious about requests from both the military and the government, clearly recognizing that military demand was unreliable and that the probable consequence of heavy dependence on it would be huge excess capacity.

Explosive military demand after the Shanghai Incident

In January 1932, just after the start of the Shanghai Incident, the Naval Technical Department ordered the five leading machine tool makers to share the production of specific-purpose machine tools for the urgent supplementary supply of consumable armaments like shells and torpedoes. This pleased the makers immensely (*ibid.*: p.515). The focus of military production shifted to that of armaments expansion, and the demand for machine tools increased sharply. The Five Majors reacted positively, unilaterally organizing the Japanese Machine Tool

Builders Union in May 1934. However, the situation was different in March 1938, when the government passed the Machine Tool Building Act in an effort to induce the active participation of the Five Majors.[20] The explosion in military production at the time required a concomitant sharp increase in machine tool supply, which was satisfied both by domestic production and by huge imports of machine tools that could not be produced in Japan. In 1939, the year prior to the US ban on machine tool exports to Japan, the total value of machine tool imports was ten times larger than that in 1936, amounting to 57 percent of the value of domestic production (see Table 1.1). Machine tool purchasing missions were sent several times to Europe and the USA to facilitate increases in imports.

1.3.3   An outline of wartime control

*The National General Mobilization Act
and the State Electricity Control Act*

Control of the machine tool industry constituted part of wartime economic control, which began at the beginning of 1937 with the Order to Control Foreign Exchange for Imports. This order was introduced to tackle a foreign exchange crisis, brought on by widespread expectations that increased military demand would sharply increase imports. Expectations of increases in military demand were aroused after Finance Minister Baba of the Hirota Cabinet (March 1936 to February 1937) announced the 1937 budgetary plan. Japan suffered from inflation and a trade deficit with the rapid increases in industrial production in the second half of 1936. The first Konoe Cabinet (June 1937 to January 1939) promulgated 'Three Principles for Finance and the Economy' at the start of June 1937. The three principles were 'production capacity expansion, recovery of the international balance of payments, and coordination of a materials demand–supply balance.' With this, the direct control of the economy began. The NGMA and the State Electricity Control Act were passed by the Diet at the beginning of 1938 as the capstone of a series of control laws and related policies.

Note, however, that the following view gained wide support concerning these Acts of early 1938:[21]

> The Army promoted the former, and the Communication Ministry the latter. Neither Act was, however, established in response to any urgent situation. … Though the Diet finally accepted the will of the military to enact these laws, despite being criticized as essentially equivalent to the Nazis' 'authority delegation law.' The NGMA was established in a short time, its passage being aided by the outbreak of the Sino-Japanese War. The NGMA was a manifestation of the military's desire since World War I for measures enabling 'war harnessing the entire power of the nation.' At the time of its

enactment nobody, even high officials of the Army, thought it necessary for managing the wartime economy.

   Under the State Electricity Control Act, control of the generation and transmission of all electricity throughout the country was unified to one company, Nihon Hassoh-den. The activities of each electricity company were limited to distribution, and each company was assigned an area in which to distribute. The Act was also based on the idea of central control, the idea being that they should avoid the waste of dual investment and excessive competition, develop large-scale water power stations, and coordinate flexibly an inter-regional electricity generation/consumption balance. At that moment no urgent need for the Act existed such that electricity demand much exceeded supply. However, 'reform' bureaucrats in the Communications Ministry pushed Communication Minister Ryutaro Nagai of the Konoe Cabinet to ensure the enactment of their plan, against which the industry was strongly opposed.

(Nakamura 1989: p.10)

Major events in economic control in 1937

The Temporary Import–Export Grading Act was enacted in September 1937 to address increases in imports. Under the Act, the government designated items that it could restrict or prohibit the export and import of. It could also issue orders concerning the production, rationing, transfer, specification, and consumption of items that used designated items in their production. The Temporary Funds Coordination Act was also enacted in September 1937, under which establishing a new company or financing long-term debt needed government approval. The aim of this Act was to preferentially promote military and basic materials industries, which restricted investment in peacetime industries such as textiles, paper, and commerce. Furthermore, with the enactment of the Act to Apply the 1918 Military Industry Mobilization Act (see Section 1.3.3), the government was authorized to 'control, use, and expropriate' plants, mines, and other establishments. In fact, the Factories and Workplaces Control Order was established under this Act, whereby major factories for military production were placed under the control of the Army or the Navy.

   In October, the Planning Agency and the Office of Resources were reorganized into the Planning Office, which took over the business of planning and coordination for 'expansion and use of total national power in peacetime.' From the October–December quarter of 1937 this new ministry took over the business of national general mobilization from the Office of Resources. It oversaw production expansion plans and made various plans, including the Materials Mobilization Plan concerning trade, finance, and labor mobilization (see *ibid.*: p.8).

The 'Revised Four-Year Plan'

The Petroleum Industry Act was enacted in March 1934, 'satisfying demand both from business as an anti-depression policy but mainly from the military as a national defense policy' (MITI 1964: p.85). The need to expand production capacity began to be debated from about 1936, and these debates led to the enactment of the Automobile Manufacturing Act and the Key Fertilizers Manufacturing Act in May 1936. In January 1939, the cabinet produced a Four-Year Production Capacity Expansion Plan for 1938–1941 (the so-called 'Revised Four-Year Plan'). This plan emphasized 'the expansion of the national defense capability' and was fundamentally premised on the policy of 'establishing self-sufficiency in the supply of key materials' in fifteen selected industries. These industries included machine tools, trains, ships, and automobiles, in addition to basic materials like steel, coal, and light metals.

Note that the plan stated that 'the government would adopt special measures to promote implementation of the Plan, particularly taking into consideration the situation concerning control and support of business, supply of engineers and workforce, financing, materials supply, etc., in each individual industry.' The plan continued that, 'whenever necessary, the government would establish new laws and ordinances and put the National General Mobilization Act into action.' Moreover, the plan also declared that the government would pay due attention to the coordination of the plan with the Materials Mobilization Plan (*ibid.*: pp.213–19).

As Nakamura (1983: pp.300–1 and table 10.10; also *ibid.*: ch. 2) describes, the plan was the finalized Production Capacity Expansion Plan, which had been inaugurated with great passion under the Five-Year Plan for Key Industries. However, the environment surrounding the plans changed greatly in the year and a half that elapsed during the process. That is, Materials Mobilization Plans took effect, but the reduced import capability inhibited plans for capacity expansion. The Ministry of Commerce and Industry criticized the Army's plans for a scale of production that could not be maintained in peacetime. Thus 'the sad fate' of the original plan demonstrated the circumstances of the time.

Following the Four-Year Plan, the government established industry laws in many industries. Examples include the Steel Manufacturing Act and the Artificial Oil Manufacturing Act in August 1937, the Machine Tool Building Act and the Aircraft Manufacturing Act in March 1938, the Shipbuilding Act in April 1939,[22] the Light Metals Manufacturing Act in May 1939, the Organic Composition Manufacturing Act in April 1940, and the Key Machinery Manufacturing Act in May 1941. The substance of all these laws was very similar (MITI 1964: pp.238–9).

Rationing system

In the March–June quarter of 1938, basic materials like cotton thread, gasoline, animal feed, ammonium sulfate, and steel were one by one placed under a rationing system. These materials stood at the heart of the Materials Mobilization

Plans. Concerning steel, the primary material for making machine tools, the Steel Control Council was organized within the Commerce Ministry as the final decision-making body for the government/private sector steel supply–demand plans (*ibid.*: p.265). All the machinery industries were organized under the umbrella of the Steel Control Council by affiliation with industrial union-type institutions that the government controlled. 'The government implemented steel rationing, and also intended to control machinery production through this control structure' (JMTBA 1962: p.126).

In July 1938, the Rule Concerning Machine Tool Supply Controls was enacted as a supplementary rule under the Machine Tool Building Act (MTBA). This rule required makers of machine tools equipped with more than thirty machine tools to supply their products to users primarily manufacturing arms and related products (*ibid.*: p.117). Prior to this rule, only the output of manufacturers equipped with over 200 machine tools was subject to a government distribution approval system under the MTBA. However, with the Rule Concerning Machinery Equipment Control of September 1939, all machinery equipment, both for new plants and for the expansion of existing plants, was placed under a requirement for government approval. In the machine tool industry, any diversion of machinery equipment into producing cutting and grinding machine tools or their components also needed government approval, which was intended to prevent the short-sighted production of low-quality machine tools (*ibid.*: p.118).

The path to the establishment of control associations

From this point, the path to the establishment of control associations like the PTCA under the Key Industries Associations Order took the following form. Many imperial orders had been issued since the outbreak of World War II in Europe under the NGMA, and calls for the Act to be revised intensified. This movement for the Act's revision was spurred by the non-passage of the 'Industry Association Bill' and other bills related to the Economic New Order aimed at reorganizing industry associations due to resistance from the private sector. Besides the opposition of many business associations and others in the business sector, there was also opposition within the government. The Commerce Ministry opposed the Planning Office, and even the commerce minister opposed the Commerce Ministry's original plan (MITI 1964: pp.454–6).

The NGMA was revised in March 1941 to enable the government to control industries. In particular, the changes to sections 16 and 18 were considered the most important of the revisions. The revision of section 16 empowered the government to make orders concerning the establishment, transfer, closure, merger, or dissolution of business. There were three basic elements to the revision of section 18: (1) the scope of the Act was expanded to cover activities outside 'general mobilization activities'; (2) the application of the establishment order was expanded from merely unions used for control purposes to unions based on the Union Law, and even more generally to associations and corporations; and (3) before the revision the government had authority to establish unions to be used solely for control purposes, and the unions were not allowed to conduct any business themselves. After the revision, the scope of the government's authority was expanded to include the establishment of any associations or corporations for control purposes, and those entities were themselves empowered to conduct business (as mentioned above, the government made almost no use of these powers in the machine tool industry; see *ibid.*: p.452).

Unified control of industry was strongly demanded, and therefore the government decided to experiment with a 'control association' type of organization in the steel industry; the Steel Control Association was established on 26 April. 'The system of internal control in the steel industry prior to the control association experiment was extremely well developed and highly organized, with control centering around the Japanese Steel Producers Federation.' This federation, established as a voluntary cartel of producers, was perceived as defective in several areas, and a control association type of organization was thought necessary. The defective areas of the federation were thought to be (1) that the standing committee was practically inactive as a guidance institution; (2) that the jurisdiction of the federation concerning various tasks remained unclear, and this caused frequent jurisdictional disputes with ministries; and (3) that the promotion of integrated steel production required the active control of the whole production process, including allocation of raw materials (*ibid.*: p.456).

All this led to the establishment of the Steel Control Association, under which a pyramid-like control system was organized (see Section 1.2.3). The Japanese Federation of Industrial Unions of Steel Products stood at the top of this system of control. Even if the government could have solved the perceived problems by establishing the association, the factors that had inhibited the effectiveness of control policies from the beginning (mentioned in Section 1.3.2) would have remained. Hence establishing the association would not have contributed much to improving efficiency in the overall machinery production sector.

The following description by Kawasaki (1943: pp.281–2) is illustrative of the situation in 1943. This description suggests that not only the Planning Office but also the Commerce Ministry had to begin by collecting basic information before making Materials Mobilization Plans for machinery products.

> Starting with the temporary control of individual items, demand–supply coordination of machines was not directed to demand–supply planning of machinery products. … Demand–supply planning of machines through that of their production materials depended much on the details of materials mobilization plans. Accordingly we had to concern ourselves with various hurdles involved in carrying out speedy and smooth planned production of

machinery products of which future demand was anticipated under the plan for the whole economy. Concerning this, the Osaka Chamber of Commerce and also machinery control associations strongly demanded the implementation of a materials mobilization plan for machinery products. In response to this, the Commerce Ministry improved the order approval system, the only demand–supply coordination system, and negotiated with the Planning Office to create a materials mobilization plan for domestic machines, incorporating the successful results of planned machinery production. The Ministry finally reached an agreement with relevant parties to make a highly concrete demand–supply plan, organizing at any cost a materials mobilization plan for machinery products. … Delegating totally to the Commerce Ministry the work to collect basic information for materials mobilization plans for machinery products, the Planning Office began the diverse preparations for making the next materials mobilization plan for 1943.

The basic character of the federation remained unchanged, because it had previously been a cartel. However, the establishment of the Steel Control Association did see the authority of the chairman, who was appointed by the government, enormously strengthened (MITI 1964: pp.456, 458).

The Commerce Ministry and the Planning Office reached an agreement to limit temporarily the governing authority of the control associations to eight industrial sectors, including steel, coal, petroleum, and machinery, until the promulgation of the Key Industries Associations Order on 30 August (which took effect from 1 September). On 30 October 1941, just after the start of the Tojo Cabinet (October 1941 to July 1944), the Rule for Designating Key Industries (Cabinet Order No. 26) was established under the order, whereby the government designated twelve industries for control, including the precision tool industry. As described below, in the meantime the Machine Tool Building Act, enacted just before the NGMA, was revised in March 1941. Furthermore, in January 1941, the government issued orders for 'experimentation and research' based on the General Mobilization Experiment Order.

1.3.4   Circumstances surrounding the machine tool industry

The situation prior to the Machine Tool Building Act

Even before the enactment of the Machine Tool Building Act in 1938, the government and the military were far from indifferent to the machine tool industry. Experience during the Russo-Japanese War and World War I meant that at least part of the military recognized the importance of the machine tool industry only too well. Before the Shanghai incident, however, this recognition of the importance of the machine tool industry did not lead to any active state policies for promoting the development of the industry. As mentioned above, the industry was in fact left in hibernation for over ten years until the Shanghai incident.

Some movement toward enacting the Machine Tool Building Act

Despite the lack of active policies for promoting the development of the machine tool industry, there was some movement toward enacting the Machine Tool Building Act and some requests for production of experimental machine tools under the General Mobilization Experiment Order. It may contribute to our general inquiry to pause here to consider issues such as the key constraints operating on government behavior at the time and how the government might have made decisions if allowed to use unabated power. More particularly:

- Why did the government even adopt policies to promote the machine tool industry?
- Why did the government adopt the policies it did and not others?
- Why were these policies not adopted earlier?
- What were the results of these policies?
- How desirable were these policies as economic policies?

In this subsection, I briefly review the history leading up to these government policies and policy instruments, namely these industry laws, focusing upon the machine tool industry, in preparation for closer examination.

With the increase in the amount of manufacturing being conducted in the economy, the policy focus of the Ministry of Agriculture, Commerce, and Industry shifted from agriculture to commerce and industry. This shift created difficulty in coordinating policies for agriculture and those for commerce and industry. Consequently, in March 1925, the ministry was reorganized, and the Ministry of Commerce and Industry (the Commerce Ministry) was established independently of the Ministry of Agriculture. The Commerce Ministry took charge of the administration of the mobilization of the munitions industry until the Office of Resources was established in May 1927 as the institution solely responsible for overseeing national mobilization efforts.

The Office of Resources, as a supervising institution, delegated authority for the execution of various tasks to other ministries. It was in charge of (1) supervising affairs concerning human and material resources control and implementation plans; (2) supervising affairs concerning research and facilities needed to establish and implement the plans mentioned in (1); and (3) general administration concerning (1) and (2) (section 1 of the Founding Act).

The cabinet decision of 22 April 1926 concerning the preparation committee for establishing the National General Mobilization Institution, on which the Office of Resources was founded, declared:

The experiences of the powers in the Western world during and after the First World War clearly show that it is imperative for every nation to prepare general mobilization ability. Therefore, nationwide surveys, particularly detailed and accurate surveys of the state of endowments and demand–supply circumstances of important resources, are necessary as the basis of plans for national general mobilization. National general mobilization serves not only for national defense but also for promoting industry development, an urgent need of the Empire, not to mention its contribution to planning social policies.

(MITI 1979: p.345)

In July 1927, the Council of Resources was established as an advisory body to counsel and advise the prime minister regarding the National General Mobilization system. The Council of Resources played a key role in constructing the general mobilization system through collecting and analysing opinions and proposals from various sources (*ibid.*: pp.344–6).

The role of the Council of Resources was assumed by the Planning Council with its establishment in February 1938 amid the reorganization of the Office of Resources and the Planning Agency into the Planning Office. In November 1929, the Order for Survey of Resources was enacted as a substitute for the Order for Munitions Surveys. This new order expanded the scope of the surveys conducted from munitions supply to include everything related to the national mobilization plans. With this order, the government completed the legal foundation for constructing and implementing its plans for 'National General Mobilization' (*ibid.*: p.349).

The Committee for Promoting Domestic Production, established in June 1926 in response to 'calls for promoting domestic production and restricting imports,' was the first advisory committee of this kind. The first issue submitted to the committee was that of clarifying 'key national industries.' The committee published its opinion in January 1927, listing key national industries, including the machine tool industry, and enumerating necessary policies.[23]

The view of the government toward the machine tool industry

Military demand revived after the Shanghai incident, and with it the machine tool industry sprang back into life, but the ministry in charge of military mobilization, at that time the Office of Resources, thought the following regarding the promotion of the machine tool industry:

We don't think it necessary to produce all industrial machines and equipment in our country. However, prompt supply of all necessary industrial machinery, even in times of emergency when supply of foreign machines may

be interrupted, requires well-developed machinery industries. To promote
the development of machinery industries we must make efforts in precision
improvement and production expansion in the machine tool industry. This is
the only way to satisfactorily supply a vast volume of products demanded in
an emergency.

(quoted in JMTBA 1962: p.111)

Even in May 1937, just before the outbreak of the Sino-Japanese War, the view of
the government had altered little:

> Since 1933, with the advance in machinery industries like automobile manu-
> facturing, aircraft production, shipbuilding, and so forth, demand for machine
> tools has increased sharply. ... Today the demand is still growing, however, we
> are rather doubtful about the future of the industry. In addition, our impres-
> sion of the domestic machine tool industry is that it is undeveloped, not only
> in terms of the variety and performance of products but also in terms of engi-
> neering technology, when compared with imported machines. ... We
> sincerely hope for the development of the machine tool industry not only to
> aid the defense of Japan, but also the future of Japan in general.

(quoted in *ibid.*: p.112)

Promotion policies for the machine tool industry

The Office of Resources began discussing promotion policies for the development
of the machine tool industry in 1935. The minister of the Office of Resources
organized the Study and Research Council for the Machine Tool Industry, which
included the participation of relevant persons from the Office of Resources and
other ministries, and from the Five Majors of the Machine Tool Builders Industrial
Union. Issues discussed included the selection of standard machine tool models
and the determination of their designs and specifications, and the desirable steps
to be taken to achieve higher market value. The outcome of the discussions were
the S-model machine tools, the designs of which the Planning Office published in
the official gazette in July 1938 (MITI 1979: p.478). However, as mentioned in
Section 1.2.10, those models were not widely accepted.

At this time, the Minister of the Office of Resources mentioned policies for
the machine tool industry in addition to those for steel, petroleum, automobiles, and shipbuilding in his 'opinion concerning necessary policies for
preparing general mobilization' submitted to the prime minister in July 1937.
In the Five-Year Plan for Key Industries, which the Army Ministry issued in
May 1937, the machine tool industry was listed as a key sector, behind only the
arms-manufacturing industry, the aircraft industry, and the automobile industry
(*ibid.*: pp.366–9).

On the other hand, the Council of Resources had been tackling the issue of the nature of 'desirable policies for expanding machine tool production capacity and increasing the availability of machine tool equipment in the wider industrial sector.' Following intensive discussions, the Council of Resources submitted its report on 30 June 1937. The report declared the need for 'effective policies both for developing skilled engineers and workers, and for improving the quality of materials and establishing a smooth system of materials rationing.' The report proposed five courses of action, including 'the promotion of the domestic production of special machine tools which were at the time fully imported' and 'the adoption of temporary measures for promoting the import of special machine tools while demand for these machine tools could not be fully satisfied with domestic supply' (*ibid.*: pp.478–80).

The Lukouch'iao Incident occurred one week after the report, and with this the demand for machine tools for munitions production accelerated. The government accordingly decided to adopt this report and enact a law as soon as possible, which led to the MTBA of April 1938. As mentioned above, during this period the government enacted laws in many industries. It was in August 1937 that the government finally adopted the budgetary plan to build the Experiment Laboratory for Machinery and began its construction. The laboratory had been strongly demanded since 1923 for the reason that 'constrained by profitability requirements, machinery manufacturers were unsuited to conduct basic research concerning high-grade machines which were in scarce demand and which required rare materials.' Construction was delayed due to shortages in construction materials, but it was finally completed in 1941, with full operation beginning in 1942 (Kawasaki 1943: pp.38–9; see also MITI 1979: p.480).

The MTBA adopted many proposals of the report, particularly the measures for promoting expansion of production capacity. Also, the Temporary Funds Coordination Act took effect in September 1937. In this, the government classified industries into categories A, B, and C, namely industries considered as important to 'armaments,' 'the balance of trade,' and 'current production capacity,' respectively. The machine tool industry was ranked Aa, that is, an industry 'to be treated with extreme preference' among industries 'which firstly either directly contributed to munitions production or had close connection with munitions production, and secondly which presently suffered or were expected to suffer from capacity shortage, and consequently in need of new plant construction, capacity expansion, and improvement in business equipment' (MITI 1964: p.165; MoF 1957: p.73).

The Temporary Funds Coordination Act was established 'to coordinate the use of domestic funds for balancing the demand–supply of materials and funds at the time of the Sino-Japanese Incident' (section 1). According to the official history of the Ministry of Finance:

Basically, financial control was supplementary to overall economic control. At the time of the enactment of this law, however, the direct control of materials was undeveloped, and therefore the financial control measures of this Act had a strong indirect influence on the control of the demand–supply of materials.

(MoF 1957.: p.67)

1.3.5   The Machine Tool Building Act: an outline

The Machine Tool Building Act

As one of a series of industry laws, the MTBA was promulgated in March 1938 and took effect in July 1938. 'The Act's objective was to radically expand production capacity in large machine tool building plants'[24] (Kawasaki 1943: p.27). I have extracted below the parts of the Act that are of direct concern to our discussion:[25]

1   Licensing for business (section 3): a business equipped with over 200 machine tools (or over fifty special-purpose machine tools) is required to be licensed by the government.
2   Preferential treatment for licensed businesses: (a) exemption of income tax, business tax, and import tax for necessary equipment (sections 7, 8, 9, and 12); (b) subsidies for depreciation (sections 10 and 12); (c) preferential treatment in fund raising (section 14); (d) elimination of potential threats posed by foreign machine tools (sections 23 and 24).
3   Control over licensed businesses: (a) a licensed business must report business plans to the government, and the government has the authority to demand changes to business plans (section 16); (b) equipment expansion and changes to equipment require a license from the government (section 6).
4   Mandatory measures concerning technological development and rationalization of management.[26] The government may issue orders regarding the following matters: (a) orders for production or equipment expansion and improvement (section 19.2); (b) orders for making and observing an inter-firm agreement (section 21.2); (c) orders for technical cooperation (section 21.3); (d) orders concerning the use of sample machines and designs (section 21.4); (e) orders concerning the transfer of business (section 21.6); (f) orders and restrictions concerning the use of designated designs, materials, components, and so forth (section 21.12); (g) orders concerning the establishment of mandatory standards (section 21.13).
5   Other relevant provisions: the government may provide for (a) orders concerning coordination of the supply of and demand for products (section 19); (b) subsidies for the trial production of machine tools.

License system under the MTBA

The Act implemented a license system whereby machine tool makers with production capacity beyond a certain level were required to obtain a government license to operate. A wide variety of preferential treatment was provided to licensed businesses. The intention behind the Act was to radically expand production capacity in the large machine tool factories. In 1936, only five companies, Shinohara and the Five Majors apart from Karatsu Metalworks, satisfied the licensing standard of over 200 machine tools. Karatsu had 170 machine tools. The next largest industry players all had fewer than 100 machine tools (Sawai 1984: pp.158–59; MITI 1976: p.458, table 140).

The Planning Office and the Commerce Ministry had in fact aimed their policies of protection and support at these six largest companies in the industry. The Diet was strongly critical of the fact that support was limited to large-scale producers, but the government responded to these criticisms by changing the nature of policy implementation under the Act to include small producers within the support (Kawasaki 1943: pp.26–7).

In addition, as Sawai (1984: p.157) describes, there was a difference in the bureaucracy's (government) and the Diet's understanding of the technological levels of individual factories. The government argued that no small producers were actually manufacturing high-precision machine tools. Diet members responded that there were indeed many small, specialized producers manufacturing excellent products. The government therefore lowered the license threshold from 200 to fifty machine tools for producers of special machine tools such as automatic lathes, high-precision screw-cutting lathes, gear cutters, and jig borers (*ibid.:* pp.155, 157; MITI 1976: p.469).

The following statement in Kawasaki (1943: pp.300–1) is representative of how the attention paid to small businesses inhibited subsequent economic control during the control associations period:

> Today everybody realizes the undeniable error of having constructed an association of producers manufacturing machines most urgently needed around an organization based on the Industrial Union Act. The initial reason behind this organizational structure was to promote the interests of small business and so 'keep the peace.' The abrupt development of wartime economic control compelled us to adopt such a benevolent or considerate stance towards small business. However, we cannot deny that industrial unions operate on basic principles such as the conference system, equal treatment, majority decision rule, and emphasis on the collective interest, and these operated to inhibit swift and efficient implementation of national policy, that is, the production expansion plan. ... This is a consequence of an equal opportunity rule and plan making based upon wrong social policy ideals. The system of control was fundamentally inconsistent with the objective of

control, the system being one without any synthesizing plan, and treating all manufacturers equally, from large to small, regardless of the level or nature of their technology.

Revision of the MTBA in 1941

The MTBA was revised in March 1941, and the revisions took effect in July. The revisions changed the character of the Act in two ways: (1) the licensing threshold of 200 machine tools was abolished, and all machine tool makers were made subject to the licensing system (section 3); (2) the Act imposed many mandatory rules concerning technical improvement and so forth, as outlined in point 4 on page 91. The question that springs to mind here is why these measures were only realized with the Act's revision in 1941, rather than from the original date of enactment in 1938.

Four factors account for the late adoption of the measures:

1   The Aircraft Manufacturing Act was promulgated on the same day as the revised MTBA. This fact implies that an urgent need for aircraft production capacity demanded the revision of the Act for mandatory measures.

2   The MTBA was first promulgated and took effect two days before the NGMA, which was enacted in 1938 but not in response to any urgent need. In fact, 'at that time nobody, even high-ranking officials in the Army, perceived it to be indispensable to managing the wartime economy' (Nakamura 1989: p.10). The Act prepared the legal foundation for national general mobilization, but the development of urgent circumstances was required to spark its actual implementation.

3   The basic policy of the time was to make every effort to import machine tools, particularly those that could not be produced domestically. The importation of machines was intended to contribute to expansion of production capacity in key industries by supplementing domestic production of machine tools and also by providing machines of technological levels beyond domestic production capability. The government conducted import materials mobilization, that is, the planned allocation of each imported machine to individual industries. The government achieved this through its power over foreign exchange by controlling import licenses under the Foreign Exchange Control Act. Machine import licenses under this Act were issued solely on the basis of the urgency of the need for any particular machine. At that time, the government held discussions with the military regarding importing machines for military supply. These discussions led to import licenses being issued only for machines used in military supply industries or heavy industries that could not be produced domestically. The bulk of items involved were machine tools, industrial machines for expanding production capacity, and precision machines (Kawasaki 1943: pp.4, 43–4). Then, in June 1940, the USA prohib-

ited exports of machine tools, and the government commenced active efforts to promote domestic machine tool production. It promulgated the General Mobilization Experiment and Research Order (the subject of which included machine tools) under the NGMA in September 1939, but as noted below the order was actually first put into operation on 23 January 1941.

4 The revised MTBA and the Key Machinery Manufacturing Act were enacted in addition to the previously existing industry laws concerning machine tool making, automobile production, shipbuilding, and aircraft manufacturing. With the Key Machinery Manufacturing Act, there were now laws covering the whole machinery industry, including the bearing industry, as we will see in Section 1.3.10.

Three points to note

It is worth noting three points here: (1) it took three years for the unsatisfactory situation under the initial MTBA to be addressed with the revision to the Act; (2) even with this revision, neither the government not the military could realize what they wanted; and (3) widespread dissatisfaction remained even after the revision, which resulted in the PTCA being established, and subsequently the Munitions Ministry and the Munitions Company Act. However, despite all these reorganizations, wartime control had very limited success.

1.3.6   The Machine Tool Building Act: an evaluation

Comparative reference to the shipbuilding industry

In our analysis of the effectiveness of the MTBA (particularly of how the enactment of the MTBA affected the nature of government and military intervention in the machine tool industry), we are once again helped by comparative reference to the shipbuilding industry. The government had a deep interest in promoting the shipbuilding industry long before the days of industry laws, and I will here briefly outline the government regulation of shipbuilding before the industry laws.

In the late 1920s, the shipbuilding industry was seriously affected by the deep depression in the economy. Eventually, the government provided three rounds of subsidies to help the industry through this situation, beginning with the 1932 First Ship Improvement Support Program. After that, national policy shifted to tonnage expansion, and the government's June 1937 Five-Year Plan for Key Industries incorporated a concrete goal specific to the shipbuilding industry. Then with the Temporary Act for Ship Control three months later, a true legal foundation for future shipbuilding control was established (sections 7 and 8).

The NGMA, promulgated in April 1938, designated ships as general mobilization material and their production and repair as a general mobilization activity (sections 2 and 3). Also, the Factories and Workplaces Control Order, which was based on the Act to Apply the 1918 Military Industry Mobilization Act, took effect in May 1938. This order placed most major shipyards under government control (Onozuka 1962: p.5). The Shipbuilding Act was enacted in April 1939, taking effect in December. Finally, the Shipbuilders Federation arranged to change its name to the Federation of Shipbuilders Unions in July 1937.

However, 'it is not too much to say that this framework of regulation imposed by the government achieved nothing at all.' Direct government control over the shipbuilding industry began with the Shipbuilding Approval System based on the September 1939 New Shipping Control Order. This system was altered in February 1940 to a license system under the Shipping Control Order (which was based on the NGMA). Despite these regulations enabling the government to actively regulate and control shipbuilding, 'no remarkable change occurred in the shipbuilding control' (*ibid.*: pp.3–11).

During the period before the Shipbuilding Control Association, 'though the ground seems to have been prepared for the unified implementation of planned shipbuilding, nationwide shipbuilding control did not actually take effect, probably because the time was not ripe. ... The government failed to convincingly carry out planned shipbuilding' (*ibid.*: pp.3–11). We have already observed the situation subsequent to the establishment of the Shipbuilding Control Association in Section 1.2.7.

Five points to note in evaluating the effectiveness of the MTBA

In evaluating the actual function and the effectiveness of the MTBA, it is important to consider the following five points, in addition to the fact that much stronger control was considered necessary several years later.

First, leading companies, particularly the Five Majors, hesitated to expand their production capacity in response to the Act. They did not value the incentives that the Act provided highly. Faced with this unenthusiastic response (attributable in part to memories of the collapse of the Navy's Eight–Eight Fleet Plan after World War I), the Naval Technical Department asked the Five Majors to state their opinions of the Act prior to its enactment. The Five Majors did so, and 'four of the Five did not hold the Act in high regard at all, with only Ikegai Metalworks responding that they would begin a big expansion program subsequent to the enactment.' Karatsu Metalworks had already accomplished a large expansion of capacity in response to the explosive increases in demand attributable to the Sino-Japanese War. Karatsu went so far as to evaluate the Act as 'of great help to newly established companies, but of no remarkable assistance to large companies that had already conducted expansion programs' (Sawai 1984: pp.158–60).

However, I do not imply that the benefit of becoming a designated company would not have covered the cost. Four of the Big Five, excepting Karatsu, and two special machine tool makers became the designated companies at the start in July 1938, and Karatsu joined in February 1939 (at this time the number of designated companies totaled sixteen). Moreover, as mentioned above, we ought to keep in mind the strong resistance to the Act exhibited in the Diet, criticizing the Act as providing too much assistance to large producers.

Second, many companies other than the Big Five actually received licenses. In total, twenty-one companies (twenty-four factories) were licensed under the Act (including four companies newly licensed in November 1940) before its revision in 1941. As already mentioned, in 1936 only six companies possessed more than 100 machine tools. In addition to these six, licensed at the start in July 1938, four more producers were licensed in October, one in December, and a further five in February 1939, most of which possessed fewer than 100 machine tools in 1936 and conducted rapid expansions of capacity.

Many of these subsequently licensed companies were new entrants to the machine tool industry, such as Toyo Machines (the Technical Engineering Division of Toyo Kohan), Kokusan Precision Tools, Shibaura Machine Works, Toyoda Machine Works (Toyota Motors), and Osaka Kikoh (JMTBA 1962: pp.119–25; MITI 1976: pp.464–6). The Technical Engineering Division of Toyo Kohan, later Toyo Machines, for instance, started construction of a mass-production plant for lathes at the end of 1936 by purchasing equipment, with inaugural production beginning in December 1937 (Mitsubishi Heavy Industries 1964: pp.15, 23).

Third, as already mentioned, by 1938 machine tool production had increased sharply. Compared with the number of machines produced and the aggregate weight of machine tool production in 1932, output levels in 1938 were roughly thirty times higher in both respects.

Figure 1.2 shows the number of machine tool factories by size of plant in terms of the number of workers, and Figure 1.3 displays the indexed yearly fluctuations in those figures, assigning 1935 a base value of 100. As these figures show, generally since 1932 but in particular since 1936, the figures regarding the number of factories in the machine tool industry increased sharply across all size categories. The MTBA was established in March 1938 and took effect in July of the same year. This Act simply could not have effectively supported and promoted such a huge increase.[27]

Three points lend support to this view: (1) even in the final stages the number of licensed producers was twenty-one with twenty-four factories, whereas the number of factories with over 100 workers had already reached ninety-three in 1938; (2) as discussed below, the aggregate production share of the licensed producers was low; and (3) the incentives provided by the Act were effective only in terms of promoting the acquisition of equipment beyond a threshold level and were ineffective regarding any other equipment of a licensed producer.

For one thing, the government's policy focus in the machine tool industry was not simply to expand production capacity and volume as such but to upgrade the

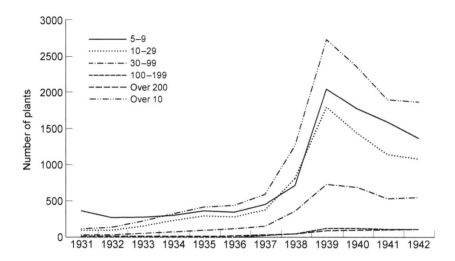

Figure 1.2 The number of metalworking machinery factories in each size[a] category, 1931–42

Source: MITI, census of plants.

[a] Size in terms of the number of employees.

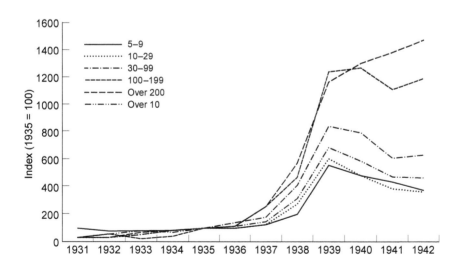

Figure 1.3 Indexed[a] number of metalworking machinery factories in each size[b] category, 1931–42

Source: MITI, census of plants.

[a] Indexed at 1935 = 100.
[b] Size in terms of the number of employees.

quality of the machine stock to include more large or special-purpose machine tools. The reality behind the sharp increases in plant number and production capacity that were actually achieved was that 'many small machine producers supplied easily made low-quality machine tools, which, unsuitable for military production, remained as idle stock throughout the country' (JMTBA 1962: p.117).

To combat this situation, the Rules Concerning Machinery Equipment Control were enacted in September 1939. The government intended the rules to restrict new plant and capacity construction by small machine producers and new entrants through the use of a license system. Thereby, the new construction and expansion of metal machine tool production capacity and also the diversion of equipment into machine tool production were made subject to government licensing.[28]

Fourth, despite the preferential treatment of licensed producers provided under the Act, the major proportion of machine tools were produced by unlicensed producers. The Steel Control Council was organized in the Commerce Ministry in February 1938 to serve as the core institution for steel control. Subsequently, the Rules Concerning Steel Rationing Control were established in June, setting up a card system to implement nationwide steel rationing control (as shown in Section 1.2.3). The details of this steel rationing system were that a card, or more correctly a certificate for allocation of steel rations issued by a control association, was necessary to acquire steel. Hundreds of associations, including industrial unions, were designated as control associations for this purpose.[29] Producers licensed under the MTBA organized the Industrial Union of Japanese Machine Tool Builders as one of these control associations.

Aside from this scheme of licensed producers, small-scale machine tool makers (predominantly producers equipped with over twenty machine tools for metal cutting and grinding, or producers with fewer machines but approved as technically competent) organized the First Machine Tool Builders Industrial Union in each major production prefecture. The National Federation of Machine Tool Builders Industrial Unions was established incorporating these prefectural unions, and it boasted 403 members by August 1940. Smaller producers excluded from both these organizations organized the Second Machine Tool Builders Industrial Union in each prefecture, whose members in turn all belonged to the Federation of Prefectural Local Industrial Unions in each prefecture (MITI 1964: pp.263–7; JMTBA 1962: pp.165–7).

The ratio of output from members of the Industrial Union of Japan Machine Tool Builders (the association of licensed producers) to that from the National Federation of Machine Tool Builders Industrial Unions in 1939 was 27.2:72.8 in terms of value and 13.8:86.2 in terms of the number of machines produced. In 1941, when the Act was revised, these ratios had altered to 41.4:58.6 by value and 23:77 by number of machines produced (Sawai 1984: p.162, table 7). It is obvious that licensed producers actually accounted for the minority of production.

Only later did the government expand the scope of its policy of increasing machine tool production to include the members of the First Machine Tool Builders Industrial Unions. Furthermore, in order both to lend support to the new subjects of government policy and to prevent production of low-quality machine tools, the government stopped allocating steel for machine tool production to members of the Second Industrial Unions in April 1940 (Kawasaki 1943: p.86)

However, the details and effectiveness of the suspension of steel allocation to the Second Industrial Unions in 1940 remain unclear. I can find no description regarding this point in the article published in October by Hashii (1940b), who was at the time chief of the General Affairs Section of the Machinery Bureau. The piece that was published in February by the same author (1940a: p.157) was written while he was chief of the General Machinery Section. Stating that 'it is obvious that with the present situation of the country we can ill afford to waste large quantities of steel in producing low-quality machines any longer,' he writes:

> at present, improvement guidance with certificate examinations by the prefectural government, and technical advice, is the national policy for small producers at the crossroads. But without strengthening through organizing unions or merging and improving their performance by themselves small businesses would not be able to enjoy their long-run prosperity.

Accordingly, at least until the late refocusing of government policy, medium-sized producers (members of the First Machine Tool Builders Industrial Unions) lay beyond the bounds of government policy. However, Materials continued to be allocated to the smallest producers, and even they thrived (*ibid.*: p.57):

> At the same time other machine makers smaller than the size required for the license also developed freely. Rises in prices and an explosive increase in demand for machine tools strongly stimulated the activities of those small makers, resulting in tremendous expansion of their production capacity.

Fifth, as we have seen, the MTBA was based on the report of the Office of Resources, in which the fourth and fifth of five proposed courses of action were, respectively, 'the promotion of the domestic production of special machine tools then fully imported' and the 'adoption of effective temporary measures for importing special machine tools in order to promote the expansion of machining capacity in key manufacturing industries while domestic supply could not satisfy the demand for these machine tools' (MITI 1979: p.478).

Private companies and the military actively imported machine tools to supplement their equipment. Several overseas machine tool purchasing missions had been conducted since 1937, resulting in the purchase of many machine tools. The Army's second purchasing mission, which visited Europe and the USA, for instance, contracted to buy 985 machines in Europe and 848 in the USA (Japan's machine tool imports in 1938 and 1939 topped 7,000 in both years). However, before all the machines from Europe had arrived in Japan, war broke out in Europe and this interrupted supply. In the autumn of 1939, the Military Air Services Department and the Department of Naval Aeronautics jointly sent a purchasing mission to the USA to purchase special machine tools mainly for aircraft engine production. Again, however, most of these orders were canceled by the US machine tool embargo in June 1940 (JMTBA 1962: pp.107–8). Toyo Kohan (later Toyo Machines), which was a new entrant to the machine tool industry with its newly built mass-production lathe plant, purchased sixty-one machine tools from abroad between the end of 1936 and the beginning of 1937. The company continued to import, and the number of machine tools ordered at the end of March 1940 was about eighty, twenty-eight of which were not received due to the June embargo (Mitsubishi Heavy Industries 1964: pp.15, 47).

Of the two, however, the fifth course of action was considered of higher priority. Accordingly, machine tool imports showed increasingly rapid growth after the outbreak of the Sino-Japanese War. Machine tool imports in 1939 totaled ¥157.16 million, which was more than ten times greater than the 1936 figure and represented 37.4 percent of domestic demand in terms of value (10.6 percent by number of machines produced and 20.2 percent by aggregate weight; Sawai 1984: pp.162–3, table 6).

On 4 June 1940, the US government declared an embargo on the export of machine tools to foreign countries in the name of US national defense. (In the summer of 1939, 'the rumor was circulating that the US would soon prohibit basic machine tool exports to Japan of such as accuracy gauges and lead screw cutting lathes. The Army therefore sent a mission to the US headed by Mr. Hayasaka, the chief engineer of Ikegai Metalworks, who acted as an advisor to the military arsenal for purchasing as many used machine tools as possible before supply might be cut.' As this description from Maekawa (1996: p.83) suggests, the US machine tool embargo did not take effect suddenly.) With this, Japan diverted the destination of its orders for machine tools from the USA to Germany. However, this source of supply also became unavailable with the outbreak of war between Germany and the USSR in June 1941.

The demand for high-precision machine tools increased steadily, and the only remaining means by which to satisfy this demand was the promotion of domestic production (Kawasaki 1943: pp.85, 166). Prior to this period, the 'promotion of the expansion of machining capacity in key manufacturing industries' under the MTBA ranked as the government policy of the highest priority. However, the MTBA failed to outline explicitly the boundaries of government authority in making directions. Therefore the August 1939 Rules Concerning Subsidies for Trial Production of Machine Tools made under the Act were actually based on proposals from the private sector and did not themselves promote domestic machine tool production (Mitsubishi Heavy Industries 1964: p.76). With these developments, the 'promotion of domestic special machine tools production' emerged for the first time as a policy of pressing urgency.

The MTBA and related policies during the period were modest

Government intervention in the machine tool industry can be summarized, as Hashii (1940a: p.55) has argued, as 'evolutionary control.' Because of both difficulty in purchasing raw materials and an unanticipated and severe interruption of imports, output volumes and supply quantities of products in other controlled sectors decreased, causing problems, and with this industry control started. The key issue in other industries was how to satisfy vast demand with extremely finite supply. In the machine tool industry, however, the primary objective was to increase the absolute volume of supply, for which the government had listed this industry for production capacity expansion plans since 1938. 'The focus was placed upon machine tools, the most urgently required given the circumstances of the state at that time, and in order to allocate products to these key sectors strong calls sounded for the control of supply.' As a result, the production of 'machine tools relatively easy to build and of a general demand character, such as ordinary lathes and milling machines,' expanded rapidly. Japan had reached a situation where 'there was no need for any consideration to be paid to the future development of these particular machine tools' (*ibid.*: pp.55, 158).

If the objective of the MTBA was to expand production of these machine tools, the Act would at first blush seem to have been effective. However, closer examination yields a much less flattering appraisal. In the first place, most of these machines were not manufactured by the well-established large producers, which were from the beginning the focus of the Act's policy. The majority were instead built by unlicensed producers, and licensed producers like Kokusan Seiki and Toyo Machines had already begun mass production in the industry before the Act was established. Second, the Act did not authorize the government to force individual producers to expand the production of any specific product, and the government did not do this. Finally, the rationing of materials may well have been effective in cutting down production in specific sectors, but it was not used to promote effective expansion of capacity or investment in R&D for realizing supply increases and product improvements in specific sectors of the industry. These points apply to the whole process of wartime control, but particularly to wartime control during the period of the PTCA.

The MTBA and related policies were thus modest. As mentioned above, regarding shipbuilding control prior to the establishment of the Shipbuilding Control Association, 'the government failed to fully commit to planned shipbuilding' (Onozuka 1962: p.11). If this was the case for shipbuilding, then given the size of product ranges, the diversity of user demand, fluctuations in product quality and producer competence, and the sheer number of producers, it is only natural that the government also failed to commit fully to intervention in the machine tool industry in the period prior to the PTCA. As shown in Section 1.2, this was also true during the period of the PTCA

1.3.7   Trial production under the General Mobilization Experiment and Research Order: history and outline

With the revision of the MTBA in March 1941, various compulsory measures were introduced to improve technology and rationalize management. If the measures outlined in the MTBA were ever actively and forcefully implemented in the industry, it was after this revision that the government issued orders for production and research 'in case of military necessity.' The Act authorized the government 'to make orders to a machine tool builder in case of military necessity. Orders available to the government were orders to produce specific machine tools, to study specific matters concerning machine tools, or to perform tasks of military necessity such as produce special equipment' (section 20). Additionally, the government was authorized 'to grant subsidies for trial production of designated machine tools within the budgetary limit' (section 22).

It was after this March 1941 revision that the supply of imported machine tools was cut and hence the promotion of domestic production of special machine tools, which had all been until that time imported, became crucial for national defense (Kawasaki 1943: p.166). Before that, the government had placed a higher priority on expanding production capacity for those machine tools that were relatively easy to produce and of general demand character while adopting measures for the temporary importation of more specialized machines.

Subsidies and orders for the trial production of machine tools

Rules concerning subsidies for the trial production of machine tools were established in August 1938 under the MTBA, 'with which the government subsidized the trial production of machine tools then unable to be built or difficult to build in Japan. The subsidy covered half of the trial production cost' (*ibid.*: p.169). During 1938 and afterwards, the government subsidized scores of trials every year, with the total budget amounting to between ¥300,000 and ¥500,000 (*ibid.*: pp.169–73; MITI 1979: pp.586–7). However, these government subsidies based upon the Act lacked concrete objectives. While they specified the models to be subsidized, the choice of models to be subsidized was determined based on proposals from private companies, particularly potential producers participating in the trials. Accordingly, the subsidy policy was at best merely a modest measure for promoting rapid domestic production of machine tools necessary at that time (JMTBA 1962: p.142; Hashii 1940a: p.76).

Also, the government issued the Imperial Order for General Mobilization Experiments and Research in September 1939, exercising authority granted under section 25 of the NGMA. This order specified that 'where necessary for general mobilization the government could order those producers engaged in the production or repair of general mobilization materials, or to managers of experiment and research institutions, to conduct experiment and research.' It provided for government orders to private companies to conduct trial production of machine tools. However, it was only at the late stage of 23 January 1941 that the government actually issued the orders.

Prior to presenting the Bill for Key Machinery Manufacturing to the Diet (which was prepared in reaction to the US machine tool embargo in June 1940), the Commerce Ministry conducted a study to identify factors inhibiting the promotion of domestic production of key machinery. This study identified four factors inhibiting such domestic production: (1) the insufficient state of basic research; (2) shortages in machinery equipment for the production of large machines, processing machinery, and equipment; (3) a shortage of precision machine tools and insufficient engineering technology; and (4) the underdevelopment of the materials industry.

In response to the study, the government decided to use measures available to it under the Key Machinery Manufacturing Act more effectively, which led to the adoption of radical policies to promote domestic production. These policies consisted of the following measures: (1) reorganization and expansion of research institutions to facilitate more active technical cooperation; (2) expansion of the licensing system for research equipment to cover large machines and precision machinery; (3) establishment of engineering technology for those machine tools that would serve as basic machinery for further machinery production; and (4) various other ancillary measures (Kawasaki 1943: pp.229–31).

The revision of the MTBA saw also the enactment of the 1941 Key Machinery Manufacturing Act, effective from January 1942. Subsidies for key machinery manufacturing research, which were based on the rules established prior to the Key Machinery Manufacturing Act, also began in the 1940 financial year. In 1940 and 1941, the ratio of the size of total research subsidies for manufacturing key machinery to total subsidies for trial production of machine tools was 13:10 in terms of the number of projects but only 6:10 in terms of the total value of subsidies granted. Accordingly, the value of the subsidy per project was smaller for the former than the latter (MITI 1979: p.587, table 3.268).

Furthermore, a liaison conference was held between the Army, the Navy, the Commerce Ministry, and the Planning Office on 16 December 1940. At this conference, it was decided to activate the General Mobilization Experiment and Research Order concerning machine tools, and the first experimental production orders were issued on 23 January 1941. These consisted of orders to twenty-one producers of 111 models. In 1942, the government issued a second round of orders to nineteen producers for twenty-two models, and a third round to six producers for six models. Moreover, in addition to orders for individual projects on key machines, the government also issued General Mobilization Experiment and Research Orders regarding models already receiving subsidies, either for trial production of machine tools or for research into manufacturing key machinery. With such an order, a project could expect to receive preferential treatment under the Materials Mobilization Plans (Kawasaki 1943: p.245).

The government asked the liaison conference to select the models and types of machine that would be targeted under the domestic production promotion policies and also to determine which producers ought to be commissioned for production (*ibid.*: p.166). Furthermore, with the suspension of machine tool imports due to the outbreak of war between Germany and the USSR, the government put into action the Key Machinery Domestic Production Promotion Plan as part of the 1941 Production Capacity Expansion Plan determined at the regular cabinet meeting on 29 August (*ibid.*: p.229).

1.3.8   Trial production under the General Mobilization Experiment and Research Order: an evaluation

Let us turn now to evaluation: the degree to which and in what direction government orders influenced the behavior of machine tool producers, and the effectiveness and the desirability of the policy of trial production under the General Mobilization Experiment and Research Order. The conclusion is straightforward: the government's influence was not substantial, and the policy was neither effective nor desirable, regardless of the standard chosen for evaluation.

Basic issues for evaluation

Ideally, a comprehensive evaluation would involve detailed information regarding the following seven questions (unfortunately, that information is largely unavailable):

1   For the trial production orders issued on the 139 models (excluding those for which the order replaced the preceding subsidy), how many actually resulted in trial production being conducted? Furthermore, what percentage of trial production started was actually completed?

2   What models and types of machine were targeted for promotion of domestic production? Did the government select those machines that were most likely to achieve policy success? What was the anticipated value assigned to particular projects, particularly in the successful cases?

3   What were the expected development costs for individual projects? What were the actual amounts of subsidies? What was the value of the other

government support, like preferential treatment under the Materials Mobilization Plans?

4   What would have occurred to these machines without trial production orders or subsidies? These machines were predominantly the subject of military demand, and accordingly their demand price must have been inherently high. Might prices have been higher without those policies? If so, how much did the subsidies offset the artificially lower price? And were prices enforced? According to the JMTBA (1962: p.143), the 'policies for promoting special machine tools for producing aircraft engines and arms were quite informal. Private companies and arsenals engaging in military production made their independent efforts to secure supplies of machine tools.'[30]

5   On what basis were the companies selected for trial production?

6   To what extent did the government intervene in the internal decision making of individual companies? For instance, did it intervene in the details of the planning and management procedure, time schedule, and intensity of trial production activities of particular companies? Did the government stipulate the priority for various models when it asked a company to complete several trials at once?

7   How strongly were orders actually enforced? Had the government sufficient competence to effectively enforce the orders?

Two surveys of machine tool trial production

The 'List of New Model Machines for Trial Production during the War,' which was compiled as the result of a survey conducted by the JMTBA and published as *The Industrial History of the Showa Era* (Toyo Keizai Shimpo-sha 1950: p.319), is a basic source of information concerning the first point above (see, for example, MITI 1979: p.609). The list includes fifty-seven models, five of which do not have any date for completion. If we assume for present purposes that those fifty-seven cases were all that were actually started, and also that trials were started but not finished in those five cases, then the ratio of completed trials to the number of trial production orders is 52:139, or less than 40 percent.

A survey was also conducted by the JMTBA regarding 'The Catalog of Machine Tools for Trial Production under the General Mobilization Experiment and Research Order' (the results appear in JMTBA 1962: pp.223–36). This survey lists slightly different figures from the first survey mentioned: seventy-eight models, four of which do not have completion dates listed. The corresponding completion ratio based on this data would be 74:139, or slightly more than 53 percent. Furthermore, this catalog lists the number of models completed in each year between 1941 and 1945 as ten, twenty-two, twenty-seven, eleven, and three.

A government evaluation of the effectiveness

Recall that trial production orders were initiated in response to the suspension of imports of special machine tools. About 70 percent of machines affected by import suspensions were machine tools to be used in machine tool production plants. Therefore the government was left with no alternative but to rely on domestically produced machine tools, and it did this through the 'general mobilization' of domestic machine tool makers (Kawasaki 1943: p.235).

In 1940, the government supervisor of machine tools listed the 'promotion of domestic production of special machine tools' as one of the important issues of the time. Yet he subsequently published the following comment, suggesting that in reality only quite a modest policy with strictly limited objects would be feasible:

> The development of high-grade machines like gear cutters, whose production requires high technology and research, has been very slow. ... The development of special-purpose machines and mechanical machines for mass production is currently unaccomplished and remains an issue for the future. ... We have however made efforts to promote this production by subsidizing trial production. The scale of the support we [the government] have provided to the industry thus far, however, has been far from adequate to achieve the rapid development of production capacity for the models now under large supply shortages.
>
> (Hashii 1940a: p.158)

Partly because of this situation, producers were ordered to copy the 'model machines' of first-grade foreign producers without modification (JMTBA 1962: p.143). As Hayasaka (1964: p.496) argues, it was often thought that a leading machine tool maker could produce a full range of machine tools individually simply by copying foreign products. However, copying imported machines is not always easy. Hayasaka reports cases of both failure (even by Ikegai) and success, despite Kearney and Trecker's comment that it must have been difficult at the time to copy the No. 2 full-universal Milwaukee K-model carbide milling machine (*ibid.*, pp.460, 510–13).

Who actually selected trial producers, and how?

Suppose we assume that the government was able to appropriately determine the models and types of machine tool for trial production. The next stage, that of selecting appropriate firms to conduct that trial production, required detailed information regarding the development competence, decision-making mechanism, and manufacturing technology level of individual companies. The key questions here are whether the government had adequate information upon which to base its selections of producers for trial production, and whether it was competent in performing this task appropriately.

> In selecting trial producers, the government took each company's experience in machine tool production, plant equipment and capacity, and technological level into consideration. As a matter of fact, however, most machine tools the subject of trial production under the General Mobilization Experiment and Research Order were for aircraft manufacturing, and trials were ordered only with those companies that had close connections with aircraft manufacturing companies.
>
> (JMTBA 1962: pp.223–6)

Closer analysis of the above-mentioned 'catalog' adds weight to our suspicion that the companies actually chosen for trial production were not selected by strictly rational means, true to the system of control imposed under the MTBA. From the catalog, which lists seventy-eight models as being the subject of trial production, we find that eleven companies unlicensed under the MTBA (e.g., Fujikoshi Kozai, Toyo Manufacturing, and Howa Manufacturing) were actually conducting trial production. Also, among twenty-one companies listed as licensed makers, nowhere do we find the names of the major licensed producers Shibaura Machine Tools and Mitsui Machine Tools. Yet eight models were allocated to Hitachi Seiki, the largest allocation, and six to Ohkuma Metalworks and Okamoto Machine Tools.

Identifying the net contribution of 'orders'

What are crucial are the details and exact meanings of terms such as 'orders' and 'ordered' and the reason why any particular 'orders' could be and actually were effective. Orders for trial production were based on the General Mobilization Experiment and Research Order, and expressions like 'ordered' and 'issued orders' were used extremely loosely. For instance, the terms were used even to refer to situations where the government simply induced trial production of special machine tools with subsidies or contracts to buy at a higher price. We must identify the net contribution of 'orders.'

As discussed in Section 1.2.13, it is hard for the government (the principal) to realize production expansion from each producer (agent) as it wishes. It is even harder for the government to ensure the realization of each producer's investment in equipment for the expansion of production as it wishes. It must be even harder to accomplish the development, design, and trial production of a specific model of machine, because any given producer accumulates and uses its competence and know-how for development, design, and trial production from a long-term point of view.

Accordingly, if a model ordered to be produced on a trial basis does not fit well with its resources, if the success of trial production would not contribute much to the accumulation of useful know-how, if the project is against its business interests, or in 1943 in particular if trial production is unlikely to contribute to an advantageous position in the postwar machine tool industry, it is only rational for a producer not to engage enthusiastically in the trial production thus ordered. We have seen above that the 'scale of the support we [the government] have provided to the industry thus far, however, has been far from adequate to achieve the rapid development of production capacity for the models now under large supply shortages' (Hashii 1940a: p.158).

Therefore, if trial production was successful, it must have been due to the government having subsequently adopted special new ideas or devices to induce producers to carry out the orders effectively. Also, selecting producers and accomplishing trials properly must have been far harder than simply realizing, for example, 'ordered' equipment investment, because of the difficulty the government would necessarily face in collecting information and accumulating the necessary know-how.

There is no reason to believe that trial production orders worked effectively

The exact details of how companies were selected for domestic production trials remain unclear. As mentioned above, we know that the liaison conference between the Army, the Navy, the Commerce Ministry, and the Planning Office made the decisions to implement the order, and we know that the Commerce Ministry studied the obstacles to domestic production of key machines. However, such a study is by its nature difficult to conduct effectively. Given that even during the period of the PTCA, coordination between the Army and the Navy and between the military and the government concerning production was far from smooth, one might wonder whether the government had the information it needed to issue appropriate trial production orders or to ensure that the orders issued were completed effectively.

An outline of the actual measures adopted by the government to implement the trial production policy bolsters these doubts. Kawasaki (1943: pp.256–9) outlines the policy measures actually adopted. Although he claims that 'effective policies to promote domestic production were adopted satisfactorily for machine tools, bearings, and automobiles,' an analysis of the policy measures reveals how weak and inactive they actually were:

(4) *Measures for promoting research*: an official in charge (a) shall always supervise research progress and make efforts to eliminate any factors that may delay progress; (b) shall keep in close communication with technical officials

and the control associations concerning domestic production promotion. The government shall also actively cooperate to promote research.

(5) *Post-research measures*: [(a)-(c) omitted]; (d) the government shall determine the selling price, paying due attention to the profitability of the producer; (e) where necessary the government will adopt a policy of restricting market participation, so as to grant a monopoly to the researcher.

Cases for illustration

Detailed information about trial production from the companies that received the orders is also scarce. Toyo Machines received an order for trial production of six models in January 1941, on three of which it had already started trial production prior to the order. Regarding two of the three, Toyo had already started trial production in 1939 and had completed it by October 1942 as part of its autonomous planning to expand production of plant equipment in order to acquire a license under the MTBA. As for the third, Toyo did actually commence trial production, intending the machine to substitute for imported machines when foreign imports were suspended. Trial production was completed in December 1941. As for the remaining three orders, Toyo started trial production of two in the autumn of 1941 and of the last in September 1942, and these machines were completed in June 1943, and April and May 1944 (Mitsubishi Heavy Industries 1964: p.78).

Toyoda Machine Works (established by splitting off the engineering division of Toyota Motors) proposed six models for new trial production under the MTBA to the Machinery Bureau of the Commerce Ministry, all of which it completed successfully. These models went into mass production after being judged high quality by the Commerce Ministry. The above-mentioned 'catalog' lists four trial models for Toyoda Machine Works, which were included in the six models. 'Toyota Motors commenced the manufacture of all of these six models for their own automobile production, which in turn enabled mass production of munitions including aircraft' (Toyoda Machine Works 1991: p.13). Thus model selection and the setting of schedules for trial production strongly reflected the interests of producers, and we rarely find proof of active intervention by the 'ordering' side, the government.

Summing up

The above discussion suggests that trial production orders made under the General Mobilization Experiment and Research Order merely constituted extensions of the preceding system of subsidy grants for trial production of machine tools and key machines. The systems of both trial production orders and subsidy grants were very similar, at least in such key areas as the character and operation of the systems and the role of the government or the state in each system. The only significant difference between the two was that the former targeted machines newly listed as appropriate for domestic production, which was made necessary primarily due to import suspension. Before the import suspensions, the relevant parties had intended to import these machines, either because of the urgency of demand or because of the difficulty associated with domestic production. Accordingly, the models newly ordered for trial production would have been those that were difficult to produce (if models were selected truly, as was argued).

In addition, some models 'ordered' to be subjects of domestic production were those models that would have been put into trial production at the initiative of the machine tool producers regardless of any government 'order.' Consequently, the fact that trial production was completed for models that the government 'ordered' does not mean that the policy measures contributed to that trial production.

The above discussion suggests that the companies conducting trial production predominantly took the initiative in model selection and setting schedules for trial production. Government 'orders' included no fresh incentives (like massive subsidies) beyond those already implemented. The state therefore had no effective supplementary measures to influence the behavior of producers, and indeed the behavior of those producers was not influenced. Therefore the net contribution of the 'orders' could not have been substantial.

1.3.9   Evaluation of the policy to promote domestic production

Two basic issues in evaluating policies to promote domestic production

Japan realized domestic production of many machine tool models. However, the issue is what portion of this can be attributed to the domestic production promotion policy or related policies intended to promote domestic production? Here I address two issues, which, in addition to the preceding evaluation of trial production under the General Mobilization Experiment and Research Order, complete the discussion in this area. First, what policies existed to promote domestic production other than orders for trial production, and to what extent did they actually contribute to promoting domestic production? Second, what was the cost associated with the policies to promote domestic production? I aim to draw conclusions on the effectiveness of policies to promote domestic production in a broad sense, that is, by considering the above two issues collectively with conclusions drawn in the previous subsections.

The policies had a strictly limited effect

In addition to trial production under the General Mobilization Experiment and Research Order, the government adopted other policies to promote the domestic production of machine tools. As we have seen above, these included subsidies for the trial production of machine tools and key machines, and orders for the production of specific machines. However, these 'policies' had a strictly limited effect. It was primarily the explosive growth in machine tool demand that led to the increased domestic production. The explosion in demand for machine tools was caused by several factors. Most basically, it reflected the expansion in armament stocks. Second, shortages of foreign currency and likely bans on further imports spurred demand. Third, the government's preferential treatment of the industry in terms of materials procurement facilitated production expansion and hence increases in domestic production unavailable in other industries.

Six points critical to an understanding of the magnitude and nature of policy costs

In the discussion below, I evaluate the desirability of the policies to promote domestic production in a broad sense, taking into account all government actions that may have contributed to the increased machine tool stock and production capacities at the end of the war. To be sure, given that the government promoted the policies to further its war aims, there is an artificiality in evaluating policy 'rationality,' but the following six points are nonetheless critical to understanding the magnitude and nature of the costs that these policies imposed:

1   Most basically, war is an absurdly inefficient use of economic resources. The economic value of any products manufactured by machine tools subsidized by wartime policies was next to nothing, and because the stocks of machine tools left after the war were specific to war production, they too had little value. Consequently, any gains in domestic production generated by the policies seldom covered the cost of those policies. Perhaps it is too much to say that all the machine tools produced domestically in haste were too specialized to be of any value during peacetime. But no one can deny that the selection of models produced deviated heavily from those that would have been produced during peacetime to meet expected demand. In turn, the constraints imposed by shortages in time and resources restricted the designs and production even of non-military machine tools.

2   Because the availability of materials, foreign currency, and labor fell during the course of the war, the production costs of machine tools (including the costs of preferential treatment like subsidies for trial production) increased. The Basic Policy of Corporate Reorganization for Strengthening War Potential (the cabinet decision of June 1943), whereby the government

diverted equipment and labor from sectors such as textiles to sectors such as machine tools where expansion of production capacity was desired, is representative of the cost of these policies to the economy.

3   Import suspensions may have promoted domestic production, but note that they raised the procurement cost of machine tools. Even under severe shortages of foreign currency, the importing of machine tools was extremely important and was promoted by policy, particularly special machine tools for production of further machine tools. The suspension of these crucial machine tool imports heavily influenced the production of both machine tools and aircraft, which should also be counted as a cost of the promotion of domestic machine tool production. However, I am not arguing that without import suspension domestic production would not have happened.

4   The combination of promoting domestic production and import suspension stalled the ability of Japanese firms in the machine tool industry to introduce foreign technical innovations and newly invented models. Japan's machine tool makers at the time badly lacked self-sufficiency, since they were manufacturing machine tools relying on foreign machines of much higher speed and quality. They were also in the situation of learning by using and reconstructing foreign machines, and they collected much information from foreign producers on the trends of more advanced technology. The suspension of foreign machine tool imports dramatically decreased the flow of information and technology into the country and necessarily raised procurement costs. Actually, because no new machines came into Japan until independence in 1952, the industry remained in isolation for more than a decade.

5   The trial production program itself stymied technological progress by ordering producers to copy the 'model machines' of the first-grade foreign producers without any modification (JMTBA 1962: p.143). This obviously reduced the gains from investments in expertise and technological innovation. To make matters worse, in picking the foreign machines to copy, the government did not even pick the most advanced machines at that time.

6   The promotion of domestic production of machine tools was carried out in total isolation from the most competitive and technologically advanced rivals, which were overwhelmingly foreign firms. Hence the conditions that would otherwise have prevented the evils of monopoly and helped to promote more efficient supply systems did not exist. When a competitive manufacturer subcontracts for components (witness today's car makers), it will generally induce the firms it selects for trial production to compete with each other, conduct trial production runs for the same model at more than one producer, and monitor their performance at regular intervals. The government adopted none of these measures. On the contrary, the policy of allowing a trial producer to monopolize the production of a model could only have resulted in further increasing the cost. Apparently, the government had not the least

idea of how to manipulate incentives appropriately to achieve improvements in efficiency. Furthermore, at least in connection with promoting domestic production, there was no discussion regarding policies for promoting the accumulation of R&D capability in individual companies or improving quality. The list of companies that could become trial producers was fixed *a priori*, which would almost inevitably have encouraged the usual evils caused by lack of competition (although the actual harm may have been mitigated by the large number of designated producers and the short control period).

Moreover

In addition to the above points, recall that the government was only able to adopt those policies when control was finally expanded to the whole economy. That in turn suggests that the costs of promotional policies for munitions-related industries were costs spread over the economy at large – and spelled huge sacrifices for the national economy. We should also consider the more direct costs of control over the entire economy. As the control measures accumulated, the institutions for implementing control became increasingly complicated, as suggested by the number of persons engaged in public service. The number of males engaged in the (non-military) public service sector increased from 547,000 on 1 October 1940 to 890,000 on 22 February 1944 (Nakamura 1977: p.147, table 19).

Moreover, agents who were the subject of control could not escape from the heavy cost burdens imposed by the red tape concerning proposals and reports. The following description from Niigata Metalworks (1968: pp.83–4) is representative of the situation:

> During the war, the government made a vast number of laws, ordinances, and rules for reorganizing industries, imposing various restrictions and controls, all in the name of directing all national power to the war effort. With the progress of the war the number of laws multiplied, and further the government revised them frequently, causing interpretation and enforcement issues which seriously troubled the company the subject of government control. Red tape such as inescapable proposals and reports inevitably increased explosively. Not only companies but also the government had to spend much time and energy to comply with the regulations of the system of control. This bureaucratization resulted in delays in government activities and also damaged business activities in individual companies. The president of our company, Mr. Ouchi's response to an inquiry from Mr. Takashi Isaka, the chairman of Japan's Economic Federation, accurately reflects the circumstances of the time. In short, Mr. Ouchi responded that inappropriate control procedures, increasing the general expense and damaging the appropriateness in materials rationing control, caused serious blowouts in the cost of supply.

1.3.10   An evaluation of the policy for promoting domestic production in the bearing industry

Let us here evaluate the policy for promoting domestic production in the bearing industry, mentioned in Section 1.2.1, for the purpose of comparison. Output in the industry was 260,000 bearings in 1930, 850,000 in 1935, 8.3 million in 1940, and 35 million in the peak year of 1944 (Annual Stat. Mach., MITI 1953).

For a long time, the government and the military had strongly demanded the domestic production of bearings and had made continuous efforts toward the preferential and exclusive use of domestic products. For example, in 1933, with a research grant for industry promotion from the Commerce Ministry and the support of the Navy, NSK imported bearing-manufacturing machines from the USA and Sweden.[31] Before 1935, however, locally produced bearings had not captured the full confidence of domestic users.

The Temporary Funds Coordination Act of 1937 ranked the bearing industry as Ab. The government adopted a policy of importing as many bearings and associated materials, such as steel alloys, as foreign currency constraints allowed. Furthermore, in response to the promulgation of the Rules Concerning Steel Rationing Control of 1938, the five major manufacturers organized the Japanese Bearings Manufacturers Industrial Union. Institutionally, this organization came under the umbrella of the Federation of Japan Machinery Manufacturers Industrial Unions.

No industry law like the MTBA was established for the bearing industry. Despite this, the government and the military heavily intervened in the industry to promote development, which would in turn benefit and promote military production. There was no industry law, but there was a basic guiding statement in the form of the Basic Guideline for the Ball-bearing and Roller-bearing Industry, which was determined on 14 June 1939. This guideline was established as an agreement between the relevant ministers. It was prepared by the Temporary Materials Coordination Bureau of the Commerce Ministry (established in April 1938) after consultation with representatives from both the Equipment Bureau of the War Ministry and the Mobilization Bureau of the Navy Ministry. The basic policy objective was self-sufficiency, for which the Army and the Navy decided to place major bearing factories under their control and management. The military oversaw expansion of production, promotion of technological improvement, and providing these major plants under its control with protection from the competition of foreign products.

Although the details of the policies adopted to achieve these goals are unknown, we do have information on the major components. Among those measures were (1) that the Army and the Navy put three major producers, NOK, NTN Corporation, and Koyo Seiko, under their joint management to serve as major supply sources; (2) that the military promoted the realization of existing capacity expansion programs of factories under its control; and (3) that the Army and Navy claimed 60–70 percent of the capacities of factories under their control for their own use. To provide some precise figures, in 1939 the military shares of available capacity stood at 37 percent for the Army and 32 percent for the Navy. This left a mere 31 percent for private demand. Regarding producers other than those three, the government provided support for the ongoing programs of Fujikoshi but gave only fledgling support to other producers.

With the US embargo on the export of machines in June 1940, demand for domestic production accelerated. However, despite efforts by the government and the military to expand bearing production in 1941, targeted companies had not realized the planned expansion. Furthermore, huge imbalances in capacity expansion had developed among the target factories, which in turn caused many problems. In response, the Diet enacted the Key Machinery Manufacturing Act in May 1941.

As we have already seen, the PTCA, the jurisdiction of which also included the bearing industry with nineteen companies, was established under the Key Industry Association Order. The primary tasks of the association were to ration materials and to control the distribution of products. The Third Section of the Temporary Materials Coordination Bureau determined the allocation of materials to the bearing industry in accordance with the Materials Mobilization Plans. Further allocations between the Army, the Navy, and the private sector were determined at the allocation conference organized by the PTCA. Once the allocation of materials between demand sectors had been determined, the War Ministry, the Navy Ministry, and the Commerce Ministry each sent their own orders for products to bearing producers in accordance with their predetermined allocations of capacity.

The industry was still expanding domestic production capacity when the US machine embargo was introduced. Bearing products of the so-called Five Majors were almost exclusively devoted to military production. Some machine tool makers, under the General Mobilization Experiment and Research Order, attempted to reproduce foreign machine tools for bearing production. In addition, some bearing producers, in cooperation with machine tool makers, similarly tried to manufacture bearing-production machines.

The above discussion of the magnitude of the contribution made and the intervention conducted by the government and the military in the bearing industry shows great similarity with the machine tool industry. Except that the share of military demand remained higher, the conclusion of Part I concerning the machine tool industry is valid for the bearing industry as well. Therefore, even if the industry had 'achieved such remarkable technical progress and an accumulation of stocks in technology and production equipment' by the end of the war, it does not demonstrate the rationality or desirability of the policy of promoting domestic production in the bearing industry.

Explosive increases in demand, the existence of supply constraints due to import suspensions of both bearings and bearing-manufacturing machines, and preferential treatment in materials supply for expansion of production were the actual policy measures that mattered. Those are the factors that contributed the most to technical progress and stock accumulation in the bearing industry. However, this policy was an inefficient economic policy, particularly as a policy for industrial development, that ultimately generated a net loss.

1.4   CONCLUDING REMARKS

Conclusion of Part I

In the machine tool industry, the state intervened only incompetently, and that incompetence continued until the end of the war. This conclusion applies to both the military and the government and is particularly true of the most forceful policies. Under Commerce Ministry (which was close to the industry) supervision, government policy may have been more reluctant to intervene directly in the industry than under military control. Otherwise, no substantial changes occurred even when the policy-making initiative moved from the Commerce Ministry to the military and to the military-affiliated government sections that had demanded stronger intervention.

The impact of government policy on machine tool manufacturing under wartime control can be summarized in the following five points:

1   Despite strong requests from the military, neither government policies nor their implementation were active or powerful.
2   The promotion policies that were actually adopted neither could nor did have a substantial impact on the development or performance of the industry.
3   Compared with the situation at the start of wartime control, by the end of the war firms had accumulated substantial stocks of machine tools and the competence to develop new products. However, that progress occurred primarily in response to the militarily driven increase in demand. The net contribution of active industry promotion policies was negligible.
4   The preferential treatment of the industry both in terms of the allocation of foreign currency to enable the import of machine tools at the early stage of wartime control, and in the allocation of basic production materials, finance, and labor to the industry throughout the wartime period were prerequisites for the increases in supply achieved in this industry. If one were to call this preferential treatment 'promotion policy,' then it is possible to say that but for the policy, supply would not have increased. Crucially, though, beyond that preferential treatment government policy had no substantial effect.
5   The cost of this preferential access to foreign currency and basic resources rose dramatically over time. Because of this, even though the stock of production equipment remaining at the end of the war was great, its economic value could never have covered its cost. Ultimately, the 'industry promotion policies' could never have been justified as rational economic policies.

Implications for the strong and effective control debate

The wartime economy in Japan was highly regulated by a series of laws, ordinances, and rules. There is a huge literature that seizes on this complex regulatory environment and concludes from it that a strong government must have had a major impact on business activities and the public's daily life. Given this orthodoxy, readers may properly ask: 'Why is what we see in Part I of this book so different from what we read elsewhere?' 'Was strong and effective control by the government of Imperial Japan only a myth?' Yes, it was indeed a myth.[32]

For the reader's convenience, let me refer to representative views. The Planning Office, for instance, was established in October 1937 by reorganizing the Planning Agency and the Office of Resources. The Planning Office:

> assumed the role of planning and coordination for the 'expansion and management of national power both in normal and war times.' This new ministry, inheriting the administration of general mobilization from the Office of Resources, took charge of the Production Capacity Expansion Plan, making plans concerning trade, funds, and labor force, at the core of which were the Materials Mobilization Plans
>
> (Nakamura 1989: pp.8–9).

> They were emergency measures first adopted in reaction to the outbreak of the Sino-Japanese War, but were subsequently expanded and gradually generalized with the expansion and progress of war. Though initially appearing to be a temporary measure, the system grew gradually, and it was about 1941 when the overall system of control of materials, funds, prices, and wages was completed
>
> (Nakamura 1977: p.111).

At the beginning of his 'conclusion' Okazaki (1988: p.130), who studied wartime control in the steel industry, writes:

> During the war Japan constructed a well-organized direction-oriented planned economic system. The government made aggregate plans through exchanges of information and successive planning and plotting with the Steel Control Association ... through which information in the lower-class organizations was taken into account in plans made, ensuring the feasibility of the Materials Mobilization Plans. The Steel Control Association took part in the successive planning and plotting process. Upon detailed information collected from individual companies, they reorganized the aggregate plans of the government into rational directions to individual companies, and also rigorously monitored the process of implementation.

Murakami (1994: p.181), studying the military production industry, argues:

> Steel was basic both to the national economy and to military industry, and the production and allocation of steel fundamentally conditioned the organization of

industry. It was clear that steel was ranked as the first among 15 items in the Production Capacity Expansion Plan, and that it was also placed at the first section among the eight sections of the Materials Mobilization Plans. The person then in charge of the Mobilization Plans confessed that 'at the start the focus of the Mobilization Plan was basically placed upon steel and the belief that "steel was a fundamental prerequisite to the materials mobilization plans" was firm within the Planning Office at that time.'

However, readers will easily see that one element lacking in these statements is the use of the word 'effectiveness.' Policy may have been made and implemented in the steel industry, but was it done effectively? Also, these statements do not examine any of the following issues:

- What were the conditions needed for policy to be effective?
- What devices were implemented to satisfy those conditions?
- Why were these devices effective in satisfying the conditions?
- Why were the relevant economic agents able to coordinate and cooperate?
- How did the people involved manage to coordinate their actions and cooperate?

In evaluating accounts of wartime government control, I urge readers carefully to ask whether they are both theoretically coherent and based on a solid empirical foundation. I also encourage them to be skeptical of conclusions drawn either from government reports and documents or from the simple promulgation of laws, rules, and ordinances.

Given the state of the existing literature, however, readers naturally take it for granted that the government intervened in the details of individual firm activities in the machine tool industry, and that what remained at the end of the war was the result of active government policy. Unfortunately, the logic unravels. The fact that the government passed laws and ordinances purporting to control business and daily life need not imply that it controlled either.

The government was simply incompetent in achieving the objective

Why then did the government fail to control or even much shape the development of the machine tool industry? Why did the policies it adopted not promote its nominal goals? Why was it so incompetent? To achieve its objectives effectively and efficiently in this case, the government would have needed detailed micro-information about the reactions of the firms involved. This requirement was particularly important in the machine tool industry. There, the problem to be resolved by the principal (the government) was so complex and so dependent on flexible reactions by the agents (the firms) that no centralized system could have coped with it effectively.

Furthermore, three factors peculiar to the time aggravated the difficulties: (1) the military was by its nature unsuited to managing an economic system, but it dominated policy making and implementation; (2) in those days, the propensity for using economic incentives effectively was strictly limited, as the very existence of the 'Economic New Order' debate explicates; and (3) the rapid changes on the battlefields prevented the government from keeping pace with its needs and implementing policies consistently.

Three types of detailed micro-information were crucial to any effective policy at the time:

1   The government needed detailed information on the kind and type of machines necessary, on the areas where existing machines needed improvement, and on the technological constraints that firms needed to overcome to develop and improve the products it needed. The policy objectives not just of increasing the production of existing machines but of greatly expanding the industry, of developing new machines, and of improving a wide variety of existing machines, made such information necessary.
2   It required detailed information on the current and potential technological capability and competence of individual economic agents, including potential entrants to the industry.
3   It needed detailed information about the internal decision-making processes of individual companies in order to draw appropriate predictions regarding the reactions of economic agents.

These were the issues that it would have needed to resolve in the machine tool industry to implement its policies effectively. Obviously, it would have been easier for the government to allocate basic materials under excess demand and standardized products between agents and through those allocations attempt to promote certain sectors at the expense of others. This is precisely the path the government did take.

The government, more precisely the relevant government section in charge, did not welcome a policy that demanded of it the achievement of the nearly impossible nominal objective. Nor did it welcome the delegation to it of additional authority, when it knew that achieving the nominal objective would be difficult and probably impossible anyway. This reluctance became apparent with delays by the government in reacting to strong demand for the achievement of certain objectives by the military. For instance, despite insistent military demands to promote development of the machine tool industry after the Shanghai incident in 1932, it was only in 1938 that the government finally established the Machine Tool Building Act. Another symbolic example is the delay in adopting long-demanded promotion policies for domestic machine tool production. These policies were realized only after import suspensions took hold. As shown above, in October 1937 the Army sent its first machine tool purchasing mission to the

USA, and in May 1938 it sent another even larger-scale purchasing mission to Europe and the USA. It took a long time to even begin discussions regarding which machines and what measures were necessary to implement policy, such that these purchasing missions could be conducted. Only after these purchasing missions were the Toyokawa Naval Arsenal and the Toriimatsu Plant of the Nagoya Arsenal established in 1939.

Such delays in reacting may reflect the following factors as well:

- Recognizing that it would be able to import machine tools over a long period of time, the government found no immediate need to promote the domestic production of machine tools.
- The government thought it feasible to import machine tools to expand production capacity when necessary to fill demand. In the 1930s, the government did not foresee such a big conflict as World War II. After the outbreak of World War II, even after the start of the Pacific War, neither the government nor the military in Japan thought the war would develop on such a large scale or continue for such a long time. The Army and the Navy of Imperial Japan seem instead to have been intoxicated with the great military advances in the initial stage of the war and wasted a year without improving military production (Okumura 1977: p.61).
- The government did not believe that any effort to promote domestic production would be effective anyway. At root, it simply did not trust the development and production capability of Japan's machine tool makers.
- Inside the government, relevant parties could not agree about the situation in the country at large or about the situation in the industry. This lack of agreement, in turn, prevented any speedy policy decisions.

It is only rational for the government, incompetent and ill-prepared, to be reluctant about undertaking projects that are difficult or almost impossible to complete. It is rational even for the government to neglect or passively to resist demands from pressure groups like the military. As a result, it is not at all surprising to observe such government behavior in an emergency situation such as wartime control. It is rational, and it is predictable – but it does not lead to efficient or even effective promotional policy.

Part II

The high-growth era

2 The machinery industries under the 1956 statutory regime

2.1 THE ISSUES

2.1.1 Introduction

Parts I and II form a pair; that is, both examine the competence of the state, and the behavior and function of the state as related to its competence. In Part II, I undertake that examination through a case study of one sector of the economy. I focus on the policies that the government implemented through the 1956 Machinery Industries Promotion Act (MIPA) in the machinery industries, particularly the machine tool industry. The MIPA was established to promote the machinery industries under the government's Five-Year Plan for Economic Independence. In examining state competence and its relation to state behavior and function, Part II draws on the conclusions of Part I concerning state intervention in the machine tool industry under wartime control. Wartime control saw a situation where the state at least theoretically had much authority to act and the responsibility to implement high-priority policies in a relatively uninhibited environment.

Core issues for discussion

Most economists agree that government intervention in the private sector can be justified only in response to market failure. However, views differ on the definition of market failure, on when it occurs, and on what we should ask of the government when a failure does occur. Furthermore, who decides what policy the government should pursue, who controls the behavior of the government and how, and how effective is the government-implemented control? Also, what are the costs of such government policy, and – even given market failure – is intervention cost-justified? Conclusions to these issues will differ case by case and should not be drawn in a black-and-white manner.

State competence and behavior in a modern parliamentary democracy necessarily involve a variety of related issues. Who defines the role that the government will play? And who defines the policy that it will pursue? Even when bureaucrats in the executive branch determine policy, presumably they do so under legislative monitoring. How much discretion does the legislature give them in deciding policy? How powerful a set of tools does it give them to carry out that policy? How carefully does it monitor their behavior? What incentives does it give them to carry out those goals? How realistic are the putative ultimate goals that it assigns them? What goals can bureaucrats most realistically pursue? If they lack the competence to pursue the goals, how are they likely to respond?

At root, the state is an organization designed to achieve a given set of objectives. Just as its organizational structure changes over time, so too do the objectives it can pursue most effectively. However, that structure and those objectives vary according to the institutional and electoral constraints on the state's activity and the various interest groups with which it interacts. At any moment, the state exists as an organization with a distinctive competence in such factors as personnel, know-how, and external relationships. Its competence is the product of past decisions and activity, both long-term planned activity and accumulated everyday experience. Necessarily, it will have more ability to intervene effectively in some sectors than in others. So long as that relative ability affects its decisions to intervene (as it would if the government were subject to even minimal cost–benefit analysis), then state competence will influence the behavior it undertakes. Following from this, the actual function of the executive in particular will depend on its competence. Put another way, even when the legislature possesses the ability to control the behavior of the executive, the parameters of the legislature's ability will be inherently limited by the bounds of the competence of the executive.

In short, the government cannot and does not become competent in doing everything, because of the constraints under which it operates and the cost–performance calculation. Even a private-sector enterprise of the highest caliber will not succeed in every industrial sector. Likewise, the government will not and cannot succeed on every issue. As I did in Part I, I will take the view in Part II that the state is an organization like an enterprise, and I will investigate the competence, behavior, and function of the state on this premise.

Why focus on the machinery industries?

In this part, I focus on the machinery industries for two reasons: (1) most obviously, the machinery industries have been crucial to Japan's postwar industrial success; and (2) because several of the machinery industries were targeted under the MIPA, I can examine the impact of government policy.

The 1956 MIPA represented the core of 'industrial policy' for the machinery industries. This was the case for fifteen years after 1956, but particularly for the first ten years. This ten-year period runs roughly from the beginning of rapid growth in the machinery industries to the time when the industry attracted worldwide attention for its remarkable success. That the MIPA was crucial to the development of the machinery industries is a view held not only by many bureaucrats but also by many business people and scholars, despite a lack of supporting evidence. According to Sugiyama (1966b: p.8), for example, the MIPA 'contributed greatly to the promotion of Japan's machinery industry.' Indeed, writes Yonekura (1993: p.286), the Act 'promoted rationalization in key industries ... which, it is not too much to say, created the very foundation for their international competitiveness.'[33]

If this view of Japanese industrial policy in the machinery industry is accurate, then past experience of Japanese industrial policy will be critically important to the former socialist economies that are now making the transition to a market-oriented model and are focusing upon achieving economic growth by developing their machinery industries. If inaccurate, then it is necessary to show clearly why and for what reasons industrial policy was ineffective, particularly in the machinery industry.

This study is also intended to serve a much broader purpose: to contribute to the general inquiry of why and under what conditions 'industrial policy' in the general sense is and can be effective (see Miwa 1995, 1996a, 1996b, 1999; Miwa and Ramseyer 2002e, 2003d). If true, the body of research that emphasizes the remarkable success of industrial policy in the machinery industry may demand a fundamental re-evaluation of the generally accepted role of government, particularly that of industrial policies. The question is whether it is indeed true.

Comparison with Part I on the machine tool industry under wartime control

The study of the machine tool industry under wartime control in Part I is relevant to the investigation in Part II for the following reasons. The MIPA placed the state in a far more inhibited position in terms of making policy decisions and in exercising authority than was the case under wartime control. Moreover, the priority of policies for machinery industries under the MIPA was far lower than was the case for these industries during the wartime period, when such policy was the nation's highest priority. Consequently, wartime control provides us with an opportunity to observe and identify the relatively 'pure' behavior of a state: that is, a state that enjoyed almost unlimited authority to intervene in the private sector and allocate low-interest loans and subsidies. It also encountered very few factors inhibiting the exercise of that authority. The circumstances under which the MIPA placed the state were quite different. In the earlier stages of the MIPA and its related policies, the state was able to exercise its authority to intervene in the private sector in a fairly unrestricted way. This was not the case in the 1960s, when a series of 'liberalizations' (such as in trade) commenced. However, even before the 1960s, the state encountered far more factors inhibiting its use of authority than under wartime control.

Neither association nor correlation implies causality. In order to analyse the role and function of the MIPA, it is grossly insufficient simply to list the authority and powers that laws and other measures granted to the government. Instead, it is important to ask how the government's exercise of the authority and powers might have been conditioned or inhibited. For that purpose, we must analyse the details of the decision-making processes within the government, particularly the relevant ministry in charge. Here, that inquiry would take us to the Ministry of International Trade and Industry (MITI) and the personnel directly in charge: the Heavy Industries Bureau and the Industrial Machinery Section. We must explain the precise objectives for which the government actually adopted the policies it did. That is, we must conduct our analysis on the premise that the authority and powers granted are not always used and that the declared policy objective will not just realize itself automatically.

In the machine tool industry under wartime control, each ministry was required to work to realize the apparent national objective, but toward that end they had almost unrestricted access to the authority and powers needed. Nonetheless, I show in Part I that the Precision Tool Section of the Commerce Ministry and the Precision Tool Control Association were both surprisingly inactive. That is, both bodies did little to promote the effective creation and production of improved machine tools by reallocating resources from other industries to the more productive machinery firms.

The conclusion of Part I concerning the impact of government action on the machine tool industry under wartime control can be summarized by five points (Section 1.4):

1   Despite strong requests from the military, the government failed to adopt active or powerful policies or to work forcefully to implement them.
2   Those policies that the government did adopt neither could nor did have any substantial effect on the development and performance of the industry.
3   What growth one does see in the industry (and the progress was indeed remarkable) occurred as firms responded to new demand. The net contribution of active policies called 'industry promotion policy' was negligible.
4   The only even plausible way in which the government promoted the industry lay in the preferential access to foreign exchange and basic raw materials, finance, and labor that it granted the industry. Through foreign exchange, the industry was able to import machine tools during the early stages of the war, and the production inputs obviously helped to keep output high. If we call such policies 'promotion policy,' then it is possible to say that but for such policies, increases in supply could not have been realized. However, the important point is that beyond such preferential treatment we observe no effective policies.

5   The cost of the preferential allocation of foreign exchange and basic materials increased dramatically over the period. Because of this, even if the stock of production equipment remaining at the end of the war was great, its economic value could never have covered its cost. Therefore the 'industry promotion policies' could never have been justified as cost-effective economic policies.

This conclusion concerning government intervention in the machine tool industry under wartime control suggests that even during the MIPA period, if the government had been granted much authority and a high degree of freedom to exercise it, it would have remained relatively inactive. Accordingly, in addition to simply listing the authority and powers available to the government, we must examine the details of the process of policy making and implementation to be able to evaluate the effectiveness of the MIPA and its related policies.

Road map and conclusion of Part II

In preparation for a more detailed investigation in Section 2.3, I first outline the policies under the MIPA over the fifteen years from the first MIPA to the third in Section 2.2. I then discuss the literature on the policies adopted under the first and second MIPAs: that is, the policy during the first ten years of the MIPA. After this, in Section 2.3, I examine the effectiveness of the MIPA and related policies in detail.

Any government policy is inherently conditioned by the circumstances in which it is implemented. The decade prior to the enactment of the MIPA was a period of transition from wartime control to the high-growth postwar era. In response to various changes, particularly economic changes, both the objectives and the content of government policies changed radically.

Shortly after Japan regained its independence in 1952, conservative political parties merged into the Liberal Democratic Party in 1955. That party then maintained its position as the ruling party until the mid-1990s. Reflecting the demands of the business community and with its political backing, the LDP-controlled government consistently pursued a market-oriented policy. It promoted liberalization on virtually every front, recovered Japan's position in the international economy (and obtained membership in the GATT and OECD), and thereby realized rapid economic growth. The MIPA took effect in 1956, and the policies based on the Act were strongly conditioned by this basic political environment. Even when there were strongly interventionist bureaucrats (possibly talkative socialists), they could hardly have introduced truly interventionist policies effectively. Such policies were against the basic discipline of the government, led by capitalist LDP politicians.[34]

Accordingly, before beginning a detailed discussion of the policies under the MIPA in Section 2.3, I briefly discuss three issues crucial to the nature of the environment in which the MIPA was enacted: (1) those factors that existed prior to the enactment of the MIPA and may have constrained and influenced the formation of policy under the Act and its effectiveness; (2) the inheritance from the wartime economic system, or the environmental similarities between wartime control and the period of the MIPA; and (3) the plan for the Machinery Industries Promotion Corporation, which was the forerunner to the MIPA. Section 2.4 is a case study in the machine tool industry under the MIPA and aims to add more detail to the previous discussion by situating it in context. In Section 2.4, the comparisons with the discussion of Part I regarding the machine tool industry under wartime control are more direct. Section 2.5 consists of a brief summary and concluding remarks.

The conclusions from Part II regarding the effectiveness of policy under the MIPA are straightforward. The core policy measure under the MIPA, from the first to the third, was a program of loans at preferential rates through the Japan Development Bank and the Small Business Finance Corporation. No other significant policies were actively implemented, and these loans were not remarkably effective. The relatively low aggregate loan amounts, the relatively small gap between the preferential loan rates and market rates, and the methods adopted to allocate loans among potential borrowers, together created a situation not much different from what would have prevailed in the absence of the program. Many argue that the state's intervention in the industries designated by the MIPA, including the machine tool industry, played a critical role in promoting the development of those industries. Such an evaluation is an obvious overestimate.

2.1.2   The conventional wisdom about Japanese growth-promoting bureaucrats

Most readers will have heard tales of the glorious success of the state in promoting Japan's economic development, particularly the role played by growth-promoting bureaucrats. Most notably, for instance, Chalmers Johnson (1982) famously fashioned his theory of the 'plan-rational' 'developmental state' on tales from Japan. In reading this part of the book, readers might wonder what they should make of the competent state behind that famous industrial policy.

The evidence from this book directly contradicts that orthodox view of Japan and its economy. For the reader's convenience, I first review the orthodox literature.[35] As a point of reference, I focus on one of the best-known recent studies, by Tetsuji Okazaki and Masahiro Okuno-Fujiwara (1999). In Section 2.5, I will return to this study to show what is actually wrong with it and therefore with the conventional wisdom.

The literature[36]

One would be hard put to prove where the tales about Japanese growth-promoting bureaucrats began, but if politicians and bureaucrats did not invent them, they certainly had every incentive to repeat them.[37] Politicians transfer rents in all modern democracies, and they transferred them in Japan. They cover their tracks in all modern democracies, and they covered them in Japan as well.

To cover their tracks, Japanese politicians in the ruling LDP recited the tales of growth-promoting bureaucrats whenever it was convenient to do so. When the economy doubled in less than a decade, they lost no time in taking credit. Had not their prime minister announced his plan to do just that? The top MITI bureaucrat (quoted in Trezise and Suzuki 1976: pp.753, 793) even compared his team to Napoleon and Clausewitz. 'In the quarter of a century since' World War II, he declared, it had created on Japan's 'cramped land area a giant economy that ranks second in the free world.'

Voters are not fools. They know that politicians routinely claim credit for bull markets that coincide with their tenure. Just as routinely, the voters dismiss the claims. Japanese politicians may have announced that they would expand the economy, the economy may have grown, and the politicians may have taken credit. Neat it may be, but voters know that it is too neat by half, because the politicians simultaneously promised to avoid central planning, and voters could tell which promises they kept.

Notwithstanding this obvious duplicity, the legend persists in academic circles. In truth, academics (and public intellectuals generally) always paid more attention to it than did voters. Take just the accounts in English. In sociology, Ezra Vogel (1979: pp.65, 71) early on discovered a Japanese 'bureaucratic elite' that 'boldly tried to restructure industry, concentrating resources in areas where they think Japan will be competitive internationally in the future.' Even in 2002, Ronald Dore could list among the 'main characteristics of the Japanese economy' a 'strong role for the state' in 'the promotion of economic growth and national competitiveness.'[38]

Following Chalmers Johnson, in political science Brian Woodall (1996) recently found in MITI the 'power, in the form of formal legal authorizations and informal "administrative guidance," to develop whatever industries it deemed critical to the health of the national economy.' And in law, Curtis Milhaupt and Mark West (2002: p.44) characterized the postwar economic environment as one of 'bureaucrat-orchestrated economic management.'

Even many economists toed the line. Kazushi Ohkawa and Henry Rosovsky (1973: p.223; reprinted from Rosovsky 1972: pp.229, 244) described Japan as 'the only capitalist country in the world in which the government decides how many firms should be in a given industry, and sets about to arrange the desired number.' Takafusa Nakamura (1995: pp.18, 91) claimed that MITI exercised 'strong administrative leadership' over firms, which enabled them to 'make daring investments in plant and equipment.' And Geoffrey Carliner (1986: pp.147, 156) declared that 'without government guidance and assistance, it is unlikely that Japan would be as strong as it is in semiconductors, machine tools, telecommunications equipment, or fiber optics.'

Given the apparently impeccable academic credentials of the tales, from time to time politically ambitious US intellectuals have put them to domestic use. Ira Magaziner and Robert Reich (both would eventually land prominent jobs in the Clinton administration) used Japan to advocate an industrial policy in the USA. In Japan, they declared, that policy 'enhance[s] the creation of wealth by improving the international competitiveness of a number of growing businesses and by easing the transition of declining businesses' (Magaziner and Reich 1982: p.6; see also Magaziner and Hout 1981; Reich 1987: p.231).

One-time chair of the Council of Economic Advisors Laura D'Andrea Tyson (Tyson and Zysman 1989: pp.xiii, xvi) was no less zealous. In 'the Japanese variant of capitalism,' she and a co-author announced: 'markets are emphasized as a source of growth rather than of short-run efficiency.' As a result, 'a primary role of government is to supply incentives to promote growth through markets.'

Such tales soon became the orthodoxy. In his standard text on the Japanese economy, Takatoshi Ito (1992: p.201) wrote that 'Japan's rapid economic growth, supported by high productivity growth in many industries, may be seen as evidence of successful industrial policy.' Indeed, even as Paul Krugman (1997: p.140) battled Magaziner and Reich over domestic programs, he found 'no question' that 'before the early 1970s the Japanese system was heavily directed from the top, with the MITI and the Ministry of Finance' working 'to push the economy where they liked.'

Tetsuji Okazaki and Masahiro Okuno-Fujiwara (1999)

Most of those authors accurately capture the secondary literature on Japan, for the same accounts appear in Japanese. The tales about Japanese growth-promoting bureaucrats have such a long pedigree that both authors and readers accept them as true without demanding evidence to back them up. Granted, most academics, economists in particular, have jettisoned the notion that omniscient and omnipotent bureaucrats masterminded the high growth in 1960s and 1970s Japan. Yet even they retain the idea that bureaucrats controlled the allocation of credit, through which they could 'push the economy where they liked.'[39] Even now most academics retain the idea that in prewar Japan bureaucrats controlled the economy effectively and the state led the economy to its remarkable development and industrial success.[40]

Okazaki and Okuno-Fujiwara (1999) was first published in Japanese in 1993, and even several years after the collapse of the Berlin Wall was immediately widely accepted as the orthodox view. The following quotation presents the essence of their view, and therefore that of the conventional wisdom more generally. I quote it here for readers' frame of reference in reading Part II.[41] I will return to their claims in Section 2.5.

Okazaki and Okuno-Fujiwara emphasize the 'relations between government and business' as one of the key components of the present-day Japanese economic system. They explain as follows:

The long-term nature of relations between employers and employees, and between individual firms, means that, should these relations once break down, business collapse and mass unemployment could result, and systemic risk could cause chronic problems. Through the process of post-war economic growth the Japanese government has sought to control private-sector economic activity in a variety of ways to minimize this danger. Each industry is supervised independently from above by a single administrative authority. These authorities use administrative guidance and other discretionary measures to achieve 'development' and establish 'order' in the industry. A typical model of the active control of 'development' in manufacturing industry (or the whole Japanese economy, for that matter) is the Ministry of International Trade and Industry's 'industrial policy', while 'order' is maintained through the Ministry of Finance's so-called 'convoy' policy directed towards financial institutions.

Industrial policy consists of a three-stage process. First comes the 'discovery' of an industry for development, using forecasts of future trends in technology or demand. For the purposes of forecasting, various forums are used to gather information and encourage its exchange, such as government councils, unofficial research groups and informal networks. At the second stage, industries selected for development and sectors earmarked for growth have to be nurtured and given support. Various means such as subsidies, tax incentives, and low-interest loans, and indirect means such as information exchange through councils, extending the role played by individual associations to provide information and balance interests within the business sectors concerned, and the use of long-term plans to make necessary adjustments within the affected industries and sectors. The third stage requires co-ordination of the allocation of funds and other resources between industries through inductive means. The allocation of the necessary facilities, and the selection and co-ordination of firms is carried out through discretionary administrative guidance against a backdrop of regulatory and financial measures.

The result of this is that all the firms in the sector have access to the same information on new business opportunities, and have a strong incentive to get ahead of others and quickly establish a foothold in the new business. This leads to excess competition, circumstances where investment and facilities are expanded beyond the individual firm's means, and to business plans that target market share rather than profits. If the business were to fail and mass lay-offs became likely, the authorities responsible for promoting the policy would have to shoulder some of the blame, and the government has held these systemic risks in check with a variety of means, including recession cartels and legislation such as the Emergency Measures to Stabilize Selected Depressed Industries Act (*Tokutei fukyo sangyo antei rinji sochi ho*), enacted in

May 1978, and the Special Measures to Upgrade Selected Industrial Sectors Act (*Tokutei sangyo kozo kaizen rinji sochi ho*), enacted in May 1983. But as private-sector firms are conscious of the existence of this government safety net, excess competition has simply continued to increase.

It is this 'managed competition' and 'planned allocation of resources' on the part of the government that can be traced back to the wartime planned, controlled economic system.

(*ibid.*: pp.11–12)

2.2   AN OUTLINE AND EVALUATION OF THE 1956 ACT: PRELIMINARIES[42]

2.2.1   Introduction

Part II studies the competence of the state, and the behavior and function of the state as related to its competence. It focuses on the machinery industries, particularly the machine tool industry, as regulated under the Act on Temporary Measures for the Promotion of the Machinery Industries (Machinery Industries Promotion Act, MIPA). I do not limit the subject of examination in Part II to the machine tool industry (as was the case in Part I) but include all machinery industries subject to MIPA and its related policies.[43] The MIPA was established on 29 May 1956 and took effect on 15 June, having a validity of five years. The validity of the Act was extended in June 1961 for an additional five years until June 1966, and then again in 1966 until the end of March 1971. I will refer to these three Acts simply as the First, Second, and Third Acts, respectively. The Act was therefore in force for fifteen years. However, when it came before the Diet a second time for extension (that is, the Third Act), there was much anxiety among Diet members that the government intended the law to be permanent. As a result, the Third MIPA, although of fundamentally similar content, was declared to be the last.[44]

The government was authorized to designate industries under the MIPA, and the Act's policies were then applied to those designated industries. Twenty-two industries were designated for the First Act and forty at the start of the Second Act; the machine tool industry was one of the industries to be designated throughout the fifteen years of the Act. As discussed in detail later, loans through the Japanese Development Bank (JDB) were the primary policy measure under the Act, although The Small and Medium-sized Firms Finance Corporation and the Small Business Finance Corporation also made loans under the Second Act. A total of ¥64 billion in policy loans was made during the period of the First and Second Acts. The machine tool industry was allocated the second largest volume, ¥7.1 billion or 11.1 percent of the total. The largest allocation was to the auto parts industry with ¥14.6 billion. Third was the tools industry with ¥3.6 billion, then the foundry industry with ¥3.5 billion, the bearing industry with ¥3.5 billion, the gears industry with ¥2.3 billion, the screw industry with ¥2.3 billion, the forging press industry with ¥2.0 billion, and the tool and die industry with ¥1.8 billion.[45]

As a preliminary to more detailed discussion in the next section, I will first introduce the history of the MIPA and outline the policies implemented under the Act, placing particular emphasis on the First Act. I will then proceed to examine the effectiveness of policy under the Act, focusing on the situation at the time of the commencement of the Third Act. The Third Act, although fundamentally similar to the previous two Acts, emphasized 'restructuring the production system.' In Sections 2.2.4 and 2.2.5, I introduce information from Atsushi Yonekura (1965b), then a senior official in the JDB in charge of loans under the MIPA.

I focus on the circumstances in 1965 for four reasons:

1   It is around this time that we can expect to find justifications for the second extension of the law.
2   We can also expect to find information on problems that remained unresolved after ten years of the Act's operation.
3   We might expect to find views and opinions of those who were engaged in planning and implementing the policy, including the details of the Act and its related policies.
4   We can expect to find much more detailed and open discussion than in the preceding periods. This is because it was a time when the form and substance of government intervention in the private sector had become extremely controversial: examples include the Idemitsu Incident and the Sumitomo Metals Incident.[46]

2.2.2   Outline of the MIPA: (1) the First Act

The MIPA took effect on 15 June 1956 as, in the government's own words:

> an element of the Five-Year Plan for Economic Independence. The Act aimed to promote the modernization of equipment, efficiency improvement and improved production technology in the machinery industries. In short, the Act aimed to promote the development of machinery industries in every facet. This Act focused on those sectors of fundamental importance to the greater economy, and also on those sectors supplying parts of general demand throughout the whole economy, whose performance had been inferior even among the machinery industries. The majority of firms that slotted into these categories were small producers, and therefore the Act played a critical role as a constructive and active policy for developing small machine producers.[47]

The policy emphasis for the machinery industry in 1955 was on three points: restructuring of domestic industries, improvement of technology levels, and promotion of small business. MIPA's five-year term was typical of industry-specific statutes, as one can see in the 1955 statute governing the coal-mining industry, the Act for Temporary Measures for Rationalizing the Coal Mining Industry, or the textile industry's Act for Temporary Measures for Equipment in the Textile Industry of 1956. Each of these Acts, together with the MIPA, formed part of policies for restructuring industry. Despite the health of the overall economy in 1955, the machinery industries were among those sectors that were depressed at that time. The MITI minister determined an annual plan for the rationalization of each specified machinery industry under the Act. The JDB made loans to implement these plans. In addition, cartels in these industries were exempted from the application of the Anti-monopoly Act if they concerned coordination of production items and production quantities necessary to implement these plans.[48]

A government order designated machines, tools, and parts under the Act. In the beginning, eighteen industries were so designated, as shown in the upper row of Table 2.1 (excluding those marked with a [a or b]). A basic rationalization plan and an associated implementation plan were established for each of these sectors. With the addition of several other industries, rationalization and promotion policies had been adopted in twenty-two industries by 1960.[49]

The basic rationalization plans for each industry were examined and approved by the Machinery Industries Council. The government then determined and publicized implementation plans for each fiscal year based on those rationalization plans. Individual producers would then propose equipment investment plans of their own in accordance with the government's implementation plans. Finally, from among these equipment investment plans proposed by the producers, the government selected plans for recommendation to the JDB for loans at preferential rates.

Basic rationalization plans were required to cover four points (section 2.2 of the Act):

1   They should specify their rationalization targets by the end of the 1960 fiscal year concerning the performance, quality, and production costs of the designated machines.
2   They should detail issues pertinent to rationalization, such as the equipment and finance required.
3   They should discuss the disposal of equipment and its relation to rationalization: i.e., which types of equipment ought to be disposed of and how.
4   They should address other issues relating to rationalization, like advances in production technology and improvements in efficiency. To give a concrete example, the rationalization targets set for the machine tool industry were 'to develop the industry to a level where demands for standard and special machine tools could be speedily satisfied at the end of FY1960, and in addition reduce production cost by more than 20% from the levels at the end of FY1955' (annual report for FY1956: p.126).[50]

Table 2.1 Industries designated under the MIPA

| | Basic sectors | | | |
Year of designation	Basic machinery industries	Industries producing general-purpose parts	Machines and parts granted import restrictions and export promotion	Processing industries
FY1956	machine tools	iron casting	auto parts	
	forging press machines[a]	diecasting	sewing machine parts	
	laboratory machinery	metal ceramics	clock parts	
	precision gauges	screws	railway vehicle parts	
	tool and die machines	gears		
	cutting tools	bearings		
	artificial grinding wheels	valves		
	electric tools	wind and hydraulic machinery[a]		
	electric welders			
	gas cutting apparatus[a]			

FY1961			
analytical instruments	steel for casting and forging	transportation machines	heat treatment industry
precision measuring instruments	steel forging	chemical machines	
industrial weighing machines	internal combustion engines	plastic machinery	
industrial furnaces	oil pressure pumps	textile machines	
casting apparatus		mining, civil engineering and construction machines	
		agricultural machinery	
		woodworking machinery[b]	
		printing and bookbinding machinery	
		office machines	
		electric communication machinery[b]	
		industrial vehicles	
		automobile machines and tools	
		railway signaling and safety appliances	

Source: Sugiyama (1966b: p.9).

[a] For designation in FY1958.
[b] For designation in FY1964.

2.2.3   Outline of the MIPA: (2) the Second Act

> The period of the First Act, 1956 to 1960, just so happened to coincide with explosive growth in the machinery industries. ... These circumstances stimulated rationalization in the machinery industries tremendously. ... The Act, a law initially valid only for five years, was to be abolished by 15 June 1961. The government decided to have the law extended for another five-year period, however, judging it a necessary measure to combat the effects of the trade liberalization that was occurring at the time. With this, the government aimed to improve the international competitiveness of the machinery industries, and to cement the position of the machinery industries as a key industrial sector, which position had been planned under the Income Doubling Plan and the associated upgrading of the industrial structure.[51]
>
> (Sugiyama 1966a: pp.8–9)

In line with these objectives, the Second MIPA expanded 'the ambit of policy by further designating industries as policy targets to bring the total to 40, to combat recent trade liberalization in the machinery industries' (*ibid.*).

The lower row of Table 2.1 shows the industries added under the Second Act.

> To facilitate liberalization in the machinery industries, the Second Act greatly expanded the number and ambit of designated industries. In addition to industries initially designated (basic machinery industries and industries producing general-purpose parts), industries producing machines like chemical machines, textile machines, and mining, civil engineering and construction machines, were additionally designated under the Act. Moreover, revising the ambit of the Act to include processing industries in addition to machinery industries, the Act designated the heat treatment industry.
>
> (Sugiyama 1966b: p.9)

Budgetary constraints

The government's ability to designate industries under the First Act was limited, by the Fiscal Investment and Loan Program in general terms, but also more precisely by the lending capacity of the JDB. The government encountered such difficulties when attempting to add such industries as the railway vehicle parts industry, the gas cutting apparatus industry, the forging press machinery industry, and the wind and hydraulic machinery industry, and also when determining the amounts of funding to be designated to particular industries. Consequently, many industries could not be designated and remained as 'candidates under consideration for additional designation.' Industries falling into this category included the grinding wheel industry, the textile machinery industry, the oil pressure pump industry, the binocular parts industry, the light alloy and copper alloy casting industry, and the gas welding industry (MITI 1990: p.572).

These budgetary constraints continued to restrict the government's discretion under the Second Act.

> In the light of budgetary restrictions under the Second Act, the designation of 13 industries of the initial 40 were determined to be terminated at the end of FY1963. These 13 industries consisted mainly of complete machinery and parts manufacturing. However, in FY1964, the designation of only three industries was terminated, which were the railway vehicle parts industry, the clock components industry, and the electric welding industry. The remaining ten industries listed for termination continued to be designated for the full period of validity of the Second Act. These industries were retained, but with partial modifications to the range of listed machine models, due to the perceived necessity of industrial policy for the promotion of exports, for strengthening international competitiveness, and to achieve technological advancement. Further, at the same time, the printing machine industry was newly designated to assist in reducing imports, and the communication machinery industry was designated both for the purpose of completing infrastructure and to provide a small business policy. ... This resulted in the total climbing back up to 39 designated industries.
>
> (Yonekura 1965a: p.33)

Increased availability of finance under the Second MIPA

'Under the Second MIPA the government greatly increased the availability of funds for equipment modernization than was the case under the First Act. This consisted of greatly expanding the availability of loans from the JDB, and also guaranteeing loans from the Small Business Finance Corporation for small producers of designated machines.' Under the First Act, the JDB lent funds for equipment modernization totaling ¥11.2 billion at the special rate of 6.5 percent per annum. Under the Second Act, the JDB lent ¥33.5 billion and the Small Business Finance Corporation ¥19.3 billion. However, the interest rate did rise from 6.5 to 7.5 percent (Sugiyama 1966b: p.10).

The Machinery Industries Promotion corporate plan was debated prior to the enactment of the MIPA. The Decision Concerning the Establishment of the Machinery Industries Promotion Corporation was made and approved on 19 December 1955 at the fourth meeting of the Machinery Section of the Industrial Rationalization Council. The council argued for the adoption of the corporate plan 'as a most powerful and appropriate measure for nurturing and developing both the basic and the parts manufacturing sectors of the machinery industry.' The plan ultimately failed, the primary cause being that, in addition to budgetary constraints, the 'plan did not address the issue of small business.'[52]

Both the ruling party and the opposition parties judged the MIPA to be much weaker and less effective than the corporate plan, and the Act suffered from the same ills as the plan. For instance, Yoshio Suzuki, chief of the Heavy Industries Bureau, commented in a Diet debate that 'it was a small business policy that merely built upon previous policies.'[53] As a matter of fact, there were 294 recipients of designated machinery loans under the First Act. Of that total, 171 companies, or 58 percent, remained in the category of small business in May 1961, having either less than ¥10 million in paid-up capital or fewer than 300 employees. What this shows is that even before the participation of the Small Business Finance Corporation, small businesses were already the principal beneficiaries of this program. That is, in terms of aggregate value, loans for small businesses accounted for 32 percent of the total. The average loan was ¥27 million. The percentage of loans of less than ¥30 million was 73 percent in number and 43 percent in value. If we compare these figures with designated machinery loans made by the JDB under the Second Act, we find that in FY1961 loans of less than ¥50 million accounted for only 18 percent of the total in number and 36 percent by value. In FY1963, loans of less than ¥80 million accounted for 26 percent of the total in number and 50 percent by value. We can therefore see that the loans made by the JDB under the First Act were extremely small and that policy under the Act was basically directed toward small businesses.

Expanded scope of policy measures under the Second MIPA

The scope of policy measures under the Second MIPA was also expanded beyond that of the First Act. The Act stipulated special treatment, revolutionary at that time, to promote mergers and joint investment, 'particularly to facilitate firm size expansion and for establishing specialization in production. These special measures included partial exemptions from corporate income tax on any income received or deemed received (contribution in kind) arising from the fact of merger, and partial exemptions from any registration tax arising from joint investment. The government also made efforts to establish specialized mass-production systems through maintaining previous orders to form rationalization cartels for producing forging press machines, and also issuing fresh orders of the same nature to five industries such as the textile machines industry' (Sugiyama 1966a: p.9). I will refer in more detail to the contents of this policy and comment on its effectiveness in Section 2.2.4. Although these special measures were provided for under the Second Act, 'the preferential tax treatments were applied only in seven cases during FY1961 and FY1965. This was largely because it was a period of little merger activity and also as the measures applied only in extremely limited circumstances, that is for example where income arose due to merger (payments from one institution to another arising from merger)' (*ibid.*: p.12).

The subject of section 6 of the MIPA was 'the minister's authority to make orders for joint operations between enterprises' and stipulated as follows: 'The MITI minister is empowered to make orders when necessary to producers of machines designated in the rationalization basic plans to conduct joint operations to achieve the rationalization of designated machinery industries, and particularly regarding the following matters. The MITI minister may make orders for restrictions on production items, quantity restrictions on individual items, restrictions on technology, and regarding purchasing methods for parts and raw materials.' The MITI minister was required to consult with the Fair Trade Commission before making orders for joint operations under section 6. The commission thought it necessary to create a special exemption from the Anti-monopoly Act for conduct arising out of and associated with orders under section 6. This was because, although section 24.4 of the Anti-monopoly Act did not prohibit rationalization cartels (joint operations between enterprises to achieve rationalization), the exemption applied only to the rationalization of individual enterprises rather than to whole industries. Accordingly, the existing section 24.4 cartel exemption under the Anti-monopoly Act was thought too restrictive to serve as a measure for rationalizing the industrial structure in the machinery industries. Furthermore, the government reasoned that producers would encounter much difficulty in reaching agreements regarding joint operations if left to negotiate merely by themselves, as complicated conflicts of interest existed. Consequently, orders for joint operations under section 6 were ranked as policy measures of top priority in the basic rationalization plans, along with measures to ensure the necessary funds and to publish standards for advancing production technology. An exemption from the prohibition of 'joint operations conduct' under section 6 was created, whereby such conduct was legal if registered, and such conduct then became exempt from the Anti-monopoly regime.

The fundamental idea underlying these orders for joint operations (which emerged more clearly as 'industry reorganization' and 'restructuring' in the Third Act) was that 'simply replacing equipment is insufficient for effective equipment modernization or for achieving rationalization targets. In addition, an appropriate production system must be established and adopt the following measures, that is, the definition of each producer's production territory, the introduction of uniform standards for parts and raw materials, and the improvement of purchasing methods of parts and raw materials' (Hidaka 1956).

All this policy theory is fine, but what is critical here is that it was in May 1959 that the first rationalization cartel under the MIPA took effect on production sector coordination, which was in the forging press machinery industry. The second case appeared in April 1962, three years later. It governed the coordination of industry sectors and the regulation of standards for preparatory machinery in the weaving industry. In short, very few cartels based on the MIPA were actually implemented. Five cartels involved the coordination of industry sectors, and five involved the regulation of industry standards. Both measures were then adopted in three industries.[54] These figures include the implementation of the regulation of standards in the artificial grinding wheel industry, which began in November 1965.

2.2.4   Problems with the MIPA: (1) industrial order issues

Regarding the role of the Second Act in combating the effects of trade liberalization, Sugiyama (1966a: p.13) comments:

> trade liberalization is now at its final stage with the liberalization ratio having reached the 95 percent level. There has been to date no remarkable damages to the industry, which we had anticipated and worried would occur, with the exception of some specific fields or models. In this sense, the Second MIPA has lived up to expectations in terms of being a measure for coping with.

Toward the end of the life of the Second Act, firms in the machinery industry, particularly the Federation of Japanese Machinery Industries, began to reflect on the industry situation. In particular, they began to discuss policies for the industry after the MIPA. The Draft Act for the Fundamental Upgrading of the Machinery Industry was published as a candidate to supersede the MIPA, and it placed much emphasis upon export promotion and support for the scrapping of obsolete equipment. The Japan Machine Tool Builders Association responded to this Draft Act and its proposals by strongly demanding that the government continue to provide support in such areas as tax and financing. The Auto Parts Industry Association also appealed for its inclusion as a listed industry for 'industrial order restructuring' loans from the JDB. Thus the issue of a replacement law for the Second MIPA grew in significance in 1965. Naturally, discussion regarding a replacement law intensified at the Subcommittee on Machinery Industries Policy at the Heavy Industries Division of the Industrial Structure Council. In response to this, the federation organized the MIPA Committee, which consisted of leaders from twelve associations that were hierarchically organized under the federation and conducted discussions from the standpoint of the industry on the details of a replacement law for the Second Act (Yonekura 1965a: p.32; 1965b: p.15).

The 'industrial order' and MITI's failed statute

It was phrases concerning the 'industrial order,' such as 'industrial order finance' and 'industrial order restructuring,' that attracted much attention with the commencement of the Third MIPA. On the content of the Third Act, Sugiyama (1966a: pp.18–19), chief of the Promotion Subsection of the Heavy Industries Section, states:

though the sphere of application has been severely limited, the Third Act maintains the basic idea evident in the preceding Acts, that is a focus upon equipment modernization and the restructuring of the industrial order. However, this Act is to be the final one, that is there is to be no further extension in five years time. Therefore, we have only five remaining years in which to solve problems, and accordingly the primary focus of the Third Act is to be placed upon solving 'the industrial order issues' regarding which we have particularly failed to make progress. Accordingly in selecting target industries more consideration will be given to industries with clear policy objectives and detailed programs concerning industrial order restructuring, rather than to those simply targeting equipment modernization. Admittedly it is important to set a clear policy objective, and then seek the cooperation of relevant industry members in achieving that objective. But we have also to improve the responsiveness of lending policy in such ways as stressing industrial order objective in financing, that is when making designated machinery loans. We must allocate a much higher ratio of policy loans to equipment investment for industrial order restructuring, and further expand the loan objects from designated machinery to include also land and building.[55]

Aside from the MIPA, a draft bill known as Temporary Measures for the Promotion of Specified Industries was prepared at the instigation of the Industrial Order Division of the Industrial Structure Investigation Group. This bill can be summarized in five points, most of which paralleled conventional MITI policies under the MIPA:

1   Although MITI made every effort to see this bill enacted, it failed in this endeavor. Under the proposed statute, the government would first have designated target industries from among ferrous alloy products, steel forging and stamping, automobiles, tires, petrochemicals, and other associated industries shortlisted by cabinet order on the proposal of individual industries.
2   'Policy issues concerning matters like coordination of standards, production specialization, equipment investment coordination, and mergers' were to be determined upon agreement between the minister in charge and industry representatives.
3   Those involved in specified industries were to be asked to make efforts toward the achievement of policy. Additionally, banks and government financial institutions would endeavor to supply all necessary funds.
4   The government would make efforts both to ensure fiscal funds and to realize tax breaks to facilitate mergers, such as partial exemptions of registration taxes and corporate income taxes.
5   Exemptions from the application of the Anti-monopoly Act for joint operations for rationalization were to be offered.

The bill was first discussed in the Industrial Structure Committee in December 1961, and the cabinet sent it to the Diet three times, the first in March 1962. However, it was never passed.

The fundamentals that underlay the draft law are important here, as they are representative of MITI's basic attitude toward policies for industry. The following quote reveals those fundamentals. Recall that it was during the period of the Second MIPA that the bill was debated, drafted, and sent to the Diet three times without success. This observation illustrates the political environment that conditioned the MIPA:

> With too many enterprises of a very small size, contemporary Japanese industry suffers from excessive competition. In short, the extremely small scale of enterprises and the excessive severity of competition are the characteristics of Japanese industry. To correct this situation it is necessary to ensure fair competition among enterprises of appropriate scale, and to increase the scale of enterprises so as to promote rationalization and strengthen the international competitiveness of the industry. Thus, first of all, we have to expand the size of enterprises by promoting concentration and mergers among enterprises. This will facilitate the economies of large-scale production. At the same time, the public–private cooperative system [the *kanmin* system] was widely discussed to strengthen the ties between government and business. Under this scheme of cooperation, the government, business, and the financial sector would collectively enter into discussions regarding standards for promoting industries and setting goals for upgrading the overall industry, with each to present arguments from their respective standpoints. Based upon these discussions, under this scheme business was to make every effort in reaching the agreed goals, the government was to supply fiscal funds with preferential tax treatments for those enterprises (business), and the financial sector to support the whole process by making available all necessary funds.
>
> (annual report for FY1962: p.119)[56]

Atsushi Yonekura: a critical review of the First and Second MIPAs

After a review of the past ten years of experience and policy performance under the First and Second Acts, the legislature passed the Third MIPA to extend the policies. The fact of this extension suggests that a closer examination of the process of review will provide information useful for examining the effectiveness of the policy under the two Acts. Critically, no effective policies were actually implemented during the first ten years of MIPA to solve the 'industrial order issues.' To be more precise, the government had never adopted preferential-type policies that restricted the allocation of resources to selected enterprises under government policy.[57]

Yonekura 1965b was published prior to the passage of the Third Act by a person in charge of policy loans under the MIPA. This work argues that although the Act made some contributions to industry, it had a variety of serious defects. It points out that:

> the MIPA, like most laws, lacked responsiveness. Measures implemented under the Act could not be made fully responsive to each stage of development in Japan's machinery industries. Therefore the implementation of measures under the Act failed to match the urgent needs of industries. Further, measures under the Act were applied uniformly in each designated industry and did not take into account idiosyncrasies within industries. In short, the Act quickly became totally outdated.
>
> (*ibid.*: p.15)

As shown below, Yonekura argues that 'the principle of equal opportunity among enterprises that was ingrained in enterprise raising policies' inhibited the achievement of an 'industrial order restructuring' that would place powerful enterprises at the core of each industry:[58]

> Established tradition inhibited policies under the MIPA to no end, and the fundamental character of the Act as an Act for small business policy was particularly difficult to overcome. The principle of equal opportunity in enterprise raising policies was not compatible with industry objectives of the time, which were that of trade liberalization and an open economic system such as the promotion of specialized production systems to strengthen the international competitiveness of industries, and the reorganization of industries to place powerful enterprises at the core. Conversely and at the other extreme, in some industries like industries for machine tools, drills, grinding wheel industries, and also some agricultural machinery industries, competition for larger market shares resulted in excessive equipment investment, which promoted further excessive (and unnecessary) competition among enterprises of the same size.
>
> (*Ibid.:* pp.15–16)

In answering 'how should the MIPA and its implementation be improved?' Yonekura continues:

> The MIPA was used for the sake of convenience and lacked any definite long-term vision, with the effect of promoting excessive competition in some industries. We have to establish a model for realizing economies of scale and avoiding excessive competition and which is acceptable to the industry, that presupposes free economic activity. It is also necessary for each industry and each enterprise to be able to state clearly their ideas concerning management

and the direction of future development. From a national point of view, the government should take the responsibility of leadership in the realization of this new model by implementing financial policies, which will reduce economic loss most effectively. Allowing fiscal funds to function as money for restructuring the industrial order is necessary to lead industries and enterprises along this direction. We should open the way for loans to facilitate change of trade or its closure, and mergers for realizing economies of scale. We should also use fiscal funds to promote the smooth procedure of mergers.

(ibid.: p.20)

MITI's implied review of the past

The view of Yonekura (*ibid.*) regarding the ten-year period of the First and the Second MIPA, that 'the MIPA was used for the sake of convenience and lacked any definite long-term vision' and 'was not compatible with objectives such as promotion of specialized production systems to strengthen the international competitiveness of industries, and their reorganization to place powerful enterprises at the core' is generally accepted as accurate. The fact that MITI's proposed bill was not passed is consistent with this view. Furthermore, the failure of the bill suggests that policies of this type were not implemented with any vigor under the Third Act. The following statement from MITI's annual report for FY1967 (p.101) implies that MITI also shared Yonekura's view:

> Under such circumstances, and having decided to fundamentally review the Basic Plan for the Promotion of the Machinery Industries based on the MIPA, we organized the General Section under the Machinery Industries Council on 1 December 1967. The General Section approved an Outline for Revising the Basic Plan at the meeting on 9 February 1968. The Outline for the revision of the Basic Plan was prepared particularly in response to the liberalization of international investment, recognized that the traditionally adopted policy to modernize and rationalize equipment within individual enterprises is insufficient. We placed the greatest emphasis upon making structural improvement plans with concrete and highly coordinating contents, for promoting structural improvement in the industry. Referring to the production scale of major producers in the world, we draw production scales and targets for their achievement for every industry as a concrete guide for structural improvement. Our policy measures for achieving the realization of target scales are the promotion of forming industry groups both for coordinating production items among members and for rationalization cartels or joint operations. To prevent these industry groups degenerating into mere abstract plans and also considering the independence

of industries, we make it a rule when making plans to specify the number of target industry groups, cartel enforcement schedules, and so forth.

'Issues associated with liberalizations in international investment and the strengthening of international competitiveness' were 'the central pillars of industrial policy'[59] in the second half of the 1960s. The cabinet decision of 6 June 1967 concerning the liberalization of inward direct investment declared that 'at this point in time a total re-examination, right down to the core, of various plans for modernization and rationalization under special laws including the MIPA is crucial. Having conducted this re-examination, which we envisage would incorporate the strengthening of policy measures in case of necessity, we should also review enforcement plans by for instance shortening the term of those plans.'

The interim report of the Special Committee on Policies for Capital Transaction Liberalization in the Industrial Structure Council of November 1967 stated that 'in order to cope with the liberalization of capital transactions, we have to immediately establish a long-term vision for structural improvement in each industry, paying much attention to the independence of industries' (for more detail, see Miwa and Ramseyer 2002e: pp.191–202).

Detailed picture of the First and Second Acts

Three points can be made concerning policies under the First and Second MIPAs:

1   Even when policies did operate effectively to promote modernization and rationalization, the effects were felt only within individual enterprises.
2   The contents of plans to promote structural improvement in each industry were insufficiently concrete and were far from coordinated.
3   Government intervention was severely inhibited by various factors that forced the government to pay much consideration to the independence of industries when establishing new plans (the so-called 'long-term visions') to supersede the 'abstract plans' of the past. Government intervention in order to 'promote' the forming of the industry groups consisted merely of the government 'specifying the number of groups to be formed and cartel enforcement schedules.'

The same applies to the 'industrial order finance' provided for the 'restructuring of the industrial order' and to the preferential tax treatment provided for mergers. In his comments on the industrial policy budget in 1966, Sugiyama (1966a: pp.9–10) describes the policies as follows:

Industrial Order Finance: In December 1965 MITI recommended the equipment investment program of two automobile companies about to merge

(Nissan and Prince) to the JDB for industrial order finance to the total of 4 billion yen. The Subcommittee on Automobile Policies of the Industrial Structure Council strongly recommended that mass production in the automobile industry be promoted through mergers and joint operations. Upon this recommendation MITI established an industrial order finance scheme for the automobile industry in FY1963. The Nissan–Prince case was the first example of the application of this scheme. In FY1966 MITI secured 7.5 billion yen in JDB loans for industrial order finance, which was 2.7 billion yen larger than the corresponding amount of the previous year. The loans were for four industries: automobiles, ferrous alloy products, steel forging and stamping, and petrochemicals. Three of these industries were under the jurisdiction of the Heavy Industries Bureau. MITI intended to 'further promote the already rising movement of industrial order restructuring with this financial support.' Importantly, no industries under the MIPA were objects of this scheme.[60]

Preferential Tax Treatment to Promote Mergers: In FY1966 the government adopted two regimes of preferential tax treatments to promote firm expansion through mergers. First, for mergers conducted during FY1966 or FY1967, the resulting value obtained from the following calculation was excluded from corporate income tax payable and apportioned over the three years following the merger: (corporate income tax) $\times$ (20%) $\times$ {(the smaller of the two values of increased paid-up capital resulting from the merger)/(the post-merger paid-up capital value)}. That is, the corporate income tax payable will be reduced by up to 10 percent for three years in the case of merger between two companies of equal paid-in capital. When the corporate income tax is 40 percent (the approximate marginal rate for corporate tax payers), for instance, this rate will be reduced to 36 percent at the lowest for three years.[61] The other regime consisted of registration taxes associated with mergers being reduced. The details of these reductions were that the rates of tax for the registration of increases in paid-up capital were reduced from 1.5/1,000 to 1/1,000, and for the registration of succeeding property reduced from 4/1,000 to 2/1,000. Further, the carryover of reserve funds for price variations from merged corporations was permitted.

Prior to these measures, partial exemptions from the tax payable on liquidation income arising from merger and from registration tax under the MIPA and the Act on the Promotion of Small Business Modernization were provided for. However, prior to the twofold regime of tax measures adopted for promoting mergers in FY1966/67, these were the only preferential tax treatment measures for promoting mergers in the industries under MITI's jurisdiction. The 'introduction of preferential tax treatments including a general reduction of corporate income tax was a daring policy measure at the time, and was expected to produce significant effects' (Sugiyama 1966a: p.10). However, in addition to the small size of tax incentives introduced with these measures, what is critical to our examination here is that such 'daring' measures had not been adopted before this period. Also, the preferential tax treatment measures that were actually adopted under the First Act were not considered by this MITI official to be 'daring.'

2.2.5   Problems with the MIPA: (2) other points of criticism

Yonekura also discusses the need for support measures to replace those provided for under the MIPA (1965b: p.15). As mentioned above, although he admitted that the Act did play some role and make some contributions, Yonekura argues that it had many defects and 'quickly became totally outdated.' Furthermore, Yonekura argues, 'the principle of equal opportunity among enterprises that was ingrained in enterprise raising policies' rendered the policy for restructuring the industrial order ineffective. Although he concedes that 'the validity of my argument may be limited to financial institutions, and may not be of general application,' it is worth introducing his views here for two reasons. First, they capture the views of many of his contemporaries. As he himself notes, 'many relevant persons have already pointed to many of these facts in the Act.' Second, they give us an 'insider' perspective that is rarely accessible to 'outsiders,' and they are consistent with other research (Miwa 1995, 1996a, 1999; Miwa and Ramseyer 2002e, 2003d). Readers will note that many of the characteristics that Yonekura discusses are common to centralized plan-oriented and interventionist policies more generally.

Yonekura's critique

The five points in the following quote, numbered (2) to (6), are the factors that Yonekura lists as 'points to be criticized' following the first point ('equal opportunity among enterprises'), quoted above.

(2) The basic rationalization plans, guiding policy loans under the Act, did not match industry trends such as demand movements and technical innovations. Further, the inflexible nature of the basic rationalization plans in terms of the very restricted propensity to further designate as necessary equipment as the objects of policy loans, inhibited the flexible enforcement of fiscal funds special loans. In particular, the initial designation under the Act totally excluded both plant buildings and equipment for purely technological research. The former, namely plant buildings, are of equal importance to machinery equipment in terms of reducing costs, improving the quality and precision of products, and maintaining uniformity in product quality. In addition, throughout 39 industries designated under the Act the renewal of

machinery equipment progressed rapidly in terms of the number of machines renewed. However, the designation of machinery equipment (to be renewed) focused primarily on standard, general-purpose machines on the market. Consequently, vast amounts of more specialized obsolete equipment remained in the industry. This was of particular concern to the then recent movements towards conserving labor.

(3) The scrapping of obsolete equipment, which is the other side of equipment renewal, was totally voluntary, that is left up to individual enterprises to administer by themselves. The Act by itself had no coercive power, and guidance provided by the ministries concerned and financial institutions was insufficient. Consequently, instead of scrapping obsolete machines, obsolete machines were simply transferred from parent companies to first-tier subcontractors, and then in turn to the second-tier subcontractors, and finally sold in the market as used machines, further suppressing already stagnant demand.

(4) Partly because of technical difficulty in expression, targets for improving quality and precision in the basic rationalization plans were very ambiguously described and generally did not explicitly state the value of the target to be achieved. Only capacities like precision and those easily expressed in numerical values were detailed on the lists, and the expression of capabilities concerning functions like easy handling and rigidity were totally ignored in many industries. As a result, although domestic machine tools reached an internationally competitive level in terms of technology concerning configuration and precision, they were seriously lacking in basic areas of technology such as easy handling, rigidity, and durability. Hence they could not be described as having persuasive originality and superiority when compared with foreign machines.

(5) Enforcement plans for each year lacked any close coordination with the basic rationalization plans. For example, introductions of technology from abroad during the past several years, though a rational step for individual enterprises, were hardly compatible with the industry-wide industrial structure policy for promoting specialized production. In addition, although based upon long-term economic forecasts, these forecasts were made in 1960 and 1961 when production, exports, and investment were all experiencing extraordinary booms. Accordingly, the basic rationalization plans by themselves deviated from the contemporary state of the industry.

(6) The basic rationalization plans overestimate the role of equipment investment both in quality improvement and in cost reduction. We observed no remarkable cooperation from producers or users, for instance, in promoting joint research, either. The basic plans and the enforcement plans were far too abstract to serve as guides and to provide goals for establishing rational

production systems and achieving the rationalization of the industry. They lacked concrete vision.

(Yonekura 1965a)

Yonekura improvements

In the section 'How should the enforcement of the MIPA be improved?' Yonekura (1965b: pp.18–21) additionally lists seven points thoroughly detailing measures that he argued should be adopted to address the inadequacies identified with the above six points:

(1) Abolishing systems to designate industries by cabinet order as objects of fiscal fund loans: once designated, an industry rarely lost its designation. Some industries designated accordingly took advantage of benefits under the Act. Other industries, though widely regarded as important, were never designated because of insufficient PR or political influence. Attaining designation required much time and vast energy. The Act ought to supply only a general outline of industries upon which policies will be focused and so maintain flexibility and the ability to designate necessary industries to receive national support as necessary.

(2) Overcoming the ingrained motifs of being a small business policy and also granting equal opportunity to large companies in equipment financing support: we ought to re-examine the character of the Act, which almost totally excludes large companies from policy focus, that is companies with over 10 billion yen in paid-up capital.

(3) Systems to designate equipment for policy support which are unable to cope with trends in technical innovation and equipment investment should be abolished: the MIPA listed many general-purpose machines and experiment/ examination equipment which specified industries were expected to use in the production process. The policy measures under the Act were implemented only regarding listed equipment. Therefore policy was unable to be responsive to the trends of the time, particularly in technical innovation. Under the present system equipment renewal was conducted by simply replacing obsolete designated equipment with new general-purpose machines, primarily expanding capacity only quantitatively.

(4) Introducing loans for technological development: the MIPA only places indirect emphasis on technological development by promotion objectives like reducing costs and improving product quality and precision. The Act lacks any provision for loans to support technological development. Even if lenders were aware of the importance of funds for technological development, without direct connection with the Act such investment could never become a consistent national policy for promoting the machinery industries.

For example, expanding JDB loans for commercializing domestic technology and the Loan System for Financing Heavy Machinery Development[62] should be restructured, altering their focus from individual projects to producers themselves. These loan regimes should also be expanded to cover all necessities, not simply matters having to do with the contract price.

(5) We have to establish a concrete vision for industrial order restructuring. We should expand the function of fiscal funds in the realization of such restructuring.

(6) We must make progress in scrapping old or obsolete equipment by implementing compulsory scrapping measures. In addition, we should introduce a new loan system which incorporates the diversion of obsolete equipment to subcontractors in order to promote more effective use of obsolete equipment.

(7) Expanding preferential treatment on depreciation: under the Act on the Promotion of Small Business Modernization, enterprises in designated industries are allowed to increase the volume of tax-free depreciation by one-third of the volume in normal cases. For instance, we should allow the same preferential treatment, irrespective of company size, to all properties acquired through a project supported by policy loans.

Overall, as a man personally in charge of MITI's policy loans, Yonekura (*ibid.*: p.15) thought highly of the Act's contributions. He states that 'the Act has facilitated the modernization of Japan's machinery industries, which had been suffering from a lack of international competitiveness and high costs and inferior quality when compared with the international standard. Japanese machinery industries are now able to cope with an open economy which began with the trade liberalizations since 1961, having been raised to the level of the international competition.' However, even to him, the Act appeared to have many 'points to be criticized' and points 'to be improved.' At this point, readers should wonder how the MIPA and its related policies could have been effective, and how they could serve as 'an excellent model of industrial policy for underdeveloped countries' (Kuroda Seiko 1995: p.129). As I explain below, the Act and related policies were indeed ineffective, and they cannot serve as a model for policy elsewhere.

2.3   THE EFFECTIVENESS OF THE 1956 STATUTORY FRAMEWORK

2.3.1   Basic issues

As I noted in Part I, several issues arise when studying the effectiveness of a policy. To start with, we must ask whether the policy is even potentially effective. We can do so by supposing that the state possesses a unified and definite will to implement the policy and also that the state adopted and implemented measures designed to achieve the policy objective optimally. On the basis of those two suppositions, we can investigate the magnitude of the contributions that might be made by such an optimal policy. That, in turn, would constitute the maximum value of the potential contribution. We can then estimate what would have been the change in value of the target function realizable by that optimal policy and compare it with the probable value without that policy or with alternative policies.

The investigation in Part I centered on the effectiveness of the policies for the machine tool industry under wartime control. That industry was also one of the targeted industries under the 1956 Temporary Measures Act for the Promotion of the Machinery Industries (Machinery Industries Promotion Act, MIPA). The Precision Tool Control Association (PTCA), which was virtually an affiliate of the Precision Tool Section of the Commerce Ministry, stood as the core policy measure for the machine tool industry. The conclusion of Part I about the policy of establishing a control association for the machine tool industry and further of controlling that industry in general was that this had zero effect. We have no reason to think that anything relevant had changed in the machine tool industry by the 1950s. Accordingly, the conclusion of Part I applies directly to analogous policy measures for this industry under the MIPA.

In addition, three basic conditions that existed in the machine tool industry were also very closely mirrored in other industries under the MIPA:

1   In each industry, there were many enterprises that competed fiercely with each other.
2   In most industries, there was a diverse range of products and a wide variety of models.
3   Technological levels and management expertise differed greatly between firms in any one industry. Accordingly, there was also great variance in the quality and performance of products on the market.

It can very plausibly be assumed that the state was unable to acquire detailed and precise information about product ranges, quality and performance of products, and production costs regarding individual companies. As we have concluded regarding the machine tool industry, the 'establishment of a control association has no rationality as a policy for achieving such urgent objectives as reducing the production costs of certain products, improving their quality and performance, or developing new products' (Section 1.2.6). Therefore the conclusion drawn in Part I regarding the state, the PTCA, and their interrelationship under wartime control also applies in a much broader context to the state and industry associations in general in the machinery industries, and the nature of their cooperative interrelationship under the MIPA.

The second step in examining the effectiveness of a policy is to ask how well the government was able to form and implement policy – the extent to which (as principal) it was able to induce firms (as agents) to follow its lead. To the degree that it was unable to do so under the MIPA, the Act would have made less of a contribution than otherwise. Several questions are relevant: did any factors, for example, constrain the range of choices available to the government? Within the government itself, was there sufficient consensus about policy and sufficient coordination in implementation that it could act as a unitary principal? Did that consensus extend to questions of detail? Did the government have the information and capabilities it needed to design the policies it wanted? And did it have the tools it needed to enforce its objectives?

By tackling these questions, we generate answers to the following issues, which in turn take us a long way in our investigation of the competence of the state and the relationship of the state's competence to the behavior and function of the state. The relevant questions are as follows:

- In general terms, what could the state do to achieve its policy objectives?
- What could the state do other than preferentially allocate key materials like foreign currency and investment funds to these sectors?
- Were these measures effective enough to achieve the designated tasks?
- If not, what reasons underlay the failure?
- Was stronger intervention necessary?
- If yes, why was such forceful intervention not implemented?
- Why were institutional arrangements for stronger control not realized from the very beginning?
- Did decisive constraints exist to realizing such arrangements?
- Alternatively, was it that the state did not think such forceful intervention would be effective?

2.3.2   Background: (1) putting the MIPA in context

I will examine the context of the MIPA, the basic character of the policies for promoting the machinery industries, and the environment in which these policies were implemented. I begin by introducing the view of a Ministry of International Trade and Industry (MITI) official (Hayashi 1961: pp.446–7) regarding 'the relative importance of policies for the machinery industries.'

It is only in the past two or three years that the importance of the machinery industries in policy making has become widely recognized. The MIPA was established in 1956, before which almost no policy focus had been placed upon the industries except for the establishment of the Japan Export–Import Bank in 1950 and the adoption of the sugar-link system.[63] Most other policies aimed at the machinery industries and their exports were those that applied to other industries as well.

According to Hayashi, the point of the policies was to expand markets, to establish mass-production technology, to rationalize production, to modernize equipment, to promote R&D, to promote exports, and to stabilize input prices. Yet none of the MITI policies were, to Hayashi, distinctive to the industry:

> Excepting rationalization in production systems and the modernization in equipment under the MIPA, policies under the Electronics Industry Promotion Act, and the establishment of the Export–Import Bank, most policies were of general application, applying to all industries, or mere candidates for the future, in which there was almost nothing peculiar to the machinery industries. Further, even most of those policy measures for the machinery industries were simply built upon pre-existing movements in those industries, with the only exception being the measure to promote mergers to increase firm size to an international level.

A decade ago, in response to an article by Hayashi (1953), then an official in the Industrial Machinery Section, Saga (1953) published an essay showing clearly that a consistently debated problem under the MIPA had also been an important issue prior to the Act.[64] Saga (1953) expresses two points of dissatisfaction with export promotion policies. First, 'there was an extensive reliance upon others' in terms of expecting support like political protection and financial subsidies from other firms and the business world. Initially, there was no recognition that the basic problem facing export promotion existed within the industry itself. Second, 'the character of industrial rationalization policy was indiscriminate and lacked definite policy programs.' Saga concludes:

> Heavy reliance of the Japanese economy upon freedom and assistance from abroad made us without our knowing it weak flowers grown up in greenhouses. We have totally neglected an opportunity to reconsider seriously and investigate fundamentally how we should lead and manage the Japanese economy, which has become snowed under by accumulated bad conditions. … Obviously there is neither a panacea nor an excellent remedy for export promotion. The only potentially effective policy is one that promotes making our own products internationally competitive through rationalizing production and management in selected industries according to well-organized

priority, and also concentrates allocation of all scarce energies to this objective. ... As shown clearly by the public construction expenditure in our country, nothing is more nonsensical than to divide such small sums of money into even smaller parcels. ... Consequently it is our most urgent and greatest task to decisively reconstruct the industry, by establishing industry rationalization programs which grant high priority to selected industries for export promotion, and adopting an industrial reorganization policy.

(*ibid.*: p.14)

Saga's argument about 'establishing industry rationalization programs which grant high priority to selected industries for export promotion, and adopting an industrial reorganization policy' is basically the same as the 'New Industrial Order' argument that began to be debated later. It is also of fundamental similarity to the view of Yonekura (1965a), who argues that 'lacking any definite long-run vision, the MIPA was used for the sake of convenience' and that 'the government should lead the industry from a national point of view with financial policies' on the principles agreeable to the industry. Thus the factors that were strongly recognized as defects of past policies, at least in some parts of MITI, in 1953, remained critical policy issues throughout the period of the First and Second MIPAs.

As a preliminary to a more detailed discussion of policy effectiveness, let us briefly examine a number of issues including a series of related policies leading up to the MIPA, the organization and formation of relevant sections in MITI, and other circumstances relevant to the Act. The decade prior to the beginning of the Act was a transitional period for Japan.[65] The direction and circumstances of Japanese society and in particular the Japanese economy were changing rapidly. In response to this, the objectives, issues, and content of government policies, particularly policies for industry, often changed and fluctuated radically. MITI, which administered the Act, was established in 1949 as a reorganization of the Ministry of Commerce and Industry, which was established as a successor to the Munitions Ministry just after the end of the war. MITI underwent radical changes and transformations in every facet of its existence, including its internal organization, its position inside the government, its own policy priorities, and the priority of its policies within the government.

Policies can be strongly inhibited by political circumstances. Since the Act and its related policies began at the conclusion of a decade of transition, a precise understanding of these political circumstances during that transitional decade is of critical importance to an examination of policy effectiveness under the Act. However, it is inappropriate to overestimate the influence of environmental conditions or to overemphasize any general economic or societal 'continuity,' that is economic or social factors that existed during wartime or even prewar and retained significance postwar.

2.3.3   Background: (2) relevant bureaux and sections within MITI

The organization of the MITI in 1956, which corresponded to the beginning of the MIPA, was based on the Cabinet Order Concerning the Organization of MITI (30 August 1952, Cabinet Order No. 390). In addition to the Minister's Secretariat, the head office of MITI had nine bureaux, and it was the Heavy Industries Bureau that took charge of the Act. Following enactment of the MIPA, the Conference for the Promotion of the Machinery Industry was established as an affiliate of the Heavy Industries Bureau, which consisted of twelve sections at the time with the Heavy Industries Section at the top of the hierarchy. The primary jurisdiction of this section covered 'matters concerning general coordination of the business of this Bureau' (section 49). Section 53, which is quoted below, stipulated the jurisdiction of the Industrial Machinery Section, which took charge of the machine tool industry.

> Section 53 The Industrial Machinery Section shall take charge of business matters listed below.
>
> (1) Matters concerning machine tools, experimental machines, and tools.
>
> (2) Matters concerning bearings, screws, and gears.
>
> (3) Matters concerning machines for the textile industry, machines for coal mining, machines for the chemical industry, machines for construction and civil engineering, and machines for other industries (excluding those under the jurisdiction of other sections).
>
> (4) Matters concerning farming tools, fishery tools, forestry tools, food processing machines, sericulture machines, brewing machines, tobacco manufacturing machines, lumber machines and saws.
>
> (5) Matters concerning iron frames and bridges.
>
> (6) Matters concerning printing and bookbinding machines, and sewing machines.
>
> (7) Matters concerning clocks and watches, phonographs, optical machines, physical and chemical appliances, and business machines.
>
> (8) Matters concerning machines and tools not subject to any other jurisdiction.

Organizational history before the establishment of MITI in 1949

The Precision Tool Section, which took charge of the machine tool industry under wartime control, existed as part of the Munitions Ministry at the end of the war on 15 August 1945. On 26 August, the Munitions Ministry and the Ministry of Agriculture, Commerce, and Industry were reorganized as the Ministry of Agriculture and Forestry and the Ministry of Commerce and Industry (Commerce Ministry). The Commerce Ministry was essentially a combination of six bureaux, three of which, namely the Commercial Affairs Bureau, the Industrial Affairs Bureau, and the Mining Bureau, had a long history, having been established in the middle of the Meiji era. The other three bureaux were established in 1939 as part of organizational reforms conducted during the period of strengthening wartime control. These latter three bureaux, the Textiles Bureau, the Fuel Bureau, and the Electricity Bureau, were organized according to the products they administered. Of the six bureaux, the emphasis was on the Mining, Fuel, and Electricity Bureaux. The Precision Tool Section did not belong to the Machinery Bureau, which had been established within the Commerce Ministry in 1939 just before the reorganization into the Munitions Ministry. Instead, it belonged to the Industrial Machinery Section of the reorganized Industrial Affairs Bureau, which consisted of five sections at this time: for industrial policy, industrial machinery, power machines, inorganic chemistry, and organic chemistry.

The International Trade Agency was established as an affiliate, in addition to the Coal Agency, to the Commerce Ministry for state-run trade by the imperial order of 14 December 1945. In addition, with the corresponding organizational reforms implemented on 10 January 1946, the Industrial Affairs Bureau was reorganized into six sections: for industrial policy, industrial machinery, automobiles, chemicals, fertilizers, and fermentation.

Reforms were also implemented on 8 November 1946 whereby five of the six original bureaux of the Commerce Ministry were organized according to the products they administered, and the Industrial Recovery Bureau and the Reparations Enforcement Bureau were added. The Industrial Affairs Bureau was divided into the Machinery Bureau and the Chemicals Bureau, the former consisting of five sections: for machinery policy, industrial machinery, electrical apparatus, automobiles, and daily necessities. The decision to reorganize bureaux according to the products administered was taken for two reasons. First, a fundamental policy during the earliest years of the US occupation was to move control functions away from the private sector and to the government. Therefore the government was forced to inherit industry control from the wartime control associations, control corporations, and control unions. Second, with the trend toward strengthening control, there was expansion in the qualitative nature of the control.

Two major organizational reforms that were conducted between this time and the establishment of MITI on 25 May 1949 are relevant to our discussion. First, along with the new measures of establishing the Telecommunication Machinery Bureau and the Daily Materials Bureau with the reform of 19 June 1947, the Machinery Bureau was reorganized into four sections: for machinery policy, industrial machinery, electrical apparatus, and automobiles. Second, the Small and Medium-sized Enterprises Agency (or simply the Small Business Agency or SMEA) was establishment on 2 July 1948 to 'generate satisfactory conditions for raising and developing small business, and improving small business management.'

The establishment of MITI in 1949

The Act by which MITI was established took effect in May 1949 and was largely in response to the occupation government's (i.e., the Supreme Commander of the Allied Powers, SCAP) emphasis on expanding exports and enhancing the connection between production and international trade. In order to realize fundamental organizational reform, the Act made the administration of international trade (traditionally handled by the International Trade Agency) the core element of general commerce administration. The Act also established the Resource Agency in order to unify the administration of the energy sectors. Furthermore, the Act implemented the restructuring of relevant government agencies in response to the reduction in overall economic control.

Here a number of points can be made:

- The birth of MITI implies above all a diversification of the basic character of institutions: a shift in emphasis away from domestic economic activity (focusing on policies to expand production amid the postwar disorder) toward international trade and policies to promote exports.[66]
- It was an opportunity to reduce the size of organizations in response to the reduction in the overall control of business that accompanied the return of economic stability.
- The organizational structure of the ministry was for the first time stipulated by law.[67]

In the beginning, in addition to the Minister's Secretariat, MITI had eight bureaux. The title of each bureau began with 'International Trade,' which was a reflection of the circumstances of the time.[68] For instance, the Machinery Bureau was called the International Trade Machinery Bureau, which consisted of six sections: for machinery policy, machinery exports, industrial machinery, agricultural machinery for private use, electrical apparatus, and casting and forging products. It also included the Telecommunication Machinery Division (wire and radio) and the Car Division (automobiles and other vehicles).

Organizational reform of MITI in 1952

The next major organizational reform was the enactment of the New Act for the Establishment of MITI on 31 July 1952. This Act followed the cabinet decision concerning 'administrative reform' of 28 August 1951, which made the following policy declaration:

> With the conclusion of the US–Japan Peace Treaty ending the occupation, we conducted fundamental reviews of the existing administrative organs and their operations, which were tremendously expanded and complicated during the war and the postwar period. The aim of these reviews was to eliminate a wide variety of complicated restrictions arising from the administrative structure and to reduce the public burden. We have decided to establish a new system of government administration which is more appropriate for an independent and democratic Japan in the post-peace-treaty era. We shall do this through restructuring the organization and function of present government administration.

At the same time, the five product bureaux were reorganized into three bureaux: the Heavy Industries Bureau, the Light Industries Bureau, and the Textiles Bureau. As shown below, the process leading to the establishment of the Heavy Industries Bureau reflects the radical and critical swings in government policy at the time.

In Japan, 'the basic source of responsibility within bureaucracy is the relevant division in the main ministry which has jurisdiction over the industry. ... Regarding any matters that fall within the jurisdiction of any given division, each division of the ministry itself personifies the Japanese government' (Kyogoku 1983: p.347). It is illustrative to make some basic observations regarding the human resources available to government division relevant to our discussion. In 1952, the number of personnel in the Heavy Industries Bureau was 204,[69] so each section had an average of seventeen members. Even if we assume that the size of the Industrial Machinery Section was twice the average, it would still have had only thirty-four members. Table 2.1 suggests that among the industries designated under the MIPA in 1956, at least nine, producing machine tools, experimental machinery, precision gauges, cutting tools, screws, gears, bearings, sewing machine parts, and clock parts, were under the jurisdiction of the Industrial Machinery Section. Therefore, again assuming that the Section had thirty-four members and further that all were fully engaged in administering the Act, the average number of government personnel per industry was at best fewer than four.

2.3.4   Background: (3) policy changes

The Japanese economy during the MIPA period

The situation of the Japanese economy when the First MIPA took effect in 1956 is well captured by the following statement, which appeared in the Economic White Paper for FY1956 and expounds the need for new policies to be developed: 'We are faced with a new era. Our growth through recovery is over. Our future growth will be sustained by modernization, and progress in modernization will only be possible through speedy yet stable economic growth' (p.42). This White Paper also includes the famous phrase, 'We are no longer in the "postwar" age.'

It was in 1954 that total GNP topped the prewar peak of 1939, but only in 1957 did *per capita* real income exceed the prewar level. The FY1957 Economic White Paper asserted the existence and emphasized the seriousness of the economic 'dual structure.'[70] Many of its general remarks were devoted to an analysis of that dual structure. The White Paper asserted that in the next ten years (the period of the First and Second MIPAs) 'we must place emphasis on policies for modernizing obsolete sectors by raising and developing medium-sized enterprises to achieve improvement in their profitability. This is how we will be able to eliminate the dual structure, that is, through modernization and growth in the economy' (pp.37, 40). The National Income Doubling Plan over 1961–70, adopted by the government in December 1961, followed this approach, emphasizing policies for small business, with the aim of eliminating the dual structure. As shown in the previous section, this plan served to inhibit the implementation of policy under the MIPA, and it also influenced the policies related to the Act.

This decade also saw extremely high growth in Japan's machinery industries, symbolized by the explosive development of the automobile industry. Eiji Toyoda, chairman of Toyota Motor Corporation, states in his memoirs that 'our first true car was the Crown, which was unveiled in January 1955' (Toyoda 1985: p.172). The number of cars produced in Japan that year was a mere 20,000. Within five years, that figure had risen to 165,000 and within ten years to 696,000. In 1968, vehicle production exceeded the two million mark. Vehicle exports reached 10,000 in 1961 but by 1965 had risen to 100,000 and in 1971 to one million.

The reductions in production costs and improvements in product quality realized in the automobile industry depended partly on cutting costs and improving quality in such automobile-related industries as parts, machine tools, and production equipment. Throughout the period, the Japanese economy suffered from chronic shortages of foreign currency. As a result, with a few exceptions most of the materials, machines, and parts used in automobile production were developed and produced domestically. Consequently, quality improvement and productivity gains were realized domestically in every area from stamping and machining to production of tyres, bearings, glass, steel, and machine tools (for details, see Miwa 1996a: ch. 4). It is important to recall here that, as shown in Part I, the machine tool industry under wartime control realized a tremendous expansion of production and improvements in quality in response to explosive growth in demand. The establishment of the Machine Tool Building Act and subsequent policies, of which the PTCA is representative, did not greatly contribute to the developments in the machine tool industry. Rather, it was the explosion in demand and the elimination of rival foreign producers through import suspensions, which were forced by the war, that were the main contributing factors.

A brief summary of Japan's postwar economic history before the peace treaty

The first decade after the end of World War II was a period of transition in Japan. The changes in both society and the economy were extremely dynamic. The objective, issues, and content of government policies also reflected this situation and fluctuated wildly. This was particularly so regarding policies for industry. Here I extract the 'Summary of Contents' from *The History of Policies for Commerce and Industry* (MITI 1985b), a brief summary of Japan's postwar economic history before the 1952 peace treaty.

Chapter 1. Period of Disorder following the End of War

The beginning of the 'postwar' period; occupation policy in the initial stage; economic disorder and inflation; policies for commerce and industry; reparation and trade issues.

Chapter 2. The Progression of Inflation and the Resumption of Production

The progression of inflation and stagnation in production; progress in reparation issues and enterprise reconstruction and restructuring; measures for production resumption and tightening control; recovery policies for major industries; state-run trades and the Trade Corporation; progress in *zaibatsu* dissolution and the establishment of Anti-monopoly Act; reforms in administrative organs.

Chapter 3. The Development of Policies for Industrial Recovery

Economic policies of the Katayama Cabinet [i.e., the first socialist cabinet in Japan]; state management of coal mines and continuation of the priority production system; diversion in the occupation policy for Japan – reparation and trade issues; elimination of concentration, and reconstruction and restructuring of enterprises; development of industrial recovery policies; policies for the recovery of major industries; establishment of the Small and Medium-sized Enterprise Agency and the Industrial Technology Agency; from recovery to stability.

Chapter 4. The Dodge Line and the Establishment of MITI

The Dodge Line [i.e., deflationary SCAP policies]; the establishment of MITI; enactment of the Foreign Exchange and Foreign Trade Management Act and trade policy; emergence of industrial rationalization policy; stabilizing the economy and loosening controls; trends in major industries and policies for international trade and industry.

Chapter 5. Policies for International Trade and Industry during the Korean War

The outbreak of the Korean War and trade policy; wartime boom and the following recession; development in industrial rationalization policy; trends in major industries and policies for international trade and industry; conclusion of the occupation and recovery levels of Japan's economy.

It is unnecessary to comment regarding the abundance, diversity, and seriousness of the tasks that faced the Japanese government during this period. Even if we limit our attention to the economic issues prior to the deflationary policies and the establishment of MITI in May 1949, they were enormous. These would have been radically different from the issues that had faced the economic bureaucrats during the war.

The very birth of MITI symbolizes the difficulty of the issues facing the government, since it implied 'above all a transition in the basic character of institutions from being focused upon domestic economic concerns such as policies for production expansion amidst the postwar disorder, to placing primary emphasis on international trade and policies for export promotion.' This transition of economic focus saw a reduction in the size of the relevant government regulatory agency for industry (then MITI) in response to a general reduction in government control over business (Shoko gyosei 1955: II, p.512).

The machinery industries before 1952

In the MITI (1985b) history above, chapter 2 refers only to five industries: steel, electricity, gas, textile, and chemicals. Chapter 3 discusses the machinery industry but makes no reference to 'commercial policy' relevant to the industry. The only relevant discussion in chapter 3 is as follows: 'The postwar recovery in the machinery industry has been realized primarily in the area of consumer goods and machines for their production (predominantly for export). The machine tool industry and the industrial machinery industry, which are regarded as occupying the core of the machinery industries, have remained stagnant. This implies that recovery in the machinery industry has yet to take place' (pp.97–8).

Some relevant discussion exists in chapter 4. There, the account relates that in May 1949 the Commerce Ministry 'launched the basic plans for the machinery industry, adopting the promotion of exports of machinery products as the primary objective.' Chapter 4 begins by stating that 'with budgetary constraints along the Dodge stabilization policy line, and further the suspension of the Recovery Finance Corporation, domestic demand for machinery, particularly capital goods, has decreased sharply. … The basic plans for the machinery industry further aim to reinforce the quantity and quality of key industrial machinery and to raise the fundamental sectors of the machinery industry. The achievement of these aims will not be easy however' (p.150).

Some relevant discussion also exists in chapter 5, which begins with the statement: 'Special procurement due to the Korean War had an extremely grave impact on the recovery of the machinery industry.' According to the account, 'With the commencement of talks regarding the ceasefire agreement, machinery production stagnated. MITI made efforts to strengthen the competitiveness of the machinery industry, adjudging that the recessive economic environment both at home and abroad, and also the inferior international competitiveness of the machinery industry, were the basic cause of the stagnation.'

2.3.5   Background: (4) industrial rationalization policy

Industrial rationalization policy
and the Industrial Rationalization Council of 1949

The so-called 'industrial rationalization policy' deserves special attention because it was the forerunner to the MIPA and led in many ways to its enactment. By a cabinet decision of 13 September 1949, the Industrial Rationalization Council was established as an advisory committee to study relevant matters. That is, 'with the establishment of a balanced budget, a uniform exchange rate, and also the promotion of sound financing policy, industrial rationalization has urgently become requisite for managing our national economy. One precondition to the effective enforcement of industrial rationalization is the establishment of guiding principles in each industry regarding future industrial structure. In the second place, rationalization is in principle intended to allow prices to speedily approach international levels.' The council was established on 24 December as a large organizational institution and at the start had, besides the general assembly, thirty-one subassemblies. These included the central subassembly, the general assembly, and many subassemblies organized by sector like the Cotton Industry Subassembly and the Synthetic Fiber Industry Subassembly. Divisional meetings were organized under each subassembly (MITI 1985b: p.126).

In the policy debates concerning economic stability conducted since 1948, many strongly advocated the need for industrial rationalization. The Dodge Line imposed the obligation of intense efforts for rationalization upon the Japanese government and business, emphasizing the policy of promoting exports to achieve economic independence. MITI, which was established along the Dodge Line, 'placed at the core of their policy' the promotion of international trade as a trade policy and industrial rationalization as an industrial policy (*ibid.*: p.125). The new International Trade Enterprise Bureau within MITI was an organ to promote this policy. The highest priority for this bureau was 'matters concerning industrial rationalization of the business under MITI's jurisdiction' (section 10 of the Act for Establishing MITI). However, two points should be noted here. First, as shown in both the Dodge Line and the cabinet decision mentioned above, the highest-priority policy objective was promoting exports, and it was the achievement of industrial rationalization that was argued to be necessary for it. Second, industrial rationalization policy was not the sole task of the International Trade Enterprise Bureau, which was also charged with administering enterprises' policies more generally.

The Temporary Industrial Rationalization Agency of 1930 versus the Industrial Rationalization Council of 1949

Accordingly, the position and role of the Enterprise Bureau were greatly different from that of the Temporary Industrial Rationalization Agency. The latter was established on 2 June 1930 and lasted until 30 April 1937 as an affiliate to the Commerce Ministry for promoting the industrial rationalization movement that developed in the late 1920s. This earlier institution had been established for the purpose of mobilizing all the sections within the Commerce Ministry's jurisdiction. It was in charge of the establishment and enforcement of uniform rationalization policy, and (by imperial order) 'to take charge of matters concerning the rationalization of industries under the management and jurisdiction of the Commerce Ministry.'

The Temporary Industry Council was established on 20 January 1930, and its objective was 'to study and discuss important matters concerning industrial rationalization and other methods of promoting industry in response to inquiry of the prime minister, and to make recommendations to ministers concerned.' This council thus had a wider and different role from the Industrial Rationalization Council. Also, as the following list shows, this prewar council received a much wider variety of inquiries. For example:

•   In which industries should we control firms in order to reconstruct our economy, and what control measures should we adopt?
•   How best can we realize efficiency gains through such improvements in production technology as unification and simplification of production standards and management methods?

- What are the desirable measures to improve industrial finance, particularly for enforcing industrial rationalization?
- What measures are to be adopted to promote the 'buy more domestic products' movement?[71]

Upon the resolution of the Temporary Industry Council, the Hamaguchi Cabinet (July 1929 to April 1931) established the Temporary Industrial Rationalization Agency, which came under the management of the commerce minister, and took charge of matters concerning industrial rationalization. The agency consisted of two divisions, one of which 'took charge of matters concerning (1) controlling enterprises (2) enforcing scientific management control methods (3) improving industrial finance and (4) other measures on industrial rationalization' (MITI 1985a: p.130).

This council, a huge political apparatus headed by authoritative figures, started its activity with an impressive resolution, and it existed until April 1937 (see Section 1.3.5), three months before the Lukouch'iao incident, which led to the Sino-Japanese conflict and wartime control. As we saw in Part I, not only did no preparation exist for wartime control at that moment but also there was no agreement even inside the military and the government about an urgent need to enact control laws, including the General Mobilization Act of March 1938 (see Section 1.2.3). The point is that what we see about the prewar Temporary Industry Council strongly suggests that the postwar Industrial Rationalization Council could do and did little if anything.

The Industrial Rationalization Council placed little focus on the machinery industries

The Industrial Rationalization Council commenced its activities in 1950, placing particular emphasis on rationalization in the steel and coal-mining industries. At that time, the domestic price of coal, particularly that of soft coal, remained above international levels. This hindered the independence of key industries like steel and had disastrous consequences for the export profitability of steel after the reduction and abolition of subsidies to compensate for the gap between internationally competitive prices and domestic prices. Thus industrial rationalization policy emphasized the steel and coal-mining industries.[72]

The council submitted its first report to the MITI minister on 23 February 1951. A synthesis of the reports of various subassemblies in the central subassembly, this report declared in Part VII:

> The development of power sources and the expansion of new ship building, together with rationalization in the shipbuilding, the coal mining, and the steel industries represent the foundations of industrial rationalization. We

must adopt policies to allocate funds necessary for the achievement of these goals and pursue these policies over the long term.

(MITI 1972: pp.66–74)

The second report of the Industrial Rationalization Council was submitted on 18 July 1952 and 'gave direction to rationalization policies proposed in the first report' (*ibid.*: p.96). A third report was submitted on 16 September 1953. In the meantime, the council also prepared 'the Basic Direction of Policies for Coal Mining Rationalization' and 'the Basic Direction of Rationalization in the Steel Industry,' which were published on 30 July 1953.

On 1 November 1953, the council underwent reorganization from a traditional vertical industry-oriented organization to a structure based on the issues involved. This reorganization was conducted for three reasons: (1) it was intended to strengthen the 'export competitiveness of Japan's industries' and enhance 'industrial rationalization'; (2) it aimed to alter the traditional focus of rationalization promotion, which was centered primarily on individual enterprises, to 'rationalization in industrial structure, restructuring the system of organization to facilitate inter-firm cooperation and connection'; and (3) the reorganization was intended to stir debate about measures for additional industrial rationalization.

With this reorganization, five divisional subassemblies were organized under the Industries Oriented Subassembly, in which only the Steel Subassembly was included among industries under the jurisdiction of the Heavy Industries Bureau. Also, the reorganization dropped the Industrial Machinery Subassembly, Electrical Machinery Subassembly, Communication Machinery Subassembly, Precision Machinery Subassembly, and Casting and Forging Subassembly (*ibid.*: pp.44–5, 109–10).

The Japan Development Bank
and the Act for the Promotion of Enterprise Rationalization

The establishment of the Japan Development Bank (JDB) on 1 April 1951 and the enactment of the Act for the Promotion of Enterprise Rationalization (law no. 5) on 7 March 1952 were the major events of industrial rationalization that occurred during the period. The Fiscal Investment and Loan Program (FILP), which showed a doubling of total loan volume over the previous fiscal year, played a leading role in the government's FY1951 expansion policy. More than half of FILP was allocated to private-sector loans, for which the JDB was the major lending route. The crucial point here is that four industries, the electricity industry (development of power sources), the shipping industry (ocean-going shipbuilding), the steel industry (rationalization), and the coal-mining industry (rationalization), accounted for almost 70 percent of the total volume of loans made. Furthermore, these four industries occupied special positions as borrowers from the JDB for a long period after 1951 and were known as 'the four industries of special policy concern' (*ibid.*: pp.75–9, 159 *et seq.*).

The most remarkable characteristic of the Enterprise Rationalization Promotion Act was that it placed the greatest emphasis on tax exemption as a measure to promote the rationalization of enterprises. In particular, the special depreciation allowance that it provided to facilitate the modernization of machinery in key industries had a far 'more significant effect' than its other measures. Its significance ranked with the measure that allowed a 50 percent increase in the depreciation allowance over three years adopted through the Revision of Special Tax Measures Act of 1951 (*ibid.*: p.209).

Under the former special depreciation allowance, the government designated thirty-two sectors as 'designated industries' entitled to use the allowance from the sixty-six originally proposed as 'sections in key industries where the modernization of machinery is considered of urgent necessity.' These designations focused on 'basic industries' like the steel and coal-mining industries but also included the machine tool industry and the bearing industry. The value of machinery newly acquired under this scheme during FY1952 and FY1956 totaled ¥103.2 billion. Five industries accounted for more than 5 percent of this sum. To give more detail, ¥35.8 billion worth of machinery was allocated to the steel industry, ¥14.9 billion worth to the coal mining industry, ¥9.2 billion worth to the petroleum refining industry, ¥6.9 billion worth to the dyeing industry, and ¥6.3 billion to the cement industry. The machine tool and bearing industries brought up the rear, each acquiring ¥1.1 billion worth of new machinery (MITI 1957: pp.88–91; 1972: pp.218–21).

The Japan Center for Productivity was established on 1 March 1955 'with the objective of promoting increases in productivity in the national economy. The movement for increases in productivity began under the leadership of this body. Thus, this year also showed remarkable developments of the enforcement of industrial rationalization' (MITI 1972: pp.113–15).

The Act on Temporary Measures for Coal Mining Rationalization

During this period, many laws for rationalizing and promoting particular industries were enacted, with these industries also being exempted from application of the Anti-monopoly Act. The Act on Temporary Measures for Coal Mining Rationalization, which was promulgated in August 1955, was the first of these laws and in a way broke the ice. The Act on Temporary Measures for Textile Industry Equipment of June 1956, the MIPA of June 1956, and the Act on Temporary Measures for Promoting the Electronics Industry of June 1957 followed soon afterwards. 'Each Act occupied the position of the fundamental law for achieving rationalization in the industry concerned, and further each law included provisions for the exemption of the application of the Anti-monopoly Act to joint operations among industry members following government instructions' (*ibid.*: p.119).

Let us for a moment concentrate on the Act on Temporary Measures for Coal Mining Rationalization. This Act 'was intended to address the high coal price, by achieving cost reductions through drastic rationalizations, that is, through a number of measures such as concentrating coal production to mines boasting the highest productivity levels, improving mine facilities, and mechanizing production' (*ibid.*: p.118). However, already at the end of 1949 (the Act was enacted in August 1955) the 'promotion of industrial rationalization' had been detailed as among the basic aims of SCAP's Headquarters for Economic Stability.

> [The Act] provided for the preferential rationing of materials to enterprises with superior productivity. This represented a great shift from the traditional practice of indiscriminately allocating rations to every enterprise. This shift in rationing measures implied a change of course from the priority production system which had been adopted previously. While the priority production system treated every enterprise in the industry equally regardless of productivity levels, what we see introduced in this Act is a 'concentrated production system' incorporating the preferential allocation of funds and materials to enterprises boasting superior efficiency within the industry.
>
> (*ibid.*: p.118)

The Commerce Ministry, in response to this shift in rationing measures, discussed the introduction of corresponding measures in the coal-mining industry. For instance, it discussed the revision of standards for rationing designated production materials, which it actually did put into practice gradually. The essence of the response of the Commerce Ministry was to determine an 'appropriate operation rate' for the industry, and they 'determined the destination of materials rationing by reference to this rate. That is, it revised or suspended materials rationing for the next period to plants with operation rates below the appropriate rate' (MITI 1985b: pp.127–8).

As mentioned above, concerning the MIPA and related policies, there was strong dissatisfaction that the government had taken no effective corrective action. As shown in Part I, we find the machine tool industry expressing the same demand under wartime control, but we see no active government corrective actions. Moreover, the first inquiries to the Temporary Industry Council, upon which the Temporary Industrial Rationalization Agency was established in June 1930, was 'what are the industries where we have to control enterprises for restructuring our economy under the present situation and what should be the direction of their control?' One of its major reports proposed concrete 'restructuring' plans such as 'mergers,' 'associations,' 'joint management,' and 'management delegation,' arguing that 'the most urgent need in our shipbuilding industry is to reduce the production cost as close to the international levels as possible by definite enforcement of equipment capacity restructuring and rationalization of business management' (for details, see MITI 1961: pp.15–31).

Summing up

The discussion in this subsection can be summarized under five points. In the 1950s, 'industrial rationalization policy' received strong backing from the government. It was this environment that was the background to the MIPA and that led to the enactment of that Act.

1   The significance attributed to postwar rationalization policy and its role was far less than that of the significance and role of the industrial rationalization movement in the late 1920s. The same goes for the position of the postwar Industrial Rationalization Council as regards the position of the Temporary Industrial Rationalization Agency.

2   In the 1950s, the policy of the highest priority was export promotion, and industrial rationalization was pushed as a subsidiary measure for the realization of export promotion policy objectives.

3   Industrial rationalization policy focused primarily on the steel and coal-mining industries. Other industries where industrial rationalization policy was also important were the electricity, shipping, petroleum refining, textile, and cement industries. The machinery industries, including the machine tool industry, were not primary targets of this policy.

4   The two pillars of rationalization policy, namely JDB loans and tax benefits, were primarily directed to steel production and coal mining. The machinery industries were not major beneficiaries of these policy measures.

5   Many laws were enacted for the rationalization and promotion of specific industries, and these laws exempted the application of the Anti-monopoly Act. Even in the coal-mining industry the government had to conduct 'the preferential rationing of materials to enterprises with superior productivity, breaking free from traditional rationing practices, which saw rations going indiscriminately to every enterprise.'

2.3.6   The continuity of the wartime economic order:
(1) wartime control and its aftermath

Two factors that might have conditioned MIPA policies

In order to investigate the MIPA and related policies and to assess their actual role and contribution, it is necessary to examine in detail two factors that might have conditioned the process of policy making and the enforcement of policy measures. The first of these concerns the nature of related institutions, including the legal system – the nature and process of transformation of the institutions related to the conduct of the government in intervening in industry under wartime control. The second involves the transformation of the institutions that coordinated the conflicts of interest between industry members and enforced policy under wartime control. This examination yields the following two conclusions.

First, the laws that provided the foundation for the wartime control regime faced at least one attempt to abolish them completely after the war. There were fundamental differences in the primary policy objectives of the postwar Commerce Ministry and the MITI. The framework within which government agencies tried to implement policy at the commencement of the MIPA was fundamentally different from the circumstances under wartime control. The government enjoyed a far smaller degree of freedom and less power with which to intervene in the private sector and enforce policy after the war than it did under wartime control.

Second, there was at least one attempt to abolish or reorganize the industry associations after the war. These associations (which had often been reorganized into control associations during the war) played crucial roles during the war as part of the mechanism of control. These industry associations, after reorganization or after being established subsequent to having been abolished or dissolved, were organized under the principle of voluntary participation. Furthermore, they did not play a control role analogous to that which their wartime predecessors had played. Industry associations underwent sweeping transformations in both name and deed.

Transition from the wartime economic regime

The transition from the wartime economic regime started with the Cancellation of Designation of Munitions Companies and Munitions Supply Companies on 15 August 1945. Five days later, the government abolished the related restrictions on the use of steel and copper (Shoko gyosei 1955: II, p.803). As MITI (1985b: p.22) put it later:

> With the end of war the Materials Mobilization Plan, the plan which conducted the fundamental coordination of the demand and supply of materials during the war, was abolished. … With the occupation policies of demilitarization and of the destruction of all war potential, the former wartime regime of control was destined to be destroyed or abolished.

Two further laws central to wartime control were repealed: (1) the 1937 Act on Temporary Measures Concerning the Import–Export of Products, repealed effective 16 January 1946; and (2) the Materials Control Order of December 1941, which was issued under the 1938 National General Mobilization Act and repealed effective 1 April 1946.[73] Many other economic laws were also repealed or revised.

'The abolition of wartime materials control focused primarily upon goods produced for military supply. Some controls that primarily focused on consumption goods escaped untouched, which reveals that the major objective was demilitarization and the maintenance of public welfare' (Shoko gyosei 1955: II, p.517). In finance, for instance, the 1937 Temporary Funds Coordination Act continued in effect, while the Financial Control Association Order (dealing with the centralized control of financial institutions) was repealed on 24 October 1945. The National Financial Control Association and the wartime Finance Corporation were dissolved on 26 October (*ibid.*: pp.482–3). Effectively, the wartime system of financial control was fundamentally transformed.

Transition regarding laws and orders related to the MIPA

Widespread changes in the regulation of the machinery industries also took place. General national mobilization laws and orders (e.g., the General Mobilization Materials Use and Expropriation Order and the Factories and Workplaces Control Order, which had facilitated state control over munitions factories) were repealed. So too were many industry-specific acts, including the Petroleum Industry Act, the Artificial Oil Manufacturing Industry Act, the Steel Industry Act, the Key Machinery Manufacturing Act, the Automobile Manufacturing Act, the Aircraft Manufacturing Act, the Machine Tool Building Act, the Light Metals Manufacturing Act, the Act for Subsidizing Arms Manufacturing Industries, the Organic Composition Manufacturing Act, the Petroleum Sales Monopoly Act, the Exceptional Wartime Administration Act Concerning Procedure and Jurisdiction, the Munitions Company Act, and the Temporary Import–Export Grading Act (*ibid.*: p.805; MITI 1985b: p.21).

In the machine tool industry, all institutions that had supported wartime production and control disappeared. This included not just rules and restrictions relating directly to military production but also controls on production materials like steel, the Machine Tool Building Act, the Key Machinery Manufacturing Act, and the PTCA. Financial controls over the industry were abolished, and government sections in charge of the industry were reduced in size and role.

Collapse of demand for machine tools

Moreover, product demand, which had grown so explosively during the war, faded. At the same time, 'arms production was prohibited, and the use of previously military-related production equipment (factories designated or controlled by the Munitions Company Act) was placed under a license system' (Shoko gyosei 1955: II, pp.583–4). In addition, as discussed in more detail in the next section, the machine tool industry was designated as a major object of reparations for war losses, with many factories being designated as objects of reparations (i.e., they were to be dismantled and shipped abroad). Machine tool production equipment in designated factories was 'only permitted to be used for the production and repair of manufacturing machines useful to the recovery of public welfare, providing of course that this did not interfere with the maintenance of equipped machine tools in good condition' (JMTBA 1962: p.161). Not until 1952 were these designations removed.[74] Thus key environmental factors that had inhibited the machine tool producers during wartime almost totally disappeared after the war, just as new complications emerged.

Summing up

The MIPA appeared after a decade of transition. On the one hand, various factors that had inhibited the machine tool industry disappeared during this period, but on the other hand the industry experienced deep depression due both to a collapse in demand and to heavy restrictions on production. The MIPA and related policies did not show any continuation of or similarity to the wartime policies.

The legal and other institutions that constituted the wartime control program were almost totally abolished. In effect, the foundation of government authority and power to intervene in the private sector to control industry disappeared. It was primarily in the materials production industries (like coal mining and steel) that some remnants of the control endured.

Observers commonly describe Japanese administration as 'vertically structured': information and policies travel between industries and the ministry through industry-specific divisions but not across the bureaucratic divisions themselves. Many argue that because of this Japan has been slow to make decisions or to change structurally. Laws, for example, are often industry-specific: the Banking Act, the Securities and Security Exchange Act, the Insurance Industry Act, the Loan Regulation Act, the Investment Advising Act, the Freight Transportation Act, the Electricity Utilities Act, and the Telecommunication Act. Most such acts involve four regulated industries (industries, one might add, that are also heavily regulated in many Western countries): energy, financial services, transportation, and telecommunications. However, note that in the manufacturing sector almost no such industry law has existed since the end of the war, with the Petroleum Industry Act of 1962 being the principal exception. Beginning with the Petroleum Industry Act of 1934, many manufacturing industries (e.g., steel, aircraft, automobiles, shipbuilding, machine tools) had been regulated by law and through control associations for years. With the end of the war, all those control associations and industry laws were abolished.

Yukio Noguchi's The Year 1940 Regime

Even today, many share Noguchi's (1995) view that 'the economic system under-lying and supporting Japan's high growth was basically the continuation of the

Wartime General Mobilization Regime.' Noguchi's book is famous for its title, *The Year 1940 Regime*; in it he writes that under the New Economic Order of the second Konoe Cabinet (July 1940 to July 1941) the government enacted many industry laws, issued the Key Industry Associations Order, and 'organized industry associations called "control associations," which were the instruments for economic control by bureaucrats.' He concludes: 'These industry associations, government corporations, and government funds, with slight changes in shape and style, still remain, increasing the number in some sectors, and play important roles both as instruments for bureaucratic control and informal regulation on economic activities and as seats for former high-ranking bureaucrats' (*ibid.*: p.9). Noguchi insists that 'the economic system underlying and supporting Japan's high growth was basically the continuation of the wartime general mobilization regime.'

However, what he argues was maintained unchanged from the wartime economic regime was 'the economic regime – particularly the institutional foundations for financial control' (*ibid.*: p.12). He emphatically does not argue that industries in the manufacturing sector were regulated under this regime. 'The Year 1940 Regime established for the wartime general mobilization' was kept untouched in postwar Japan,' he writes (*ibid.*: p.12). He concludes: 'The continuation in the government's institutional structure from prewar Japan was strong enough to surprise us. Only the military authorities disappeared, and all the ministries except for the Ministry of the Interior remained almost unchanged .... Perfect continuation from the wartime regime even of seniority rule in promotion inside ministries was maintained' (*ibid.*: p.76). For this conclusion he takes the Ministry of Finance as an example, arguing that even the name of each bureau never changed.

The picture is completely different when we take government policy toward the manufacturing sector by the Ministry of Commerce and Industry (later, MITI), instead of financial regulation by the Ministry of Finance, upon which Noguchi's argument mostly depends. In the Commerce Ministry, we observe strong continuation in human resources, but in other areas the continuation is less obvious. First, the basic objective and role of the ministry's jurisdiction completely changed, from industry development and control to export promotion. Second, the bureaux changed drastically and repeatedly in number, organizational structure, name, and role. All industry laws were repealed and control associations abolished outside the energy sector, and those trade associations that survived were obliged to transform radically their role, character, and leadership.

2.3.7   The continuity of the wartime economic order : (2) abolition of control associations

Abolition of control associations

Control associations were organized in each industry with the Imperial Order for Key Industry Associations of August 1941. This order was based on the National

General Mobilization Act. To retrace briefly from Part I, if we take the PTCA as an example, it was organized around enterprises in industries under the jurisdiction of the Precision Tool Section of the Machinery Bureau in the Commerce Ministry. The primary task of control associations was to supplement the administrative capacity of the government, and associations were affiliated to government sections in charge of the industries (in the case of the PTCA, the Precision Tool Section). In fact, the most significant role of control associations was to allocate production materials between association members according to the Materials Mobilization Plans, the objective being to achieve an expansion of military production of 'precision tools' including machine tools. The 1943 Exceptional Wartime Administration Act Concerning Procedure and Jurisdiction determined the scope of administrative authority that was delegated to control associations. The PTCA was a large organization with six divisions and twenty-five sections organized to exercise control over business. In the beginning, 318 machine tool makers, forty tool producers, nineteen bearing manufacturers, and four precision tool producers joined the PTCA.

With the wide-ranging abolition and reorganization of the wartime legal controls, various kinds of private organ that were involved in some aspect of the wartime control were designated for dissolution. Of all the control associations that were organized in each industry under the Key Industry Associations Order of August 1941, the control associations for automobiles (24 November), rubber (7 December), and railway track (20 December) dissolved voluntarily before the close of 1945. In 1946, the control associations for leather (23 January), steel (11 February), cement (21 June), and light metals (28 September) were similarly dissolved. In place of these associations, conferences and industry associations were newly organized but remained purely private institutions. Even in the steel industry, as a result of negotiations between the General Headquarters (GHQ) of the occupying forces and the Commerce Ministry, the 'Memorandum Concerning the Dissolution of the Steel Control Association' was issued on 11 February 1946. Under this memorandum, the association was dissolved and the Japan Steel Conference was established. As for the remaining control associations, the 'order for their dissolution came on 6 August 1946' (MITI 1985b: p.21).

The case of the gear industry

The gear industry provides another example of the change in circumstances of industry associations from prewar to postwar. The following outline gives some indication:

(1) The Tokyo Gear Producers Industrial Union was established with 62 members as a voluntary association in April 1938. The establishment assembly was held in July 1939. The background to the establishment of this

Union was that under wartime control it became necessary to promote cooperation and the exchange of information between industry members. Under the Commerce Ministry's guidance, the Union was established after discussions which were held over one year. In the Kansai District also the Osaka Gear Industrial Union was established in April 1939.

(2) With the October 1942 order from the Munitions Ministry[75] for the organization of a national union, these two unions were merged into the Japan Gear Industrial Union, which was renamed the Japan Gear Industry Control Union in January 1943.

(3) With the end of the war the Control Union was dissolved. After reorganization, the Japan Gear Industry Association emerged as a voluntary association in December 1945. The operation and function of this new association was, at the most, to collect and submit information concerning the industry upon the request of the Commerce Ministry. The association was renamed the All Japan Gear Industry Association in 1948, whereupon it commenced nationwide operations to assist in the industry's recovery.

(4) On 5 June 1958, the Japan Gear Industry Association was established as a corporation, with seventy-four members.

(Japan Gear Industry Association 1990: pp.12–14)

Postwar trade associations versus wartime control associations

Note that although trade associations (often called 'industry associations') may have exercised critical roles in industries designated under the MIPA, no direct continuity existed between those trade associations and the former wartime control associations. Furthermore, the postwar associations differed fundamentally from the wartime control associations in terms of both their organization and their role in policy enforcement.[76]

The process of government wartime control over business ceased totally with the abolition of the legal foundations for wartime control. Each control association either dissolved voluntarily or was dissolved by order. Purely private organizations, called 'conferences' or 'industry associations,' were established in many industries to replace control associations.

It is thus incorrect to assume that the role of industry associations and their relationship with the government under the MIPA was the same as that of the control associations and the government under wartime control. For example, at one time the PTCA had an extremely large bureau with six divisions and twenty-five sections. Yet we should note several facts:

- By the last days of the war, it had shrunk in size as successive officers resigned, and it eventually ceased to function (JMTBA 1962: pp.159, 222; see also Juyo Sangyo Kyogi-kai 1944). It was abolished after the war and reorganized into the Japan Machine Tool Builders Association, membership of which was voluntary.

- On 26 August 1945, the Munitions Ministry and the Agriculture and Commerce Ministry were abolished and the Commerce Ministry and the Agriculture and Forestry Ministry were revived. Instead of the Machinery Bureau (which existed from June 1939 until the Commerce Ministry was reorganized into the Munitions Ministry) the former Industrial Affairs Bureau of the Commerce Ministry was revived. The machine tool industry was one of the industries under the jurisdiction of the Industrial Machinery Section of this bureau. In May 1949, the Commerce Ministry and the Trade Agency were reorganized into the MITI, and the machine tool industry was placed under the authority of the Machinery Policy Section of the Trading Machines Bureau (MITI 1962).
- Both the Materials Mobilization Plan, upon which wartime control was carried out, and the Army and the Navy (which virtually implemented the control) were abolished.

These changes were not mere formalities. Rokuroku Sangyo, one of the leading machine tool builders, tells of a day in January 1946, after the abolition of the PTCA, when industry leaders were busy planning a new industry association. The Commerce Ministry held an abolition ceremony in the morning and an opening ceremony for the new association in the afternoon. It held the ceremony with thirty-six machine tool makers at Hakone Spring. At that moment, the manufacture of machine tools was under a license system, and the thirty-six makers present at the opening ceremony received licenses. Makers without licenses were unable to secure raw materials to survive. Hearing the complaints, the GHQ investigated and revoked the system entirely (*Oyou Kikai Kogaku* (Applied Mechanics), August 1989: pp.143–4).

Okazaki and Okuno-Fujiwara's continuity claim

Many people share Okazaki and Okuno-Fujiwara's (1999) view that 'economic recovery in Japan in the early years after the war exploited systems for planning and control system that had been created during the war years.' They argue that 'the institutions that supported this policy [industrial policy] also derived from the wartime or early postwar periods. The industrial associations that took over from the control associations were recognized [*shonin* in the original, literally 'approved'] in the 1948 Business Organizations Act [*Jigyosha dantai ho*, Trade Associations Act], and broad-based networks of business organizations [i.e., industrial associations] were formed' (*ibid.*: p.33).

However, the Trade Associations Act was enacted as a supplement to the Antimonopoly Act, and its objective was to prevent coercive activities by trade associations. This objective appears clearly in section 1, which details the Act's objective to be 'to clearly define the legal bounds of activities for trade associations, and to enforce their notification to the Fair Trade Commission.' Section 17 of the Act also provides that the provisions in the Anti-monopoly Act and 'the authority of the Fair Trade Commission as regards the Anti-monopoly Act should not be interpreted as being in any way affected or altered by the provisions in this Act.' Thus the Act simply clarified those activities of trade associations that lay beyond, that is were not prohibited by, the Anti-monopoly Act. In this light, the statement by Okazaki and Okuno-Fujiwara that trade associations were approved by the Trade Associations Act is misguided. Nothing prohibited the formation or the existence of trade associations, even just after the war (see FTC 1997: I, pp.37–9).

Control associations had been established under the Key Industry Associations Order to supplement the administrative capability of government sections in charge of industries. They were then abolished immediately after the war. Even when there was the appearance of 'continuity' between the wartime and postwar regimes, such as in the organizational structure and membership of associations, there was relatively little 'continuity' in substance and government policy (Miwa 1997a (1): pp.74–6; 1998c: parts II, III-6, III-7).

Okazaki and Okuno-Fujiwara base their view on the example of the steel industry. The Material Mobilization Plan was based on steel. Because of this, the steel industry occupied a special position in wartime control, and steel remained more heavily regulated than the rest of the manufacturing sector after the war. As a result, any interpretations based on the steel industry will cause serious misunderstanding.

Did wartime control alter the fundamental nature of firms?

Readers may well argue that the wartime controls altered the fundamental nature of Japanese firms, and that those controls would therefore continue to affect the way firms behaved even after the formal termination of the controls. Many industries, particularly those heavily related to military supply such as the machine tool industry, were indeed influenced by wartime control. Under the wartime control regime, not only direct control and government intervention but also demand explosion and strong requests for product improvement influenced the industry, the latter particularly resulting in rapid growth of incumbent firms and new entrants. As we saw in Part I, the impact of direct government intervention was limited in the number of companies, in the scope of actual intervention, and in the length of the period of strong intervention. The issue here though is the degree and areas of influence. Admittedly, during the immediate postwar period the machine tool industry did suffer from a huge imbalance in supply and demand due to its war-induced expansion of capacity and in machine tool stockpiles, together with drastically decreased demand due to the disappearance of military buyers. Although miserably depressed, the market dominated the postwar Japanese economy, and only those firms best suited to market conditions could have survived.

However, I do not agree with Okazaki and Okuno-Fujiwara (1999: p.8) and Okazaki (1999: p.117) that the wartime controls resulted in an economy where shareholders have 'very little influence … in corporate management.' Because of those controls, they reason, 'Both the power and role of shareholders were reduced, the status of management and employees rose, and main banks (and in the capacity as capital providers, loan consortia) replaced the leading shareholders as monitors.'

Observers routinely argue that the ownership of Japanese firms is dominated by 'friendly' (or 'stable') shareholders who voluntarily choose to be friendly to the current management and do not force managers to promote shareholder welfare. In fact, friendly shareholders have all the rights of any other shareholder, and – while agency slack is not zero – Japanese managers do work to promote shareholder welfare. Indeed, 'friendly' shareholders are friendly precisely because incumbent managers generally look after their interests (Miwa 1996a: ch. 11). Although some observers suggest that the 'characteristic feature' of Japanese firms, particularly the roles and rights of shareholders, differs greatly from that of foreign firms, particularly US firms, others disagree. Clark (1985: p.56), for instance, reasons that even in the West, 'to an experienced corporate lawyer who has studied primary legal materials, the assertion that corporate managers are agents of investors, whether debtholders or stockholders, will seem odd and loose.'

Basic logic suggests that investors would not continue to buy stock in firms that disregarded their welfare. If greater ownership interests could increase their returns, they would buy bigger stakes. Neither institutions nor budgets constrain their optimizing behavior. Where for fifty years scholars had claimed that the dispersed shareholdings in large US firms allowed managers to ignore shareholder welfare, Harold Demsetz and Kenneth Lehn (1985) found the claim implausible on its face. Firms that raise their funds on competitive capital markets should choose ownership patterns close to their firm-specific optimum or die. If so, Demsetz and Lehn continued, then any attempt to regress shareholders returns on ownership structure will yield insignificant results. And so they found. The Demsetz–Lehn logic applies straightforwardly to board composition. Miwa and Ramseyer (2003a) found that even in Japan in the 1950s firms chose ownership patterns close to their firm-specific optimum, and also (2002f), focusing on outside director appointments, that in the 1980s and 1990s Japanese firms chose board composition levels close to their firm-specific optimum.

To be sure, under the wartime regime a munitions company was required to appoint 'a responsible person' who answered to the government and who could not be dismissed without government approval (although the government could dismiss him). However, neither the military authorities nor the Munitions Ministry could have contributed much to increasing production, as neither had serious production management capabilities (for that matter, if government officials could have improved company performance, the socialist economies would not have collapsed). Even if such intervention had been potentially effective in Japan, the wartime controls were not in place long enough to have changed fundamentally the firms involved, and they would have lost effectiveness when the government lost the authority on which it had been able to rest its power.

2.3.8   The history of the MIPA: the Machinery Industries Promotion Corporation plan

The death of the Machinery Industries Promotion Corporation plan

The MIPA draft was prepared in great haste following the failure of the Machinery Industries Promotion Corporation plan. Both the ruling party and the opposition evaluated the draft MIPA as being much weaker and of far less potential effect than the corporation plan. As a result, many contemporaries doubted that it would have much effect (MITI 1990: p.569).

MITI went to great lengths to have the corporation plan enacted. For instance, the Machinery Section of the Industrial Rationalization Council, at its fourth meeting on 19 December 1955, formally resolved that its 'adoption was the most effective and appropriate measure' available. The Federation of Machinery Producers in Japan, which also enthusiastically promoted the enactment of the plan, appealed directly to the finance minister and the MITI minister. Despite these efforts, however, at the sixth meeting of the Machinery Section on 30 January 1956, the Machinery Industries Promotion Corporation plan was finally abandoned.

It was following this abandonment that the Heavy Industries Bureau prepared 'An Outline of the MIPA' on 20 February. The MIPA Bill was presented to the Machinery Section promptly on 29 February. On 2 March, the cabinet decided to present this bill to the Diet, and this occurred on 6 March. The bill was passed in both Houses unanimously and took effect on 15 June (MITI 1990: pp.565–70). The clear identification of the causes of failure of the corporation plan, and of the differences between the plan and the MIPA, tells us much about the nature, role, and limitations of the MIPA and related policies.

The corporation's objective

In describing its proposed machinery industries promotion in 1955, the Heavy Industries Bureau wrote that the corporation's objective was to 'promote the modernization of old and obsolete production equipment, to improve the quality of machinery products, to reduce production cost, and to promote the modernization of the production structure in the machinery industries.' The Machinery Section, which had been newly organized under the Industrial Rationalization Council, discussed the corporation plan four times. They concluded that it 'should be adopted and accorded the status of a highly desirable and appropriate measure, and hence be implemented with vigor.' The corporation was to be a government-funded organization with first-year working capital of ¥3.4 billion. These funds would be allocated from a number of sources, including the general budget and from rental revenue that the government would earn from machines that the corporation would rent to private firms.

The first order of business for the corporation was to be the selection and purchase of machine models approved by the Machinery Industries Promotion Council (tentative title), which were then to be lent to applicants under the modernization plans. The objective of these operations was to drastically reduce the interest payments and tax burden of enterprises by allocating them machines to rent. This 'big favor' to enterprises was designed 'to accelerate the modernization process by alleviating burdens associated with enterprises facing difficulty in raising finance for their own allotment.'

The second order of business for the corporation was to be the scrapping of 'old or obsolete equipment.' This scrapping program was intended to be effected by collecting old equipment from enterprises and replacing it with new rented machinery from the corporation. The corporation was then to sell the old machinery to 'other enterprises of a lower class' or simply to scrap it. Initial plans projected the scrapping of old equipment to the tune of 1.5 times the aggregate weight of the new modernized machinery allocated to enterprises. Finally, the third order of business for the corporation was to be the promotion of domestic production of machinery. The corporation was to bear part of the 'risk' associated with the production of machines domestically by undertaking to buy all domestically produced machines for one year. The operations of the corporation were to be centered on eighteen industries whose performance was judged to be seriously affected by 'old or obsolete equipment' (MITI 1990: pp.561–3). There is a striking similarity between industries intended to be the subject of policy under the corporation plan and those under the MIPA.

The corporation plan versus the MIPA

If one compares the corporation plan with the MIPA, the primary differences between the two lie in the following areas: (1) the scale of and methods by which finance was provided (or planned to be provided) to subject enterprises; (2) the decision to lend machines already selected and purchased by the corporation instead of simply lending part of the purchase cost to the firms and leaving them to purchase machines individually; (3) the magnitude of preferential treatment that was (or was planned to be) provided to enterprises; and (4) the industries and enterprises covered under the two regimes. The MIPA was established in circumstances where the corporation plan had been promoted enthusiastically by MITI, the Industrial Rationalization Council, and the industries concerned. Therefore there was almost no alternative other than to alter the MIPA to at least in some ways accord with the regime proposed under the popular corporation plan.

One of the reasons for the abandonment of the corporation plan is as follows:

> At the stage of ironing out budgetary details, the Corporation Plan was discussed in detail. Details of the plan that received particular attention were (1) whether a new independent organ such as the Corporation should be established; (2) whether existing financial institutions would be able to fulfil the same objective and hence render the Corporation unnecessary; (3) whether investment through the Corporation would be appropriate, particularly from the point of fairness; (4) whether investment through the Corporation would not be too 'loose.' In the end, the harsh situation of the national budget received much emphasis and the Corporation Plan was not adopted.[77]
>
> (MITI 1990: p.565)

By 'harsh situation of the national budget,' the quotation refers to the fact that funds could not be secured from the General Account in the budget. It was thought necessary to establish the corporation through public expenditure due to the deep-rooted view that loans through the then-existing long-term credit banks or government-affiliated financial institutions like the JDB would be insufficient. Therefore, when one compares this view with financing measures later adopted under the MIPA, one realizes that the fundamental and core objective of the corporation plan was not mirrored in the MIPA.

The MIPA was finally adopted, but...

MITI's evaluation of the situation under the MIPA at that time was as follows:

> Although the strict lending requirements that accompanied JDB loans were drastically eased, the very fact that modernization was being implemented through JDB loans and therefore inevitably being subjected to lending standards and finance examinations, inhibited the effectiveness of the modernization process. Further, individual enterprises have been forced to bear the risks associated with the modernization program in the form of loans. Accordingly, when compared with the corporation plan, which intended to promote drastic modernization through actively overcoming this difficulty by adopting the measure of lending machines, nobody can deny that the policies under the Act are inferior both in scale and effect speed for realizing equipment modernization.

Moreover, under the MIPA regime MITI had initially planned to secure a total of ¥10 billion worth of loan funds over three years, ¥3 billion of which was to be spent in the first year. The reality, though, was that the total budget for loans during FY1956 (the first year) was merely ¥1.5 billion, and the interest rate on these ten-year loans was 6.5 percent per annum (MITI 1990: pp.564–7).

The following points were raised during discussions in the Machinery Section of the Industrial Rationalization Council and very likely influenced the above conclusion:

1   The policy objective was identified as the promotion of the rationalization of the machinery industries, including the automobile and the electrical machinery industries, and also enhancing the international competitiveness of these industries. Toward that end, it was thought desirable to promote and support the best factories in these industries. The lack of measures oriented toward small businesses and the consequent problem of unemployment were raised in response to these initial policy proposals.

2   Many argued that the policy objectives could be achieved by using existing financial institutions, pointing out that existing government-affiliated financial institutions were suited to tasks such as these.

3   There was strong criticism that the MITI's intended promotion policies were unfair, arguing that enterprises borrowing machines from the corporation would receive excessive preferential treatment.

Shifting our attention now to the MIPA, it was passed with the unanimous support of the Diet after the failure of the corporation plan. Both the ruling party and the opposition parties evaluated the Act as potentially much weaker and less effective than the corporation plan, pointing to three areas of weakness: the insufficiency of funding; the allocation of investment risk to individual enterprises; and the process of examination necessary for financial approval (MITI 1990: p.569). Debate in the Diet 'repeatedly centered upon how the Act would be disadvantageous to small businesses not designated under the Act,' and the Upper House made an additional resolution demanding that special consideration be paid to 'the possible effects on competitiveness of small business not designated.' During the debates, Heavy Industries Bureau Chief Suzuki went to great lengths to explain that 'the MIPA was in essence simply a small business policy along the traditional line.' Suzuki replaced the reference to the best plants with 'average-sized small business' and 'medium-sized machinery plants' (*ibid.*: p.570). As mentioned above, the selection of enterprises to be policy objects was severely inhibited by the restrictions associated with the JDB budget for loans.

2.3.9   Policy enforcement under the MIPA:
(1) role of industry associations

Room for industry associations to undertake crucial roles in policy implementation

As explained in Section 2.2.2, each industry designated under the MIPA was required to prepare and submit a basic plan for rationalization to the Machinery Industry Council, which discussed and authorized such plans. The implementation plan for each year was determined on the basis of these basic plans, and these plans then served as the basis upon which MITI made recommendations for JDB loans for rationalization of equipment at special rates.

A basic plan was required to detail four points (section 2–2): (1) the objectives for rationalization as of the end of FY1960 concerning the performance, quality, and production costs of the designated machines; (2) matters concerning the equipment necessary to achieve rationalization, such as the kinds of equipment to be introduced and the finance required to do this; (3) matters concerning the management of the equipment needed for rationalization, such as equipment to be disposed of by scrapping, diversion, or other methods, and the methods of disposal; and (4) other important matters concerning rationalization, such as advances in production technology and improvements in efficiency.

As mentioned above, the government sections in charge of the MIPA were understaffed. The Industrial Machinery Section, for instance, had taken charge of at least nine MIPA industries at the start in 1956. If we relate this workload to the average of seventeen people in each government section, then even if we generously assume that all section personnel were fully engaged in MIPA-related business, less than two people were on average allocated to each industry. This situation left ample room for industry associations to undertake crucial roles.

Cases from the tool and die industry and the gear industry

The precise definition of 'industry associations' and 'industry' is not always clear. It is not always true that any particular enterprise belongs only to one industry and one industry association. The position and role of the associations in each industry differed greatly and changed over time. The Machinery Industries Council organized within itself a section to correspond to each designated industry. Such sections were to serve as advisory organs, and they almost completely determined the details of enforcement programs and rules.

In the tool and die industry, for instance, where no industry association had ever existed before the commencement of the MIPA in June 1956, major producers in Tokyo, Nagoya, and Osaka had already begun discussions regarding the establishment of an industry association prior to the commencement of the

Act. In March 1956, for example, industry players organized the First Round-Table Conference to discuss the modernization and rationalization of the precision tool and die industry. These discussions led to the birth of the Tool and Die Round-Table Conference, which was a voluntary association of private companies. This conference was designed to prepare an indigenous promotion program for the industry. In fact, a variety of scholars,[78] users, and industry representatives participated in the operations of the Tool and Die Section of the Machinery Industries Council. Consequently, Yonekura (1993: pp.263–4) argues that ' "the Basic Rationalization Plans for Tool and Die Production" were completed as the result of the general will of producers, scholars, and users, who discussed technology, production plans, and appropriate management styles, and also clarified the standards by which objects would be selected under the MIPA.'

The gear industry was required to define the precision standards for gears as a prerequisite to designation under the MIPA. To this end, the All Japan Gear Industry Association, which was established in 1948, organized a technology committee with the commencement of the Act. The outline of the basic rationalization plan for the gear industry was approved in October 1956, and the Japan Gear Industry Association was established in June 1958 as a corporation with seventy-four members.[79]

Roles played by industry associations

A basic rationalization plan was a general plan regarding the entire industry concerned, and it did not detail the investment plans or production plans of individual companies. Individual enterprises were instead to make their own plans by reference to the objectives and policy measures detailed in the basic rationalization plans. The rules for JDB special loans stipulated that special loans would be provided for projects that required funding to achieve the objectives detailed in the basic plans and for which the MITI minister recommended preferential treatment. Once the basic rationalization plan was approved, this became the foundation on which the rationalization enforcement plan for each year was determined and on which MITI made company recommendations to the JDB.[80]

It is quite common in Japan that industry associations play key roles in making and enforcing government policies for industries, and 'rationalization' policies provide a good example. In postwar Japan, policies for industries were determined and enforced placing heavy reliance upon close relations between the government and industry members, and these relations were achieved through industry associations. This is true not only of the manufacturing sector but also of non-manufacturing sectors (Miwa 1996a: part III, particularly ch. 8).

As shown in Part I, the same can be said regarding the prewar and the wartime periods. This is illustrated by the roles played in the machine tool industry by the PTCA, its predecessors the Japan Machine Tool Producers Industrial Union and the All Japan Machine Tool Industrial Union, and also the Machine Tool Producers Union. In the shipbuilding industry, the Shipbuilding Control Association, the Federation of Shipbuilders Union, and the Shipbuilders Federation similarly illustrate the process.

The Industrial Rationalization Movement, which began in the late 1920s,[81] was symbolized by the establishment of the Temporary Industrial Rationalization Agency in June 1930. One primary concern of this agency was the control of enterprises, particularly the issue of 'imposing appropriate control over small manufacturers.' The agency had six standing committees organized under it. One was the Control Committee, and its task was to research and collect information about the industry generally and individual companies in particular in order to determine which industries ought to be controlled and the appropriate mechanisms for their control. Here again, 'temporary committees were established in many industries, consisting primarily of industry members, in order to research and discuss concrete methods for improving control in each industry. The government organized these committees gradually, industry by industry, after determining whether a committee would be appropriate for any particular industry by focusing upon the attitudes of relevant industry enterprises and other matters concerning the industry' (MITI 1961: p.70). The government and individual companies 'strongly demanded the reinforcement of cartel control or cartel-like control with legal means.' This pressured the Control Committee to adopt the 'Resolution concerning Legal Rules on Company Controls' in December 1930. Along a similar line, the government established the Act concerning the Control of Key Industries, promulgated on 1 April 1931 (MITI 1985a: pp.136–7).

Industry associations undertook crucial roles

The basic rationalization plan was a creature prepared by the relevant section of the Machinery Industries Council in cooperation with representatives from every corner of the industry. The sections of the Machinery Industries Council consisted of many industry players, and the basic rationalization plan was by nature the result of compromise between these players. Without a government (or other authority) with coercive power, policies determined on the basis of such a plan could never have been effective in achieving industrial rationalization or industry reorganization if those policies stressed the role of the technologically most advanced firms in the industry.

Also, as mentioned above, even in the coal-mining and steel industries, which were the principal objects of industrial rationalization policy, overcoming the principle of equality in the rationing of resources was a complex and never-ending issue. Throughout the period of the First and Second MIPAs, the lack of a definite policy vision was the subject of criticisms that the Act was used only where convenient; that had long been pointed out as a basic defect of the Act.

The effectiveness of incentives provided under the Act varied greatly both across industries and enterprises and over time. This makes evaluation very difficult. Here I simply introduce the case of the bearing industry and suggest that the incentives provided under the Act were not decisively important and further that recipient companies did not attach top priority to these incentives. In September 1956 the Bearing Section of the Machinery Industries Council started preparing a basic rationalization plan in accordance with the MIPA, aiming to complete it by 1960. However, agreement could not be reached on the details of this plan. Prior to the completion of the basic plan the economy entered a boom, and companies launched huge programs of investment and equipment based on their own plans, which generally followed the MITI's outline for rationalization. It was only after these developments that the basic rationalization plan, after discussions at the Bearing Section, was made public by the MITI minister on 20 November 1959.[82]

2.3.10   Policy enforcement under the MIPA: (2) company recommendations by MITI and JDB loans

Individual companies made decisions regarding their own investment and production plans, making general reference to the objectives and policy measures detailed in the basic rationalization plan for their industry. Individual companies would apply to the MITI minister for recommendation for special loans from the JDB. The MITI minister determined the rationalization enforcement programs each year upon the basic rationalization plan and recommended companies to the JDB for special loans.

Our examination centers on four points here:

1   What were the criteria upon which the MITI recommended an enterprise for special loans?
2   Besides these publicized criteria, was there room for the use of discretion when making recommendations?
3   What proportions of projects recommended were actually adopted by the JDB and received special loans?
4   If the JDB did not adopt all the projects recommended, which projects did the JDB actually select and upon what criteria were these selections made?

Although our examination here suffers from a serious lack of information regarding all these issues, the information that I will introduce below is sufficient to draw a conclusion.

We find what we predict

As shown above, policies for promoting machinery industries under the MIPA were badly inhibited due to a stated limit placed on funding. Therefore the government had to select the industries from among those designated as policy objects to receive finite funding grants. The limit on the total amount of funding available accordingly meant that there was also a funding quota allocated to each industry. The MITI made recommendations for funding within this framework. Loans were provided at a special rate, which was lower than the market rate. Therefore it was only natural that every company planning investment in equipment hoped to acquire as much funding via JDB loans as possible. This resulted in huge excess demand for JDB loans. The economic boom, which operated to accelerate a company's investment plans, only added to the demand for JDB loans.

On the other hand, as a result of circumstances leading up to the Act, it was impossible to place any emphasis on the most powerful or technologically advanced companies, typically big companies, in the basic rationalization plans. Furthermore, the policy enforcement scheme relied heavily on close relations between industry associations and the government, and this did not give the MITI any breathing space to pursue other selection criteria and other objectives.

Consequently, it was well understood that an application for a JDB loan to the MITI might well not be adopted, and further that even a MITI recommendation would not necessarily lead to funding being granted, despite the satisfaction of the explicit selection criteria. Furthermore, it was necessary for the selection criteria, which were inevitably revealed in the resultant allocations of funding, whatever they were, to portray an appearance of impartiality and fairness so as to satisfy applicant enterprises. That is, funding allocations could not appear to be ill-balanced or favoring the big or most advanced firms.

For comparison, Table 2.2 lists separately the total amount of designated investment in equipment (that is, those projects detailed in the basic rationalization plan as targets for machinery investment funding and so eligible for JDB loans), the total amount of funding applied for, the total amount of funding recommended by the MITI, the total loans actually made, and a variety of relevant ratios for each year between FY1956 and FY1963. The average ratio of funding applied for to total eligible investment projects under the First Act was 67.5 percent. The average ratio of funding recommended to funding applied for was 75.2 percent. The average ratio of funding granted to funding recommended was 79.9 percent. Finally, therefore, the average ratio of funding granted to total eligible investment was 40.6 percent.

Why were the remaining 59.4 percent of total eligible investment projects excluded from such an advantageous financing opportunity? The ratio of the amount of funding granted to the amount of funding recommended represents the highest ratio. However, this fact does not suggest that the MITI played a decisive role in selecting objects for funding and that the JDB would automatically

Table 2.2 Policy loans under the MIPA: JDB loans (million yen)

	[1]	[2]	[3]	[4]	[A]	[B]	[C]	[D]	[E]	B/A(%)	C/(%)B	D/C(%)	E/D(%)	E/A(%)
The First MIPA	1956,1957	17	14	142	12,361	9,469	8,468	6,764	4,812	76.6	89.4	79.9	71.1	38.9
	1958	22	12	54	3,985	3,094	1,595	1,320	1,185	77.6	51.6	82.8	89.8	29.7
	1959	22	17	113	11,058	8,045	4,635	3,465	3,221	72.8	57.6	74.8	93.0	29.1
	1960	22	19	113	9,774	7,050	3,979	2,494	2,006	72.1	56.4	62.7	80.4	20.5
	1956–1960			422	37,178	27,658	18,677	14,043	11,224	74.4	67.5	75.2	79.9	30.2
The Second MIPA	1961	40	39	206	45,258	30,906	18,776	9,377	7,392	68.3	60.8	49.9	78.8	16.3
	1962	40	39	153	30,277	22,401	12,680	7,562	6,730	72.8	57.5	59.6	89.0	22.2
	1963	40	39	100	24,081	17,664	9,758	7,476	7,495	73.4	55.2	76.6	100.3	31.1
	1961–1963			459	99,616	70,611	41,214	24,415	21,617	70.9	58.4	59.2	88.5	21.7

Source: Yonekura (1965a: p. 36).

Note: [1] Fiscal year of recommendation; [2] number of industries designated; [3] number of industries recommended; [4] number of projects recommended; [A] total amount of designated projects; [B] total amount of designated equipment investment; [C] total amount of funding applied for; [D] total amount of funding recommended by MITI; [E] total loans actually made.

accept these selections. This is because there were always close relations and exchanges of information between the parties concerned, such as the MITI, the JDB, industry associations, and individual companies.

No information is available to conclude a detailed study of each company's decision-making process regarding making an application for funding so as to reveal reactions and behavior of eligible enterprises to these government funding policy measures. However, one simple observation is that the ratio of the amount of funding granted to the amount of eligible investment was relatively high during the first year but began to decrease gradually in following years. One plausible explanation for this trend may be as follows. After funding allocation during the first year of the scheme, it became apparent not only that an application would not always be recommended but also that a recommended project would not always receive funding. At the same time, individual companies learned much about the process of application for JDB funding from their own experiences and observations gained from going through the application process.[83] Accordingly, companies revised their strategies in order to be more competitive in following years.

The next description, from *35 Years of Aisan Industries Co.*, is a case in which, undeterred by two straight years of failure, a company continued to apply for and finally acquired JDB funding. Many others must have diverted their endeavors to securing funding elsewhere or to other areas of business activity.

> We commenced our efforts to acquire special funding for rationalization by submitting filled questionnaires to the Motor Vehicle Section of the Heavy Industries Bureau of MITI. We collected materials in order to prepare our rationalization plan in accordance with the Basic Rationalization Plan of the Auto Parts Manufacturing Industry, which was published in February 1957. … We applied for special funding in both FY1957 and FY1958, but were unsuccessful. Finally in FY1959 we gained recommendation from MITI as an auto parts manufacturer under the MIPA for special funding from the JDB.
>
> (Aisan kogyo 1973: pp.59–60)

Explanation by the MITI

The process of selection adopted by the MITI when deciding which enterprises to recommend for special funding was detailed as follows:

> There are two stages involved in the selection of excellent plants under the basic rationalization plan. These stages are a technical examination by the Heavy Industries Bureau of MITI and a finance-based examination by the JDB. Technical examinations were conducted by the Association for Machinery Advancement, which was especially established to implement the MIPA. Technical examinations were conducted primarily by officials and engineers

from the section in charge, and were headed by an assistant section chief. Also, persons responsible for management and technology in the applicant enterprise were interviewed and various materials were required to be submitted by applicants. The section in charge based its selections upon materials and information submitted to it and the results of interviews conducted. The section placed particular focus upon the technological prowess of the enterprise, particularly the capability and quality of engineers and management. What was closely examined in selecting machines to be introduced was the extent to which such introduction could potentially reduce labor-hours and also the ratio of rejected articles, and further improve the accuracy of finishing. The selection of excellent plants was relatively easy in industries which exhibited a well-organized industry association. On the other hand, finance-based examinations conducted by the JDB placed emphasis upon the profitability and persuasiveness of demand forecasts and rationalization plans, and accordingly the capability of the enterprise to repay the loans.

(MITI 1990: p.576)

Our primary concern here is what the government could have possibly done to implement policy, and further the nature of the roles performed by industry associations and members in cooperating to achieve policy implementations. We must remember here that government sections in charge consisted of very few personnel, two or possibly four at most for each designated industry, even when assuming that all section personnel devote their entire energies to implementing policy under the Act. For three reasons, it is implausible to think that the MITI enforced policies to restructure the industrial order beyond the extent of the basic rationalization plans.

1   The policies had to be adopted and supported by the majority of industry members in order to have any real effect.
2   The policies were aimed primarily at small businesses and actively avoided allocating any sizeable preferences to the more technologically adept and powerful companies.
3   As shown above, throughout the decade observers routinely complained that the program lacked 'any definite long-term vision,' and accordingly it has to be said that 'the MIPA was used only when convenient' (Yonekura 1965b: p.20).[84]

2.3.11   Policy enforcement under the MIPA: (3) loans by the JDB

JDB loans under the MIPA

The JDB staff, operating under the bank's own constraints, 'made determinations regarding loans and guarantees completely by themselves. Accordingly, it was left to the JDB alone to determine matters such as the identity of borrowers, purposes to which funding would be allocated, the amounts of loans and guarantees, and the terms of loans and guarantees. ... Under the JDB Act and the JDB constitution, the JDB was permitted to provide loans and guarantees only in circumstances where repayment of funds borrowed was certain.[85] Consequently, the JDB adopted, and was required to adopt, a policy of fully examining both the financial situation of each applicant and the technological aspects of projects of the subject of funding applications, and then made loans and guarantees only to those enterprises which were certain not to default' (JDB 1963: pp.4–5).

With regard to loans under the MIPA, on 3 March 1956 'MITI and the Ministry of Finance reached an agreement concerning machinery loans to designated enterprises. The agreement was such that the total budget for loans for FY1956 would be ¥1.5 billion, the lending rate 6.5 percent per annum and term of loans ten years. Further, the agreement stipulated that loans could cover the entire purchasing cost of machinery and that the requirement of security could be waived.' The JDB, which took complete charge of loans, 'prepared an "Outline for Dealing with Loans to Designated Machinery Industries" in August 1956. The Outline accorded with the essence of the agreement reached between the two Ministries concerning the conditions under which funding would be provided, that is the total budget, interest rates and loan terms. ... With the organizational reforms conducted in May 1958, a division called the Third Business Division was established within the JDB to deal exclusively with designated machinery loans' (*ibid.*: p.296).

Focus of investigation

Our investigation here focuses upon four points:

1   Was the JDB expected to make active efforts toward the selection of technologically advanced firms for special funding, and accordingly did it make active efforts to promote the 'restructuring of the industrial order in line with a concrete long-term vision'?
2   If the JDB was expected to make such efforts, was it plausible for the bank to achieve these goals, given the numerous institutional constraints under which it was placed?
3   Assuming that it was possible to expect this of the JDB, did the bank possess sufficient competence concerning these tasks?
4   Did the bank actually make any net contributions to policy goals?

It is not easy to provide answers to any of these issues. However, it is clear that if the conclusions regarding the first two issues are negative, then the only plausible conclusion is that the JBD could not develop or acquire the relevant competence, meaning that the bank was incompetent and thus made little or no contribution.

The JDB's competence, behavior, and actual contribution

After the budget concerning the fiscal investment loan program was approved, the Economic Planning Agency prepared an annual 'Basic Enforcement Policy concerning the Investment of Government Funds to the Industry,' which required cabinet approval. However, this document includes only very general references to political concerns that were judged worthy of consideration when making loans from government-affiliated financial institutions, including the JDB. In accordance with this statement of basic policy, the finance minister then determined annual funding plans for government-affiliated financial institutions such as the JDB. These funding plans would determine the allocation of loans from government financial institutions among designated industries by broad industry categories. The finance minister was also authorized to conduct inquiries regarding reports and examinations made under the JDB Act.

Under these circumstances, coupled with the requirements in the constitution of the JDB concerning the precautions that the bank must take to ensure repayment of loans, the obvious conclusions for the first two issues above are both negative. This in turn leads us to conclude that the competence that the bank was expected to develop and possess was not what would make an active contribution to 'industrial order restructuring in line with a concrete long-term vision.' Rather, the competence expected of the bank was that of judging whether applicants for funding could foreseeably repay their loans.

The MIPA by itself failed to embody the policy goal of 'industrial order restructuring in line with a concrete long-term vision' and accordingly the basic rationalization plans prepared in each industry under the Act contained no such visions. What is more to the point, the parties directly involved in promoting policies under the Act, including the MITI and designated industries, failed to reach agreement on this point and failed to acquire wide public support for this policy goal. It is therefore implausible to conclude that the JDB, which operated under much stricter institutional constraints and possessed a much weaker battery of incentives than the MITI, could have developed the relevant competence to contribute to the relevant policy goals.

JDB loans to the machinery industries

Since the establishment of the JDB in 1951, loans through the bank were allocated predominantly to a small number of 'key industries.' Outstanding loans in FY1956 totaled ¥383.5 billion, and three industries accounted for 92.3 percent of this figure. These three industries and their funding allocations were 52.9 percent for the electricity industry, 31.9 percent for the shipping industry, and 7.5 percent for the coal-mining industry. Manufacturing industry accounted for a mere 5.9 percent, 2.2 percent of which went to the steel industry, 1.0 percent to the chemical industry, 0.9 percent to the textile industry, and 0.7 percent to the transportation equipment industry. The machinery industries were allocated only one-tenth of the total allocated to the chemical industry, which was 0.1 percent of total funding (JDB 1963: materials, pp.24–5).

The JDB's constitutional requirement that loans and guarantees be very safe meant that the bank primarily developed competence in the capacity to judge the degree of risk involved in the loans. However, what we can conclude from this and from the fact that extremely little money was allocated to the machinery industries is that at least in the earliest stages of the MIPA, the JDB must have had close to zero competence in monitoring risk in the machinery industries. Accordingly, the passage quoted above ('With the organizational reform in May 1958, a division called the Third Business Division was established within the JDB to deal exclusively with designated machinery loans') is an accurate description of the JDB's organizational response.

The following statement from Yonekura (1965a: p.36) also illustrates this point. Recall that the First MIPA started in 1956.

> The JDB acquired knowledge and expertise regarding the machinery indus-
> tries from five years' experience in providing funding to these industries
> under the First MIPA. The Bank had established an internal system for
> dealing especially with funding applications from machinery industries.
> Further, the Bank made active efforts to shorten the process of determina-
> tion concerning funding. It did this by participating in interviews of funding
> applicant enterprises conducted by the government, and by working to
> promote better mutual understanding between ministries concerned. Since
> 1962 the JDB had determined lending standards for designated machinery
> industries taking into consideration the finance-based concerns, and the Bank
> clearly declared the character of funding under these standards as policy
> funding, intending to increase the priority of loans. In FY1964, for instance,
> the Bank judged the urgency and appropriateness of applicant projects upon
> three standards, with which it intended to focus upon achieving the drastic
> reform and strengthening management of enterprises to make them respon-
> sive to an open economic system. These three standards upon which the Bank
> made funding decisions were (1) propensity for joint operations – to achieve
> the restructuring of production, (2) propensity to promote exports, and (3)
> technological development of applicant enterprises.

This quote is suggestive of three points:

1   It was only during the period of the Second MIPA that the JDB, having acquired a certain level of knowledge and expertise concerning the machinery industries, established an internal system to deal with these loans.

2   It was after the establishment of this internal system that the bank took part in government selection interviews and made efforts toward better mutual understanding.[86]

3   It was after FY1962 that the bank, having determined lending standards taking finance-based matters into consideration, clearly stamped the character of lending as policy lending. Before this, the bank's examination of enterprise funding applications was primarily finance-based.

The actual results of loan repayments were extremely good

The actual loan repayment rates were extremely good. At the end of November 1964, the number of outstanding JDB loans for designated machinery was 745, total value ¥22 billion. Only 'six projects (loans), that is less than 1 percent of the total, showed any instances of default in repayment, and these cases of default were due to business depression or difficulties in raising funds. When compared with other industries the object of JDB funding, including "key industries," the repayment record in this industry was one of the best' (Yonekura 1965a: p.38).

The final matter on which I wish to comment here is the special loan rate of 6.5 percent that applied to designated machinery funding under the First MIPA. First, 'the special rate of 6.5% was applied with few exceptions only to funding for key industries such as electricity, shipping, and so forth. A higher rate of 8.7% applied to funding directed to other industries. As at 31 March 1962, funding allocated at the rate of 6.5% accounted 87% of aggregate JDB funding, with almost all remaining funding being conducted at the higher rate of 8.7%' (JDB 1963: p.6). Therefore, although a special loan rate was applied to industries under the MIPA, this rate was not so low as to constitute extraordinarily preferential treatment. Second, under the Second MIPA it was not a special rate but the basic or standard JDB loan rate of 8.7 percent that was applied to funding allocated to designated machinery industries (Yonekura 1965a: p.35). That is, after the Second Act, designated machinery industries were subject to the standard JDB loan rate, which was close to the market interest rate.

2.3.12   Policy enforcement under the MIPA: (4) the pump-priming effect of JDB loans

Most literature emphasizes the positive pump-priming effect of JDB loans under the MIPA. Examples of such literature follow, namely Industrial Structure Investigation Group (1965: pp.149–72), Sugiyama (1966b: p.10), MITI (1990: p.579), Hashimoto (1993: p.58), and Yonekura (1993: pp.274–5). However, none of these sources provides much logic or evidence. Instead, they leave the following questions unanswered: (1) What was the precise definition of the pump-priming effect? (2) What was the nature of the generating mechanism that the pump-priming effect apparently entails? (3) What is the evidence upon which this mechanism is judged to have been effective? (4) What was the scale of the effect?

I conclude below that the pump-priming effect, if it ever did actually exist, could not have been significant. I further conclude that JDB loans could have had no greater effect than to provide borrowers with a direct subsidy: (the difference between the policy loan rate and the market rate) × (loan value) × (loan term). It is another matter whether these measures had a significant impact on the equipment investment behavior of enterprises, how these measures affected the behavior of firms not receiving subsidies, including potential market entrants, and the net effect produced regarding particular industries and the overall Japanese economy. These questions require further careful investigation.

The pump-priming effect of JDB loans

It is necessary to roughly grasp the argument that emphasizes the benefits of the pump-priming effect of JDB loans. I therefore introduce here the brief explanation that appears in MITI (1990: p.579).

The pump-priming effect is 'the effect obtained by investing public funds to improve the financial status of borrowing firms to increase the maximum sum that can be borrowed beyond any corresponding credit limit applied by private financial institutions.' In addition to reducing the debt burdens of enterprises by providing long-term credit at below market rate, the above-mentioned two-stage examination was of great benefit to private financial institutions. That is, this examination process not only provided a substitute for those of private banks, cutting their examination costs virtually to zero, but also reduced their lending risk by concentrating their funding on safe projects approved by the JDB examination. This pump-priming effect enabled some enterprises to undertake investment in equipment by borrowing from private banks with which there had been no transaction history, or rather only limited transactions for operating funds. Moreover, in many cases it was a condition of JDB funding that borrowers would increase their capitalization. This provided an avenue by which managers could relatively easily persuade shareholders to accept proposals to increase capitalization.

The pump-priming effect of JDB loans could not have been significant

The two-stage examination process that accompanied JDB loans included a technical examination and a finance-based examination, as mentioned above. In reality, though, could this examination process and therefore JDB loans have actually generated the results that the pump-priming effect model suggests? We have already seen above that it was only about halfway through the period of the

Second MIPA that the JDB acquired detailed knowledge about the machinery industries. In addition, the examination process of the JDB focused primarily upon loan safety.[87] The JDB adopted the strict practice of 'taking security, be it real or personal or other property, and required guarantees for loans' (JDB 1963: materials, p.14).

It is important to realize that simply because the JDB judged an enterprise to be a good credit risk, it does not follow that this judgement necessarily reduced the lending risks of private financial institutions. For example, if the JDB takes a security interest in the assets of a borrower, the risk associated with the loans of other lenders must correspondingly increase. It is accordingly implausible to argue that the safety-first doctrine that was adopted by the JDB in funding allocation could have 'cut the examination costs of other lenders virtually to zero.'

Moreover, JDB examinations, focusing as they did upon credit risk, could not have provided any useful information regarding the future growth potential or long-term profitability of borrowers. Furthermore, I can find no grounds to believe that JDB loans promoted the cooperation of shareholders in order to increase the capitalization of borrowing institutions. Prior to any JDB funding decision, a funding applicant and the JDB must have exchanged detailed information and carefully discussed whether the bank should require an increase in capitalization as a condition of making a loan. Applicants pessimistic about the feasibility of shareholders agreeing to increases in capitalization must have firmly resisted JDB proposals to place this condition on funding. Some enterprises must have abandoned applications for funding to avoid this condition, expecting to gain funding from future applications to the JDB. Consequently, it is not at all strange to find that in most cases in which a capitalization increase was stipulated as a condition of funding, capitalization increases were realized. This most likely simply reflects the situation that only those enterprises that could realize capitalization increases continued funding applications and obtained funding from the JDB.

During FY1956–FY1960 (the period of the First MIPA), JDB funds financed 30 percent of the total equipment investment eligible for JDB loans. As for the remaining sources of funds for investment in equipment, 45 percent was self-financed, and 25 percent was borrowed from financial institutions other than the JDB. These institutions were other government-affiliated financial institutions like the Small Business Finance Corporation and private, particularly long-term credit institutions, like long-term credit banks, trust banks, and insurance companies. The primary focus of the MIPA was generally placed upon basic machinery and uniform components, and JDB loans under the Act had an even stronger focus upon these sectors. Of these two broad categories, the basic machinery sector received the larger allocation of JDB funding. With regard to the sources of finance for investment in basic machinery, 32 percent originated from the JDB, and 51 percent was self-financed, which left only 17 percent to be found from other sources. Therefore, in the case of investment in basic machinery, with the percentage of funding from private financial institutions alleged to be induced or primed by the JDB funding scheme so small, the pump-priming effect of JDB loans must also have been insignificant (*ibid.*: p.298).

More basically, a borrower that was safe enough to be able to offer security and satisfy the conditions of JDB funding was probably a good enough credit risk to obtain funding from private financial institutions anyway. Such borrowers could borrow from private financial institutions as well as the JDB and conduct profitable investment projects whose expected rate of return would cover the cost. However, as we know from the figures above, JDB borrowers financed only part of their investment projects with JDB funding. This means that even when the subsidies reduced the average funding cost by 1 percent, for instance, they did not influence the borrower's marginal cost and therefore left the size of investment unaffected.

Moreover, borrowers usually made investments other than those financed by JDB loans, and any impact of reductions in average finance costs in one area were inevitably spread over the entire investment portfolio. To provide some idea of the insignificant effect that JDB funding must have had, the percentage of total investment in equipment financed by JDB loans in the auto parts industry during the periods of the three MIPAs, that is FY1956–FY1960, FY1961–FY1965, and FY1966–FY1970, was 2.2 percent, 4.8 percent, and 2.1 percent, respectively (average, 2.7 percent). In the machine tool industry, the corresponding figures were 14.7, 5.5, and 0.5 percent, respectively (average, 3.6 percent) (JDB 1976: p.460).

We have also to consider the following issues, remembering that conclusions regarding them will depend on environmental factors, particularly the competitive conditions of markets to which enterprises supplied products. First, did the MIPA subsidies supplied to borrowers actually improve the financial status of borrowers by reducing their debt burdens? Second, if so, to what extent were those debt burdens reduced? The MIPA and related policies were primarily directed at those sectors dominated by small businesses, and the policies and therefore the allocation of loans among both industries and enterprises were implemented indiscriminately as 'a traditional small business policy.' Thus most of the benefits of subsidies granted under the MIPA, as a result of fierce competition between firms receiving subsidies, must have ended up in the pockets of users and consumers of their products.

The pump-priming effect model
is similar to the main bank monitoring model

Many observers bring to these issues a sense that Japanese finance follows the main bank (monitoring) theory articulated by Okazaki and Okuno-Fujiwara (1999: p.10) and others. These writers insist that in contemporary Japan bank monitoring influences the management of individual firms, and that banks have 'high monitoring capability and also the efficient monitoring mechanism of the main bank system.' The pump-priming effect and the main bank monitoring models have similar academic pedigrees and in many ways reinforce each other.

Okazaki and Okuno-Fujiwara refer to Ueda (1999) and suggest that Ueda shares their view. They suggest that Ueda argues that the high monitoring capability of contemporary Japanese banks owes much to the monitoring skills developed and improved in the prewar period by the Industrial Bank of Japan (IBJ) and to the diffusion of these monitoring skills to other, particularly government-affiliated, financial institutions during and after the war. If true, the claim tracks the JDB pump-priming argument. Unfortunately, however, the basic assumption of this argument, that the prewar IBJ developed high monitoring skills, is untrue (Miwa and Ramseyer 2000b).

Do Japanese banks – banks that now suffer from a such a flood of bad loans and non-performing loans that they threaten the very existence of the Japanese financial system – possess 'high monitoring capability'? Did they ever possess it? Since the financial crisis in the 1920s, Japanese banks have adopted the general practice of demanding security interests and guarantees before making long-term loans or purchasing corporate bonds. This caused a shift in the focus of bank examinations and monitoring away from examining the profitability and management of the proposed project to examining the value and degree of risk associated with collateral and the guarantors stipulated. At least until very recently, there has been no change in this basic business strategy. During the second half of the 1980s in Japan, most loan collateral (and also in substance the subject of guarantees) was land. With the collapse in real estate prices since 1990, Japanese banks have been flooded with bad loans (Miwa 1996a: pp.120–2; Miwa and Ramseyer 2003f).

This misunderstanding about Japanese bank lending policy has led to misunderstanding about the role of the JDB as well. It has led observers to overstate both the monitoring capability of the JDB and the pump-priming effect of their loans. The same is true of the main bank argument. In essence, observers argue that institutions like the government and the main banks have predetermined roles as the leaders of relevant economic agents (like other lenders), select the borrowers to favor, and then monitor those borrowers. They further claim that this delegated arrangement substitutes for and is more economic than the investment of resources to these ends by the individual agents (lenders) involved. However, this argument contradicts a standard common-sense view that a decentralized market economy itself provides appropriate incentives for information-gathering activities and therefore selects better subjects for funding than the government or any main bank (particularly any main bank that enjoys a stable monopolistic position). Effectively, these pump-priming and main bank theories simply assume that governments and large banks have the ability to beat the market in predicting company performance.

Okazaki and Okuno-Fujiwara (1999: p.11) also argue that a variety of schemes for information collection and exchange, such as government councils, unofficial research meetings, and private networks, have worked well in Japan. They particularly emphasize the role of industrial policy as a means of collecting and exchanging information regarding the '"discovery" of an industry for development, using forecasts of future trends in technology and demand.' In the process, they miss the possibility that the rational response of any participant is simply to free-ride. It is against the best interest of any firm with valuable relevant information to share that information. For our purposes, note simply that nobody has ever officially documented the claims, particularly in the postwar Japanese machinery industries.

The assumption that the Japanese government or main banks have such superior monitoring capability that they can beat the market is consistent with the common view that the Japanese economy and Japanese firms are somehow unique (for critical commentary, see Miwa 1996a; Miwa and Ramseyer 2001c). The same also applies to the pump-priming effect, 'signaling effect,' and 'cowbell effect' in small business policies, which are discussed later in this book. Most of these views simply 'interpret' and 'theoretically explain' stylized 'observations.' They lack careful and critical examination of whether the industrial policy or system actually worked effectively.

Although many observers argue that main banks rescue distressed firms, I have shown (Miwa 1996a) that those main banks that lend to firms experiencing financial trouble tend instead to withdraw from those firms. They do not function as the 'lender of the last resort' as some observers describe them. Rather than rescue, they run for cover. If this is true, then it is irrational for other lenders to delegate a monitoring function and costs to main banks. Even if the main bank possesses both high monitoring capability and more information than other banks, other firms will not rely on the main bank. On the other hand, this running-for-cover behavior is perfectly consistent with rational profit-maximizing behavior on the part of any bank (Miwa and Ramseyer 2001b, 2001c chs 5 and 6, 2002a, 2002d, 2004b).

2.3.13   Summary of Section 2.3

The conclusion of the discussion above can be summarized briefly. The core policy measures under the MIPA were loans at preferential rates through the JDB and the Small Business Finance Corporation. No other measures of any significance were actively adopted. Furthermore, these loans were not remarkably effective. This was because, judging from the scale of funding provided, the minimal difference between the interest rates of preferential MIPA funding and the market rate, and the indiscriminate manner in which the funding was allocated between borrowers, the policy measures did not enhance the circumstances of the affected firms much beyond normal market conditions. Many argue that the state's intervention in the industries designated under the MIPA, including the machine tool industry, played a critical role in promoting the development of those industries. They clearly overestimate this role.

The machinery industries designated under the MIPA, exemplified by the machine tool industry, did not satisfy the conditions necessary for effective policy measures. Even during wartime control, the government did not attempt to overcome the basic problem of acquiring detailed information concerning product ranges, the quality and performance of products, and the production costs for individual firms in the machine tool industry. Under the MIPA, this problem never even made it on to the MITI agenda.

Our conclusions regarding issues identified in the second step of investigating the effectiveness of policy (Section 2.3.1) are also clear. That is, when we address these issues in the light of policies for the machine tool industry under wartime control discussed in Part I and then in the light of policies under the MIPA, and we compare the results, we learn much about policies under the MIPA. The authority and power that the state enjoyed during the postwar period was far less significant than during wartime. The scope and force of government intervention in private business activities was reduced. Moreover, comparisons with industries like energy, food, and basic materials reveal that the scope and force allowed to the government to intervene was even less in the machinery industries. Parties in the wartime government never reached a clear agreement regarding which industries or particular enterprises would be promoted through preferential policy treatment. After the war, government organizations were reduced in size, so the capacity and competence of the government to make and implement policies to promote industry were accordingly further restricted. Compared with policies for the machine tool industry under wartime control, when both international trade and the distribution of materials were placed under government control, the policy measures available to the postwar government were incomparably limited. The postwar government lacked both competence and effective policy measures, and its policy had an extremely low priority relative to promotion policies for the machine tool industry under wartime control. It was therefore only natural and rational for the postwar government to refrain from active intervention in the inter-firm allocation of basic materials, in inter-firm trade relationships, and in internal company decision-making processes.

2.4   THE MACHINE TOOL INDUSTRY UNDER THE 1956 STATUTORY REGIME

2.4.1   Introduction

This section provides a case study of the machine tool industry under the MIPA. It is intended to give life to the discussion thus far. Where appropriate, I compare the situation under MIPA with the industry under wartime control.

The machine tool industry, or the metal machine tool manufacturing industry, was designated under the MIPA for over fifteen years, throughout the period of the First to the Third Acts.[88] Under the First Act, twenty-two industries were designated. This number increased to forty with the start of the Second Act. Thus, the machine tool industry was only one of many industries designated.

Additional reasons for focusing on the machine tool industry under the MIPA

In addition to serving as a case study, it is desirable to examine the machine tool industry under the Act more closely for four reasons:

1   Because the machine tool industry produces machines that in turn manufacture machines, the development of this industry is fundamental to the development of machinery industries generally.[89] Accordingly, policies under the MIPA that were aimed at the development of machinery industries placed an exceptionally strong emphasis on the machine tool industry.

2   The machine tool industry accounted for 11.1 percent of total loans (¥64 billion) provided under the First and Second Acts. This was second only to the auto parts industry, which received 22.8 percent. Thus the machine tool industry was not only designated in form but also actually received substantial funding so as to be considered in substance a policy object under the Act.[90]

3   Even at the time of the extension to the Third Act in FY1966, the machine tool industry was judged to still require further support. 'Though developed to a stage where it was able to compete with foreign machines in domestic markets and even to expand exports annually,' this industry was classified as an industry still suffering from serious problems, resulting in below average export performance (Sugiyama 1966b: pp.13–18). However, this industry showed very rapid growth and even surpassed the production value of West Germany in 1981, and it became the world leader in 1982 after surpassing US producers. In the 1980s, the export ratio was around 30 percent. Among all the industries designated under the Act, this industry realized the most remarkable success.

4   This industry was extremely obsolete and fifteen or twenty years behind international technical standards at the commencement of the First MIPA. This was a result of the suspension of the inflow of technological information and newly developed machines during the war, the long-lasting depression in the industry during the postwar disorder, and the excess volume of machine tool stocks and production capacity. Consequently, the government was faced with a serious policy dilemma: should it prioritize the interests of the general machinery industries as users by importing technologically advanced machines or focus on developing the domestic machine tool industry by protecting the domestic market from outside competition, namely by restricting imports.

A detailed investigation of the government's decisions in this area reveals its real policy focus for the machinery industries generally and the machine tool industry specifically. According to Hayashi (1961: p.460):

> The inferior technological level of Japan's domestic machine tools and also the insufficient capital accumulation of machine tool manufacturers, when coupled with restrictive Japanese policy toward the import of machine tools from European countries and the USA, combine to operate as a huge constraint upon producers' efforts to overcome technological backwardness through modernizing machine tool equipment. Under such restrictive circumstances, to expect the development of capacities so as to enable competition with imported machines and competition in export markets is, I dare say, not dissimilar to the 'bamboo-spear tactics'[91] adopted during the war. In short, the policy of developing the machine tool industry by restricting machine tool imports serves only to sacrifice the machinery industries in general for the singular benefit of the machine tool industry. When one considers that the machine tool industry amounts to a mere 1% of the machinery industries in terms of product value, such a policy places too much emphasis upon this industry's development to be a balanced policy for the overall machinery industries.

2.4.2   Overview of the machine tool industry

I display here a figure, in addition to Figure 1.1 and Table 1.1 in Sections 1.1.3 and 1.3.1, respectively. These figures and this table provide an overview of the machine tool industry. Figure 1.1 displays machine tool production from 1930 to 1994, in terms of both the number of machines produced and aggregate weight. Table 1.1 shows the demand for and supply of machine tools over the period 1935–68. The information concerning the period prior to 1945 is included for comparison with the postwar situation, particularly the period of the MIPAs.

Five points to note

It is convenient to note five points here:

1   The industry experienced explosive growth after 1955, almost comparable to the period of growth that occurred beginning in 1931. That is, during the seven years from 1931 to 1938 output grew by thirty times in terms of the number of machines produced and by fifty times in terms of aggregate weight. The corresponding figures for the six years from 1955 to 1961 were 6.3 and 16.7 times, respectively.

2   Compared with the prewar peak (1938 in number of machines produced and 1943 in aggregate weight), output in 1955 was a mere 27 percent in terms of number of machines produced and 5 percent in terms of aggregate weight. It was not until 1960 that production surpassed the prewar peak in terms of the number of machines produced, and not until 1967 in terms of aggregate weight.

3   The industry experienced rapid growth during the period 1950–5, output expanding by 4.5 times in terms of machines produced and by 2.2 times in terms of aggregate weight. During the decade to 1955, including the seven years from the end of the war to the return to independence of Japan in 1952, this industry suffered a long and severe depression. It was dealt many serious blows, including the disappearance of the military, which was by far the biggest source of demand. Furthermore, restrictions were also placed on production activities and the designation of plants for reparations.[92] In addition, the sale of stocks of used machine tools from munitions companies,[93] particularly from arsenals, low demand for new machine tools due to the stagnation in equipment investment in demand sectors, and huge excess capacity, added to the difficulties of the situation.

4   To meet the explosion in demand before World War II, machine tool imports increased sharply during this period. As a result, the import dependence ratio (i.e., [total value of imports] ÷ [total value of domestic demand]) remained high. In the six years from 1955 to 1961, machine tool imports increased by 9.6 times in terms of value. This in turn saw the import dependence ratio stand still at 32.9 percent in 1961, although this figure represented a significant decrease from the 57.7 percent level that had been reached in 1955. By contrast, exports remained lackluster, and in 1955 the value of imported machine tools surpassed the value of domestic production by 10 percent. In 1966 and 1967, the value of exports exceeded that of imports due to the sharp decline in imports that accompanied Japan's depression of that time. But it was not until long after this period that exports exceeded imports with any regularity.[94]

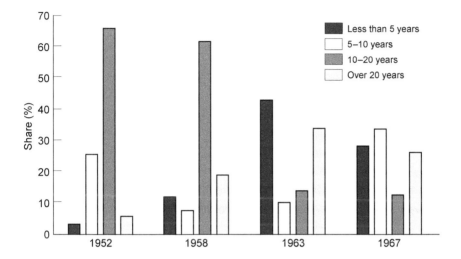

Figure 2.1 Age of machine tools in the metalworking machinery manufacturing industry[a]

Source: MITI, report of the census of machine tool equipment (1st–4th surveys)

[a]factories with more than thirty employees.

5   Machinery in this industry at the beginning of the period of rapid growth was
     obsolete, the result of long-term chronic stagnation coupled with little new
     investment in equipment. As shown in Figure 2.1, not only in 1952 but also
     in 1958 under the MIPA, the percentage of machine tools less than ten years
     old was less than 20 percent. Thus the MIPA launched a campaign of rapid
     growth in the machine tool industry with machine tools that were predomi-
     nantly prewar and wartime models, or imported during these periods.[95]

Size distribution of machine tool manufacturer plants

Figures 2.2 and 2.3 show fluctuations in the number of industry establishments organized by the number of personnel employed (data obtained from the census of
manufacturers). The data express not the number of enterprises but the number of
'establishments' (generally, one factory constitutes a single 'establishment').
Excepting a small number of large enterprises, most enterprises consisted of but one
establishment. Figure 2.2 shows the number of establishments by staff size (those
with more than ten employees) in the metal machine tool manufacturing industry for
1949–93. Based on data in Figure 2.2, Figure 2.3 displays the fluctuations between
1949 and 1965, taking 1955 as base 100.

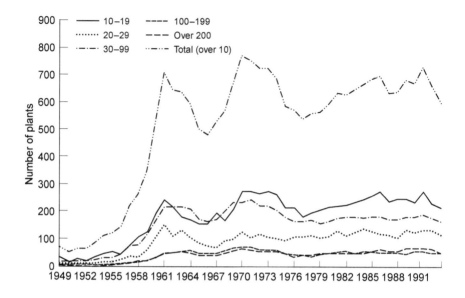

Figure 2.2 The number of machine tool factories in each size[a] category, 1949–93

Source: MITI, census of manufacturers.

[a] Size in terms of the number of employees.

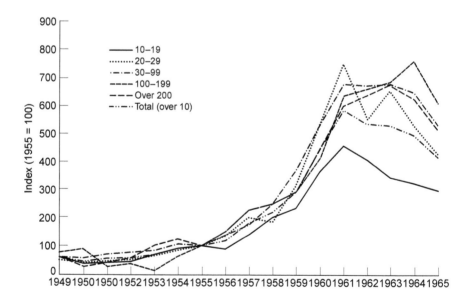

Figure 2.3 Indexed[a] number of machine tool factories in each size[b] category, 1949–65

Source: MITI, census of manufacturers.

[a] 1955 = 100.
[b] Size in terms of the number of employees.

Four observations follow from these figures:

1   During periods of rapid growth, the number of firms increased with industry size.
2   During periods of rapid growth, increases in the number of firms occurred across every workforce size category.[96]
3   As shown in Figure 1.1, the size of the industry in terms of both the number of machines produced and aggregate weight, after a brief lull during the first half of the 1960s, increased again in the second half of the 1960s and then stabilized.[97] The number of establishments had reached a peak by the end of the period of rapid growth in 1961, and since then both the number of establishments and their size distribution have shown stability for over thirty years.
4   The number of establishments employing more than ten people exceeded 700 in 1961.

As shown in Table 2.2, the average number of projects recommended to the JDB for funding annually during the First MIPA period was about 100. If we suppose that firms in the machine tool industry accounted for 20 to 30 percent of these 100 projects, then less than 5 percent of the establishments employing more than ten people could have received the recommendations for funding.[98]

The Japan Machine Tool Builders Association

As shown in the previous section, trade associations or industry associations played key roles in preparing and implementing policies under the MIPA. The representative trade association in the machine tool industry at the start of implementation of the Act was the Japan Machine Tool Builders Association (JMTBA).

The wartime control exercised by the Precision Tool Control Association (PTCA) 'nominally continued until September 1946. After the war, however, this control association was virtually dissolved, and association members organized new organs in their own respective industries. Machine tool builders organized the Japan Machine Tool Builders Society, which was an association primarily for the purpose of enhancing the profitability of private companies' (JMTBA 1962: p.161). It was on 1 December 1951 that the present JMTBA was established as a voluntary nationwide trade association. The JMTBA was established by reorganizing the East Japan and West Japan Machine Tool Builders Societies, established in 1949.

After the war, the machine tool industry was listed as one of those industries to be destroyed, having been declared an industry that contributed to the military economy. Also, a major portion of the industry was for a long time designated as objects of reparation payments. The relevant wartime association, the PTCA, focused primarily on the machine tool industry and was established as an organ for managing the wartime economy. Shortly after the start of its activities, the

Machine Tool Society, established in November 1945 to focus on machine tool exports, was ordered to purge three directors, including the chairman. It was eventually ordered to close.[99]

The increase in the number of machine tool makers that accompanied the explosive growth of the industry saw the number of JMTBA members increase (Table 2.3). The number of members at the start of FY1955 was fifty-four, but this had increased to seventy-six at the end of FY1960, and then to 107 by the close of FY1963. During these years, seven firms left the association. The number of members increased particularly after 1960 due to the fact that many firms were established in the machine tool industry during 1958–60 and joined the association only after a few years in business.[100] Consequently, the number of new industry entrants meant that although the Big Five (Hitachi Seiki, Ikegai Metalworks, Okuma Metalworks, Toshiba Machines, and Toyoda Machine Works) increased output rapidly (for instance, assigning the total output for 1956 a base value of 100, the output value of the Big Five had increased to 200 by 1958 and to 800 by 1962), their share of production to the total output of the industry decreased sharply, from 55.3 percent in 1956 to 37.3 percent in 1958, and further to 31.4 percent in 1962 (Japan Long-Term Credit Bank, Research Division 1966: p.30).

Table 2.3   Number of members of the Japan Machine Tool Builders Association

	Fiscal year								
	1955	1956	1957	1958	1959	1960	1961	1962	1963
Number at beginning of year	54	55	58	60	63	65	76	92	103
New entries during year	4	3	2	5	2	11	18	11	4
Exits during year	3	0	0	2	0	0	2	0	0
Number at end of year	55	58	60	63	65	76	92	103	107

Source: JMTBA, adapted from Japan Long-Term Credit Bank, Research Division, 1966: p.30, table 27.

Machine tool vintage in the machine tool industry

Reflecting sluggish long-term demand and production in the economy, investment in equipment in the machine tool industry was extremely limited, the result of which is revealed in the age structure of machine tool equipment in the industry (see Table 2.2). The percentage of machine tool equipment less than five years old in March 1952 was only 2 percent. By September 1958, that figure had risen to 12 percent, but the percentage of equipment between five and ten years old was only 8 percent. Thus, even in 1958, when the period of the First MIPA was half over, this industry was still equipped with machine tools produced mostly before and during the war.[101] It is widely agreed that 'the model and performance of a machine tool becomes obsolete in seven years on average, and in ten years at the maximum.'[102] The machine tools that were produced during the war and hence in use during the period of the First Act 'depended heavily on imported machines designed primarily in the 1920s in Europe and the USA and were not 1930 model machine tools' (Mishina 1958: p.106). Therefore machine tool production, at least under the First MIPA, was conducted with extremely old and obsolete equipment.

2.4.3   Policies under the MIPA

The metal machine tool manufacturing industry was under the jurisdiction of the Industrial Machinery Section. The basic rationalization plan for the metal machine tool industry and their implementation program for FY1956 was submitted to and approved by the Machinery Industry Council meeting at the end of 1956 (published in the official gazette on 15 March 1957).[103] The basic rationalization policy for the metal machine tool industry involved 'the promotion of equipment modernization, increasing the production volume for each model and reducing the number of models each producer possessed by promoting concentration. These policies were intended to improve the quality and performance of metal machine tools and to reduce their production costs.'

Six goals in the basic rationalization plan for FY1960

The basic rationalization plan for FY1960 included the following six goals:

1   To develop the capacity to supply products speedily and sufficiently to satisfy all the demand for listed products[104] existing at the end of FY1960.
2   To increase product quality and performance beyond the Schulenger standard, DIN and JIS (Japanese Industrial Standards). These standards had already been realized for high-performance products supplied by Japan's machine tool makers. The list detailed those figures as desirable targets, but manufacturers were expected to make products of a higher quality and performance.

3   To generate the funding needed to install listed equipment, which would require funding to the tune of ¥5.5 billion plus additional sums for the supplementary investment.

4   To reduce production costs to more than 20 percent below costs at the end of FY1955[105] (2 percent of this figure was to be achieved by reducing the cost of purchasing materials, 5 percent by reducing direct production costs, 3 percent by reducing the failure rate, and 10 percent by reducing indirect costs and management costs).

5   To scrap or use for other purposes old equipment that had been replaced by new equipment.

6   To rationalize production in three areas: (a) the promotion of specialization in production by the concentration of producers in each field; (b) the promotion of uniform standards for parts used in production, and the rationalization of purchasing methods; and (c) the advancement of production technology by establishing a research institution for joint use.

Thus, the basic plan listed machine tools to be supplied domestically. It then detailed the quality and price levels to be achieved in domestic production as prerequisites to ensure competitiveness with imports. In addition, the plan proposed measures to achieve the requisite price and quality levels.

While this was fine in theory, however, as shown in Section 2.2, concerning points (5) and (6) the policies were ineffective in almost every industry designated under the MIPA. For instance, Kato (1960: p.355), an official in the Heavy Industries Section of MITI, describes the machine tool industry as follows:

> The production lot of each individual firm concerning each product is extremely small in this industry in Japan, primarily because each firm produces too many products. Upon reflection, the Special Council for Discussing Production Sectors was organized in the industry, which, however, due to severe and complicated conflicts of interest among industry members, did not work effectively.

This description suggests three points: (1) many recognized the importance of economies of scale to be realized by specialization; (2) however, MITI did not intervene actively in the private sector to achieve the realization of economies of scale; and (3) the indigenous efforts of the industry were not effective due to the complicated conflicts of interest between industry members.

The basic plan was nothing more than an industry forecast

The basic rationalization plan included an equipment investment plan for the industry. The achievement of the objectives detailed in this plan was the primary aim of the First MIPA, which placed policy emphasis on modernizing old and obsolete equipment. However, with the explosive growth in demand for machine tools after 1956, the objectives of the plan were realized within three years, whereupon the plan was revised and the objectives upped twice (in FY1959 and FY1960; Table 2.4). The above-mentioned figure of ¥5.5 billion, the amount needed to install designated equipment, was revised and increased to ¥10 billion in FY1959 and to ¥13.5 billion in FY1960.

Table 2.4   Basic rationalization plans for the machine tool industry (million yen)

		Basic plan (initial stage)		First revised plan (FY1959)		Second revised plan (FY1960)		
		[1]	[2] [A]	[1]	[2]	[1]	[2] [B]	(B/A) x100
Designated machines	Machine tools	800	5,000	1,200	9,100	2,000	12,510	250
	Metalworking machinery other than machine tools	30	70	30	70	25	60	86
	Laboratory and testing equipment	140	200	300	430	300	430	215
	Other equipment	130	230	130	400	90	450	196
	Total	1,100	5,500	1,660	10,000	2,415	13,450	244
Equipment other than designated machinery			486		3,000		3,750	722
Total			5,986		13,000		17,200	287

Source: JMTBA, adapted from Japan Long-Term Credit Bank (Research Division, 1966: p.32, table 12).

Note: [1] number of machines to be newly introduced; [2] value of machines to be newly introduced.

The basic plan under the Second Act, which emphasized the strengthening of international competitiveness through promoting mass production by expanding the scale of firms and establishing specialized production, planned to implement investment in equipment equivalent to ¥18.5 billion by FY1965. In fact, investment in the industry totaled ¥20 billion in FY1961, which exceeded investment during the whole period of the First Act. However, Investment during the period of the Second Act decreased sharply after this, and by FY1965 only 55 percent of the initial investment target had been realized.

In each case, the fundamental policy initially adopted in the basic rationalization plan deviated greatly from what was in fact implemented and achieved. However, this deviation did not result in the product shortages that would likely have occurred if the plan had been enforced faithfully and enthusiastically. This reveals that the basic plan was nothing more than an industry forecast. I return to this issue below.

The role played by the JMTBA under the MIPA

The machine tool industry was no exception in that, because of the limited size of the government section directly in charge (the Industrial Machinery Section) and the number of designated industries over which that section assumed charge, the government could never have played a leading role in this industry in making and implementing the basic rationalization plan and annual implementation programs. In addition, the trade association in this industry, the JMTBA, had fifty-four members even at the commencement of the MIPA in 1956. This is far beyond a convenient number for reaching and maintaining tight agreements between members. Also, within several years the number of association members had doubled and the shares of production of large firms in the industry had decreased sharply, which illustrated the instability of the association's structure. It is also implausible, therefore, that such a trade association, playing such a critical role as it did actively resolving conflicts of interest between members, could have led the industry in a direction decisively different from that of the market, for instance by making a clear determination that JDB loans should be preferentially directed to a select group of firms satisfying specific conditions.

Plans and forecasts in postwar Japan

Observers can find phrases like (long-term or long-run) 'plan', 'forecast,' 'objective,' and 'goal' in a wide variety of postwar Japanese government documents. Many then conclude that Japan must have had an extremely interventionist government, and that the Japanese economy must have been centrally directed. However, most of the plans had no more substance than weather forecasts or wishful thinking.

These forecasts, particularly the demand–supply forecasts, were typically made by the industry association. Being long-term forecasts, they were usually expected to be revised as necessary. We observe the same phenomenon in the equipment investment coordination program that MITI enforced in connection with its 'long-term credit plans,' which it based on an industry's long-term forecast. Firms in the steel industry, for example, regularly underestimated demand and had to revise their 'plans' upward during the year. Notwithstanding these misjudgements, the economy never suffered from shortages – as it would have if the plans had been binding. Given that the plans were in fact simple forecasts, by the time demand expanded producers had already raised the quantities they supplied (Miwa 1996a: ch. 9).

In the postwar period, the Japanese Economic Planning Agency has always prepared medium-term plans for the national economy, on average a five-year plan that is revised every two to three years. Many argue that this is a symbol of the command-style character of the Japanese economy. Yet those who were directly concerned with 'plans' tend to overemphasize their importance, and official documents have the same tendency. Many draw direct conclusions based upon these exaggerated and self-serving accounts. As Komiya (1990: p.284) points out, 'Japan's national economic plans are more correctly interpreted as long-term forecasts, with some element of wishful thinking by the plan-makers.' Also 'nobody considers the national economic plans as rigid, binding plans which must be followed by the government. … There is not much substance in the national plans which can be usefully referred to by the government ministries and agencies when making important policy decisions in their respective fields. … Economic plans are similar to a long-range (one- to three-month) weather forecast which is announced once or twice a month.'

For some time after the publication of the Income Doubling Ten-year Plan in December 1960, it became fashionable among larger firms to publish their own overall long-term management plans projected over a five- or ten-year period. When making company plans, the rate of growth of the national or relevant sector was taken for granted, and each company added a plus factor to the industry average rate of growth, hoping to increase market share for itself. But here again in practice few companies paid much attention to their long-term plans in making actual investment decisions since most such plans turned out to underestimate their growth potential (*ibid.*: p.286). Before the oil crisis of 1973, government plans consistently underestimated growth potential. However, as I have concluded previously (Miwa 1996a: ch. 9), MITI's investment coordination program in the steel industry, for instance, which was based on long-term plans prepared in accordance with its 'long-term credit plan,' had only negligible impact, if any, on the investment behavior of individual companies.

In emphasizing the continuity in economic planning between the prewar and postwar economic systems, Okazaki and Okuno-Fujiwara (1999: p.18) again misunderstand the basic character of postwar economic planning. They argue that:

> Overlaying the economy with a web of legally based controls was in effect hampering the resource-allocation function of the market. To replace it, a range of economic plans were drawn up by the government that provided criteria for running the controls. Once the Materials Mobilization Plan (*Busshi doin keikaku*) of January 1938 had started to come into effect it was followed from 1939 with a Foreign Trade Plan, a Funds Control Plan, a Labor Mobilization Plan, a Transportation and Electric Power Mobilization Plan, and a Production Capacities Expansion Plan.

Crucially, they do not try to measure how much impact even those wartime plans had on the behavior of individual firms. However, in Part I, I find that that impact, despite its high priority in the government, was trivial.[106]

2.4.4   Policy effects

The term 'machine tool' is a general term that encompasses a wide variety of machinery products. Each producer has strengths and weaknesses in various types and models of machine, and hence producers usually specialize in producing one or several types of machine in the area of their strengths.[107] The number of producers is relatively large for machines such as engine lathes, milling machines, vertical drilling machines, radial drilling machines, and vertical cylindrical grinders. However, for thread grinders, jig boring machines, broaching machines, and hobbing machines, the number of producers is more limited.[108] Furthermore, within the market for each type of machine tool, the demand for precision and performance is extremely diverse, and accordingly the level of design and production technology also fluctuates widely with machine type. The barriers to new market entry therefore differ greatly, depending on the particular market. As a result, the number of products supplied is truly diverse, and substitutability between products meeting different demands is limited. Hence, the competition between producers supplying products for different demands is also limited.[109]

Potential policy effectiveness was so limited in the machine tool industry

I pose the question here whether policies for the machine tool industry under the MIPA could possibly have done anything other than provide indiscriminate monetary subsidies. For example, could the Act have promoted only selected groups of products or firms? The answer to this question is no, for three reasons: (1) the section in charge (and MITI generally), the trade association, and the JDB and the Small Business Finance Corporation as sources of policy funding all lacked the will, competence, and legal mechanisms that they would have needed to do so; (2) the priority assigned to MIPA policies was unclear in the general scheme of national policies but not of high priority—in particular, there is no evidence of any widespread public support for such a targeted approach; (3) as a result of the two previous points, the government lacked the means to realize such an objective.

A detailed discussion concerning these three points has been conducted above, but the following quotation reiterates the logic: 'even before the commencement of the Act, policies under the MIPA were destined to be those for small business. Loans to large firms were extremely exceptional under the First and the Second Acts' (JDB 1976: p.452). Consequently, discriminatory policies that preferentially allocated funds to the more technologically advanced firms were a political impossibility, even if the government had had the competence to implement such a policy.

By contrast, during the war discriminatory and preferential policies for the machine tool industry had been enforced with the support of the nation: 'with time the struggle to secure products from first-grade builders grew more intense. As priority was allocated to military demand, particularly that for aircraft production, civil demand machines were forced to be content with tools from second- and third-grade builders' (JMTBA 1962: p.137). Under the MIPA, the government did not adopt such policies as to preferentially promote the production of 'first-grade builders.'

Moreover, under wartime control, although 'the promotion of the domestic production of special machine tools that were then totally imported' was adopted as a fundamental long-term policy, the government 'adopted effective temporary measures to promote the import of special machine tools whose demand could not be fully satisfied by domestic supply.' With the progress of the war and the accompanying increase in the difficulty of importing foreign machines, the focus of policy shifted to 'promoting the domestic production of special machine tools.' By contrast, under the MIPA, the promotion of domestic production of machine tools, if it can be said to have existed as a policy at all, never became a policy of high priority. Furthermore, machine tool imports were liberalized at a greater pace than was the case for other machinery industries.[110]

As shown in Section 1.3.2, following the Shanghai incident in 1932, the government and the military both asked the major machine tool makers to increase production and expand capacity. However, the producers remembered the collapse in demand after World War I and were reluctant to agree. Therefore the government had to provide strong incentives to the producers, and it did so through the Machine Tool Building Act.

Makers of machine tools found themselves in a similar situation at the beginning of the MIPA after a decade of difficult postwar transition. Toyoda Machine

Works, established in 1941 as a Toyota Motors spin-off, became one of the five major machine tool makers in the 1960s, but in 1953 machine tools sales were only 20 percent of its total. The company history describes the effort it took to refocus the firm from textile machines to machine tools. After the war, in addition to drastically cutting the number of employees, the firm had been forced to delve into the manufacturing of every kind of metal product, including cooking pots and plows, in order to survive. With the expansion of textile production in Japan, it discovered a new and lucrative market and grew to be one of the largest suppliers of textile machinery. Then, in 1952, Toyota Motors, which in 1955 still owned more than 20 percent of Toyoda Machine Works, asked it to make auto parts. Note that in 1952 most Japanese saw manufacturing passenger cars as a high-risk venture. They remembered, perhaps, the famous 1950 pronouncement by the chairman of the Bank of Japan: 'it is useless to develop the automobile industry in Japan. Now is the time of the international division of labor, and we can buy cars from the USA.'

The effect of JDB loans to the machine tool industry under the MIPA

Under the MIPA, the machine tool industry received JDB funding to the tune of ¥2.63 billion during FY1956–FY1960, ¥3.765 billion during FY1961–FY1965, and ¥480 million during FY1966–FY1970. This funding represented 14.7 percent, 5.5 percent, and 0.5 percent, respectively, of the total value of the investment in equipment in the industry during those periods (and 3.6 percent over the full fifteen-year period; JDB 1976: pp.454–60). As shown in the previous section, the economic impact of these loans, even with interest rates below market rates, was not substantial.

Some observers refer to the data in Figure 2.1 and claim that the MIPA funding grants did promote equipment modernization (e.g., JDB 1963: p.39). Yet the impact of JDB funding can only be measured by comparing the actual industry performance against the circumstances that would likely have existed had there been no such funding scheme. An increase in equipment investment will raise the percentage of new machines among machinery stock. Yet the equipment investment behavior of machine tool makers is overwhelmingly influenced by expected future demand for their products, and a slight variation in credit interest rates will not generally have a significant impact on investment behavior. It is clear that investment during the period was by no means fully attributable to government policy. It is unreasonable to conclude directly from Figure 2.1 that the impact of JDB funding on investment in equipment was substantial.

I do not propose to identify the actual impact of policy, which is a difficult and unprofitable task since the net impact seems to have been negligible. Rather, I limit myself to three points.

1   The initial equipment investment target for the machine tool industry under the First MIPA was ¥5.5 billion, but this was revised and increased by a factor of 2.5 during the period of this First Act. This revision was conducted in response to changes in the investment behavior of machine tool makers, which in turn was caused by explosive increases in demand for machine tools.

2   As mentioned in the previous section, the bearing industry, for instance, where there was a failure to reach agreement regarding details of the industry's basic rationalization plan, actively invested in equipment without policy support during the 1955–7 boom.

3   As shown in Figure 2.4, the automobile industry, which was outside the jurisdiction of the Act, introduced new equipment much more rapidly than did the machine tool industry. Investment in equipment in the car industry was in response to the rapid growth of the industry.

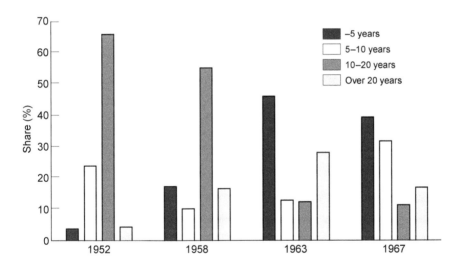

Figure 2.4 Age of machine tools in the automobile and auto parts manufacturing industries[a]

Source: MITI, report of the census of machine tool equipment (1st–4th surveys).

[a] factories with more than thirty employees.

2.5   CONCLUDING REMARKS

Conclusions of Part II

The main conclusion of Part II, which has examined the MIPA and the policies based on this Act, can be stated as follows. The fundamental policy measure adopted under the MIPAs, from the First to the Third, was loans at preferential rates through the JDB and the Small Business Finance Corporation. No other substantial policies were used. These loans had little effect due to the small magnitude of funding, the limited difference between the preferential interest rates of the loans and market interest rates, and the indiscriminate manner in which funding was allocated between borrowers. In total, the policy measures provided little benefit, and they failed to create an economic environment that differed to any extent from what would have ensued otherwise. Many argue that state intervention in the industries designated under the MIPA, including the machine tool industry, played a critical role in promoting the development of these industries. That overstates the case.

Whether directly or indirectly, whether through 'self-regulation' or the 'autonomous coordination' of industry associations, the government did not intervene actively in the industries it purported to promote. The 'promotion policies' that it did adopt could not potentially have had – and did not have – a significant effect on company behavior. The public did not share a widespread consensus about the objective of the MIPA (or the need to 'restructure the industrial order'), and neither did the government. All this made the postwar policies far less effective than those during wartime, and as shown in Part I the wartime policies did not have any substantial effect either. Because of the lack of substantial public support, many in government believed that melding MIPA policy into 'traditional small business policies' was the only way to make the policies palatable. This in turn ensured that the government had less authority and power in the industry than it did during wartime. The industry did grow during the postwar years, but not because of government policy. It grew because supply responded to booming demand.

Fundamentally, whether during wartime or under the MIPA, the machinery industries (and the machine tool industry) did not satisfy the basic preconditions for government intervention to alter market conditions to promote an industry. If these conditions are not met, then even a government possessing a clear policy will and enforcing policies of optimal effectiveness will not succeed. In this sense, the policies that were implemented under the Act belong to a policy set where implementing effective 'promotion policies' or 'support policies' is inherently difficult by nature.

Yet the postwar government faced a skeptical public. With the end of the war, and the postwar disorder and decade of postwar transition that followed, public attitudes regarding the government's role in terms of actual policy, policy issues, and government organization changed dramatically. This change, which was revealed in the first half of the 1960s both by the government's failure to enact the economic regulation it wanted and by the Sumitomo Metals and Idemitsu Incidents, affected the content and enforcement of the MIPA. It was no longer easy for the government to adopt policies of a discriminatory and preferential nature to the advantage of some industries or some group of firms within an industry.

Policy under the MIPA thus lacked widespread consensus and support for the policy objectives to be pursued. This was so not only within the government but also among general groups in the community. Policies under the Act therefore lacked the strong support both of other government sections, including other sections within MITI, and of the general public. Debates held about policy lacked substance, the available policy measures were limited, and the authority delegated to the government was highly restricted. Effectively, this tied the hands of the government and left it with only policies of limited potential effect. Although a few industries during the postwar transition period may represent exceptions, most postwar policies for individual industries were enforced under such restrictive conditions. In the majority of cases, an individual industry or a group of industry associations asked the government to 'support' the industry. The government sections in charge then cooperated with this request. In reality, however, acquiring the 'support' of the government, in whatever form it was presented, received much more attention than the actual realization of alleged 'policy objectives.'

Therefore, the desultory consequences that followed were largely inevitable. First, those policies that attempted to enforce strong or discriminatory preferential treatment toward any individual industry or group of firms were almost always ineffective. Second, the objectives of these industrial 'policies' were rarely concrete. Third, the question of 'restructuring the industrial order' was much discussed but never decisively acted on.

Given an inherently difficult task and a skeptical electorate, the government took but timid steps. That timidity was itself a rational response. For the task assigned, it was incompetent and ill-prepared. Even during the war, it hesitated to comply with military requirements. Under peacetime conditions, it equivocated even further. What happened was the consequence of rational choices of the parties involved – the government sections in charge, the industry associations, and the firms themselves.

Implications for the industrial policy debate[111]

Many readers will have approached this book with preconceptions similar to those of Krugman (1997: p.142): 'There is no question that before the early 1970s the Japanese system was heavily directed from the top, with the MITI and the Ministry of Finance influencing the allocation of credit and foreign exchange in an effort to push the economy where they liked.' Many Japanese also share this view, and Okazaki and Okuno-Fujiwara (1999: pp.11–12), quoted in Section 2.1.2, typify the academic response. Given this orthodoxy, readers may properly ask: 'Why is what we see in Part II of this book so different from what we read elsewhere?' 'Was there a glorious industrial policy that disappeared?' 'Or was it a myth all along?' Yes, it was indeed a myth.

Okazaki and Okuno-Fujiwara

Consider again the Okazaki and Okuno-Fujiwara (1999) discussion. I do not raise it because it is unusually wrong but because it captures the conventional wisdom so nicely. Okazaki and Okuno-Fujiwara argue that Japanese firms and workers maintained unusually long-term ties, and that because of these ties the 'systemic risk' in the economy posed a large risk of 'business collapse and mass unemployment.' To 'minimize this danger,' they explain, the government used non-binding 'administrative guidance' to promote high-growth sectors. It did so through 'government councils,' in which it gathered information about the technologies and industries with the greatest potential for growth. In response, firms shifted their investments to these targeted areas. Unfortunately, this targeted growth created the risk of 'excess competition' and caused firms to compete for market share at the expense of profitability. To hold the resulting 'systemic risks in check,' the government then adopted a variety of antitrust exemptions.

In evaluating this account, I urge readers to ask carefully whether it is theoretically coherent and has a solid empirical foundation. I also encourage them to be skeptical of conclusions drawn either from government reports and documents or from the simple promulgation of laws, rules, plans, control associations, and trade associations.

Policy coherence

Okazaki and Okuno-Fujiwara posit a coherent policy. Yet journalists and commentators frequently note the pernicious effects of the 'vertical' organization of the Japanese bureaucracy. Not only do bureaucrats not coordinate their policies with colleagues in other bureaux, they seldom cooperate, and they often do not even communicate with each other. Predictably, policy incoherence ensues. Or so at least we are routinely told.

By contrast, Okazaki and Okuno-Fujiwara would have us believe that Japanese bureaucrats successfully overcame the effects of that organizational verticality. Bureaucrats conceived and implemented coherent 'industrial policy' and a coordinated 'convoy system,' they write. How, one wonders, did they do so? Today, politicians regularly intervene in the policy-making process to promote constituent interests. Did they not intervene in the early postwar years? Was someone able to restrain them? If so, who?

Okazaki and Okuno-Fujiwara write that the Japanese government accomplished the 'co-ordination of the allocation of funds and other resources between industries.' Who carried out the coordination? How did they overcome the 'verticality' so often claimed to stymie policy coherence in Japan?

Active control

Okazaki and Okuno-Fujiwara claim that a 'typical model of the active control of "development" in manufacturing industry (or the whole Japanese economy, for that matter) is the Ministry of International Trade and Industry's "industrial policy".' In other words, not only did the Japanese *try* to control the economy. They actually did.

Yet in reading accounts such as this, consider carefully the empirical evidence. Presumably, Okazaki and Okuno-Fujiwara claim that ministries like MITI actually controlled the economy and used that control to try to promote growth. But what policies did it hope to advance? What measures did it adopt that might have accomplished those goals? Could the measures have accomplished what Okazaki and Okuno-Fujiwara argue the government actually accomplished?

'The allocation of the necessary facilities, and the selection and co-ordination of firms,' explain Okazaki and Okuno-Fujiwara, 'is carried out through discretionary administrative guidance against a backdrop of regulatory and financial measures.' Yet 'administrative guidance' is non-binding. How is it that the government was able to induce firms to comply through non-binding measures? What do Okazaki and Okuno-Fujiwara mean when they describe the government as implementing the guidance 'against a backdrop of regulatory and financial measures'?

In any event, which regulatory and financial measures did Okazaki and Okuno-Fujiwara have in mind? In which cases did the government use guidance to allocate facilities, pick firms, or force them to coordinate? What do we make of such notorious policy failures as those involving Nisshinbo Textiles, the Idemitsu Kosan petroleum firm, or Sumitomo Metals (discussed at length in Miwa and Ramseyer 2002e)?

Picking winners

In claiming that the government identified and promoted growth industries, Okazaki and Okuno-Fujiwara begin by ignoring the obvious counterfactual. Suppose the government had not created an industrial policy. What would have happened? Would the industries identified in the policy have grown more slowly? Would the economy have developed in a different direction?

According to standard theory, a decentralized capital market regularly identifies the industries and firms with the greatest growth potential. In effect, Okazaki and Okuno-Fujiwara are claiming that the Japanese government outguessed the market. What evidence do they have of this?

If the government did outguess the market, what enabled it do so? Okazaki and Okuno Fujiwara write: 'For the purposes of forecasting, various forums are used to gather information and encourage its exchange, such as government councils.' Again, however, sellers in decentralized markets have strong incentives to anticipate and respond to buyer preferences. By doing so, they automatically push production toward higher-valued services and products. Do Okazaki and Okuno-Fujiwara assert that the Japanese government was able to shift production more efficiently and expeditiously than the market?

Government councils

Given the prominence of 'government councils' in the literature, I urge readers to ask a few skeptical questions. Realistically, could these councils have accomplished what Okazaki and Okuno-Fujiwara attribute to them? After all, the councils did not start with the information. Instead, they had to obtain it, and to do so they had to convince firms to disclose it voluntarily. What induced firms to disclose crucial information?

According to Okazaki and Okuno-Fujiwara, the councils collected information about which firms, technologies, and industries had the greatest growth potential. Yet why would any firm disclose such information to the government and (thereby necessarily) to its competitors? Would not a rational firm keep its own information secret and try to free-ride on the information its rivals disclosed? In turn, would not the logic of the prisoners' dilemma then cause the council's entire efforts to acquire information to unravel? Would the council not find itself with no valuable information? And would that not lead firms to dismiss cursorily the value of any information that the government did provide?

In effect, Okazaki and Okuno-Fujiwara posit a simple economy populated by egregiously badly managed firms. After all, not only do they assert that firms volunteered information about new and profitable business ventures in a public forum. They claim that the council members agreed that those ideas represented high-growth ventures. And they further claim that the council was then able to convince firms to re-route their investment and production away from projects they had thought most profitable and instead toward projects championed by the council.

Could Japanese firms in the late twentieth century have been run by executives who missed business opportunities so obvious that government councils could discover them and then be able to convince those executives to pursue them? One should wonder. These are firms that regularly (and rightly) vetoed new ideas that their employees proposed. They vetoed them because they knew that if the ideas were as good as their proponents claimed, the odds that their competitors might have missed them were trivial. Notwithstanding (or perhaps precisely because of) that inherent skepticism, they regularly introduced new products, new technologies, even entirely new fields. Would companies such as these have shifted investments because of information about growth opportunities introduced by a government council?

Pork barrels?

Okazaki and Okuno-Fujiwara claim that the government promoted growth and development through a wide variety of policies. If true, those policies would have represented a radical departure from the international norm. Hundreds of studies in modern political science and economics document the extent to which rent-seeking and pork-barrel politics dominate economic policy in advanced modern democracies. Yet Okazaki and Okuno-Fujiwara would make Japan the exception. In Japan, they argue, the government instead adopted policies that effectively and efficiently promoted growth and development. What enabled it to pursue such exceptionally enlightened policies?

   Fiscally, the postwar Japanese government primarily targeted small firms, and firms in the coal, electricity, ocean-going shipping, textile, agriculture, and construction industries. Was this allocation growth- or development-enhancing? Given that economic growth is a public good, would firms have supported growth-promoting programs anyway? Were the programs that the government did implement large enough to have affected national growth rates? Were they structured to affect investment decisions on the margin?

Saving losers

Okazaki and Okuno-Fujiwara tell us that firms had such a 'strong incentive' to exploit the opportunities disclosed by the government councils that they engaged in 'excess competition.' As a result, their 'investment and facilities are expanded beyond the individual firm's means.' The question is how the councils could plausibly have discovered such good projects. Why would the information have led to 'excess competition'? Indeed, what is 'excess competition'? Is it different from any other case where firms compete to exploit positive net present value projects? And which industries at what periods did Okazaki and Okuno-Fujiwara have in mind?

   Indeed, we learn that through this 'excess competition' firms adopted 'business plans that target market share rather than profits.' Why would a firm pursue a market share that lowered profits? And what does it have to do with whether the firm learned of the plan on its own or through the government anyway? More basically, policies that raise market share usually also make money. Okazaki and Okuno-Fujiwara seem to posit cases where the two goals conflict. Which cases do they have in mind?

'If the business were to fail and mass lay-offs became likely, the authorities responsible for promoting the policy would have to shoulder some of the blame,' write Okazaki and Okuno-Fujiwara. As a result, 'the government has held these systemic risks in check with a variety of means, including recession cartels.' The claim is broad, and it raises both questions of scope and questions of international comparison.

Okazaki and Okuno-Fujiwara potentially attribute enormous responsibility to the government. Which industries, for example, do they believe the government promoted? Was it responsible for protecting firms in all? The government maintains bureaux that at least nominally supervise virtually all industries. Is the government 'responsible' for preventing bankruptcies everywhere?

Here too Okazaki and Okuno-Fujiwara beg the comparative question. When firms face excess capacity, democratic governments the world over routinely provide aid. Whether with economic justification or not, they routinely adopt measures to cut unemployment and promote economic activity. Did the Japanese government adopt measures that differed fundamentally from measures that other governments adopted? Did the aid that Okazaki and Okuno-Fujiwara cite really minimize the dangers of 'systemic risk'? Could the measures that they cite have minimized any serious disruptions? And what do they mean by 'systemic risk' anyway?

Why Japan? Why the 1960s?

Let us return, finally, to two fundamental comparative questions. First, why Japan? Suppose that the Japanese government actually maintained the 'industrial policy' that Okazaki and Okuno-Fujiwara attribute to it. Why was it able to do so? Why did other advanced economies not use it? Perhaps more to the point, why did the governments in the Soviet bloc not use it (or use it successfully)? At least such governments could have drawn on a much more centralized and powerful state apparatus.

Second, why the postwar years? Do Okazaki and Okuno-Fujiwara claim (like most other proponents of the Japanese industrial policy hypothesis) that the formerly effective industrial policy no longer works? We doubt that they claim the government still picks winners and rescues losers. To what do they attribute the decline? If the system worked so well for so long, why did the government abandon it? Would not voters have wanted it to continue?

Good instincts will take us a long way here, and good instincts are not country-bound. The 'innumerable regulatory actions are conclusive proof, not of effective regulation, but of the desire to regulate,' write Stigler and Friedland (1962: p.1). Moreover, explains Ronald Coase (1964: p.194), 'what ... regulatory commissions are trying to do is difficult to discover; what effect [they] actually have is, to a large extent, unknown; when it can be discovered, it is often absurd.'

No 'plan' prepared by a government institution and backed by its instructions will materialize automatically. If 'plans' and 'instructions' worked as well as the proponents of Japanese industrial policy seem to assume, the former socialist economies would not have collapsed in such a miserable manner.

And yet, many readers will no doubt respond: 'where there is smoke, there must be fire.' Without some substance to the industrial policy, we would not have the literature that we do. For the many non-Japanese Japanologists who are addicted to the notion of Japanese 'uniqueness,' this response is nothing if not convenient. But for every proverb there is a counter-proverb, and here there is one as well (as I noted in the Preface): 'If one dog barks at his shadow, a hundred dogs will bark at his voice.' About the enduring legacy of the Gardiner Means obsession with 'administered prices,' George J. Stigler (1988: pp.111–12) had much the same thing to say:

> It is fair to say that [its] persistence is a remarkable tribute to [its] palatability to ruling political thought. Once an idea is widely accepted, it is guaranteed a measure of immortality. Its decline in popularity is more often due to changing interests than to contrary evidence, no matter how powerful that evidence may be.

Part III

Contemporary Japan

3   Policies for small businesses[112]

3.1   THE ISSUES

> One of the most striking features of recent Japanese public policy, viewed both in comparative context and against the backdrop of Japanese history, has been the fluctuating but generally pronounced bias toward the small across a range of industrial, trade, and credit-policy sectors, often at the expense of the large.
>
>   (Calder 1988: p.312)

This statement, with which Kent Calder begins his chapter on 'Small business policy,' reflects the dominant academic view of Japanese small business policy. Coupled with the following three facts, this view often leads scholars to conclude that small business policies have played a tremendously important role in the economic development of Japan: (1) the pace of economic development in Japan has indeed been rapid; (2) the role of the government has appeared to be significant; and (3) small enterprises are thought to have contributed much to Japanese economic development. Because of this academic focus on small business policy, governments and development strategists particularly in transitional economies and in developing economies have now become interested in Japanese small business policies as lessons for their own planning strategies.[113]

    Learning about Japanese small business policy, people in the governments of transitional economies ask: 'How did such a huge number of active small businesses come into being?' 'What were the conditions for their creation?' 'How did government policy contribute to their success?' 'What were effective policies?' They would thus receive the following message with surprise and disappointment: in Japan the government has consistently suffered from an 'excessive' number of small businesses, and how to create small businesses has never been a policy issue. Accordingly, we can draw no lessons for creating small businesses from the Japanese experience (Miwa 1995, 1999).

    Granted, few scholars still posit a monolithic 'Japan Inc.' However, as we have seen in Part II, that does not stop them positing a 'Japanese (-style) system,' a 'Japanese (-style) economic system' or a 'Japanese (-style) enterprise system.' As they revise their views of Japanese industrial policy, they may also re-evaluate their ideas about 'the Japanese (-style) system.' Yet, curiously, we are now observing a new product – a development model called the '(East) Asian Miracle,' exported from Japan by those in and around the Japanese government to the economies in transition. These writers argue that the postwar Japanese experience can be instructive, and they suggest a strongly interventionist role for government. The World Bank (1992) and a series of World Bank research projects on the Japanese experience resulting in Aoki and Patrick (1994) and Kim *et al.* (1995), are representative examples.

Like much that is said about Japanese industrial policy generally, most of what is said about Japanese small business policy is misguided. The efficacy of these polices has been extremely limited. Active small enterprises have not been created through well-organized, effective small business policies from the government. In this chapter, I provide detailed information on the nature of those policies, how they have been implemented, why they have been ineffective, and why ineffective policies have been enforced.

Two purposes of Chapter 3

I focus on policies for small business in this chapter for two reasons. First, there is strong demand worldwide for detailed information on the actual picture of Japanese small business policies and their contribution to the country's postwar economic growth. Unfortunately, as shown below, this demand is based on the totally false idea that the policies have been effective. Therefore, the first purpose of this chapter is to identify the error: postwar Japanese government policy was not effective toward vital small businesses.

The tale of effective small business policies in Japan has been exported widely as part of the postwar Japanese experience, which, like the tale of an effective 'main bank' system, at least potentially leads to harmful consequences. For instance, taking Japan's 'main bank' system as a reference, the Bank of China, that country's central bank, issued its 'basic rule for loans' in June 1996. This stipulates that a company receiving a loan has to establish a 'main bank' relationship with a bank in the district where the company is registered. For this purpose, the bank issued its 'main bank regulation rule' in August. Under a 'bank–company cooperation agreement' between a bank and a company, the main bank is obliged to provide the borrower with financial services concerning settlement, liquidity, funds to improve technology, and so forth. The scheme started in mid-1996 with 300 companies among the 1,000 firms selected by the state for their economic strength. The bank appointed a main bank for each company on the basis of its loan and settlement history. The Industry and Commerce Bank was appointed as the main bank to 240 of the 300 firms.[114]

The second but more basic purpose of this chapter is to show how deeply state competence conditions both policy debates in the political marketplace and the policies actually adopted and implemented. Being deeply conditioned by state competence, every policy (in a democracy) is adopted and implemented in response to voter demand, often creating a gap between what the government can achieve and what it is allegedly pursuing. This gap has long been greatest in small business policies.

Backed by the wide but vague support of the public, which will allow certain sacrifices in efficiency for the sake of preferences for weak small firms, small business policies have consistently been a powerful and effective political slogan. Few parties or cabinets have been able to buck the demand for such policies. In this sense, the postwar demand for small business policies shares the same basic character as the wartime demand for the 'expansion of production,' 'domestic production,' 'development,' and 'improvement' of machine tools discussed in Part I.

Road map

This chapter is divided into four parts. Section 3.2 is a preliminary section, where I discuss three basic areas in which to investigate the competence of the state and point out three reasons why small business policies have been ineffective. In Section 3.3, I discuss the small business policy of the central government, the history of small business policies, the 'dual structure' view and small business policies based on this view, financial or funding policy, a policy evaluation focusing on the indiscriminate character of policies, and the menu of small business policies. Section 3.4 introduces the role of local governments in small business policy enforcement, taking as an example the commercial and industrial policy of the Hyogo prefectural government, and then discusses the preferential allocation of orders for public construction to small businesses. Section 3.5 provides a general evaluation of small business policies.

3.2   PRELIMINARIES

The subject of this chapter is policies for small business. The study focuses upon their contribution to Japan's economic development. Since I conclude that small business policies have shown only small if any potential and exhibit negligible efficacy, I place more focus on their propensity to succeed than on their actual achievements. The primary reason for the inefficacy of small business policies is their extremely limited potential in the sense that even with wide political backing the policy objective demanded is difficult to achieve, rather than the process of policy making itself or its implementation. This point is probably already clear to readers of the preceding parts of this book. Let us begin by discussing the basic issues concerning an evaluation of small business policy.

3.2.1   The competence of the state

The state is an organization lacking braking mechanisms

The state neither is almighty nor has a crystal ball or Aladdin's lamp. Just like an individual or an organization such as a firm, the state incurs costs in doing anything. The state has limited areas in which it is competent, resulting in it having strong and weak points. In short, there are some tasks to which the state is suited and some to which it is not. The intervention of the state in the private sector can be justified only where the state achieves the objective more efficiently than the market. Therefore, assigning to the state a task beyond its competence will result in very high costs and is thus undesirable for the public.

The critical point is that the state (this applies to the state in general and to individuals within the state), unlike an individual or a private firm, lacks the following braking mechanisms to reject tasks to which the state is unsuited. Market competition will defeat a private firm and the firm will not survive if it attempts tasks to which it is unsuited. Even if trying to fulfill a task would not endanger its survival, it will not pursue unprofitable tasks. Even when a firm might have undertaken an unprofitable task, it will make every effort to escape from it. In other words, the profit incentive plays an essential role as a brake.

Lacking in incentives of the same kind, few such braking mechanisms operate on the state. On the contrary, at least in Japan, the cost of a policy corresponds to the magnitude both of the budget and of the personnel, and therefore of the power, of each government section. The state is an organization that lacks a strong incentive to pursue the efficient achievement of tasks, and as a result it may fill even demand for which it is not competent.

Once, at least, it was said that the task of elite bureaucrats, called career bureaucrats, was to enact new laws and to organize new industry associations. In fact, Japanese bureaucrats hold their positions at the pleasure of the cabinet, and the cabinet holds power at the pleasure of the electorate. Voters will reject parties that systematically pursue egregiously inefficient policies, and facing that threat politicians will restrain bureaucrats who also do that. Potentially, the public in a modern democracy thus functions as the electoral equivalent to the market constraint on private-sector firms. However, as the large literature in public choice and modern political economy demonstrates, this electoral market generally constrains inefficient state behavior less effectively than competitive economic markets constrain inefficient firm behavior. In the small-business sector, that constraint on state behavior in Japan has been almost non-existent – and I use it here to illustrate the mechanisms that a government may adopt where the electoral market imposes almost no brake on inefficient policy.

What is feasible for the government is limited

The question then becomes 'what can and should we expect of the government?' Such a question will necessarily include the following five mutually related components. (1) What is allowed of the government? (2) What is feasible for the government? (3) What competence has the government? (4) To what extent can we control the members of the government in order to improve consumer welfare? (5) To what extent does the government's decision-making process track the interests of consumers?

The government is not allowed to do everything. Although it will differ over time and with circumstances, the choice set of policy variables allowed to the government is strictly bounded. This point becomes clearer when we take as examples the government authority to collect taxes, to restrict property rights, or to give orders to the private-sector workforce. Theoretically, if there was no limit in discriminatory treatment and in tax collection by the government, it would be able to pursue policies that transfer huge amounts of income from the public at large to a specific group of people or firms. The choice set of policy variables allowed to the government is necessarily wider in an 'emergency' like wartime. Defining the choice set is itself a big political issue. What is critical here is the simple fact that the choice set is bounded. If the choice set is limited in practice, even an otherwise almighty government may not be able to pursue an effective policy.

The set of tasks that the government can feasibly achieve is limited, just as it is for an ordinary firm. In the case of a profit-maximizing firm, at any one moment, the firm calculates the maximum profit it can earn from a project, which by definition is never exceeded by its actual profit. It then discounts that potential maximum by the likelihood that it will earn less and compares that expected return with its probable costs. Likewise, a government will set its goals by reference to the maximum value it could earn from a given function. In a world of scarcity – which is to say, the world we live in – it cannot do everything simultaneously. It cannot produce unlimited amounts of both guns and butter.[115] Lacking magical powers, it generally cannot improve the productivity of private-sector firms or make them realize what they could achieve without government intervention (otherwise they would have done it on their own). Shifting the decision-making unit out of private hands into government seldom, if ever, improves the situation. Nonetheless, as Mancur Olson classically noted, it is in the nature of the political marketplace that small concentrated interest groups sometimes obtain inefficient policies that profit them at more than offsetting costs to the broader public.

The competence of the government determines the roles and activities it is suited to perform

A firm with superior technology, an efficient firm, is able to produce more outputs from a given amount of factor input. Likewise, a government with superior competence will achieve a higher objective function value when manipulating the policy variables available to it within the policy choice set. Every firm and likewise every government will have strengths and weaknesses, that is competence in some areas but not in others. Even Toyota Motors cannot achieve huge success within a short time when entering fields where such companies as Sony, Orix, or Seven-Eleven Japan have long been profitable.

The competence of a firm or the government will in turn determine the roles and activities that they are suited to perform. For instance, the government is far more competent and suited to providing community-wide services such as diplomacy, quarantine, fire services, and the maintenance of public order than it is to, say, providing meals for people of various tastes, or to competing in markets like swimwear, shoes, handbags, neckties, or electronics, where consumers differ by size, taste and resources, and products are subject to the vicissitudes of style and technological change.

As shown in Part I, the government made every effort to promote the development of the machine tool industry during the wartime control period. This objective constituted government policy of the highest priority, and accordingly the government was allowed the highest degree of freedom in terms of policy variable choice, something that cannot even be dreamed of in peacetime. The achievements of the government in its intervention in the machine tool industry were very limited. This was due to there being very little potential for achievement. That is, this industrial sector was unsuited to government intervention, and government competence was unsuited to intervention in this industry.

The 'evil of monopoly' emerges

Bureaucrats and officials in governments are ordinary people who behave rationally. They are not special types of people who automatically, under any conditions, devote themselves entirely to the interests of consumers.

Managers in a firm make every effort to mobilize the energies and skills of employees in order to attain maximum achievement of the firm's objectives. Otherwise, a firm will be plagued by low efficiency, low product quality, and also an identity crisis. A precondition to realizing the objectives of any firm is the strong support of consumers. This fact of a competitive market leads managers to work in the interests of consumers – else they do not remain managers.

Such a mechanism does not automatically function for government, which often undertakes requested tasks for which it has no competence. The electoral market being what it is, the government often has only greatly attenuated incentives to provide goods and services efficiently or to respond to consumer demands. In cases where the government is guaranteed monopolies or relevant costs, 'the evil of monopoly' emerges more clearly. A monopoly accompanied by authority or legal foundation will mean that the government can autonomously allocate 'tasks' to itself, forcing consumers to accept the situation.

Although firms and consumers do not engage in trades from which they cannot expect to earn a net benefit, one cannot say that about every activity involving the government. It is not always easy to induce governments to enforce only policies that improve aggregate social welfare. If it is sometimes possible to reach consensus among the relevant firms in an industry, it is enormously difficult to reach any agreement among a large number of individual voters. Democracies have long struggled with this issue to reflect the interests of consumers in policy effectively. The achievement of this objective, and also ensuring that governments make continuous efforts toward this objective, is not easy.

Summing up

Let us sum up the discussion thus far with five points:

1   The political decision-making process entails the influential voices of various interest groups jockeying with each other for position and advantage, so 'pork barreling' becomes more or less inevitable. Consequently, policy variables that are practically available to the government become extremely limited.
2   The government has no crystal ball and is not a magician. Like a private enterprise, what is feasible for the government is strictly bounded.
3   The government has its strengths and weaknesses; there are roles that it is unsuited to perform and those to which it is better suited, and these are determined by its competence. Asking the government to undertake a role unsuited to it costs much.
4   Individual bureaucrats, and for that matter the entire government, sometimes undertake tasks requested of them regardless of whether they are suited to them. In addition, they often lack strong incentives to improve efficiency.

5   It is not easy to realize or maintain a situation where every policy is loyal to the interests of consumers.

It should now be clearer that when addressing the issue 'What can and should we expect of the government and to what extent?' we must take great care. Small business policy is no exception.

3.2.2   Three points basic to state competence in small business policy

It is desirable to note three points when investigating the competence of the state in pursuing small business policies.

Small businesses occupy the predominant position in the Japanese economy

First, small businesses, in terms of the number of both firms and employees, occupy the predominant position in the Japanese economy. Many readers may think of such large firms as Toyota, Nissan, and Honda in the automobile industry and NEC, Hitachi, and Sony in the electronics industry as representative of Japanese firms. Some may have the perception that large firms such as Toyota, and therefore their production systems, which are famous for their 'just-in-time' delivery of parts for production, cover most of the Japanese economy. On the contrary, most Japanese firms are small, and more than half the added value is generated by small firms. This predominance of small firms in Japan has a long history, and their share has not changed for at least thirty–forty years.

A comparison of large Japanese firms and their US and European counterparts reveals that Japanese firms are rather small and have far fewer employees in relation to sales. In 1991, Toyota's annual sales amounted to about half those of General Motors and a third more than Volkswagen's, yet Toyota employed less than one-tenth (72,000) the number of GM workers (751,000) and less than one-third the number of Volkswagen workers (266,000). As shown by Scherer and Ross (1990: p.63, table 3.3), in 1985, employment in Japan's top ten and top twenty leading companies as a percentage of total industrial employment was 7.3 and 9.9 percent, respectively, remarkably lower than nine other nations, including the USA (13.1 and 18.6 percent, respectively), which was the lowest among these nine nations (see Miwa 1996a: pp. 9–11, for details).

Most Japanese firms are small, and most Japanese workers are employed in small firms. The total number of establishments in the whole Japanese private sector (excluding agriculture and fisheries) was 6.5 million in 1991, and 99.1 percent were small businesses. Private-sector employees totaled 55 million, and small businesses accounted for 79.2 percent of the workforce. Limiting our attention to the manufacturing sector, we see almost the same picture. There were 857,000 manufacturing entities in 1991, and 99.4 percent of these were small businesses. Of the 14.1 million manufacturing employees, 73.8 percent worked in small businesses. Corresponding figures in the manufacturing sector in 1957 were 99.6 and 72.3 percent, suggesting the continued predominance of small businesses.[116]

What happened to Japan's economy was a normal outgrowth of market forces

Another important point concerns the role of government in promoting the rapid growth of the Japanese economy. Concurring with the majority of economists, I think that what did happen to Japan's economy was not miraculous but a normal outgrowth of market forces. As discussed in Part II, the dominant view of the Japanese economy, at least before the 1970s, was that the government had contributed tremendously to the growth of Japan's economy. The government, MITI in particular, was often identified as the headquarters of 'Japan Inc.,' and its policies were thought to represent one of the main engines powering Japan's rapid economic growth. However, careful and systematic research of Japanese government policies began in the 1980s, and scholars, especially economists, have begun to ask what the government actually did and to identify the effect of those policies. The main subject of research has been 'industrial policies,' and scholars have found few substantial effects traceable to any industrial policy.[117] This, in turn, has forced a revision of the traditional view.

What should be pointed out is that there were an 'excessive' number of firms in almost all Japanese industries, especially in those that exported many of their products. Competition was severe even in the early days of industrial policies, that is in the 1950s and 1960s. Even in those days, days that advocates of the effectiveness of industrial policies might call 'the heyday of industrial policy,' the central slogan of industrial policy was 'elimination and prevention' of 'excessive competition' (e.g., Morozumi 1966). In most cases, at the request of a majority of firms in a specific industry, the government simply intervened in the market to restrict competition. For instance, most exemption clauses to the Anti-monopoly Act that were critically reviewed or eliminated during this period were introduced before 1960.[118]

Neither deconcentration policies, such as *zaibatsu* dissolution and the Act for the Elimination of Excessive Concentration of Economic Power, nor the introduction and enforcement of the Anti-monopoly Act in 1947 had much effect in reducing this so-called 'excessive competition.'[119] Thus Japanese economic growth should be interpreted as a normal outgrowth of market forces. This chapter is an attempt to examine closely the contents and identify the economic effects of policies for small business in Japan, along the lines of recent studies of industrial policy.

The meaning of 'effectiveness' in evaluating policies

My third point concerns the meaning of 'effectiveness' in evaluating policies. In this chapter, I focus on the effectiveness of small business policies in promoting Japan's economic development. Concomitantly, I table any examination of the effectiveness of these policies as 'social policy' or as policies for equity and social stability.

3.2.3   Three factors decisively conditioning the effectiveness of small business policy

Basically as a result of the first point mentioned in Section 3.2.2, three factors decisively condition the effectiveness of small business policy. The first two restrict the potential effectiveness of the policy, and the third conditions its actual effectiveness:

1   It is usually easy to enter markets where there are many small firms, and the keenest competition faced by small firms comes from other small firms in the same industry. Therefore, even if subsidies for small businesses are huge, most of those benefits are eventually passed on to the users and consumers of small business products via market competition. As shown below, the most important small business policy measures have been financial, primarily the provision of loans at below market rates. Unless competition between small firms is restricted effectively, even a huge sum of tremendously preferential loans to small businesses will provide negligible benefits to those businesses.[120]

2   In the greater economy, most firms are small and most workers are employed by small firms, which makes the realization of policy, that is providing preferential treatment for small business, very difficult. This holds despite the fact that small firms, constituting as they do the majority of the economy, enjoy copious political power to influence policies in their interest. Having no crystal ball, the government collects the funds for its small business policies from economic agents other than small firms. Because of the excessively high ratio of small businesses and employees in small businesses, the remaining sectors (large firms) are inadequate to generate the funds for an effective small business policy. Thus, small business policy is decisively conditioned by the simple fact that nobody can subsidize almost everybody.

3   Because of the huge number and the diversity of small businesses, coordinating the interests of relevant parties is complicated, making the inherent nature of small business policy of the 'pork barrel' type. The many firms and their employees are distributed over a wide range of industrial sectors. As a result, policy for preferentially allocating resources to a specific industry or to a specific group of firms within an industry rarely attracts support from the majority of small firms.

The first two factors make effective small business policy unfeasible in any economy. In addition, under democratic political systems such as Japan's, small business policy inevitably becomes 'pork barreling.' In Japan (as in most modern democracies), the predominance of small businesses in the economy has generated concomitantly large political influence, and that influence has pushed the government to extensively develop small business policies and emphasize their importance.

3.3   THE POLICIES OF THE CENTRAL GOVERNMENT

3.3.1   Policies for small businesses

Government policies for small businesses began in prewar Japan as social policies, not economic policies. In other words, the government imposed them for reasons of 'equity' rather than 'efficiency.' At least until the beginning of the 1970s, postwar small business policies reflected this character (Miwa 1996a: pp.45–48). As shown above, the Diet, in enacting the Machine Tool Building Act in 1938 and the MIPA in 1956, instructed the government to show strong 'consideration' against adverse influences on small businesses. Under wartime control as well, 'consideration' to small businesses from the social policy point of view functioned as an obstacle both to establishing efficient wartime control and to its smooth operation.[121] The policies for small business during this period were designed to address the 'medium and small enterprises problem.'

The government's 1956 Economic White Paper is famous for declaring that 'we are no longer in the postwar period.' The Economic White Paper of the following year asserted the existence and emphasized the seriousness of the 'dual structure' of the Japanese economy. Much of the general remarks was devoted to an analysis of the dual structure, and the importance of small business policy was strongly affirmed. The words 'dual structure' suggest that there are two distinct sectors in the economy and that one sector consists of small, traditional enterprises with low productivity and low wages, and the other of large enterprises with modern technology, high productivity, and high wages. The 'medium-sized and small enterprises problem' is closely related to the concept of 'dual structure' and suggests that large firms in the modernized industrial sector subordinate, control, and exploit small firms in the traditional sector. This view explicitly assumes that large firms have and can exercise the power to exploit small firms, whose freedom of choice is tightly restricted and likened to a 'hold-up' situation, that is a situation where small firms are held at gunpoint. Many Japanese have identified this situation as a 'social problem' to be addressed by government intervention (see Miwa 1996a: ch. 3, for critical review).

Several important milestones in small business policy occurred in the early postwar period. For example, the Small and Medium-sized Enterprise Agency (SMEA) was created in 1948 as an extra-ministerial bureau of MITI, and the People's Finance Corporation and the Small Business Finance Corporation (SBFC) were founded in 1949 and 1953, respectively. However, it was not until the late 1950s that small business policies attracted public attention. The 'dual structure' emphasized by the 1957 Economic White Paper struck a responsive chord among the public and gained immediate acceptance. 'Dual structure' became one of the most popular phrases of the time. In 1963, fifteen years after the establishment of the SMEA, the Small and Medium-sized Enterprise Basic Act (hereafter, the Small Business Basic Act) was enacted on a wave of public support and enthusiastic political backing. It required the government to conduct fact-finding surveys on small businesses and to submit an annual report (the so-called White Paper on Small and Medium-sized Enterprises in Japan, or the Small Business White Paper, first published for fiscal year 1963) to the Diet on trends among small businesses and measures taken to assist them. From this period, policies for small businesses began to be implemented systematically.[122]

Ironically, the rapid economic growth in the 1960s extinguished the flame of support for the dual structure view, and it faded rapidly. By 1970, the Small Business White Paper was subtitled 'The Transformation of the Dual Structure and the Increasing Variety of the Medium and Small Enterprises Problem.' Either the situation surrounding small businesses or the public's image of small business had changed. As I summarize below, it was the public's perception that had changed. There was great divergence between the image and reality of small businesses, and the image of small businesses has changed more radically than the reality. In short, the problem that small business policies were ostensibly designed to address did not exist. If the elimination of the 'dual structure' is the standard for measuring the effectiveness of small business policies, those policies could never have amounted to 'effective' policies.

3.3.2   The 'dual structure' view and small business policies

Small business policies were systematized during the decade after the mid-1950s, symbolized by the enactment of the Small Business Basic Act in 1963. Those policies were designed to eliminate the 'dual structure' under which large firms supposedly exploited a large number of small firms. Most supporters of the 'dual structure' view asserted that 'excessive competition' was inevitable because there were too many small businesses. Accordingly, elimination of barriers to small business entry was never an objective of small business policies.

Four points inconsistent with the 'dual structure' view

As I have discussed previously (Miwa 1996a), the 'dual structure' view that underlay Japan's small business policy was totally misguided. Four points emerge here for discussion.

1   The Japanese economy grew rapidly even before the 'dual structure' was apparently 'dissolved' by about 1970. In this environment, both small and large firms grew steadily. This implies that large firms provided stable demand for the products of rapidly growing small firms. Such a fact is not consistent with the notion that large firms exploited small businesses.

2   As shown in Table 3.1 and Figure 3.1, the profitability of the smaller firms
     has been much higher than that of large firms. This too is not consistent with
     the argument that small firms were exploited by large firms.[123]
3   As shown in Figures 3.2 and 3.3, between 1954 and 1991, that is before and
     after the time of the supposed 'structural change,' both the number of estab-
     lishments and their employment in every size category increased constantly.
     This too is inconsistent with the argument that small firms were exploited, as
     rational entrepreneurs would not enter markets in which they would be
     exploited.
4   Although it is widely believed that a 'loan-concentrating mechanism' in the
     financial sector targeted loans at large firms rather than small businesses,[124]
     perpetuating the notion of 'dual structure,' as shown below, such a mecha-
     nism in fact never existed.

Three propositions against the 'dual structure' view

These four points (or even just one or two) invite three propositions:[125] (1) the
assertion that a large majority of small firms were 'exploited' before the early
1960s is inconsistent with reality; (2) the assertion that they have been exploited
in more recent years is likewise inconsistent with reality; (3) 'structural change,'
in the sense of a dramatic reduction in the proportion of small firms being
'exploited,' never occurred.

Summing up

In short, the problem that small business policies were ostensibly designed to
address did not exist. Moreover, the magnitude of policy measures was small, and
small business policies were implemented indiscriminately among a huge number
of small firms. This means that they neither potentially had nor did have a major
impact on the small business sector as a whole.

3.3.3   An illustration: loans for small businesses

The SBFC, together with the Cooperative Bank for Commerce and Industry,
founded in 1936, became the principal means by which the government channeled loans to small firms.

Three basic facts about loans to small businesses

However, those small business policies had no substantial effects (see Miwa 1995,
for details). There is wide agreement that the most important small business policy
measures were financial, in which these government-affiliated financial institutions
were the central players. I will take loans by these institutions as an illustration.

Table 3.1 Rate of profit on equity (paid-up capital) of corporate enterprises before tax, all industries

Firm size by equity (¥ million)	Profit rate (five-year running average) (%)						Number of years below average profit rate		
	1953–59	1960–64	1965–69	1970–74	1975–79	1980–84	1960–84	1960–74	1975–84
2–5	22.4	32.4	30.7	34.6	22.2	16.1	7	0	7
5–10	20.9	34.1	31.4	35.4	23.0	17.8	6	0	6
10–50	21.2	28.7	31.2	35.5	24.4	20.9	1	0	1
50–100	18.7	25.3	26.7	30.4	23.1	24.4	2	0	2
100–1,000	13.1	20.5	23.3	25.6	22.0	22.3	12	10	2
Over 1,000		16.2	19.8	21.3	17.8	19.5	23	15	8

Source: Ministry of Finance, Hojin kigyo tokei nenpo (Financial Statement of Incorporated Business), annual, adapted from Miwa (1990: p.13, table 1.1).

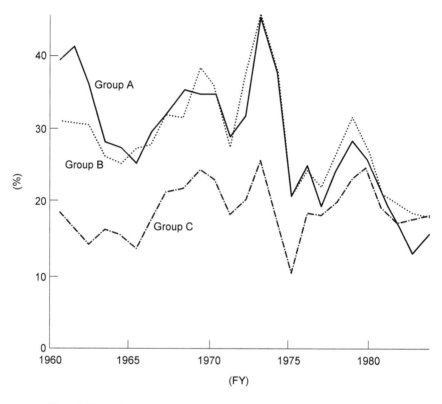

Figure 3.1 Rate of profit on equity (paid-up capital) of corporate enterprises before tax, all industries

Source: Ministry of Finance, *Hojin kigyo tokei ninpo* (Financial Statement of Incorporated Business), annual, adapted from Miwa (1990: p.13, table 1.1).

Group A: Enterprises with 5–10 million yen in capital
Group B: Enterprises with 10–15 million yen in capital
Group C: Enterprises with more than 1 billion yen in capital

First, during the twenty-year period 1960–80, these institutions provided only 10 percent of the total amount that small businesses borrowed from all financial institutions. Taking five-year intervals, these figures were 8.7 percent in 1960, 8.8 percent in 1965, and 9.3 percent in 1970. They finally exceeded 10 percent in 1975, reaching 12.8 percent in 1975 and 12.6 percent in 1980.

Second, in most cases the SBFC loan rate was a self-designated 'base rate' that was equal to the long-term prime rate. Small firms are not always able to borrow at this rate in the regular financial market, especially when the market is tight, and SBFC loans necessarily included a subsidy to small businesses. However, this subsidy amounted to only 0.5–1 percent of loans.

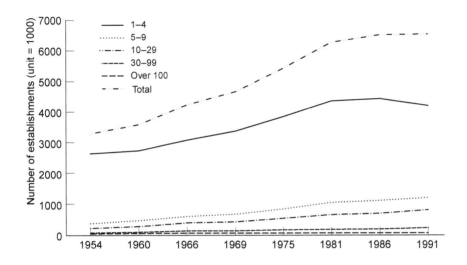

Figure 3.2 The number of non-agricultural establishments in each size[a] category, 1954–91

Source: Administration Management Agency, census of establishments.

[a] Size in terms of the number of employees.

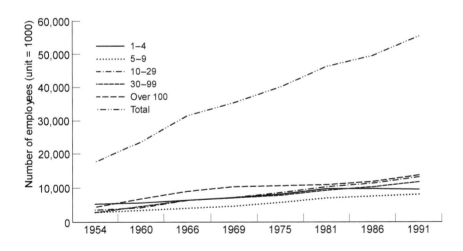

Figure 3.3 The number of people engaged in non-agricultural establishments in each size [a] category, 1954–91

Source: Administration Management Agency, census of establishments.

[a] Size in terms of the number of employees.

Third, supporters of the view that loans to small businesses were effective assumed the existence of a financial dual structure that seriously handicapped small firms. Such an assumption is unfounded. As shown in Figure 3.4, the proportion of equity to total capitalization of large firms was consistently higher than that of small firms over time, and had gradually fallen to the level of small businesses by 1970, when support for the dual structure view weakened. Thus it was small firms rather than large firms that could make advantageous use of the financial market, and this advantage is thought to have gradually disappeared by 1970.

Even loans to small businesses, the most important small business policy measures, were based on the erroneous assumption of a financial 'dual structure.' Those policies provided only 10 percent of the total amount of funds that small businesses borrowed from all financial institutions, at a rate slightly lower than the market rate. If policy loan rates were 1 percent lower than the market rate, then representing as they did only 10 percent of total funding, they could have lowered the average borrowing rate by a mere 0.1 percent. It is impossible to evaluate that as a remarkable policy effect. Consequently, loans to small businesses could not have been an effective policy measure.

The effectiveness of loans to small businesses depends on the state of the capital and product market and the relation between small businesses and large firms. In many cases, small business sectors are so competitive that loans to small

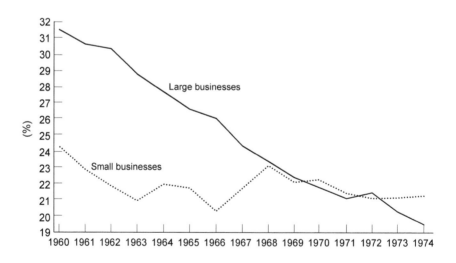

Figure 3.4 Equity/capitalization ratio, 1960–74

Source: Bank of Japan, *Financial Statement of Small Business in Japan* for small businesses and *Financial Statement of Principal Enterprises in Japan* for large firms.

businesses at lower interest rates benefit only the buyers of their products, including consumers and large firms. This suggests that this 0.1 percent reduction still overestimates its policy effect.

A strong pump-priming effect?

The following rebuttal of the above evaluation has received wide support: the argument that policy loans had a strong 'pump-priming effect,' 'signaling effect,' or 'cowbell effect,' or more simply, that such policy loans had the effect of stimulating private banks to lend to firms receiving policy loans. Even if the ratio of policy loans to total borrowing had been less than 10 percent, the argument runs, their effects have been far greater than this figure suggests in terms of priming other loans. Consequently, it is argued, loans to small businesses had a tremendous effect on small business promotion, and on Japan's economic growth.

Supporters often called this effect 'qualitative supplements,' in addition to the 10 percent 'quantitative supplements.' Recall the critical review of the argument in Part II (Sections 2.3.11 and 2.3.12) on the effectiveness of loans from the Japan Development Bank (JDB).

Three arguments against the pump-priming effect view

I cannot agree with this view for three reasons:

1   Most policy loans are provided under a general loan scheme at a 'base rate,' and the financial doors are open to any small business. For instance, the SBFC provides its loans directly through its approximately sixty offices and indirectly through private financial institutions, which number 846 (15,131 branches). SBFC offices and agents are open to any small business, and borrowers can negotiate with them directly. In other words, they need not have any recommendation from a third party such as the local government, the Board of Commerce and Industry, chambers of commerce and industry, or other financial institutions.

2   The SBFC and its agents check loan applications and security presented by its borrowers more severely than do private institutions. What we saw in Part II (Sections 2.3.11 and 2.3.12) concerning the JDB loans applies to the SBFC. The corporation adopted as a rule 'to take real estate and personal property, or other assets as a security' and to ask, 'in principle, to give surety for the loan' (subsections 7 and 8 of section 4 of the Rules). Furthermore, the system is such that if a default occurs on an indirect loan, the agent bears 80 percent of the loss (section 8 of the Rules). Coupled with the low default rate of its loans, these facts suggest that the loans at lower interest rates are directed at risk-free small borrowers through allocating

funds under a strict standard, thus subsidizing those which could have borrowed from private banks in the first place.

No incentive is provided to the persons directly in charge of lending at the financial institutions, either to identify the small businesses with the highest business potential or to bear the risks associated with lending to riskier firms. The financial institutions that those persons belong to have no incentive to change by themselves either in their business model or in their organizational design for information collection in order to facilitate their members' activities. Obviously, the government could and did take no action in correcting the program.

3   Even if the government selects firms with its own standards, why and how can it promote economic growth? An underlying, seemingly tautological, assumption of belief is that in Japan the government always has the ability to beat the market, which is, at least, still open to careful investigation.[126]

3.3.4   Overview of small business policies

Although many studies of small business policies address 'policy ideas,' 'policy targets,' and 'policy measures,' few consider 'policy effects.' Among those who do, Hajime Takaki, former chairman of the Central Cooperative Bank for Commerce and Industry, observed soon after the depression of the early 1970s:

> There are so many different policy measures for small business policies that most of us would be amazed to discover how tiny the scale of each policy actually is. Policy efforts have been wide but thin. It is as though the government waters large flower pots with small sprinkling cans. ... In the present severe depression, there is a strong demand for such policies for small business in order to encourage their owners and managers. ... Each policy is well designed and sensitive; however, the scale of government's policies is too small to have any real effects.[127]

Takashi Yokokura: a standard view

However, a more standard view would be similar to that expressed by Yokokura (1988). First, Yokokura argues that small business policies until the 1950s were but one facet of social policy and consisted of financial and cartel policies. In the 1960s, policies to assist the modernization of small business facilities were but one facet of industrial policy. In the 1970s and 1980s, modernization policies emphasized human resources, technology (information), and industrial adjustment policies such as assistance for firms to change their line of business.

Second, small business policies tended to be indiscriminate in focus and in the policy measures they used. This was in part because of the great variety of disadvantages ostensibly faced by small businesses but was also due to the operation of political-economic mechanisms.[128] Nonetheless, the indiscriminate application of small business policies, such as in the designation of industries under the Modernization Promotion Act of 1963, inevitably weakened their collective impact (effectiveness). This Act was enacted as an embodiment of the Small Business Basic Act of 1963 in order to modernize small businesses in each industry. The number of industries designated in the five years ending in fiscal year 1967 was 137. By 1975, the number had increased to 232.

Third, small business policies relied primarily on the use of financing, operating through the market mechanism, rather than competition-restricting measures and direct subsidies, which eliminated the protective policy element aspect of small business policies. 'In the case of financing, it differed from a direct subsidy in that firms had to repay the principal and pay interest, while the market mechanism was utilized so that financing was not provided to firms without the ability to repay' (*ibid.*: p.532). This contrasts sharply with agricultural policies, which depended on the use of import restrictions and direct subsidies.

Yokokura (*ibid.*: p.524) has commented that:

> If … one compares the amount and content of the budget for small business policies with that of agriculture and fisheries, the other sector that along with small business has been labeled 'pre-modern,' then the following differential can be observed. Subsidies for agriculture, forestry, and fisheries in the 1980 General Budget came to 1.9 trillion yen (including funds for land improvement and other activities to improve the infrastructure), while 1980 Fiscal and Investment and Loan Program (FILP) investments came to 890 billion yen. In contrast, 1980 General Budget subsidies for small business policies came to 61 billion yen, while 1980 FILP investments came to 3.4 trillion yen. In contrast to the huge subsidies expended on agriculture, those for small business are small, and the dependence is on FILP investments.

Two points about Yokokura's view

Two points can be made about this view. First, Yokokura's first point characterizes small business policy with policy objectives and policy slogans, which have no relation to the effectiveness of the policies or with the degree and direction of any policy impact. As discussed above, the effectiveness of small business financial policies was limited. Cartel policies in small business sectors to eliminate 'excessive competition' were not effective enough even to achieve the objectives portrayed by these slogans. As shown in Parts I and II, issues such as the 'promotion of industrial rationalization' through 'reorganizing industries' and 'restructuring the industrial order' have long existed, having originated during the prewar period. Small business modernization policy could never have been selective and discriminate either.

Table 3.2 Summary of special fiscal treatment for regional development, by prefecture

Prefecture	I [a]			II					III								
	1	2	3	1	2	3	4	5	1	2	3	4	5	6	7	8	9
Hokkaido						•	•	•		•	•	•	•	•	•	•	•
Aomori						•	•	•		•		•	•	•	•	•	•
Iwate						•	•	•				•	•	•	•	•	
Miyagi	•					•	•	•					•			•	
Akita	•					•	•	•		•			•		•	•	•
Yamagata						•	•			•		•	•	•	•	•	
Fukushima	•					•					•	•	•	•	•	•	
Ibaraki					•							•	•	•		•	
Tochigi												•	•	•			
Gunma													•	•			
Saitama													•				
Chiba						•							•	•			
Tokyo										•							
Kanagawa																	
Niigata				•						•	•	•	•	•	•	•	

Toyama	Ishikawa	Fukui	Yamanashi	Nagano	Gifu	Shizuoka	Aichi	Mie	Shiga	Kyoto	Osaka	Hyogo	Nara	Wakayama	Tottori	Shimane	Okayama	Hiroshima	Yamaguchi
•	•	•	•	•	•	•	•	•				•	•	•	•	•	•	•	•
•	•	•	•	•								•	•	•	•	•			•
•	•	•	•	•	•	•	•	•		•	•	•	•	•	•	•	•	•	•
•	•	•	•	•	•	•	•	•		•		•		•	•		•	•	•
•	•	•	•	•	•	•	•	•		•	•	•				•	•	•	•
•	•		•																•
	•						•		•	•		•		•	•		•		•
							•					•		•	•	•	•	•	•
•	•	•	•	•	•	•	•	•	•	•	•	•	•	•	•	•	•	•	•
•	•			•	•		•					•		•	•	•	•	•	•
•	•	•	•	•	•		•			•		•		•	•	•	•	•	•
		•	•		•		•					•				•	•	•	•
•			•	•											•	•	•		
•	•	•		•	•	•	•	•	•										
		•				•	•	•	•	•	•	•	•						
			•																

Table 3.2 Contd.

Prefecture	I[a]			II					III								
	1	2	3	1	2	3	4	5	1	2	3	4	5	6	7	8	9
Tokushima	•					•	•	•		•			•	•	•	•	
Kagawa						•	•	•		•			•	•	•	•	•
Ehime	•					•	•	•	•	•			•	•	•	•	•
Kochi						•	•	•	•	•			•	•	•	•	
Fukuoka	•			•		•	•	•	•	•	•		•	•	•	•	•
Saga						•	•	•		•	•		•	•		•	
Nagasaki		•			•	•	•	•	•	•		•	•	•	•	•	
Kumamoto	•					•	•	•	•	•	•		•	•	•	•	•
Oita	•					•	•	•	•				•	•	•	•	•
Miyazaki	•			•		•	•	•	•	•			•	•	•	•	•
Kagoshima							•	•	•	•			•	•	•	•	•
Okinawa								•									
TOTAL	8	8	9	17	7	37	26	43	14	26	7	24	41	44	27	44	22

Source: adapted from Japan Regional Development Corporation (1991) *Chiiki keizai tokei yoran* (Outline of Statistics for Regional Economies), pp.16 –17.

[a] The policies in this table are classified as follows:

I. Policies for improvement of the function s of large cities

    1. Metropolitan district

    2. Kinki district

    3. Chubu district

II. Policies to promote industry

    1. New industrial cities

    2. Specified areas for industrial reorganization

    3. Developing areas

    4. Technopolises

    5. Areas that encourage introduction of new industry

III. Policies to promote special areas

    1. Special soil areas

    2. Isolated islands

    3. Coal -mining areas

    4. Areas of heavy snowfall

    5. Mountain areas

    6. Underpopulated areas

    7. Newly developing areas

    8. Isolated areas

    9. Peninsular areas

Second, because of rules regarding decision making and the policy implementation process, policies in any democratic state almost always become 'indiscriminate,' and pork barreling sets in. Depending on various factors, such as the idiosyncrasies of particular political systems and the historical and cultural environment, the content, form, and seriousness of the 'indiscriminateness' varies over time and across countries, industries, and policy types. There is nothing exceptional about small business policies in Japan being extremely 'indiscriminate.'

'Indiscriminateness' appears not only among industries but also among regions

As shown below, central government's small business policies are implemented by or in combination with local governments. As a result, 'indiscriminateness' appears not only among industries but also among regions. The Japanese government has enthusiastically enforced 'regional policies' to 'vitalize regions.' Although not explicitly, these policies always have had in mind small firms as their actual beneficiaries. Table 3.2, which is a summary of the special fiscal treatment for regional development by prefecture, clearly shows how indiscriminately special fiscal treatments have allocated public resources between regions.[129]

3.3.5   The small business policy menu in Japan

Let me here catalog, for the convenience of readers, the 'basic measures' adopted as small business policies in Japan. These are the 'basic measures' found in *Outline of Small Business Policies* (SMEA 1992).

Four points on the small business policy menu

Readers should keep four points in mind:

1   I refer here to many Japanese 'policies' and 'policy measures.' Their titles often make little sense even in Japanese and therefore are hard to translate into English. Many of these policies are simply new versions of older ones and contain new phrases with only nominal differences in meaning. This proliferation of policies with only slight variations has resulted from the political and administrative conditions in Japan.

2   Although the SMEA was established to promote small businesses, it is not the only government institution that does so. The Ministries of Labor, Construction, and Transportation, the Fair Trade Commission, MITI, and local governments all have small business policies. Limiting attention to small business policies for individual industries, the SMEA's *Outline* refers to the Life Industries Bureau of MITI (policies for the textile industry, promotion

policies for traditional arts and crafts industries, and promotion policies for daily necessities industries), the Resource and Energy Agency (policies for coal-mining regions and policies for small mining firms), the Ministry of Agriculture and Fisheries (policies for small businesses in the agricultural and fishery industries), the Ministry of Transportation (policies for small trans- portation businesses), the Ministry of Welfare (policies for businesses in industries related to the environment and health), and finally the Ministry of Construction (policies for small construction businesses and policies for small realty firms).

3　No clear definition of small business policy exists, and accordingly the following list is not necessarily exhaustive. For example, the MIPA discussed in Part II was explained by the person directly in charge as 'a traditional small business policy.' Policies like the Large Store Act, the licensing system for liquor retailers, exemption clauses introduced to the Anti-monopoly Act in 1953 for resale price maintenance of branded and printed products (which occupied the center of the recent deregulation debate and are discussed in Chapter 4), show a strong small business policy color (see, for example, Miwa 1997e). Prohibitions against the establishment of medical institutions and the holding of farmland by business firms also share the same character (*ibid.*: §8-3).

4　As discussed in the next section, in addition to enforcing small business poli- cies as part of or in combination with those of the central government, local authorities such as prefectural governments adopt their own small business policies, which are not included in the list.

The menu of policy measures for small business

1　*Finance*: financial assistance is provided by three government-affiliated institu- tions – the SBFC, the People's Finance Corporation, and the Central Cooperative Bank of Commerce.

2　*Credit supplements*: to obtain a loan from a financial institution, it is helpful for a small firm to have its loan guaranteed by a credit guarantee association, which in turn applies to the Small Business Credit Corporation to insure the guarantee.

3　*Small business taxation*: corporate income tax is reduced; preferential tax treat- ment to promote investment by small businesses is provided.

4　*Cooperatives*: aid is provided for the joint business activities (such as joint production, joint processing, joint sales) of about 50,000 cooperatives.

5　*Consulting and finance*: management consulting and guidance are provided by specialized personnel in the prefectural governments.

6   *Personnel training* (human resource development): a variety of training programs and basic training courses are organized by prefectural government institutions for small businesses.

7   *Technological development*: technical training courses are provided in institutions for small businesses and technical assistance by prefectural and other public research institutions.

8   *Promotion of small enterprises*: management consulting and guidance by personnel at the Board of Commerce and Industry and chambers of commerce and industry; special loans for management improvement; special loans for equipment modernization.

3.4   THE POLICIES OF LOCAL GOVERNMENTS

3.4.1   The commercial and industrial policies of Hyogo Prefecture

Small business policies and local governments

Most policies of the central government are implemented through or with the assistance of local governments. In most cases, however, the central government decides the general scheme of each policy. Local governments that consider the scheme useful then develop more detailed plans and compete to have their specific plan adopted by the central government. The selection of proposals often appears to be very politicized, which may be the reason for the indeterminate focus of those policies.

Policy implemented by the central government is the result of collaboration with local governments. This division of labor reflects the recognition that the effectiveness of such policies depends on the circumstances surrounding them, and that these circumstances differ greatly by region. Each local government also has its own indigenous small business policies. As a result, there are a wide variety of policy objectives and forms among the actual policies of local governments, the weight of which is also different.

Compared with financial policies, it is more difficult to evaluate the effectiveness of other policies, such as technical assistance by prefectural and other public research institutions, management guidance by specialist personnel, and the provision of management consulting and guidance by specialist personnel.

However, coupled with the following two points, what I have learned on various occasions, and scattered materials also suggest that the overall effectiveness of these other policies is no different from that of financial policies. There is wide agreement that the most important policy measures for small businesses were financial policies. Also, as shown below, the number of persons engaged in small business policies has been so limited that they simply could never have achieved effective policy implementation.

Hyogo Prefecture

To better understand the implementation and effect of policies, let us focus upon a prefecture, Hyogo Prefecture, in which Kobe is the largest city. Its population is 5.4 million, 4.4 percent of the total Japanese population. Several indicators show that its economic power is 4–5 percent that of the whole country. The prefecture is located in the Kinki district, which is located in the central western part of Japan and consists of seven prefectures. This prefecture has both densely populated, highly industrialized urban areas and sparsely populated areas that have agricultural bases or are located in mountainous regions.

The number of establishments (excluding agriculture and fisheries) was 274,000 in 1986, 99.1 percent of which were small businesses. Of these establishments, 47.9 percent were wholesaling and retailing entities, 23.9 percent were engaged in the service sector, and 12.6 percent were manufacturing entities. Of the total workforce, 77.8 percent were employed in small businesses. The manufacturing sector employed 27.5 percent of the total workforce, 69.6 percent of whom were in small businesses.

The Bureau of Commerce and Industry

The Bureau of Commerce and Industry (BCI) within the prefectural government is in charge of small business policies for the region. As of 1992, this bureau had a staff of 360, 4.2 percent of approximately 8,500 prefectural employees (in 1967, the corresponding numbers were 404, 5.0 percent, and 8,000). The BCI has seven divisions (five in 1967), and the Industrial Policy Division, the New Industry Location Division, the Finance Division, and the Industry Division are directly involved in small business policies.

In addition, the General Coordination Division has indirect involvement in small business policies. Of the 360 BCI employees, 166 are in the central office, and seventy-five are in divisions with small business connections. In addition to the divisions in the central office, two subordinate institutions deal with small business policies. These are the Institute for General Guidance for Small Businesses, which is subordinate to the General Coordination Division and employs nineteen people, and Hyogo Prefecture's Institute for Industrial Research, which is subordinate to the Industry Division and employs 118 people.

No significant difference between the policy priorities of central and local government

Three groups of policy measures were at the core of BCI policies in 1992: measures to upgrade the industrial structure; measures to stimulate regional economies; and measures to promote successful small businesses. The budgets for each group reveal the predominance of the third group of policy measures, which included two significant items: ¥57.6 billion for financial assistance and ¥14.4 billion to assist the growth of small businesses. Policies for small businesses are the core of local government policies for commerce and industry, at the center of which stand financial policies. There is thus no significant difference between the small business policy priorities of central and local government.

The Finance Division of the BCI

BCI's Finance Division contains four subdivisions, three (as of 1992, fourteen employees and three managers) of which implement policies directly related to small businesses. The Finance Subdivision (four employees) is responsible for a wide variety of tasks, such as providing information on government loan systems and miscellaneous financial guidance. The Credit and Cooperative Subdivision (seven employees) takes charge of financing through cooperatives and tasks related to the credit guarantee system. The Equipment Modernization Subdivision (three employees) is in charge of tasks related to loans for modernizing equipment.

An illustration of the division of roles between central and local government

Let us consider the policies for modernizing the equipment of small businesses as an illustration of the division of roles between central and local government. Of these four measures, the budgetary burden for measures 1 and 3 is borne equally by the central and prefectural governments, while that for measures 2 and 4 is wholly funded by Hyogo Prefecture:

1   *Loans for modernizing equipment*: as of 1992, ¥1.6 billion; in line with the Small and Medium-sized Enterprise Modernization Promotion Act.
2   *Expansion of funds for loans for the promotion and modernization of local industries*: ¥550 million.
3   *Equipment-leasing system*: in line with the equipment-leasing system established in 1966, the central and prefectural governments provide loans to an equipment-leasing agency (a public service corporation). The equipment-leasing company then purchases machinery and leases it to small enterprises. Loans associated with leasing totaled ¥1.65 billion.
4   *System for leasing high-technology and energy-saving equipment*: the Hyogo Prefecture equipment-leasing agency purchases equipment and leases it. Total purchases of leasing equipment were ¥700 million.

Technical assistance

Besides financing policies, the most conspicuous measures among the small business policies in Japan are the various activities called consultation, diagnosis, guidance, advice, and assistance. Here I explain the scope of the 'technical assistance' granted through Hyogo Prefecture's Institute of Industrial Research, which comes under the control of the Industry Division of the BCI. The Industry Division, with seventeen employees and six managers (personnel data from 1992), consists of two subdivisions: the Manufacturing and Mining Promotion Subdivision with four employees; and the Local Industry Areas Promotion Subdivision with four employees, and two offices. Fifteen of the institute's workforce are office workers, ninety-nine are technical experts and workers, and four are technical support staff. In addition to the Center for Industrial Research, which employs two-thirds of this staff, three technical centers of a similar scale, for machinery and metals (sixteen employees), textile products (fifteen employees) and leather products (thirteen employees), are subordinate to the institute.

The origin of the Institute of Industrial Research came with the establishment of the Industrial Experiment Station by the prefectural government in 1917. The newest technical center (for leather products) was established in 1948, and the total number of employees was 126 in 1967. The technical centers then had twenty, twenty-one, and seven employees, respectively, suggesting that little changed in twenty-five years.

These types of institution and technical center are not peculiar to Hyogo Prefecture. Every prefecture has its own such institutions, the origins and roles of which are quite similar. As in the case of Hyogo Prefecture, which has special interests in specific industries such as textile and leather products and established technical centers for them, each prefectural government has institutions for specific industries (usually local industries). The effectiveness of those technical assistance policies can be evaluated in part by the ratio of the total number of technical personnel to the number of small businesses. In the case of Hyogo Prefecture, there were 118 technical personnel for 272,000 establishments (34,000 in manufacturing alone). Consequently, even if these policy measures were effective, their overall impact could not have been great.

3.4.2   Preferential treatment of small business in public facilities construction

There is wide academic agreement that the most important small business policy measures were financial. However, there is another view of significant weight, which argues that preferential treatment of small firms in the construction of public facilities is at least as important a small business policy measure (from the point of view of small construction firms) as policy loans. In order to illustrate the size, direction, and forms of distortion that small business policies would produce when powerfully enforced, I will briefly describe two phenomena that are now attracting wide attention as policy distortions: *uwauke* (literally, 'reverse subcontracting') and *marunage* ('complete or blanket outsourcing'). Essentially, both refer to the use of a small firm as a front organization that obtains the contract then arranges for another (larger) firm to do all or most of the work.

Three points as background information

Three points should be noted as background information:

1   The ratio of public facilities construction to total construction demand in Japan is about 40 percent. The ratio rose during the 1990s and in FY1994 reached 45.3 percent, or ¥81.43 trillion in monetary terms.

2   In monetary terms, more than 80 percent of all construction of public facilities is ordered by local governments: in 1993, 40.2 percent by prefectural governments and 43 percent by governments of communities like cities, towns, and villages. Even if the central government sets a basic framework for the preferential treatment of small businesses, it is local governments that actually enforce it as small business policy.

3   The emergence of and increase in *uwauke* and *marunage* has paralleled the emphasis on preferential treatment of small businesses in the construction of public facilities, which is based on the Small Business Basic Act of 1963. The number of construction companies, primarily small companies, rose dramatically in the decade from the second half of the 1960s (the number of 'licensed' construction companies increased from less than 100,000 in March 1965 to 350,000 in March 1975).

Uwauke *and* marunage

The term *marunage* became popular in Japan in the wake of the bribery scandal involving bureaucrats in the Ministry of Welfare and the construction of nursing homes in Saitama Prefecture in 1996. In the construction industry, this term, together with the term *uwauke*, had been popular for a long time, but they began to appear in the mass media after 1996. *Uwauke* describes the situation where a small construction company taking on a project to construct public facilities subcontracts the work to a larger company. *Shitauke* is the Japanese term for subcontracting, in which a larger company subcontracts to smaller ones. Here, though, the normal direction of subcontracting is reversed, and hence *shita* (down or downward) is replaced with *uwa* (up or upward). Small contractors often delegate all the work of an entire construction project to a subcontractor, which is called *marunage*. However, if the main contractor does practically nothing in construction, they violate section 22 of the Construction Industry Act, which prohibits such 'blanket outsourcing.'

Basic questions for discussion

These practices raise the following questions:

*   Why does a small contractor rely on *uwauke*?
*   Why does it blanket subcontract?
*   Why does a large company engage in *uwauke* instead of becoming a main contractor?

- Why does a buyer, or a local government, not contract directly with a large company, which otherwise would be engaged in *uwauke*?
- Why do local governments not check *uwauke* and *marunage*, at least the latter of which violates section 22 of the Construction Industry Act?
- Which players would be likely to profit from stronger restrictions on *uwauke* and *marunage*, and which would be likely to lose?

Illustration: the case of the road-paving industry

For illustration, I take the case of the road-paving industry, where *uwauke* and *marunage* are most prevalent. Reports in industry journals and the mass media convey the following facts:[130]

- The *uwauke* and *marunage* phenomena commenced with the Small Business Basic Act of 1963 and the Act for Securing Business on the Public Demand for Small Business (so-called *Kan-koju-ho*) of 1966, the latter of which was based on section 20 of the former, and stated that 'the state must take necessary measures to increase the business opportunities of small firms, concerning the procurement of products and services by the state and so forth, in order to expand demand for products and services of small firms.' With these laws, governments, local governments in particular, commenced new and strengthened existing preferential treatment of small local businesses involved in public facilities construction but excluding non-local small businesses.
- The number of road-paving companies had increased from 479 in 1966 to about 10,000 in 1975 and about 70,000 by 1995. The increase in the number of enterprises in this industry has been the most dramatic, matched only by the dredging industry. As shown in Figure 3.5, the increase was particularly dramatic in the categories of ¥10–50 million and ¥50–100 million in paid-up capital, where the dependence of firms on the construction of public utilities was the highest.
- One of the leading journals of the industry, *Douro kensetsu* (Road Construction), in a symposium in its January 1984 issue, focused on *uwauke* and *marunage* and suggested that most firms in the industry have recognized their wide prevalence.
- The suggested mark-up between the price offered by the government and the *marunage* price is 10 percent at the minimum, which suggests that main contractors, usually small local companies, take more than 10 percent of the 'construction cost' as their profit.
- In order to increase work for small businesses, governments divide construction projects into unnecessarily small parcels, meaning that construction costs soar.

- The spread of *uwauke* and *marunage* has invited a huge number of new entrants that are incompetent in road paving.

Today *uwauke* is a contract between a small main contractor incompetent in road paving and a large paving company, rather than between two competent paving companies, one small (main contractor) and the other large (subcontractor).

Six points about the prevalence of **uwauke** *and* **marunage**

Uwauke and *marunage* are the consequences of factors like the present procurement systems or 'policies,' as well as the fact that government agencies are the buyers. It is widely recognized that 'policies' to secure business opportunities, rather than business itself, for small firms, particularly those in the region, have a strong tendency to exclude firms that are competent in efficient and appropriate works. The market reactions to these policies are *uwauke* and *marunage*.

The 'opinion' of the Administrative Reform Committee of 12 December 1997, which was submitted to the prime minister, declares: 'The excessive preferential

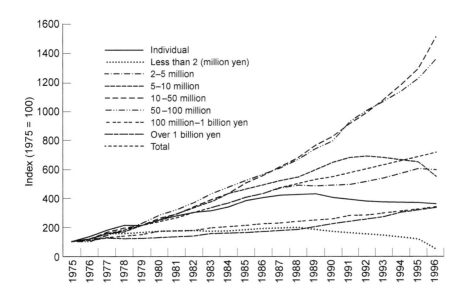

Figure 3.5 Indexed[a] number of road-paving companies in each size[b] category, 1975–96

Source: Ministry of Construction.

[a] 1975 = 100.

[b] Size in terms of paid-up capital.

treatment of small construction companies and of local companies, coupled with those systems, have caused the prevalence of the so-called phenomena of *uwauke* and *marunage*, causing public facilities construction costs to skyrocket.' Under the Act to establish this committee, the prime minister and the cabinet immediately adopted the opinion. Thus, this is now the formal view of the Japanese government.[131]

Six points can be made at this stage of the discussion:

1   Simply prohibiting *uwauke* and *marunage* is against the buyer's interest, since it forces incompetent contractors to finish works. Even if the buyer could prevent a deterioration in quality, the firm with the higher costs will finish the work. Although the direct cost to government might be unchanged, forcing supply to inefficient firms is against the interest of consumers, decreasing their total income.

2   Dividing projects into unnecessarily small parcels increases construction costs, regardless of who finishes the work.

3   Providing highly profitable opportunities through *uwauke* and *marunage* has created a flood of new entrants to the market, which in turn has led to strong demand for the maintenance and further expansion of such opportunities.

4   The situation requires someone to 'coordinate' the demands of relevant parties, controlling their behavior and allocating works between them. This in turn potentially leads to a variety of collusive practices. The apparent involvement of politicians in the collusion is thought by many to corrupt the political process as well.

5   Even competent small construction companies, making efforts in their proper business, are badly affected by a flood of incompetent new entrants. Under the present situation, competence in construction work does not necessarily mean prosperity for a company, which hinders the entry and growth of excellent small businesses.

6   The morale of construction companies, regardless of their size, diminishes to zero under the present situation, and it has fatally affected the development of the industry.

Countermeasures that focus only on the tip of the iceberg are harmful

The prevalence of *uwauke* and *marunage* is merely the tip of the iceberg, suggesting a greater evil lying below the surface. Understanding the mechanism that creates these phenomena and identifying their real causes is the issue of primary concern. Countermeasures that focus only on the tip of iceberg are harmful, since they do not address the problems identified in the above six points.

In response to the 'final opinion' of the Administrative Reform Committee in December 1997, the Three-Year Plan for Promoting Deregulation of the government, which was revised at the end of March 1998, declared that the Ministry of Construction, the Ministry of Home Affairs, and the other ministries procuring public facilities construction would survey the actual circumstances of *uwauke* to eliminate *uwauke* and *marunage*, and that they would ask local governments to follow suit. For the first time, the government thus formerly recognized the existence of *uwauke* and promised this survey. The government has also asked local governments for their cooperation. Recall that most construction of public facilities is in the hands of local governments, which are not directly controlled by central government.

Have policies for small construction companies been effective?

It is an empirical question requiring careful investigation whether policies for small construction companies like the preferential treatment of small construction companies in construction of public facilities have been effective in the sense that they finally benefited the majority of small construction companies on average, rather than a select few. The dramatic increase in the number of companies, including many paper companies, was invited by the prevalence of *marunage*, and competent road-paving companies were badly affected by competition with incompetent companies. These observations suggest that the market mechanism has been seriously distorted and that the flood of new entrants is not the consequence of higher profitability and healthy business activities.

Apparently, the first and third of the three factors discussed in Section 3.2.3 that decisively condition the effectiveness of small business policy also apply to this case. Competition in sealed bidding is sometimes said to be rigged in collusion with either politicians or bureaucrats, and if so this could dramatically raise the cost of public construction. However, whether the resulting cash flow, or 'rents,' ultimately goes to the main contractor is another question. Competition and jockeying for the position of contractor also determines the final profit allocation.

As a result, most small construction companies are not highly profitable, and the allocation of public utilities construction contracts both between regions and between groups of construction companies is indiscriminate. That governments do not always maximize social welfare is clear in this case. Despite the high social costs involved, correcting the problem caused here by government 'policies' requires enormous time and energy.

3.5   CONCLUSION: AN OVERALL EVALUATION OF SMALL BUSINESS POLICIES

Although the scope of Japanese small business policies is extensive, they have not effectively supported small businesses. Neither, therefore, have they stimulated overall economic growth. Any lessons to be learned from the Japanese experience are therefore negative: it is of no use to imitate Japanese policies for small businesses. To learn why so many small firms now exist in Japan, it is necessary to search for causes and mechanisms beyond government policies.

Some observers, especially non-Japanese, have been impressed by the existence of the SMEA and the wide variety of its policy measures.[132] However, this ignores the fundamental nature of Japanese administration, with its vertically integrated but horizontally largely uncoordinated structure. In Japan, almost every industry has a counterpart in government. For instance, the Steel Industry Section and the Automobile Section of MITI and the Securities Bureau in the Ministry of Finance. These government sections devote all their efforts to protecting, encouraging, and supporting firms in that industry. Therefore, almost all industries are systematically and continuously protected and supported by the government. The case of small businesses is no exception. The problem springs from a simple fact that nobody can protect and subsidize everybody (see Miwa 1996a: ch. 8, for details).

Basic conclusions of Chapter 3

Readers may wonder why the government's policy menu has been so extensive, why small businesses have been so enthusiastic about these policies, what the basic characteristics of these policies are, and whether the persons in charge of small business policies held any doubts regarding their effectiveness. Although this book has not considered these questions, I will close this chapter by briefly addressing these issues.

First, the basic and common character of policies for small businesses has been 'social' and not 'economic.' Second, although the policies have not been effective in improving consumer welfare, each policy functioned as a subsidy for some small businesses and had redistributional effects. The enthusiastic response to these policies from some political groups follows from this fact. As is often the case with political movements, the enthusiastic support for 'new' policies for small businesses has sometimes come from the professionals in the movements rather than from the small businesses themselves.

Third, the primary task of the bureaucrats in charge of an individual policy is to make detailed plans in response to political demand and to enforce these plans, which are approved by the Diet. Even when bureaucrats have doubts about the effectiveness of these policies, they generally refrain from expressing these doubts openly.

That is, they cannot explicitly reject political demands, for instance by saying that policy is unsuited to its objective or that there is no appropriate way to achieve it.

As discussed at the beginning of Section 3.3.4, although many studies of small business policies address 'policy ideas,' 'policy targets,' and 'policy measures,' very few consider 'policy effects.' This observation is consistent with the view that many studies of small business policies stand on the same side of the fence as the people in charge of the policies, who fully comprehend the ineffectiveness of their policies. Like the 'main bank literature industry' and the 'Japanese industrial policy literature industry' mentioned above, there now exists a 'small business policies research industry' as a result of a demand-creating supply mechanism.

How can such an 'ineffective' policy survive?

Almost always, a new policy requires a new law and a new organization with new employees. These employees, in combination with supporters of the policy, will resist any later attempt to reduce the size of government that will accompany any abolition or revision of the policy. As a result, in Japan as anywhere else, it tends to be easy to expand government organizations but difficult to reorganize them and almost impossible to downsize them. Small business policies are no exception, and the trend of expansion and the extensive menu of policies are a direct reflection of this logic concerning government organization. The state is an organization that lacks a strong incentive to pursue the efficient achievement of tasks. As a result, it periodically undertakes tasks for which it is congenitally unsuited.

Backed by the wide but vague support of the public, which will allow certain sacrifices in efficiency in the name of preferentially treating small firms that are weak, emphasizing small business policies has consistently been a powerful and effective political slogan since the prewar period. Whoever might most enthusiastically demand it, any political party or government has been able to do nothing but swallow demands to emphasize small business policies and further expand them. In this sense, demand for small business policies shares the same basic character as demands for the 'expanded production,' 'domestic production,' 'development,' and 'improvement' of machine tools discussed in Part I.

What if a king controlling the necessary enforcement machinery were to order all doctors within his realm to develop the elixir of life? Eschewing any judgement on the feasibility of this task, the doctors would obey the order and devote themselves to R&D. The behavior of bureaucrats is basically the same. Once one discovers the elixir that the public, or more correctly the supporters behind the king, demand, the similarity becomes more apparent. So often one hears the following statement within the walls of the Diet: 'Yes, it might be logical or the ideal, but remember that we, or I, must be elected.'

Even today, 'eliminating the disadvantage of small firms' comes first in 'The Basic Outline of Small Business Policies,' focusing on counterbalancing small business handicaps due to socio-economic constraints. The primary policy measures for this objective are financial and preferential tax treatment measures, management guidance, policies for establishing well-balanced subcontracting relationships, and policies connected with the Act for Securing Business on the Public Demand for Small Business. I am not arguing that any small business policy is necessarily ineffective. However, any policy that is based on the assumption that 'small firms are the weak' and designed to correct that 'imbalance' is obviously going to be ineffective, no matter who implements it and no matter where it is enforced. Small business policy can be effective only when we abandon these policy assumptions.

No signs for change ?

The Administrative Reform Committee, which stands outside the vertical bureaucratic structure, submitted its 'final opinion' to the prime minister in December 1997. Both the prime minister and the cabinet committed themselves to paying the highest respect to this opinion. The following statement, which is included in the introductory section to this opinion, has now been accepted by the government as its basic policy; it symbolically represents the past history, present state, future, political environment, and actual nature of small business policies:

> The uniform application of rigid protective policy to small firms, assuming that 'small business is weak' hinders efficient resource allocation within the whole economy, and is not necessarily in the overall interest of small business. Like in today's public utilities construction, excessively equal allocation of works among small firms might appear to be fair, but it has evils as well. It restricts free competition. It provides survival opportunities for firms idle in cost reduction efforts. It further invites new entries from inferior firms. Consequently, it deprives both superior small firms intending to prosper upon making serious efforts and newly born small firms of growth opportunities. In short, it seriously damages the vitality of the small business sectors.

This statement is hardly the type that one would expect from a bureaucracy that was integrated into the traditional vertical structure. However, it was the politics under the present political decision-making system that resulted in the creation of the committee and gave it the freedom to offer powerful 'opinions' to the prime minister, and to have its activities supported and encouraged.

4 Who actually determines the substance of policies and how?

4.1   THE ISSUES

Introduction

As George Stigler (1975: pp.112–13) observed (see Section 1.1), neither of the following two views of the state provides a logically coherent basis on which economists can make responsible policy recommendations. The first view of the state, which reflects a 'cynicism' that has been generated by 'historical reality,' emphasizes 'the imperfectibility of the political system, of its susceptibility to the well-placed minority, of its tardiness in adopting new technologies, of the bureaus that are forgotten islands of indolence, of the carelessness (or worse) of the public's rights by eminent politicians in advancing their private fortunes.' The alternative view is based on 'unreasoning optimism' and sees the state as 'dictated by the *necessities* of optimal economic organization: an institution of noble goals and irresistible means.' Stigler's points about views of the state as a whole also apply to individual economic policies.

But if the state is not 'an institution of noble goals and irresistible means,' how does it go about making policy? That is, who, after all, actually determines the substance of policies? Even though the Diet is bestowed with national power of the highest order, can it determine the substance of policy? If it cannot, why can the Diet not achieve this? Is it then the cabinet, supported by the majority of Diet members, or the prime minister, who determines policy? What about the majority group within the ruling party? Do coalitions of small 'politically powerful' groups ultimately control political decision making? Is it the case that a well-placed group of minorities, forming the famous politicians–bureaucracy–business triangle, is the answer in Japan? However, most readers will have already fully recognized the danger of relying on such convenient, simple, and schematic explanations.

Example of a company

An examination of the power structure in large exchange-listed companies may provide an insight into the above issues and a useful comparative model for understanding the state. If we relate the shareholders' meeting to national elections and the board of directors to the Diet (or the cabinet), do meetings of shareholders actually control the decisions of company management? How much actual control over company decisions lies with the board of directors or the president or the chairman (the prime minister)? The degree of difficulty in reaching an agreement between board members, as is the case with Diet (or cabinet) members, particularly a tight agreement upon which the active cooperation of members can be established and maintained, will be particularly serious on issues where the future outlook of relevant parties differs greatly and their interests conflict.

Furthermore, the enforcement of any agreement reached in such circumstances will suffer from the implicit but strong resistance of uncooperative members. Coalitions between some board members and groups of employees change nothing. A declaration by the president to side with a powerful minority group and to let this minority determine the details of a policy, with disobedience being heavily punished, will not substantially improve the situation, even if a close watch is kept within the company.

What is a 'policy'? What does it mean to 'determine' a policy?

Unlike choosing between a white and a black ball resting on a desk, determining the substance of policy is neither simple nor obvious. The determination of the following questions concerning any policy is rarely easy: 'What is a "policy"?' 'What does it mean to "determine" a policy?' 'And when can we identify that "a policy has been determined"?'

Furthermore, there are additional issues, such as the following: 'Are the concrete substance and details of policy determined when the Diet enacts a law?' 'If they are, is this always desirable?' 'Is a Diet that cannot (or at least does not) determine policy details competent to oversee the enforcement process?' 'Suppose that the Diet decides not to determine policy details. Is this case one where the Diet has determined policy?' 'Quite often even a ministry that is delegated direct authority concerning a particular policy determines *ex ante* only general rules, leaving the fine details of policy to be thrashed out by the accumulation of decisions applying policy to individual cases. Where this is the case, exactly who determines the "substance and details" of policy and when?' Thus the issue of 'who determines a policy and when?' requires the initial clarification of 'what is the nature of the policy to be determined?'

Determining the substance of a policy and its details is a consequence of the input of many 'relevant parties' over a long period. Accordingly, the answer to the issue of who decisively influences the determination of 'the substance of a policy' will vary depending upon the definitions assigned to the terms 'the substance of a policy,' 'determination,' and 'influence,' which will obviously differ from case to case. I think it is safe to say that most readers would agree that the answers to the following questions are not obvious: 'What is a "policy"?' 'What is the precise nature of the predominant policy-determining institution "government"?' 'And what is the ambit of the conception of "government"?'

Case study for this chapter

This chapter uses a case study of an actual event to examine these issues. The case study should provide insight into the anatomy of the policy decision-making process and the behavioral patterns of participants. I use the term 'anatomy' since I will not analyse the actual mechanism itself. Decision making depends on various factors, such as the targeted issue, time constraints, and the political environment, and I do not assert that the discussion that follows is in any way a blanket representation of the political decision-making process in postwar Japan. However, it is basically consistent with the decision-making process involved in the 'policies' upon which I have focused in the preceding chapters.

I served as a member of the Deregulation Subcommittee (DS) of the Administrative Reform Committee (ARC) for three years to March 1998, and as a member of the Deregulation Committee of the Government Headquarters for Administrative Reform Promotion from February to May 1998. While serving on these committees, I participated in the planning, decision-making, and enforcement processes regarding actual policies for 'deregulation.' This provided a golden opportunity to examine the many facets of 'policy,' particularly the decision-making process and how that process conditioned policies.

As an illustration, I will use the matter of the re-evaluation of resale price maintenance (RPM) exemptions for publications under the Anti-monopoly Act. Due to the massive campaign by the Japan Newspaper Companies Association (JNCA) to maintain the exemption, it became a politically prominent issue during the period. Consider the issue, then, as a laboratory experiment in the interaction of the parties involved and in the impact of a variety of external shocks (see Miwa 1997b, 1997c, 1997d, 1997e; Miwa and Ramseyer 2003b, 2003e). Because I focus on the *process* of policy making, I ignore the propriety of the policy itself – the actual efficiency or inefficiency of RPM in the publishing industry.[133]

Two points to note

Note two points at the outset. First, government policies vary greatly depending on the issues targeted, even when we limit our attention to the decision-making process. Here I discuss the process connected with 'deregulation.' Under the vertical structure of Japanese administration, sections of relevant ministries tend to attach importance to the interests of the majority in the relevant industry. Most deregulatory issues in contemporary Japan remain unsettled primarily because of successful efforts by the majority of players with vested interests in the relevant industries. The actions of these majority players have been supported by the relevant government sections. In this case, however, the standpoint of the relevant government section conflicted with that of the majority players in the industry.

Second, in most cases that came under heated deregulation debate during the three-year period after 1995, including the case discussed below, proponents of regulation argued that the regulations in place were 'social' regulations rather than 'economic' regulations. The basic principle in re-evaluating ongoing regulations and that underlay the government's recent Deregulation Promotion Program was 'the blanket abolition of *economic* regulations, with but a few exceptions, and the reduction of *social* regulations to the necessary minimum' (see Miwa 1997b: §II).

'Economic' regulation versus 'social' regulation and 'economic' value versus 'social' value

This 'abolish economic but not social regulations' principle implies that those regulations that most view as 'economic' are now being abolished, and that the supporters of those regulations that remain will claim that they are 'social.' However, many doubt if there have ever been any regulations that cannot be asserted to be 'social.' Even regulations concerning cartels, after all, were nominally associated with 'social values' like 'industry order,' the 'stability of supply,' and the 'stability of society.'

Normatively, I see no reason to distinguish between 'social' regulation and 'economic' regulation. Government intervention in response to market failure is justified when it guides the economy to a more desirable state than would be the case under free-market conditions, thus creating benefits beyond its cost. Government intervention cannot be justified simply because the benefits associated with intervention are of 'social' value. Even if the policy objective is the realization of 'social' rather than 'economic' value, when the benefits created by the intervention do not cover its cost, the intervention is harmful to the economy (see Miwa 1997b: §I and §II).

However, in the political decision-making process, as shown below, this distinction has great significance. The slogan 'social regulation' is most frequently used in political campaigns to generate wide public support. Apparently, this sometimes works because many people implicitly assign a higher value to 'social' values than to 'economic' values.

The 'social' values that political entrepreneurs most frequently emphasize are those of safety, health, culture, environment, stability, equity, and public disclosure or accountability. Usually, those who ascribe a high value to these 'social' values do so by implicitly denying the relevance of the costs associated with the values. For instance, suppose that a child drowns in a swimming pool. Many will place much 'social' value on the prevention of any repetition of such accidents and so argue that regulation for this purpose is 'social' regulation. However, even they will usually recognize (however uncomfortably) the relevance of the cost if someone introduces regulations to prohibit swimming entirely or prohibit the construction of swimming pools more than 50 centimeters deep. Those regulations, they will conclude, are inappropriate or excessive, however 'social' they may be.

Whether 'social' or 'economic,' normatively desirable regulations are those whose benefits cover the costs. Yet those who are influenced by appeals to the 'implicit social consciousness' sometimes recognize – however vaguely – that they have effectively rejected that 'economic' calculation. Medical care offers another illustration. Politicians sometimes seem to claim that we should introduce a system whereby everybody will be able to enjoy medical care of the highest quality everywhere and at any time. The benefits of such a system must be balanced against the magnitude of the value of the sacrificed goods and services (the cost). Such a system would very likely require that all citizens engage in medical care by becoming doctors and nurses, making it impossible to secure minimum food requirements. When advocates of such a system conduct such a cost–benefit analysis, they will realize the inherent impossibility, and thereby also realize that social and economic issues cannot be so easily dichotomized after all.

It is to this 'implicit social consciousness' that proponents of regulation appeal when they argue for the establishment, powerful enforcement, and maintenance of regulations, even where the actual regulation may have become stronger or been maintained longer than is socially desirable. Often this 'implicit social consciousness' is linked to a vague distrust of the market. Proponents then appeal to that distrust by arguing that 'this regulation is of special value and is exceptional,' that 'we should reject such irresponsible re-evaluation of regulations based on economic considerations,' or that 'anarchy reigns in a free market' (see, generally, Miwa 1997b: §II, 1997e, 1998b). In the case study discussed below, appeals to this 'implicit social consciousness' were indeed successful.

Road map to Chapter 4

Section 4.2 of this chapter details the provisions of the Anti-monopoly Act dealing with abuses of positions of authority and responsibility and so sets the scene for the issue to be investigated in this chapter: who actually determines the substance of policies and how? Section 4.3 provides an outline of the political decision-making process. Section 4.4 illustrates the importance of government sections in charge of policy, which lie at the very core of the process, and also the various councils that have supplementary roles. Section 4.5 discusses the measures and 'safety nets' that relevant parties adopt to realize and maintain their interests within the political decision-making process.

The following three sections then illustrate the discussion in the preceding sections. Section 4.6 deals with the campaign to oppose the abolition of business tax exemptions for newspaper companies. Section 4.7 deals with the process, and Section 4.8 the result, of the JNCA's campaign against the re-evaluation of RPM exemptions for publications under the Anti-monopoly Act. Section 4.9 sums up the discussion.

This chapter has two appendices. Appendix 1 provides an outline of the RPM exemptions for publications under the Anti-monopoly Act and a brief summary of the relevant government commentary. Appendix 2 extracts a publication of the Fair Trade Commission (FTC), entitled 'The treatment of RPM exemptions for publications,' published on 31 March 1998.

4.2   THE DETERMINATION OF 'POLICY' SUBSTANCE: ANTI-MONOPOLY ACT REGULATION OF ABUSES OF POSITIONS OF AUTHORITY AND RESPONSIBILITY

Who actually determines the substance of government policy and how? How do we define the phrase 'determination of policy'? For instance, to what extent is the 'substance' of a policy determined at the time of legislation? Who determines any remaining details of the 'substance' of a policy? When, where, for whom, how, and why is the substance determined in the way it is? In order to illustrate these basic issues more clearly, I discuss the Anti-monopoly Act regulation of abuses of positions of authority and responsibility.

The Mitsukoshi case

The leading case is the Mitsukoshi case (FTC decision on 17 June 1982), and a brief outline of this case (following Itoda 1995: pp.165–6) follows. As I focus here on the *process* of decision making, I ignore the obvious questions about why Mitsukoshi chose the negotiating strategies that it did, and whether it makes economic sense to ban those strategies (see, generally, Posner 1976: pp.171–84, 205–7).

> *Facts of the case*: Mitsukoshi is a famous Japanese department store, and has long promoted out-of-store sales through the business and personal connections of employees. This system is called the 'recommendation sales' and 'R strategy' system. Further, Mitsukoshi has also 'encouraged' employees to sell movie or show tickets of productions in which Mitsukoshi has participated, or of Mitsukoshi's own 'traveling abroad' programs. Mitsukoshi established an in-house special-purpose organization to achieve sales goals along these lines. Toward that end, Mitsukoshi appealed to its trade relationships and urged its suppliers to purchase these products. In effect, its suppliers were forced to accept these requests if they wanted to maintain their trade relations with Mitsukoshi. Likewise, Mitsukoshi asked its suppliers to bear the costs of any remodeling that it conducted in its stores. Again, in order to preserve trade relations with Mitsukoshi, suppliers bore these costs. Mitsukoshi gave no reasons or clear foundation for the calculation of the cost burden. Mitsukoshi also required its suppliers to bear the costs associated with special events or celebrations such as the 'Fireworks Festival' and the 'Ginza Festival,' which are events that Mitsukoshi 'sponsored' but are not directly connected with sales promotion.
> *Holding – the application of the Act*: Mitsukoshi asked its suppliers to purchase goods and services and to bear the costs of events and celebrations, which suppliers unwillingly accepted. Such conduct falls within the ambit of

designation 10 of 'unfair trade practices,' that is 'to trade relying on a superior trade position with suppliers, on terms unduly detrimental (in monetary terms) to suppliers when compared with normal trade customs,' and so violates section 19 of the Anti-monopoly Act, which prohibits 'unfair trade practices.'[134]

Six points to note

There are six points worth noting from this incident concerning 'who actually determines the substance of a policy and how?'[135]

1   This is a decision of the FTC, which is an administrative institution established to enforce the Anti-monopoly Act. If any party concerned was not satisfied with the decision, a suit in a higher court, the Tokyo High Court, was always available. No such appellate suit was brought, however, and the decision was enforced. There still remains a possibility that in a similar case a firm (in the position of Mitsukoshi) will bring an appellate suit in the Tokyo High Court and win. In short, the decision did not represent a final determination of 'policy' regarding 'abuses of positions of authority and responsibility.'

2   Section 45 of the Anti-monopoly Act provides that 'any person may, if that person considers that a situation which violates this Act exists, report the said fact to the FTC and request that appropriate measures be taken.' Given the various barriers to private litigation under the Anti-monopoly Act in Japan, however, if the FTC decides not to take the 'appropriate measures,' the Act and policy under it have no effect. Thus, even when such a rule exists, whether it is enforced largely depends upon the FTC. Let us take the enforcement of a speed limit as an illustration. The speed limit on highways in Japan is set at 80 kilometers per hour. However, as a regulation or a policy, it is not enforced with any rigor.

3   The relevant provisions are as follows. Section 19 provides that 'Entrepreneurs shall not employ unfair trade practices.' Section 2-9 defines the term 'unfair trade practices' to 'mean any conduct falling within the ambit of the following paragraphs, which has a tendency to impede fair competition and which is a conduct designated by the FTC.' Paragraph (v) of section 2-9 is one example of conduct defined as 'unfair trade practices' by section 2-9; it details conduct that consists of 'utilizing one's position of unjust bargaining power when transacting with another party.' 'Unfair trade practices' were prohibited in the 1953 amendment of the Act. There has been no amendment to the relevant provisions of the Act since then, which implies that there has been no direct participation of the Diet in determining these policies since 1953. The Act further stipulates that 'the

chairman and the commissioners of the FTC shall perform their respective duties independently' (section 28).

4   As we have seen, the section 2-9 definition of 'unfair trade practices' requires, among other things, that the FTC designate the conduct to be deemed an unfair trade practice. The FTC's designations are detailed in the Unfair Trade Practices Notification (General Designations). These designations of conduct were made public on the establishment of this prohibition in 1953 and remained unchanged through the time of the Mitsukoshi case. They have since been revised only once, in 1982. So we see that it is the FTC that decides how and when designations should be revised and so apparently determines policy.

5   Of conduct designated under the Unfair Trade Practices Notification (General Designations), designation 10 was applied to the Mitsukoshi case. This prohibits conduct that consists of 'trad[ing] relying on a superior trade position with suppliers, on terms unduly detrimental [in monetary terms] to suppliers when compared with normal trade customs.' What are the precise meanings of words and phrases such as 'relying,' 'superior trade position,' and 'terms unduly detrimental to suppliers when compared with normal trade customs'? Why did the conduct of Mitsukoshi fall within the bounds of this designation? This designation had rarely been applied before the Mitsukoshi case. Accordingly, not only the details but also the broad substance of this designation remained unclear. What was also unclear was whether this designation was a workable one and whether the FTC intended to enforce it. In addition, although the term 'abuses of positions of authority' is a popular one, it appears neither in the Anti-monopoly Act nor in any conduct designated by the FTC.

6   Note two further points. First, the alleged conduct of Mitsukoshi was by no means peculiar to Mitsukoshi. It was only that Mitsukoshi had long conducted itself in such a way and hence became the target of 'social criticism' for 'forced sales.' Until this case, the conduct had not been targeted by the FTC under any provision of the Anti-monopoly Act. Second, Mitsukoshi immediately began a campaign against the FTC once the FTC had made the allegation. However, Mitsukoshi's stance changed with the onset of two events. One was the resignation (or rather ousting by the board) of the president of the company, Mr Okada. The second was the emergence of a scandal (unrelated to this incident) in which Okada was involved. The escalating 'social criticism' that flourished in the mass media against the 'forced sales' and the president's scandal seriously constrained the behavior of Mitsukoshi. These factors in turn affected the substance of government policy under the Anti-monopoly Act prohibitions.

Summing up

As the discussion above suggests, the issues of who actually determines the substance of government policies and when, where, for whom, how, and why this is done are seldom simple or obvious. As readers will appreciate, this also applies to the discussion in Part I about promotional policies for the machine tool industry under wartime control and in Part II concerning the MIPA and its policies for the machinery industries. In addition, the small business policy discussed in the previous chapter is no exception.

4.3   AN OUTLINE OF THE POLITICAL DECISION-MAKING PROCESS

Three scenarios for illustration

Let me begin by outlining some actual dialog dealing with the political decision-making process:

(A)   *Question:*   Why should we not change the system to allow corporations for profit [*eiri hojin*, business corporations] to open medical institutions?

        Answer: Medical care is directly connected with human life. We should not grant licenses to such organizations as motivated by profit incentives.

(B)   *Question:*   How about allowing convenience stores to sell highly safe over-the-counter medicines like cold medicines and painkillers, particularly for those suffering from colds at night or toothaches on the weekend?

        Answer: Some of today's over-the-counter medicines have strong side effects and cause allergies. Allowing convenience stores to trade in such medicines is dangerous, even regarding over-the-counter medicines.

(C)   *Question:*   Why do we not free the restrictions that currently exist regarding employment agencies? The current system is one of 'positive restriction,' that is it strictly regulates the occupations which can be the subject of employment agency services. Why do we not reform this system to be one of 'negative restriction,' that is a system which regulates employment agency services to stipulate occupations that cannot be the subject of employment agency services, such as extremely dangerous professions? Also, why do we not liberalize salary restrictions on employment agency services?

        Answer: Employment agencies deal with humans, who we should not treat like commodities. In Japan there has been a long history of employment agencies, called *kuchiire-kagyo*, emerging in the Edo era. Accordingly, we should pay the greatest attention to protecting workers, the weak minority, from the tremendously high referral fees of these employment agencies.

These exchanges are factual and have been extracted from official hearings of the DS of the ARC. The answers are those given by a bureaucrat from the relevant ministry in response to questions from subcommittee members (see Miwa 1997e: pp.22–7). Given the 'implicit social consciousness' discussed above, even a hint of the need to introduce competition to improve efficiency encounters strong resistance in areas deemed to involve 'social' regulations.

Four issues to note

The following issues emerge from the three scenarios above:

- Do the answers given reveal the true reasons behind these regulations?
- Who is it that these answers satisfy?
- These explanations appear to have been effective in justifying or at least in maintaining these regulations. Why is it that such justifications have been so effective?
- Will these justifications continue to be effective in the future?

Answers to these questions may differ greatly across cases, depending upon the circumstances involved. An investigation into the actual decision-making process, and the political economic factors affecting this process, is thus indispensable.

Flowchart of the policy-making process

The process of realizing regulatory change – not only that for the relaxation and elimination of regulations but also concerning the strengthening and creation of regulations – differs greatly depending upon the circumstances. A typical case (here, a hypothetical case involving the enactment of a new law or the revision of an existing law) would involve the following process:

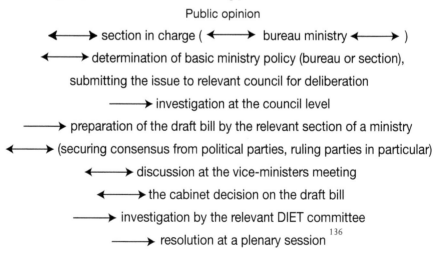

Public opinion

⟷ section in charge (⟷ bureau ministry ⟷)

⟷ determination of basic ministry policy (bureau or section), submitting the issue to relevant council for deliberation

⟶ investigation at the council level

⟶ preparation of the draft bill by the relevant section of a ministry

⟷ (securing consensus from political parties, ruling parties in particular)

⟷ discussion at the vice-ministers meeting

⟷ the cabinet decision on the draft bill

⟶ investigation by the relevant DIET committee

⟶ resolution at a plenary session [136]

As Kyogoku (1983: pp. 347–8) points out regarding Japan:

> The basic unit of bureaucracy when the allocation of responsibility is concerned is the division in the main ministry that has jurisdiction over the industry. ... For matters within a given jurisdiction, each division of the ministry by itself personifies the Japanese government. ... Subsection chiefs of each section bear an essential part of policy planning work, and the section chief, integrating the section's activities, possesses actual power concerning the launch of a policy plan. He also holds actual power regarding the promotion or obstruction of consensus regarding policy plans of other sections. ... That relevant section is characterized by its exclusive monopoly concerning matters within its allocated jurisdiction. Accordingly, policy plans concerning matters falling within the jurisdiction of that section are considered 'pure' or 'orthodox' policy plans only when they have autonomously and 'voluntarily' emerged from within the section.

Five points to note about sectional jurisdiction

Because of the strategic importance of the position of the relevant section within Japan's vertical administrative structure, the following five points become critical in addressing the four issues outlined above:

1   Because the ministerial section in charge possesses 'actual power concerning the launch of a policy plan,' its discretion regarding the need for a plan marks the beginning of the process.
2   In those cases where the section with jurisdiction decides that proper policy requires the enactment of a law or the revision of existing laws, it will launch a plan on the assumption that it will be approved by the Diet. Unless either the ruling party (or some of the ruling parties) or the Diet committee that potentially would be responsible for the bill supports the plan, the realization of the plan will involve great difficulty. The lack of support for a plan in either of these areas will almost always spell failure for the plan, or success only at the cost of grave compromise. The same applies to plans that are strongly opposed by other ministries.
3   Trends in 'public opinion' also affect the judgement of the relevant ministerial section in any launch of a policy plan. The degree of influence attributable to 'public opinion' will differ depending on the circumstances, including factors like the issues targeted and the political environment. However, the 'public opinion' that I refer to here is rarely that of the general public or the average consumer.
4   With regard to regulations that are relevant to specific industrial sectors, the voice of the majority in the industry, transmitted via trade associations to the

relevant ministerial section, represents the 'public opinion' that matters. This 'public opinion' will influence the judgement and decisions of the section through discussions in the relevant council, negotiations and coordination with other ministries (often with other sections in the same ministry), and industry contacts within political parties, which then trickle through to the section.

5   The objective for which the relevant section's decisions are made and its relation with that of the bureau and the ministry that control the section are unclear. I omit discussion of how the personality and temperament of the key people concerned, such as the section chief, the bureau chief, and the minister, are relevant to our discussion.

With regard to the relative importance of these five points, nothing happens without an initial decision by the ministerial section to launch a policy. Also, decision making within a section will reflect above all the 'public opinion' – which will often be dominated by the interests of the majority in the relevant industry. Furthermore, the relevant section, and the ministry, have no interest in establishing and maintaining any specific regulation for its own sake; nor are they interested in exercising authority, including 'control,' over industries.

The Administrative Reform Committee and its Deregulation Subcommittee

The ARC was established in order to 'monitor' the process of government review of the Deregulation Promotion Program. The committee set up the subcommittee as its task force to perform this monitoring role. Accordingly, the DS was granted authority to require the government (the ministerial section with jurisdiction over the regulation) to explain the details of any individual regulation and to prepare an official statement detailing the effects of regulatory changes and future plans. The three question-and-answer scenarios above were some of those officially conducted at the subcommittee's hearings.

Four characteristics typical of explanations given

The explanations that the ministerial sections gave in response to the questions by the ARC shared four characteristics:

1   Where deregulation was not politically feasible, the section tried to invent a 'theory' or 'reason' to justify the maintenance of the regulation. The bureaucrats were not always able to do so. Sometimes, they could not even persuade themselves or members of the industry, leaving many to wonder about the origins and persuasiveness of the official reason for the regulation.

Matters were more complicated where the section believed that deregulation was necessary and possible, even if not easy to realize. The maintenance of friendly relations with relevant industry players is essential to the smooth operation of the daily activities of the section. Section bureaucrats are therefore eager to prevent the worsening of relations, and they make every effort to be sensitive to the interests of industry members. They pretend to be sensitive to the industry by consistently pretending that they have no choice but to accept the proposed deregulation. Under these circumstances, the trade associations standing between industry members and consumers often share the sentiments of the section bureaucrats.

2   It is only recently that the fundamental ideology of 'abolishing all economic regulations and reducing social regulations to the necessary minimum' that underlies the government's Deregulation Promotion Program has become widely accepted in Japan. Until very recently, the ideological justifications underlying many regulations classified as 'social' regulations were seldom questioned in Japan. As a result, there was seldom a need to invent reasons to justify the maintenance of 'social' regulations in situations like hearings of the DS. Consequently, in some cases those supporting the maintenance of the regulation, typically section bureaucrats and industry players, had never discussed the details of the regulation, including its costs and benefits. They seem never to have considered clarifying the reasons behind the regulation, and they responded to inquiries merely by asserting that the regulation was 'social' and therefore indispensable.

3   Because of the lack of any widespread support for public discussion about the grounds for regulation, the details of the 'social regulation' claims were never discussed. In the past, when industry members coordinated their private interests (in, for example, the deliberative councils), they placed little emphasis on the interests of consumers. The phrases such as 'social regulation' that appeared in the council reports were mere decorations to disguise the efforts to coordinate the interests of the relevant parties. Even today, in some cases people in charge of regulation apparently see no need to discuss the need for regulation; the medical services, legal services, education, newspapers, and broadcasting industry are the most egregious examples (see Miwa 1998c: p.292, note 18 for the newspaper example).

4   Because of this traditional lack of justification for a regulatory regime, many misconceptions persist. In such cases, the reasons now advanced to justify the regulation are very unsatisfactory indeed. Sometimes, the transparency of the lack of justification leads to change. The opposition of the Justice Ministry to abolishing the prohibition on stock options is an illustrative example. The ministry's justifications were vapid – and the Diet abolished the prohibition in 1997 (*ibid.*: p.292, note 19).

4.4   BUREAUCRATIC SECTIONS AND
DELIBERATIVE COUNCILS

Observers emphasize the resistance of bureaucrats, particularly those in the supervising ministerial section, as critical to the progress of deregulation. As Kyogoku (1983: p.347) argues:

> Although official power and authority are allocated between state institutions, such as within a ministry or between ministries, where the real power lies is elsewhere. In fact, real power runs in a way downhill, that is it is delegated by the cabinet to the meetings of vice-ministers, and from the meetings of vice-ministers to the departmental councils of individual ministries, and then often the departmental councils will leave matters to be determined by informal coordination between section chiefs.

Under these circumstances, the ministerial section with jurisdiction over a regulatory regime occupies a strategically critical position. As a result, the popular arguments regarding the resistance often put up by such sections is not totally untrue. However, such arguments are a source of grave misunderstanding. Attention must also be paid to factors conditioning the decision making of such sections, such as their objective function, the incentive systems provided to their members, and precisely which interests in society are represented by the 'public opinion' that influences their behavior.

Trade associations and retired bureaucrats

Under this system of vertically integrated (and horizontally uncoordinated) administration, the regulation of industries falling within its jurisdiction forms a key part of a ministerial section's administrative activities. Accordingly, the maintenance of close connections and cooperative relations with firms in these industries is fundamental to the smooth daily activities of the bureaucracy. Trade associations, or industry associations, effectively lie between the section and the firms. The function of such trade associations is to serve as a go-between between the two groups. On the one hand, they represent the section to firms; on the other hand, they represent the interests of the industry to the section. There is more, however, for the associations also represent the interests of the industry to other government agencies, politicians, and the general public.

With regard to issues such as deregulation, the government can ill afford to jeopardize these relations by paying insufficient attention to the interests of trade associations and of the industry they represent. The oft-observed retirement of bureaucrats into well-paid positions in the trade associations as senior directors (known as *amakudari*, *pantouflage* in French) symbolizes the pervasive-ness of these relationships.

The principal–agent chain

Chains of principal–agent relationships often operate in both directions. Depending on the circumstances, in other words, a party may act either as a principal or an agent. For some cases, the government (more particularly the ministries and rele-vant councils, or the Diet, the politicians, and the political parties) may be an agent of the electorate. For others, it may be the principal. Much the same can be said of the relations between the government and the trade associations and between the trade associations and industry.

Both the electorate and the business community try to influence the govern-ment to favor their own interests. Both politicians and ministries, which influence and are influenced by one another, attend to the demands of industry and consumers (voters) and then try to promote their own interests. Accordingly, one cannot always assume that these relationships are one-sided.

The question of the composition of 'public opinion' and whose interests it actually represents, those of consumers or industry, will greatly depend on the issues concerned and the circumstances. Even where the ministry accepts the demands of consumers against the view of industry, the ministry will take into account the influence of the particular industry and its members on government as a whole and make appropriate efforts to satisfy or appease the industry. In many cases, it may make large concessions to gather industry support on an issue.

The resistance of bureaucrats

Even in the contemporary situation, where the principle that only a minimum standard of justifiable social regulation will be maintained has taken root, the same applies. For example, councils, organized in combination with the launch of a policy, are essentially a setting for negotiation and jockeying among relevant parties. Councils are rarely intended to generate real and final decisions.

Typically, a council exists for a very long period, often several decades, and holds meetings as the occasion demands. Council members are primarily repre-sentatives of relevant groups with vested interests. To these members, the ministry adds people whom it believes 'fully understand the role of councils' and whom other members are willing to accept. The same applies to those who join the councils temporarily for specific issues. Consequently, the final report of a council will rarely deviate from the basic direction anticipated when the council was established, often several years earlier (see Miwa 1993a: ch. 6, 1996a: ch. 8; Miwa and Ramseyer 2002e: ch. 3, 2003e).

Even today, 'public opinion' may dramatically influence policy making by the ministry. The ministry will pay close attention to trends in 'public opinion' and take into consideration the political feasibility of its plans.

However, deregulation intended to promote the interests of consumers always tends to face difficulty from several factors, one being the vertical structure of Japanese administration. Another is the decision-making system of the Japanese Diet, which is often dominated by politicians loyal to vested interest groups. Finally, the incentive system under which bureaucrats work also represents a barrier to consumer-oriented deregulation. However, it is an exaggeration of the role of bureaucrats to argue that the difficulty of deregulation arises from the resistance of bureaucrats.

Bureaucrats are often thought to play the part of the 'villain,' but this is in part because the general public and 'public opinion' demand this. By playing the villain, bureaucrats sometimes contribute to the smooth operation of administration. The media (for instance newspapers) prefer to assign the villain's role to bureaucrats rather than to private firms out of concern for their advertising revenues. In fact, the real 'villain' is almost always in industry rather than the bureaucracy. Yet assigning the part of the villain to bureaucrats will evoke no reaction. In many cases, however, the media blame the bureaucrats out of simple ignorance and misunderstanding.

Councils tend to be conservative

Quite often the ministry is obliged to (often this obligation is stipulated in the law) or promises to seek the opinion of the relevant council and obtain the consent of its members before proceeding with reform.[137] The same applies to situations where it decides to maintain the *status quo*. As the typical duration of a council is long, the consent of the relevant parties, particularly private firms, concerning the membership and role of the council is fundamental to its smooth operation and good performance. Necessarily, it is also fundamental to the effective administration of the ministry. As a result, the members, the issues discussed, the means of operation, the direction of the discussion, the schedule, and the conclusions reached will reflect the preferences of the interest groups that most dominate the ministry. That dominance will also be influenced by the history of the industry, any idiosyncrasies in the industry, and the broader political environment.[138]

Moreover, the opinion of the industry (expressed primarily through the trade association) is formed, maintained, and altered as a result of 'intra-industry politics' between firms, groups of firms, and sector or regional groups within the industry. These 'politics' will tend to reflect the unanimous consent of members. As such, they tend to be extremely conservative, advocating the maintenance of the *status quo* in terms of both the council membership and the membership-selection procedure.[139] Likewise, the industry's opinion (particularly the opinion expressed through the industry association) will usually be conservative regarding the launch of any new policy or changes to any existing policy.

Changes to council membership and its role can potentially affect the consensus among industry members, among the relevant industries, and between the industries and the government. Smooth administration depends on this consensus, so not only the interest groups directly affected and the council members representing their interests but also the other groups and the remaining council members will tend to oppose any changes to the *status quo*.

The *status quo* of the council membership and the procedure for the designation of members is a result of political compromises. Any changes to that membership upset those compromises and potentially introduce unpredictability into the industry. However, restoring 'order' to the decision-making process can cost time and energy. This is true even of so-called 'neutral' council members.

'Public opinion' and the interests of consumers

The opinion that the ministry values so highly when preparing policy plans is thus the opinion formed and expressed through councils. As a result, under the present system policy plans will strongly reflect the interest of relevant industries rather than the interest of consumers.

Naturally, the substance of discussion at council meetings and within industries, and also the expressions used there, differ greatly from the accounts presented to the external world. The information that ministries release to the external world, including the ARC, to justify the maintenance of existing regulations is not a direct reflection of what takes place at council meetings. The contrast between '*social* regulation' and '*economic* regulation,' for example, is not a contrast that appears in the internal council debates. Although the characterization of regulation as 'social' is the primary weapon used by ministry bureaucrats and industry members to explain and justify existing regulations to the external world, it is not a characterization they make within the councils. There, the expression 'social regulation' is not used, because it is not necessary.

4.5   DEVICES FOR REALIZING AND MAINTAINING THE INTERESTS OF RELEVANT PARTIES

The ministerial sections in charge make policy decisions that reflect 'public opinion.' Every interest group tries hard to establish and maintains in public an opinion that benefits its own interests. What they do toward that end varies greatly by issue, by environmental factors like the opinion of the general public, by the relative influence of groups opposing and supporting the issue, and by any other obstacles that may block a desired objective.

Until recently, on 'social regulation' issues those supporting the regulation could simply ignore the opposition. In these cases, the opinion favorable to the industry had existed for many years and was largely taken for granted. That favorable opinion, in turn, had allowed members of an industry to work only to coordinate their interests within the industry.

'Public opinion' and the opinion of the general public

However, efforts to shape 'public opinion' to support the existing regulatory regime do require at least some support among the general public. The basic discipline of 'reducing social regulations to the necessary minimum' has gradually gained wide acceptance among the general public.

The general public has begun to demand clearer justification for existing regulations. Previously, never demanding any justification, most people just accepted the result of interest coordination between the relevant parties. As a result, the public 'approved' and 'supported' regulations without thinking about them. Once people began to demand clear justification for the regulations, however, the proponents of regulation had to show that the broader regulatory benefits to the public outweigh their costs. Benefit to the industry is now but part of the issue.

Once this occurs, the distinction between 'social' and 'economic' regulation becomes irrelevant. 'Social regulation' is an expression useful only to those defending existing regulations, because such expressions appeal to the 'implicit social consciousness' of the public. When the appeal works, proponents can argue that a particular 'regulation is desirable for consumers because it increases social values.' There are many supporters of this confused view, not only among the public but also among the sectors demanding maintenance of regulation. The point is perhaps well illustrated by the hypothetical example (introduced in Section 4.1) of a ban on all swimming pools more than 50 centimeters deep.

Use of the 'social regulation' rhetoric is now disappearing as the public becomes better informed. Demands for the detailed justification of social regulations and open discussions about them in order to examine whether they are justified will further damage the effectiveness of the rhetoric. The power to judge whether a regulation is in fact a 'social regulation' and to determine the appropriate details of regulation has gradually moved from being monopolized by relevant industries to the public.

Diet members loyal to specific interests and political parties

The basic unit of political decision making is the political party, whose behavior will reflect the political preferences of its supporters. To assemble support from the majority, a party will create a coalition of supporters by log-rolling a variety of voters. Some constituencies within the log-roll will bring in a large number of loyal voters; other constituencies will heavily contribute resources that the party can use to attract other voters. For a party that hopes to control the legislature, however, the preferences it promotes will tend to be close to those of the median voter. Consider – as a rough approximation – the political preferences of the median voter to be 'public opinion.' If the public is open to the use of an expression such as 'social regulation' but relatively careless about what it means, then a majority party will have freer rein to use regulation to favor those constituencies (industry groups) that contribute the resources (rather than votes) that the party needs. In Japan, this means that the majority party will be able to offer regulation to those Diet members loyal to specific industries (known colloquially as *zoku-giin*). If, given the recent increased support for the basic principle of 'reducing social regulations to the necessary minimum,' political parties recognize that paying devotion to this principle will actually or potentially increase their electoral success, their behavior will change.

The reactions of any political party to the behavior of industry representatives in the Diet will vary tremendously across issues, but it is critical to note three points here:

1 If a particular issue is not in the interests of the general public, parties will refrain from making clear party policy statements and allow industry loyalists to behave freely in their own interest within the party's discipline.
2 If an issue arouses serious conflict from coalition parties or from within the party, or alternatively if it becomes the focus of the general public's interest, the party will be forced to make clear policy statements. In turn, this will strongly constrain the behavior of the industry loyalists within the party.
3 In the case of a coalition cabinet, where the decisions of each party in the coalition must be coordinated, the relationship between the decisions of each party and the behavior of party members is more delicate and complicated. Even decisions built around the consensus of responsible persons in each party may have to be changed at the final moment.

Diet members loyal to the industry groups will generally try to avoid the constraints imposed by the parties, which will occur when an issue becomes a prominent one for the general public or other party members, particularly other coalition members. At the same time, however, those loyalists will make every effort to push the adoption of their position by the party, and they will do this by acquiring the support of other party members. Such action will in turn help to mitigate party discipline.

Nine hurdles to deregulation

At every stage of the process leading to the revision of a regulation, supporters of the regulation will place hurdles. Suppose that a ministry agrees that a law should be revised and decides to launch an effort to revise it. As discussed above, the ministerial section with jurisdiction over the regulation will not want to launch a revision effort if it thinks it unlikely to pass. If it is proposing a revision that the industry opposes, it will do so only if it thinks the industry's efforts to block the revision will be ineffective. It will thus propose the revision only if it first is able to cut a deal with the industry associations to support the revision, or if it has the ability independently to implement the revision.

The relevant ministerial section potentially faces at least nine types of hurdle; and the ability of proponents of regulation to characterize the regulation as 'social regulation' will bolster the strength of each.

1   To obstruct cabinet agreement, cabinet members can be lobbied to oppose the plan.
2   This can also be done at the party level by persuading either the party in power or in opposition to oppose the plan. If the parties at least show some consideration of the opposing view, then revision becomes more difficult to achieve.
3   Diet members can be mustered to strongly oppose the revision at the decision-making institutions within the ruling parties, for instance at the Policy Research Council and the Executive Council of the Liberal Democratic Party.
4   Diet members, usually members of opposition parties, can be mustered to strongly oppose the plan in the relevant Diet committees.
5   Many avenues exist by which the ministry can be convinced to abandon the revision. These avenues include securing the cooperation of various people such as Diet members, members of other ministries, and members of the mass media.
6   Other bureaux, and often even other sections in the same bureau of the same ministry, can be required to oppose the revision by obstructing any agreement or consensus within the relevant ministry, or even within the relevant bureau.

7   Members of the councils can be recruited to oppose the revision and so obstruct any agreement of the councils. A unanimous agreement is very rarely reached between council members concerning a plan to substantially revise existing regulation. This is due to understandings that exist about the nature of the council and its membership, the procedure for the designation of members, and the role of both the council itself and individual members. Accordingly, council meetings are usually occasions where the relevant parties negotiate and coordinate with each other to establish their own interests and the interests of others behind them. Once any member decides to stop a policy plan at any cost, it is not difficult to see to it that the council report includes arguments against the plan. Furthermore, unless the council reaches an agreement, the relevant ministerial section will encounter difficulties in proceeding to the next stages with the plan.

8   There is an implicit understanding in some standing councils that no member should bring up an issue for discussion unless every member agrees. Sometimes, there is also an implicit understanding that only conclusions unanimously supported will be drawn.

9   Campaigns to influence public opinion on various fronts can be conducted, since public opinion remains relevant at every stage of the process. Campaigns can vary depending on the circumstances but will almost always involve targeting politicians, bureaucrats, council members, including 'neutral' members, 'eminent' public figures (so-called 'opinion leaders'), consumer unions, and the mass media.

The ultimate target is, of course, the public, although it is rarely targeted directly. In some cases, particularly where regulations will be successfully maintained, campaigns will comprise a combination of obtaining the passive approval of the public by keeping them ignorant through poor disclosure of details and of obtaining the active cooperation of influential persons like politicians. Continuous and daily efforts to obtain support from various sectors will provide the foundation for launching an active campaign in an 'emergency' and consequently for securing the support for maintaining regulations in any 'emergency.'

At the request of the JNCA, in the autumn of 1995 all newspapers nationwide jointly launched a campaign against the re-evaluation (and abolition) of the RPM exemptions for publications under the Anti-monopoly Act. Representatives of the association, presumably after negotiation, mustered supporting opinions from representatives of every political party, for which newspapers reserved space every day. Their campaign reached a peak in early December 1995, when each newspaper allocated two pages to this campaign, which they called 'reports' rather than advertisements. This long-lasting, spectacular but obviously one-sided campaign stimulated public interest in the exemption, which may appear to be inconsistent with the view expressed above. Indeed, the association did seem to miscalculate, not recognizing that the public would not be satisfied by the invocation of 'social regulation.' They had enjoyed the good life of a stable monopoly for too long and believed they could kill the repeal movement with a single blow by convincing the DS and the FTC to abandon moves towards abolition. The subcommittee was making the conclusion on the issue at the very peak of the campaign (see Miwa 1997e: Appendix). I return to this topic in Sections 4.7 and 4.8.

4.6   ILLUSTRATION 1:
THE CAMPAIGN AGAINST THE ABOLITION OF
ENTERPRISE TAX EXEMPTION FOR NEWSPAPERS

Two campaigns by the Japan Newspaper Companies Association

The next three sections attempt to illustrate the essence of the preceding discussion by examining two factual campaigns. Section 4.6 introduces the campaign by the JNCA against the abolition of enterprise tax exemptions for newspaper companies. Sections 4.7 and 4.8 focus on the campaign by the JNCA to oppose the abolition of RPM exemptions for publications under the Anti-monopoly Act.

As shown in the Appendix, subsection 4 in section 24-2 of the Act, which was enacted with the 1953 amendment, exempts the application of the prohibition on RPM for publications. The government decided to review the Anti-monopoly Act almost half a century after its enactment, focusing particularly on the exemption clauses in the Act. Having resulted in the abolition of many exemptions, the re-evaluation process reached its final stages in the mid-1990s. Even at that point, though, one of the remaining issues was the RPM exemption for publications.

To abolish an RPM exemption, the government had at least three alternatives: (1) it could revise the Act, eliminating section 24-2 in its entirety, or subsection 4, which contains the exemption; (2) it could revise the FTC's interpretation of the term 'publications' in subsection 4 to exclude newspapers; and (3) it (again through the FTC) could declare RPM by newspaper companies to be invalid, arguing that 'the exemption is grossly injurious to the interest of consumers,' which is grounds for invalidity under the Act (subsection 1 of section 24-2). The approval of the Diet would have been required only for the first alternative. Despite this, though, the first alternative was chosen for political reasons.

Opposition by the JNCA to the abolition of the RPM exemption

The opposition by the JNCA to the abolition of the RPM exemption began in autumn 1994, when the FTC organized the Subcommittee to Examine RPM Issues under the Study Group for Government Regulations and Competition Policy (officially named 'Study Group for Government Regulations and Competition Policy Concentrating on the Investigation of the RPM Issues'). The movement began to intensify in July 1995, when the interim report of the subcommittee was published. Also in July, the DS of the ARC identified the abolition of the RPM exemption for publications as a major antitrust issue, which fueled the movement.

The movement reached a peak just before 7 December 1995, when the DS was scheduled to submit its opinion to the prime minister. Since mid-November 1995, the presidents of the major newspaper companies had been visiting powerful politicians to muster support. Newspapers and other media institutions allocated space and time every day to the views of politicians recruited to the JNCA cause.

On 27 November, the JNCA issued a memorandum urging the continuation of the exemption under the joint signature of the chairman of the JNCA (who was also president of *Mainichi Shimbun*) and the chairman of the Special Committee to Preserve RPM (who was also president of *Yomiuri Shimbun*)[140]. According to the memorandum:

> the abolition of RPM exemptions will have grave consequences for the newspaper home delivery system, which has existed since the Meiji era. This will have the effect of halving the number of newspaper issues. Additionally, publishers of quality books and magazines, and also bookstores, will be forced into bankruptcy. Unless we, the newspaper companies and publishers, unite against this absurd argument within the next week, we will pay the consequences for ever.

In response, two-page spreads appeared in newspapers with headlines like 'Destruction of the Foundation of Print Culture' (*Asahi Shimbun*, 3 December), '[RPM] Supports the Development of Democratic Society' (*Nihon Keizai Shimbun*, 5 December), and 'RPM of Publications Protects Freedom of Speech, Preserving Culture' (*Yomiuri Shimbun*, 6 December). In the *Nihon Keizai Shimbun*, a popular storyteller wrote how he 'fear[ed] the suppression of freedom of speech.'

The abolition of enterprise tax exemption for newspaper companies

The JNCA memorandum also referred to the 'enterprise tax exemptions.' 'We are afraid,' it explained, 'that the RPM exemption matter will follow a similar course to that of the earlier enterprise tax exemption matter, which, although we succeeded in postponing the conclusion for a year, ultimately resulted in enterprise tax exemptions being abolished.'

During 1951–4, seven industries, led by the newspaper industry, succeeded in having the enterprise tax (i.e., the prefectural income tax) law revised by the Diet to obtain enterprise tax exemptions for businesses within the relevant industries.[141] In 1985, more than thirty years later, the government proposed to abolish these exemptions to achieve equity in the tax burden. A partial abolition was achieved: that is, in the form of a transition clause by which enterprises that had previously enjoyed full tax exemptions would be taxed on only half of their corporate income, but this measure was to end in three years. This 'transitional' period was extended for a further two years in 1988 and again for one year four times after 1990. In 1994, the government finally decided to abolish these tax exemptions completely. Thereafter, enterprises in these industries would be taxed on their full incomes. This was to be introduced by gradually increasing the percentage of income to be taxed to reach 100 percent by April 1998. Despite continued campaigns by the JNCA to have the exemptions extended, these tax exemptions were finally eliminated, and by the end of March 1998 these enterprises were paying tax on 100 percent of their income.

The JNCA's long-lasting campaigns against abolition

The fact of the existence of these tax exemptions for these industries, and also the government's attempt to abolish them and the JNCA's long campaigns against their abolition, received very little publicity. It rarely appeared in mass media like newspapers and television. Even today, very few people know that these exemptions ever existed, although they did for forty years.

It is appropriate, I believe, to introduce the commentary on this issue by Naohiko Jinno, professor of public finance at the University of Tokyo. Jinno is particularly well versed in the events leading up to the decision taken in 1985. He recognizes that the two campaigns conducted by the JNCA, that is the campaign against the elimination of enterprise tax exemptions and that against the re-evaluation of RPM exemptions, were basically the same.[142]

First, according to Jinno, the JNCA's campaign to preserve the tax exemption was hard and obstinate. Everybody concerned was deeply impressed by the magnitude of their power and behavior in criticizing the government decision. In the end, the JNCA gained more than ten years of extensions to the transition clause after the decision was taken in 1985 to abolish the exemption.

Second, politicians were said to be heavily involved in the JNCA's campaign to oppose the government's 1985 decision to establish and then extend the transition clause. The blatant inequity associated with the exemptions and extensions meant that the campaign received very little media attention. Presumably, the pre-1985 campaign to maintain the exemption was just as vigorous.

Third, Jinno was surprised by the biased coverage (or non-coverage) of the campaign. Precisely because the JNCA's arguments and issues reflected poorly on the media, they rarely if ever found their way into print. However, the newspapers were eager to print detailed reports of the other groups that supported the exemptions, and the activities of groups with relatively little political power.

Fourth, Jinno was amazed at the attitude evident across the newspaper industry that it was somehow special and beyond any notion of egalitarian treatment.

A historical coincidence for the 1985 revision of tax law

The coalition cabinet of the Liberal Democratic Party (LDP) and the New Democratic Club took power in 1983–4, and Seiichi Tagawa of the New Democratic Club was appointed the minister of home affairs. Without this historical coincidence, the 1985 revision of tax law might never have been realized. Tagawa had long been critical of the fact that the public had been kept ignorant of the tax exemption. Tagawa attributed this to the negative attitude of the Diet, the Taxation System Research Committee in particular, and the newspapers' collusion in failing to report all relevant affairs, despite this exemption being one of the most extreme tax preferences, rivaling those for doctors and religious groups.

This enterprise tax is a local tax, and exemption from it was accordingly realized by revising the Local Tax Act, which comes under the jurisdiction of the Ministry of Home Affairs and hence that minister. In combination with Masayuki Fujio,[143] chairman of the Policy Research Council of the LDP, Tagawa opened the way for abolition of the tax exemption for mass-media companies like newspaper companies.

> Some LDP members did not want to touch this matter, fearing revenge from the mass media. When I explained my proposal as the minister in charge of the matter at the Local Administration Committee of the House of Representatives, there was a loud roar from young members of the ruling party: they barked at me 'Never propose what you know is infeasible!
>
> (Tagawa 1995: p.149)

Four points to note

It is critical to keep four points in mind here:

1   Politicians must make active efforts to promote political issues that are subject to controversy in order to see that these issues are addressed. In the case of the re-evaluation of RPM exemptions, there were no such political entrepreneurs in the Diet before March 1998. It was a major aim of opposition groups to prevent the appearance of such entrepreneurs.
2   There is a representative of the newspaper industry on almost every council and research group in the cabinet and within individual ministries. Like the representatives of other industries, a newspaper industry representative will behave in the interests of his industry on relevant issues.
3   The tax 'transition clause' was adopted only after the resignations of the two people who had played key roles in the abolition of the exemption: Tagawa at the Ministry of Home Affairs and Fujio as chairman of the LDP Policy Research Council.
4   It took the reappearance of Tagawa in 1994 to fight the multiple transitional extensions and finally to end the exemption in April 1998. According to Tagawa, he decided to return to his campaign only after the JNCA monthly *Newspaper Research* rejected the paper he had written (at the JNCA's request) on the exemption (see Miwa 1998a: p.296, note 41; Tagawa 1995: pp.150–3).

The JNCA and the newspaper industry

Even today, few people know that the exemption ever existed, even though it existed for over forty years. The same is true of the vigorous campaign to preserve the exemption and of the activities of politicians representing the newspaper industry. Had the media not collectively monopolized the means of public disclosure, the public would not have been ignorant. Aware of the exemption, it might have pushed more quickly and more effectively for abolition of the exemption.[144]

Perhaps because of its own power, the JNCA relied on few of the other devices that industries typically use to protect advantageous regulation. There was, for example, no ministerial section specializing in newspaper affairs. Neither was there a sitting policy council. Instead, people (particularly industry insiders) routinely refer to the newspaper regulatory regime as 'public' or 'social' rather than 'economic.' The newspapers themselves have been able to enforce this apparent consensus through the JNCA's collective control over the media.

Readers might wonder how TV stations behaved in this dispute. In Japan, most TV stations and networks are under the control of newspaper companies. In the Tokyo area, five terrestrial TV stations are controlled by national newspaper companies: NTV by *Yomiuri Shimbun*, TBS by *Mainichi Shimbun*, Fuji TV by *Sankei Shimbun*, TV Asahi by *Asahi Shimbun*, and Tokyo 12 by the *Japan Economic Journal*. Each of these stations represents a key nationwide broadcasting network, and only the public broadcasting network lies outside this system.

**4.7   ILLUSTRATION 2:
BACKGROUND TO THE JNCA'S CAMPAIGN
AGAINST THE REPEAL OF RPM EXEMPTIONS FOR
PUBLICATIONS IN THE ANTI-MONOPOLY ACT**

The JNCA's campaign

The JNCA campaign against the repeal of the RPM exemptions for publications in the Anti-monopoly Act became apparent to the public after the summer of 1995. The JNCA acted in concert with two other trade associations, the Japan Book Publishers Association and the Japan Magazine Publishers Association. However, the JNCA was the leader, and the others followed its lead.

The JNCA organized an active campaign in which its member companies worked to preserve the RPM exemption. All members of the JNCA acted in concert, along with the book and magazine publishers associations and their members. None reported any material against their interests: for example, opinions supporting the abolition of the exemption clause, or the unanimous support of major consumer unions for abolition. Many consumer unions were very critical of the JNCA's campaign, pointing to the misunderstandings and lying of the JNCA. The JNCA obviously did not allow such views to be reported.

The DS of the ARC, which later became a major target of the JNCA's campaign, published a document discussing the pros and cons of the major issues of the year, including the re-evaluation of RPM exemptions, on 27 July 1995. However, this debate too barely made it into the papers. The *Asahi Shimbun*, for instance, allocated only a few lines to this entire document (Administrative Reform Committee 1996: p.101; Miwa 1997e: ch. 1).

The basic strategy of the JNCA campaign

The catchphrases used in the campaign involved 'the right to knowledge,' 'the public,' 'culture,' and also 'freedom of speech' and 'freedom of the press.' Like the American obsession with motherhood and apple pie, the phrases are hard to challenge. Just as with 'safety,' 'health,' 'life,' 'welfare,' 'the environment,' and 'equity,' few people will instinctively challenge campaigns expressed in these phrases, and the agenda underlying these expressions will remain unchallenged. As with campaigns to protect vested interests more generally, the JNCA campaign styled itself as one of universal validity. As far as possible, it used the above catchphrases to circumvent inquiry and criticism into the details of issues.

Unlike most other industries, the newspaper industry could block external inquiry and criticism because of its control over primary reporting. Because its members monopolized reporting, they apparently believed that they would be able to keep most of the public ignorant of the real issues. Imagine the result if other powerful pressure groups in Japanese society, such as the Japan Medical

Association, the Japanese Federation of Bar Associations, the Central Association of Agricultural Cooperative Unions, or the Japanese Federation of Labor Unions, had tried similar tactics.

The twofold foundation of the JNCA campaign

The government's explanation for the 1953 RPM exemptions was given by then-chairman of the FTC, Masatoshi Yokota, who emphasized that the exemptions were intended primarily to secure minimum profits for retailers on certain daily products and publications (the House of Representatives' Committee on Economic Stability, 5 March). Later, on 9 March, the emphasis was placed again on daily products. The FTC chairman explained that it had included the exemptions because it believed that manufacturer-stated prices were only 'suggested prices' and not being mandatory would not violate the Anti-monopoly Act (for a full quotation, see Appendix 1; see also FTC 1995; Miwa 1997c).

The foundation of the JNCA's campaign was twofold. First, it tried to cultivate wide public support for the notion that they should rank 'social' concerns above 'economic' concerns. Second, it possessed and used the most powerful measure of control over the flow of information to the public, that is control over the media. The JNCA hoped to obtain support for the RPM exemption by using this appeal to the 'social' value of the exemptions. Moreover, by using expressions such as 'the right to knowledge,' 'suppression of freedom of speech,' and 'the public,' it tried to argue that the regulation and policies giving preferential treatment to the newspaper industry were somehow fundamentally different from other regulations and policies. By thus distinguishing them, it hoped to avoid the then-widely accepted principle of 'reducing social regulation to the necessary minimum.'

Consequently, the JNCA ignored the public's demand for explanation as to the substance of exactly why these regulations were 'social.' This in turn left the public dissatisfied and stimulated their interest in this issue. Apparently, the JNCA miscalculated, since in the long term it runs against the interest of those advocating the regulatory *status quo* to stimulate the public's interest in this issue. In this regard, the JNCA's recent campaign against the re-evaluation of RPM exemptions differed from the previous campaigns of this association. An examination of this difference illustrates the anatomy of the policy decision-making process.

The crucial factor behind the outcome

The decisive factor behind the outcome in this case was that the RPM exemptions for publications were stipulated in the Anti-monopoly Act (subsection 4 of section 24-2), rather than in other laws such as industry laws. In part because of this, RPM in the newspaper industry, for instance, is valid only on some conditions being fulfilled. For example, the industry cannot collectively decide to adopt RPM. RPM is legal only if competitors can freely decide not to use the scheme.

The statutory location is significant, because the FTC has jurisdiction over the Anti-monopoly Act. The primary role of the FTC is to enforce competition policy, antitrust policy in particular. Accordingly, unlike typical ministries, which allocate responsibility for specific industries, the FTC need not pay much attention to the maintenance of close and friendly relationships with individual industries.

Instead, the FTC saw the 1990s deregulation as a vindication of its work. Recall that the government declared administrative reform and deregulation to be one of its primary policy issues. Toward that end, it had prepared the Deregulation Promotion Program in which it adopted the fundamental principle of 'reducing social regulations to the necessary minimum.' Emphasizing antitrust policy as fundamental to this program, they actively promoted the repeal of the many exemptions that had long hampered antitrust enforcement. The abolition of these exemptions has been a long-established goal of the FTC, to which it had devoted much effort over several decades. Naturally, the FTC accelerated its efforts under this deregulation program.

The cabinet issued the Three-Year Program to Promote Deregulation on 31 March 1998 and summarized the accomplishments of the Deregulation Promotion Program, which it had enforced over the preceding three years. It had earlier declared that during FY1998 the 'abolition' or 're-evaluation in order to achieve the abolition' of most exemptions in the Anti-monopoly Act would be conducted. Toward that end, it would introduce a bill to revise the Anti-monopoly Act in the next ordinary session of the Diet.

Section 24-2, subsections 4 and 1 of the Anti-monopoly Act

Subsection 4 of section 24-2 of the Anti-monopoly Act provides:

> legitimate conduct of an enterprise whose business is publication or by an enterprise whose business is to sell publications, in order to fix and maintain with an enterprise that buys publications, the resale price thereof, shall be exempted from the application of this Act.

Subsection 1 then limits the exemption to conduct that is not 'unreasonably injurious' to consumers. That is, the exemption applies:

> unless such conduct is unreasonably injurious to the interest of general consumers, and the conduct is performed by an enterprise whose business is to sell the commodity, against the will of the enterprise that produces the commodity.

The breadth of the term 'publications' is unclear, since the following commodities are expressly excluded from application of the subsection: video cassettes, laser discs, computer programs, and databases.

Councils for examining RPM issues

These points, namely the breadth of the term 'publications' and the matter of injury to consumers, were among the objectives of the government policy to 'limit and clarify the scope of publications for RPM exemptions,' which was part of the wider Deregulation Promotion Program that the government hoped to complete by the end of March 1998. The target for completion at the start of the program was the end of December 1998, which the cabinet soon brought forward by nine months as part of its measures to advance the program.

To these ends, the FTC formed a new Subcommittee to Examine RPM Issues under the Study Group for Government Regulations and Competition Policy. Unlike typical ministerial councils or study groups, which are for the purpose of coordinating interests between relevant parties, FTC councils or (sub)committees usually include no members from individual interest groups. Most of the ten members of the FTC subcommittee were instead university professors, primarily law professors. (I joined the subcommittee as one of a few members of the incumbent study group.)

Symbolically, at the meeting of the Special Committee for Deregulation of the House of Representatives on 5 June 1996, Tsuneo Watanabe, president of *Yomiuri Shimbun* and chairman of the JNCA Special Committee for RPM Preservation, appeared as a representative of the JNCA. He criticized this subcommittee and the DS of the ARC, arguing that they merely amounted to privately organized study groups. As such, he explained, they were not entitled to wield authority. However, the former was organized under a cabinet decision, and the latter was established by a committee established by statute. Oddly enough, there was no criticism of Watanabe's official statement either at the meeting or in subsequent reports in the media. In fact, despite claims by Watanabe, the newspaper industry has been extremely eager to have its representatives participate in the 'private' study groups.[145]

If left alone, the JNCA could expect these committees to strongly recommend the abolition of the RPM exemptions. Once such a conclusion was published, the preservation of the exemptions would arouse much controversy. Therefore, the JNCA was forced to intervene before any such report was published. This deviated from the traditional tactics and measures used in its campaigns.

Five further points for understanding the JNCA's response

In addition to the fact that the FTC administers the Anti-monopoly Act and its RPM exemptions, note five points.

1   Unlike other industries, as described above the newspaper industry has no ministerial section dedicated to its affairs. Accordingly, there is no minister to systematically represent its interests in cabinet or other government meetings. Additionally, there is no ongoing communication between any government section and the FTC regarding this industry.

2   Again unlike other industries, the newspaper industry has no standing council dealing with its affairs. As a result, the subcommittee that was organized for the re-evaluation by the FTC did not include any industry representative. The JNCA made every effort to influence subcommittee members, but in vain. Soon after the subcommittee was formed, all its members received visits for 'persuasion' from JNCA representatives. In my case, a director in charge of sales and the sales bureau chief of *Asahi Shimbun* came to my office under the guise of 'collecting information.' The JNCA was unable to explain successfully the reasons for preserving the RPM exemptions at a formal meeting conducted with the subcommittee. On the morning of 3 March 1995, the subcommittee invited representatives from the JNCA to meet the subcommittee to exchange information. The JNCA defended the RPM exemptions by simply repeating the word 'public.' Repeatedly, the committee demanded more detailed explanations of what it meant by 'public' in order to gain a fuller appreciation of its argument. Finally, a director of *Mainichi Shimbun* replied: ' "public" means that every person needs a newspaper every day.' When a committee member (it was I) noted that 'every person needs toilet paper every day. Are you arguing that the RPM exemption should be expanded to the toilet paper industry?' silence followed. Later an *Asahi Shimbun* editorial (26 August 1995) proclaimed that 'the foundation of newspapers is our mission.' The editorial criticized my stand, but only in (literally) sanitized form: i.e., it ascribed to me the view that 'if newspapers and books are cultural, so is soap. Soap makes us feel refreshed.' Such is editorial delicacy, apparently. At least two persons from *Asahi Shimbun* had been present at the meeting between the subcommittee and JNCA representatives (see Miwa 1997e: pp.222–3).

3   In July 1995, the subcommittee published its interim report in order to disclose the discussion to date for public comments. Most believed that the subcommittee would recommence discussion within a few months and that a conclusion consistent with the report would be forthcoming. Most also believed that the Study Group for Government Regulations and Competition Policy, under which the subcommittee was organized, would accept the subcommittee's conclusion, and that this conclusion would then be adopted by the FTC.

4   The DS of the ARC selected the RPM exemption repeal as one of the major issues to be addressed in FY1995. As is the case with most other issues, unless something exceptional occurs, the committee in due course presents its 'opinion' that the exemption be eliminated to the prime minister. The Act founding the ARC demands that the prime minister 'respect' the opinion of the committee (section 4), and it was expected that the cabinet would pay the highest respect to the committee's opinion. Thus the issue was beginning to travel beyond the reach of opposition from any politician. It was also becoming less easy for the FTC to neglect the opinion of the ARC.

5   Particularly in the summer of 1995, major consumer unions began to express clear support for deregulation. Consumer unions in Japan have not tradition-ally supported deregulation, having a fundamental dislike of the free market. For many economists, it seemed that these unions were actually against the interests of consumers. In this case, however, they unanimously supported the elimination of RPM exemptions, particularly for publications.

Faced with these factors unfavorable to the preservation of the RPM exemptions, the JNCA was forced to take extreme measures to challenge the deregulation movement, particularly because this industry had neglected to establish the hurdles to deregulation typical in so many other industries – hurdles that accom-panied the traditional industry-specific administrative structure in most ministries.

The basic strategy of the JNCA campaign and its primary target

The basic strategy adopted by the JNCA was to make the best use of its most powerful weapon, that is the means to control and manipulate information flows in society. It manipulated the supply of information by publishing only what was consistent with its interests. Beyond this, it pressed its case through massively organized media campaigns.

On the request of the JNCA, many influential politicians joined its campaign, expressing their support for the preservation of RPM exemptions. The JNCA displayed its power and threatened supporters of abolition, inducing the public to give up abolition before the movement gathered any momentum. Apparently, the JNCA was prepared to swallow the inevitable ill-feeling and consequent distrust of newspapers among better-informed readers.

The primary target of the campaign was the FTC. In contemporary Japan, competition policy has wide public support, and nobody challenges it without cost. Once the FTC had launched an action to revise the Act to abolish RPM exemptions, it would be hard to stop such action and kill any resulting bill. The cost to the JNCA of lobbying politicians to kill any such bill would be extremely high. Similarly, once the FTC's Subcommittee to Examine RPM Issues had reached a clear conclusion for abolition and submitted it to the FTC through the Study Group for Government Regulations and Competition Policy, the cost to the FTC of not trying to revise the Act would also be great. Consequently, the JNCA targeted the subcommittee to forestall such clear conclusions regarding the need for abolition.

If the subcommittee, having already published its interim report in July 1995, had restarted discussions with the same members, there was little possibility that a contrary conclusion to that of the interim report would have been reached. Naturally, the focus of the campaign by the JNCA was to see that members of the subcommittee were replaced. Only by changing the composition of the subcommittee could it expect a different conclusion to be reached.

Something extremely unusual occurred there

Many expected the subcommittee to restart discussions in the autumn of 1995, several months after the publication of its interim report, and that it would publish the final report several months later, presumably by the end of March 1996. In fact, it was another study group that restarted the discussions, seemingly right from the beginning, in February 1997, one and a half years after the publication of the interim report.

It was not the Subcommittee to Examine RPM Issues but the Study Group for Government Regulations and Competition Policy that restarted discussions. The organization under which the subcommittee was established, the so-called parent committee, was of the same name. That parent committee had a long history and at that moment was examining competition policy issues in regulated industries like airlines, electricity, and gas, and I was a member. Oddly enough, however, the FTC organized this study group totally apart from the old subcommittee and added several new members to this new group who were 'intimate with industry conditions' and who were supposed to be friendly to the JNCA.

The FTC invited most members of the parent committee to join the new study group with no clear explanation of its role. Despite receiving that invitation, I refused to join. The first meeting of the new study group was almost totally occupied with the election of a chairman. It is a common understanding that the organizing ministry (in this case the FTC) will explain to the people it invites to a council or study group what the organization will do, and whom they expect to nominate as chairman. In this case, the FTC proposed Professor Tsuruta, who was the chairman of the parent committee, as chairman. However, the new members, in combination with 'incumbent' members who also belonged to the parent committee as representatives of the newspaper industry, challenged the selection of Tsuruta, but in vain. So something unusual was already occurring at the start of the new study group.[146]

4.8 ILLUSTRATION 3:
THE JNCA'S CAMPAIGN AGAINST THE REPEAL
OF RPM EXEMPTIONS FOR PUBLICATIONS
IN THE ANTI-MONOPOLY ACT

The cabinet decision of 31 March 1998

This cabinet decision adopted the Three-Year Program to Promote Deregulation, a decision that was based on the determination of the Government Headquarters for Promoting Administrative Reform of the same day. This determination concluded that the 'final opinion' of the ARC, therefore the determination of the DS, be adopted in full. A working group, The Deregulation Reform Committee, was organized in February 1998 and was controlled by the Government Headquarters for Promoting Administrative Reform. This committee included former members of the DS of the ARC, both of which were disbanded in December 1997 following the expiry of the three-year term of their existence. This committee, of which I was a member, was supposed to take over the role of the DS and accordingly to monitor the implementation of the Three-Year Program to Promote Deregulation.

The following determinations were made and were scheduled to be implemented by March 2001:

> resale price maintenance is *per se* illegal in light of the Anti-monopoly Act. The ongoing RPM exemption clause for publications (books and magazines, newspapers, and music records and music CDs) allows exemptions to this principle. However, the preservation of these exemptions requires 'particularly persuasive reason.' Upon further discussion of the issues outlined in the Final Opinion of the ARC, the government will take adequate steps. Immediate and precise steps will be taken in the interests of consumers, which will involve the correction of various evils in distribution and trade customs which exist under the ongoing RPM system.

It is expected and required that the FTC will take appropriate action. This accords with the previous government Deregulation Promotion Program, which adopted a policy of 'limiting and clarifying the scope of publications for RPM exemption' at the end of March 1998.

On the same day, the FTC published the statement 'The Treatment of RPM Exemptions for Publications,' which is extracted in Appendix 2. This statement declares that from the viewpoint of competition policy the exemption should be abolished. However, although not originally so intended, some continued to argue that the RPM exemption promoted the growth and diffusion of culture. Emphasizing both that RPM should not be adopted and operated jointly by publishers and that it should neither unduly injure the interests of consumers nor be taken against the will of the publisher, the FTC statement demanded that relevant parties take appropriate actions to correct existing evils. In addition, the statement disclosed other regulatory changes designed to encourage price competition in the newspaper industry. Thus the program, in combination with the FTC's policy declared in this statement, does have substance.

Obtaining a cabinet decision

I will not go into a detailed analysis of the 'actions' taken between March 1998 and July 2003 or try to forecast future developments. Simply, we have observed no changes to section 24-2 of the Anti-monopoly Act. However, the object of this chapter is merely to provide an anatomical description of the policy-making process in contemporary Japan. I will focus on the process leading up to the Cabinet Decision on 31 March 1998.

The final opinion of the ARC, mentioned in the Deregulation Promotion Program, was presented to the prime minister on 18 December 1997. That final opinion declared that 'we find no "particularly persuasive reason" for preserving the existing RPM exemptions for publications. For reasons explained below, at the beginning of FY1997 the DS identified as its goal for the year the determination of a cabinet decision that accorded with the final opinion. The cabinet did decide on 20 December to 'pay the highest respect to the opinion,' and it continued to state that 'we will take appropriate measures.' The 31 March cabinet decision was a natural consequence of the final opinion of the ARC.

The ARC was allowed to present opinions to the prime minister, but with regard to remaining deregulation issues the ARC confronted the ministerial council in charge of the relevant issue. Generally, the conclusions reached by the ministerial councils conflicted with the stance of the ARC. This created something of a quandary, and it fell to the secretary-general of the Management and Coordination Agency to try to coordinate these conflicting views. Reaching a conclusion that accords with the view of the prime minister is seldom easy – and it was not easy here.

The Cabinet Act stipulates that 'upon policy decision of the cabinet, the prime minister directs and controls the individual sectors of administration' (section 6). This enables the prime minister to direct and control individual ministries only if there is a cabinet decision to respect the ARC's opinion. Toward that end, the DS of the ARC, emphasizing the realization of its opinions, focused on acquiring a supporting cabinet decision.

The road to the cabinet decision

Several hurdles had to be cleared before the desired cabinet decision could be obtained. First, the DS (and the ARC) had to take the relevant politics and the political process into consideration when presenting their opinions on each issue. The achievement of a cabinet decision requires the acknowledgement of the issue at the Ruling Parties Policy Coordination Conference, which presupposes approval of the issue in each party in the ruling coalition. In the Liberal Democratic Party (LDP), by far the largest ruling party, the party's approval of a cabinet decision requires the acknowledgement of both the Study Group of its Policy Research Council (PRC) and its Executive Council.

For an opinion of the ARC to be acknowledged by the PRC, what is of critical importance is the approval of the LDP's Headquarters for Promoting Administrative Reform[147] and of the relevant subgroup of the PRC. Once the headquarters approves, the ARC can expect to be able to rely on its efforts for the realization of the opinion, including its influence on the relevant subgroup of the PRC.

If a conflict of opinion between the ARC (or the DS) and the relevant ministry remains unresolved, the relevant subgroup of the PRC will generally oppose the ARC and side with the ministry. That in turn will make it hard to obtain the support of the PRC in general. Even if that support is obtained, the Executive Council presents another level of difficulty. Accordingly, reaching an agreement with the relevant ministry, which can then try to persuade the relevant subgroup of the PRC, is a necessary precondition to obtaining the cabinet decision that the ARC desires.

The subgroup of the PRC to which the relevant Diet members loyal to a particular industry belong will strongly reflect the interests of that industry. Accordingly, even if the bureaucrats in the relevant ministry share the view of the ARC, if there is little chance of acquiring the support of the relevant PRC subgroups, then the ministry will have no choice but to oppose any cabinet decision supporting the ARC.

When negotiations with the ministry took a turn for the worse, the ARC was forced to make a choice between alternatives that lay between the two extremes of pushing hard to have its opinion adopted and enforced and giving up entirely. Pushing hard was chosen on the assumption that its opponents would give up, because they would not dig in and oppose the opinion if the government's deregulation program would be destroyed as a whole. Before this happened, they would be isolated and attacked by others in the PRC, the Executive Council, and the cabinet.

The direct counterpart in negotiations was the ministry. When a challenge by the ARC failed, then what the result looked like was 'the defeat of deregulation by the resistance of bureaucrats,' which is a term close to the hearts of those in the press. The reality of the situation is that 'bureaucrats consistently retreat against the resistance of industries and the Diet members tied to specific industries.'

However, it is certainly true that each political party has its own policies. In the LDP, for instance, the Headquarters for Promoting Administrative Reform plays an active policy role. Neither the PRC nor the Executive Council amount to 'dummy' institutions authorizing conclusions reached by subgroups of the PRC and the ministries. In the past few years, the political issue of 'administrative reform and deregulation' has attained such a high priority that it has resulted in the establishment of the ARC. Consequently, any 'opinions' of the ARC could expect strong support from the ruling parties.

On 18 December 1997, the PRC and the Executive Council of the LDP decided to support a cabinet decision adopting the ARC's final opinion. Furthermore, the Ruling Parties Policy Coordination Conference followed with its support on 19 December. The fruit of these acknowledgements was the cabinet decision of 20 December, which declared that 'we pay the highest respect to the final opinion of the ARC … and we will take appropriate action.'[148]

The FTC was the government institution that administered the final opinion of the ARC on the RPM exemptions for publications. Following the cabinet decision, the prime minister was authorized to use his 'authority to direct and control the individual sectors of the administration.' This then led to the publication by the FTC of its Program of Activities and comments related to the abolition of the RPM exemptions on 31 March 1998.

Actual steps to the final opinion

The DS selected the major issues to be addressed for each fiscal year in the spring. After a long process, including negotiations with relevant parties, the DS presented its 'opinion' on the selected issues to the prime minister through the ARC. Forty-seven issues were selected for address in FY1995, forty-six in FY1996, and twenty-two in FY1997. On most of these issues, the DS presented concrete opinions to the prime minister in December of each year. The only exception was the re-evaluation of RPM exemptions for publications, concerning which the DS postponed drawing any concrete conclusions twice, in 1995 and 1996. These postponements were part of the strategy adopted by the DS, taken in response to factors such as the characteristics of opposing groups, the height of hurdles to be cleared in the policy-making process, and the state of public opinion in the policy-making process.

The 'opinion' presented by the DS concerning this issue at the close of the first round of the DS in December 1995 was as follows:

> resale price maintenance is *per se* invalid in light of the Anti-monopoly Act, which lays down the fundamental rules for this matter. Any exception to these fundamental rules of the Act requires a particularly persuasive reason.

The opinion continues that 'as a major issue for investigation, we will pursue discussion and examination of this exception.' It was this opinion that the opposition campaign by the JNCA targeted at its peak.

The 'opinion' of the DS had progressed to the following stage by the end of the second round in December 1996:

> The system of newspaper home delivery meets the needs of consumers. Even giving due consideration to this fact, including the relation between the present distribution system and RPM, we find no decisive reason justifying the maintenance of the RPM exemptions for publications as a ground for exceptional treatment under the Anti-monopoly Act.

The opinion continues:

> we will continue to investigate this issue from the standpoint of consumers and draw a conclusion. We will focus our investigation on the existence of any 'particularly persuasive reason' for preserving the RPM exemptions, conducting separate investigations for each individual sector in which the RPM exemption applies. We will also promote further discussion of the issue among the general public.

The final round in 1997

The investigation in the DS in FY1997 proceeded in the light of the above circumstances. The DS devoted enormous energy to this issue, much more than it devoted to the other issues. In addition to the previous efforts to collect information through the Prime Minister's Office and embassies abroad, in May 1997 two members (including myself), together with office members, were sent to Europe and the USA to study the state of the issue there. After issuing a document detailing the pros and cons in June, the DS held a series of open discussions for three hours each week. Three out of a total of ten meetings were devoted to this issue, with music records and CDs being discussed at the meeting of 17 July, books and magazines on 9 October, and newspapers on 23 October. The DS began to prepare its final opinion at the beginning of November (for more details, see Miwa 1997e: ch. 1).

As before, the DS organized several internal subgroups, called 'working groups.' The subgroup in charge of this issue started to finalize its work in September, much earlier than was the case for other issues. Many advised the DS, and even some DS members were concerned that, because of the 'political power' and 'social influence' of newspapers, pursuing the abolition of the RPM exemptions for publications would have a detrimental effect on the greater activities of the DS and the ARS, and accordingly hurt the deregulation effort more generally.[149]

As with all issues, after the exchange of opinions among members, this subgroup began to prepare a draft opinion. Anticipating both hard negotiations with relevant ministries and industries and 'information exchange' with politicians, draft opinions are usually mere starting points, and there is a long process that follows until the preparation of the final opinion. The DS anticipated exceptionally hard and complicated negotiations in the case of the RPM exemptions. Accordingly, the DS prepared a detailed strategy on the style and content of the draft opinion, the likely environment and schedule of negotiations, and the selection of the personnel who would be involved in the negotiations.

The DS held regular three-hour meetings every Thursday afternoon. At the meetings, each subgroup reported its activities to the DS. At the meeting of 13 November 1997, the DS discussed the draft opinion of each subgroup concerning most issues before the DS. On the matter of RPM exemptions for publications, however, only the basic policy was introduced at this meeting. The draft opinion was presented on 20 November. Once approved by the DS, this draft opinion provided the starting point from which negotiations with the relevant government institutions began.

The last stage

The draft opinion on this matter was first submitted to the FTC and the Agency for Cultural Affairs, and negotiations commenced with these agencies. The Agency for Cultural Affairs forwarded the draft opinion to the relevant trade associations, including the JNCA, which placed strict limits on the circulation of the draft opinion. Even within the newspaper industry, apparently only the people in charge of sales for ten to twenty companies saw the opinion.

Most of the issues before the DS were settled on 27 November, and the remaining issues, other than the RPM exemptions, on 2 December. However, the DS withheld its final opinion on RPM exemptions from its final report, which was published on 4 December. Space in this report for its opinion on RPM exemptions remained blank.

On 4 December, the DS was still negotiating with relevant parties concerning RPM exemptions, and the blank space was finally filled on 8 December. During the period for preparing the final opinion, that is from September to December, the DS discussed this issue on every occasion, even though its members had reached an agreement on the fundamental points at an early stage. In line with the agreement, the DS continued to negotiate with relevant parties, and the final report detailed the discussions of the DS regarding the matter, concluding that the DS found no 'particularly persuasive reason' to preserve the exemptions.

I will not go into details of whom the DS negotiated with and how agreement was reached with the relevant parties. Suffice it to say that neither the FTC nor the Agency for Cultural Affairs played a major role in the process. The control and management of information on both sides of the negotiation was very tight. All parties were concerned that any fragments of leaked information would lead to reports in the media about this complicated issue, creating disorder and confusion and making any 'agreement' extremely difficult.[150] This was of particular concern to those seeking to have the exemption maintained.

Agreement was reached at an early date that the final decision would be deferred until 8 December, and this fact was kept secret. A basic agreement was reached on the evening of 3 December, and the final agreement was settled late in the evening of 5 December, a Friday. This agreement was made public on 8 December as the final opinion of the DS.

Between December 1997 and March 1998

The government published a Three-Year Program to Promote Deregulation and an official statement (see Appendix 2) on the RPM exemptions issue. The latter was based upon the final opinion of the ARC and the proposals by the FTC Study Group for Government Regulations and Competition Policy Concentrating on the Investigation of the RPM Issue (published in January). The program of the government and the official statement of the FTC were both published on 31 March 1998.

Also, between the time of publication of the ARC's final opinion in December 1997 and the government program in March 1998, each ministry with jurisdiction over relevant issues presented its action program for 'monitoring' in response to the ARC's final opinion to the newly organized Deregulation Committee of the Government Headquarters for Promoting Administrative Reform. The committee consisted of seven former members of the DS, which had been disbanded in December. Its primary task was to 'monitor' the realization of the final opinion. I was a member of the committee.

The policies of the FTC and the Agency for Cultural Affairs on the RPM exemptions issue were also 'reviewed.' Finally, the cabinet decision of 31 March 1998 determined the Three-Year Program to Promote Deregulation. This decision had to pass through the internal procedure for acknowledgement by ruling parties as described, as was the case with the cabinet decision to pay the highest respect to the December 1997 final opinion of the ARC.

Any decision-making process is long and complex, and many figures participate

During November and December, newspapers reported every day that the JNCA and other associations presented their opinions and requests to various influential organizations and persons to preserve the RPM exemption. Nothing differed from the behavior of other trade associations in this regard, except that the actions of the JNCA were 'reported' in newspapers, which was part of its campaign tactics. This demonstrates the power and influence of the JNCA.

On 18 March 1998, in the final stages of preparation of the Three-Year Program to Promote Deregulation, newspapers reported that the LDP Newspaper Distribution Meeting (the association of LDP Diet members friendly to newspaper distributors and publishers), chaired by Keizo Obuchi, had adopted a resolution at its general meeting. The resolution asked that 'the importance and necessity of the RPM system be recognized and accordingly that the preservation of the RPM exemptions should be included in the program.' On the same day, the same request was made to the Agency for Cultural Affairs and the FTC.

Although perhaps not as extreme as in the case of the abolition of RPM exemption, any policy-making process is long and complex. Many figures participate, both individuals and collectives, directly and indirectly. The process is one where various interests and power figures jockey and collude through negotiation, coordination, and compromise to maximize their own gains. Consequently, any policy that is finally adopted is strongly conditioned by the process. In the case of the re-evaluation of newspaper RPM exemptions, the explicit abolition of these exemptions was the objective. This could have been realized by deleting the exemption clause in the Anti-monopoly Act (section 24-2, subsection 4) or by declaring that newspapers no longer fell within the scope of the definition of 'publications' for the purpose of RPM exemptions. The exceptionally long and complex process in this case strongly influenced, both in substance and in appearance, the government program and the FTC statement published on 31 March 1998.

Obviously, newspapers and other mass media were the major players in the process. This was clearly revealed in the way that – even after March 1998 – very few people understood the basic issues involved or the resolution reached at the end of March 1998. To the end, the press was able to distort the information the public acquired and to inhibit the extent to which it understood the issue (see, generally, Miwa 1998a).

In reality the battle is over

After 1997, rumors circulated that the issue of RPM exemptions for publications would die a natural death. The essence of this rumor was as follows. First, (as in Germany) under the political circumstances of the time it was not feasible explicitly to abolish the RPM exemptions for publications in the near future. However, the grounds for justifying the preservation of RPM exemptions presented by proponents of the exemption had been completely refuted. Second, The FTC declared that neither RPM conducted jointly by publishers nor conduct that forced publishers to accept RPM (many newspaper sales in Japan are made through sellers who are members of a very strong trade association) would be exempted from the Anti-monopoly Act. Third, the two key complementary arrangements that had traditionally been 'justified' on the very same grounds as the RPM exemptions would soon be critically re-evaluated.

To start with, the FTC would re-evaluate the 1964 designation of unfair trade practices specific to the newspaper industry. Under this designation, the FTC had defined the sale of products in the newspaper industry, directly or indirectly, at different prices across regions or across readers, and all sales below list price as unfair trade practices that violated the Anti-monopoly Act. In addition, the FTC would critically re-evaluate the 1964 regulation on 'offerings' in the newspaper industry that effectively prohibited non-price competition in the industry (see Appendix 2).

These events effectively destroyed the conditions underlying the effective enforcement of RPM. The FTC officially demanded that traditional inflexible trade customs and institutional arrangements be re-evaluated. More importantly, the industry was overflowing with discontent against the *ancien régime*. In reality, the battle is over. Proponents of RPM exemptions may argue until they are blue in the face, but the arguments now amount to little more than a political performance.

4.9   CONCLUDING REMARKS

Regardless of the definition of 'policy' and 'policy decision making,' the reality of the policy-making process is that it is long and complex, and many figures participate. Regardless of the definition of 'the government' or 'the state,' that definition can never be limited to those officially internal to the government or the state. Even when the government succeeds in unifying the intentions of its internal agencies, the policy-making process and enforcement of policy cannot be limited to these government agencies. This applies to any individual within the government, the prime minister for instance, and also to small groups.

During the war, the government adopted a policy of developing a powerful system of wartime control to meet the demands of the military. However, the government was unable to acquire sympathy and cooperation from many influential persons in the policy-making and enforcement processes and so was unable to achieve all its objectives. The need to implement this policy within a short time made it all the more difficult. The promotion of the machinery industries under the MIPA did not satisfy the basic preconditions for acquiring sympathy and cooperation from relevant interest groups. Also, government small business policies have consistently amounted to big political performances, positing problems that are simply impossible to solve.

When we address the issue of who actually determines the substance of policy, we must begin by defining the terms 'policy' and 'determine.' Similarly, any investigation of the 'competence,' 'behavior,' and 'function' of the state requires that we define the terms 'state,' 'competence,' 'behavior,' and 'function.' The issues not only of who actually determines the substance of policy but also why, when, where, for whom, and how is seldom easy. The Diet, or men of influence, might 'determine' a 'policy' in ways that serve their own interests, inhibiting the realization of the true objective of the 'policy.' At least, 'decisions' concerning 'policy' must take into consideration the feasibility of the policy objective.

The first step in any investigation of the competence of the state, and further the behavior and function of the state as related to its competence, is to address the following issue and recognize the following fact. Namely, the relevant issue is that of who actually determines the substance of policy. The relevant fact is that the actual policy-making process is long and complex, and many people participate.

APPENDIX 1   OUTLINE OF THE RPM EXEMPTIONS FOR PUBLICATIONS AND LEGISLATIVE INTENT

The issues raised in connection with the RPM exemptions for publications are related to section 24-2 of the Anti-monopoly Act, particularly with subsection 4 of this section.

Section 24-2 of the Anti-monopoly Act (resale price maintenance contracts)

(1) The provisions of this Act shall not apply to legitimate conduct performed by an entrepreneur who produces or sells a commodity, the uniform quality of which is easily identifiable and which is designated by the Fair Trade Commission, with another entrepreneur who buys such commodity, in order to fix and maintain the resale price thereof (this term means hereinafter the price at which the latter entrepreneur or a third entrepreneur who purchases from him sells such commodity): Provided, however that the foregoing shall not apply if the said conduct tends to be grossly injurious to the interest of consumers in general, or if the relevant conduct is taken by an entrepreneur whose business is to sell the said commodity against the will of the entrepreneur who produces the said commodity.

[...]

(4) Legitimate conducts performed by an entrepreneur whose business is to publish publications or by an entrepreneur whose business is to sell such publications, in order to fix and maintain with another entrepreneur who buys such products, the resale price thereof, shall be treated as provided in subsection (1).

The Anti-monopoly Act, enacted in 1947 during the Occupation, was amended extensively in 1953 with the end of Occupation. This program of amendments, often called 'eviscerating amendments' by opponents, included the introduction of provisions for a series of exemptions to the general provisions of the Act. Exemptions for RPM contracts (24-2), for recession cartels (24-3), and for ratio-nalization cartels (24-4) were among the best examples.[151] By the beginning of the 1960s, the Anti-monopoly Act was effectively in legal hibernation. Public recognition of and accordingly their interest in this Act, and therefore in the provisions for RPM exemptions (including that for publications), were extremely low. Since then, the Anti-monopoly Act has gradually come to be accepted and supported by the general public, so the exemptions to the Act have been re-evaluated and gradually reduced. It has been a process of reincarnating the shape and position of the Act as a fundamental premise to a market economy, and closing various loopholes. With the repeal of some of the exemption provisions in the Act and in other laws that provide for exemptions to the Act, the scope of the remaining exemptions has been significantly reduced. The elimination of exemptions to the Anti-monopoly Act formed part of the fundamental principle of administrative reform, pronounced by the cabinet decision of 15 February 1994 entitled 'Future Measures for Promoting Administrative Reform.'

It was in the first half of the 1960s that the public developed a strong interest in RPM contracts and their regulation, which forced the FTC to change its stance regarding RPM regulations under the Anti-monopoly Act. First, manufacturers of cosmetics, over-the-counter medicines, and synthetic detergents all secured RPM exemptions from the FTC under subsection 1 of section 24-2 of the Anti-monopoly Act, the so-called 'designated RPM,' to prevent sales at low prices. These industries immediately began to aggressively establish and maintain the controlled distribution of their products. These developments saw consumer interest in the Anti-monopoly Act, the potential problems raised by RPM in particular, and also consumer expectations of the FTC, deepen greatly. 'Creeping inflation' during this period further stimulated the public's interest and expectations regarding this Act and the countermeasures by the FTC.

The Nippon Suisan case, which occurred in 1964, was one where the FTC adopted a policy of prohibiting RPM as constituting trade under an undue binding condition, violating designation 8 of the General Designations issued by the FTC concerning unfair trade practices. Soon afterwards, the FTC commenced the powdered milk case, which was fought out over nine years and ended in the Supreme Court. The final decision of this case, handed down in 1975, held that RPM was illegal *per se* under the Anti-monopoly Act. This decision was in line with the FTC's policy. In 1982, the General Designations regarding unfair trade practices were revised, the first revision since the establishment of the regime in 1953. These revisions saw the FTC designate 'resale price fixing' explicitly as an unfair trade practice (designation 12), that had been treated as part of 'trade under an unduly binding condition.' At the same time, the FTC began to reduce the number of RPM designations made under subsection 1 of section 24-2 of the Anti-monopoly Act, the so-called 'designated RPM.' Since April 1997, these designations have been completely abolished.

Section 24-2 was also enacted as part of the 1953 amendments to the Anti-monopoly Act. Masatoshi Yokota, chairman of the FTC, gave the following explanation of the legislative intent of the RPM exemption clause to the Committee on Economic Stability of the House of Representatives on 5 March 1953.[152]

We recognize that RPM will kill competition both among wholesalers and among retailers. In this sense, certainly creating RPM exemptions might undermine the basic spirit of the Anti-monopoly Act. Some might think that we place too much emphasis on the protection of manufacturers. ... However, consistent with guaranteed minimum wages for workers and minimum prices for farmers, we propose to ensure minimum profits for retailers. This was the primary purpose behind the creation of the RPM exemptions. ... Virtually the same reasoning holds for publications, and we allow resale price maintenance contracts both for the daily products which FTC designates, and for publications.

The debate of this issue in the committee meeting of 9 March was mostly devoted to the general legal position of RPM and the exemption for daily products.[153] The FTC chairman's response to a question by Takaichi Nakamura as to why special emphasis had been placed on publications is extracted below. However, it is essentially consistent with the explanation above. No emphasis was placed on the 'social value' of the exemptions, a topic so close to the heart of the JNCA, and its favorite expressions 'right to knowledge,' 'culture,' and 'public' were not used. Even the word 'newspaper' fails to appear.

Actually, our intention is simply to declare that the ongoing fixed price system does not violate the Anti-monopoly Act. ... We designate as an unfair trade practice 'trade under an unduly binding condition,' that is, to trade with partners upon various conditions, threatening to stop trade unless trading partners observe stated conditions. ... But as far as we're concerned, we saw [RPM in (newspaper) publishing] as simply the publisher's hoped-for price. So we didn't discuss whether it was an Anti-monopoly Act violation. The point of these provisions is to make it clear that there's no need to ask whether such practices violate the Anti-monopoly Act. Since it is in that spirit that we're adding provisions regarding the RPM of daily necessities, it seemed good to make the point clear about [RPM in (newspaper) publishing] as well – it's in that relatively light sense that we added the exemption.

APPENDIX 2   THE TREATMENT OF RPM EXEMPTIONS FOR PUBLICATIONS, THE FTC, 31 MARCH 1998

The FTC has discussed the propriety of abolishing the RPM exemptions for publications as a part of reviewing the exemptions to the Anti-monopoly Act regulations. We have requested the Study Group for Government Regulations and Competition Policy Concentrating on the Investigation of the RPM Issues, chaired by Toshimasa Tsuruta, professor of economics, Senshu University, to investigate various aspects of the issue. This study group have recently submitted to us the following proposals.[154]

(1) From the viewpoint of competition policy, we recommend the abolition of the RPM exemptions for publications, finding no persuasive reason for preserving the RPM exemptions for publications.

(2) It is emphasized by some that the RPM exemptions for publications have indirectly protected copyright holders and those engaging in the distribution of publications. Though this was not an effect originally intended by the exemptions, we should take this point into consideration from the viewpoint of cultural and public policy. Accordingly, we consider that any immediate abolition of the RPM exemptions for publications may be problematic.

(3) We hope that relevant industries will begin to adopt serious counter-measures to correct the evils of the existing system.

The FTC, upon receipt of this proposal and the final opinion of the ARC (December 1997), discussed the issue, hearing opinions from relevant parties, and reached the following conclusion:

1. The FTC has interpreted the scope of the term publications in subsection 4 of section 24-2 of the Anti-monopoly Act to include books and magazines, newspapers, music records, music tapes, and music CDs.

   As declared in the proposals of the Study Group, from the viewpoint of competition policy, direct efforts should be made toward the abolition of the RPM exemptions for publications. However, some also emphasize that, though not originally intended by the RPM exemption regime, one beneficial effect of the regime is the promotion and diffusion of culture, and we think it necessary to carefully examine any potential consequences of the abolition of this regime. Therefore, we will continue to discuss the abolition of RPM exemptions for publications, including its potential consequences, and after a certain interval we will draw conclusions as to whether these exemptions should be maintained or totally abolished.

Until we draw our final conclusions concerning the above point, the FTC interprets and will apply the exemption provisions so as to limit the publications to the above six items.

2. The choice of whether to use the RPM exemptions and the method of utilization is left totally to the voluntary decision of individual publishers. But the exemptions should never be used collectively by publishers. Moreover, utilization of the exemptions should never constitute gross injury to the interests of consumers and should not be used against the will of publishers (a proviso to subsection 1 of section 24-2). The reality of the circumstances though is that RPM exemptions for publications have been adopted in relevant industries inflexibly and uniformly, which has inhibited any responsiveness to the needs of consumers, and further obstructed consumer convenience. This has had a negative influence on distribution.

   We recognize the importance of swiftly and appropriately correcting the evils identified by the Study Group, and accordingly the FTC will take the following actions.

   (1) In the interest of consumers, the FTC will request relevant industries to implement the following corrective measures and enforce the steady realization of these measures.

   - measures to realize more flexibility in the use of RPM exemptions, for instance the adoption of time-limited RPM and partial RPM.
   - measures to increase variety in price setting, for instance introducing discounts of various kinds.
   - measures to secure the autonomy of individual publishers in their use of and the form of RPM.
   - measures to promote retail sales to consumers, for instance the provision of service stamps.
   - measures to promote the diversification of distribution channels such as out-of-store shopping and direct sales to consumers, and corresponding diversified price settings.
   - measures to correct evils in trade customs, including the promotion of the clarification and transparency of trade relations, to realize smooth and rational distribution.

   (2) To prevent RPM exemptions for publications grossly injuring the interests of consumers, the FTC will rigorously enforce the proviso in subsection 1 of section 24-2, and so make efforts in correcting the inflexible and uniform use of exemptions. For this purpose, in case of necessity, we will conduct surveys and

monitor the circumstances of actual use. In addition, we will increase the measures to promote competition by reviewing the regulation on offering giveaways. The FTC will also re-evaluate the specific regulation [*tokushu-shitei*] concerning unfair trade practices in the newspaper industry [designated in 1964] to ensure that inflexibility in price setting is not compromised.

Moreover, the FTC will act strictly and swiftly against collective RPM conduct, unfair trade practices, and so forth, in order to secure fair and free competition in the relevant industries.

Conclusion

The competence of the state determines the effectiveness of state policy. The purported need for state action has been a constant refrain in economic policy debates, and it was a refrain that called forth the splendid scorn of Adam Smith. However, Smith distrusted not the competence of the state but its motives. As Stigler (1965) read him, Smith believed that in most cases the state could efficiently achieve what it wanted, including mistaken ends. As a result, he made little of inept or inefficient state conduct. Crucially, he offered no evidence that the state could achieve its goals, and neither did most of his intellectual heirs, however religiously they repeated his claims. Ultimately, it fell to Stigler 200 years later to launch the empirical enterprise we so desperately needed. I wrote this book to continue the enterprise that Stigler began.

To study the competence of the state, I have focused on state intervention in several industries during several periods. In Part I, I examined the machine tool industry under wartime controls. If ever there were circumstances that would have given regulators the resources they needed, they were present here. Nonetheless, despite all the advantages that they enjoyed, regulators largely failed to accomplish their goals. Whether during the expansionist late 1930s or the desperate early 1940s, they simply failed to affect industry performance.

Consistent with Part I but contrary to widely held belief, in Part II I concluded that the state has done no better with the machinery industries since the mid-1950s. Again, it contributed almost nothing to industrial growth. Faced with resistance from the public, resistance from other government agencies, inadequate funds, and inappropriate statutes, the bureaucrats charged with industrial policy failed to promote development.

In Chapter 3, focusing on small business policies, I provided detailed information about a variety of contemporary issues. I asked what policies have actually been adopted, how they were implemented, why they were ineffective, and why ineffective policies were selected? In short, I asked who championed the ineffective policies, and why. Finally, in Chapter 4 I dissected the political decision-making process by examining the recent efforts of one politically powerful trade association. Through this example, I asked who actually determines the substance of policy; what 'policy' is; when and in what situations a person becomes identified as a 'decision maker'; where the boundaries of the state lie; and who should be regarded as its members.

All this implies that in discussing government policy we should keep in mind the following. The state often adopts and implements policies that reduce economic welfare; even with the best of intentions it frequently lacks the ability to do what it wants; although it generally claims that its policies benefit the public, to implement policy it needs the cooperation of a variety of relevant parties (diverse elements of the public, segments of the business community, bureaucrats, and politicians); these parties often find it hard to coordinate their actions; they generally distort the flow of information in the process; the majority of the public and scholarly community lack any interest in the competence of the state and naively accept official announcements; and demand creates its own supply – with literature supporting the state-is-competent view appearing continuously, effectively forming a 'Japan's industrial policy research industry.'

Chinese commentators observed centuries ago that 'if one dog barks at his shadow, a hundred dogs will bark at his voice.' So it is here. More recently, Stigler (1988: pp.111–12) noted that the persistence of a doctrine 'is a remarkable tribute to their palatability to ruling political thought. Once an idea is widely accepted, it is guaranteed a measure of immortality. Its decline in popularity is more often due to changing interests than to contrary evidence, no matter how powerful that evidence may be.' Unfortunately, for most of the twentieth century the Japanese economic tradition was actively hostile to the fundamental economic premise of rational behavior, and the media too fed the myth of state competence.

In this book, I argue that there has been nothing peculiar about Japan, particularly the Japanese state, its active members such as politicians and bureaucrats, and the contribution of the state to economic growth. Whether during the imperial period or in the 1950s and 1960s, self-interested behavior has been a constant theme: 'across a wide variety of institutions, across a wide realm of behavior, across a wide expanse of time, across a wide range of relations – across all of this, people scheme, exchange, calculate, and think' (Ramseyer 1996: p.165). To the degree that the reader is unfamiliar with standard rational-choice and economic theory, and to the degree that she is familiar with the conventional wisdom about Japan, she may have found the argument in this book hard to follow. Yet if she found it hard, I hope she takes the same path that my young friend from Australia took when he read the first draft: 'In reading the book,' he remarked, 'I was constantly reminded of my own personal opinion of Japan, which I formed when for the first time I was in Japan several years ago. It is "Do not look for what is different, but look for what is similar." If one analyses Japan from the assumption that Japan is fundamentally similar to other countries, then many similarities come into view. If readers look for what is similar, then they take a big step towards debunking the many myths and stereotypes that have been created about Japan and Japanese industrial policy.'

At the beginning of the 1950s, even Stigler accepted the conventional wisdom about the role of economists in the formation and implementation of economic policy. That is, he thought, economists understand well efficient methods to organize economic life. From the many inefficient policies actually conducted in our society, he reasoned, we can conclude that what political leaders needed was a good course in economics.[155] However, Stigler soon changed his mind. This 'new focus of economic studies of regulation changes the economists' role from that of reformer to that of student of political economy. … Until we understand *why* our society adopts its policies, we will be poorly equipped to give useful advice on how to change those policies. … A measure of restraint in our advice on policy would seem to be dictated by a sense of responsibility on the economists' part, and not only by the sense of caution of the body politic to whom we address the advice' (Stigler 1975: p.xi).

Let me emphasize that in terms of competence the Japanese state has been little different from most of its contemporaries. The imperial government during wartime could not efficiently achieve what it wanted, but neither could most other governments. I agree with Stigler (*ibid.*: p.xi) that 'of course, we shall not, and need not, abandon all policy advising until we have all of the mysteries of the political regulatory process. The very measurement of the costs and benefits of a policy will influence opinion and policy: one perfectly tenable hypothesis is that a society supports its economists simply because they provide complex kinds of information with speed, elegance, and increasingly more tolerable accuracy. … The traditional theory of economics is most helpful when it is applied directly to the understanding of the regulatory process.'

Stigler (*ibid.*: p.113) concludes:

> Neither the cynicism of the first view of the state nor the unreasoning optimism of the second view provides a basis on which the economist can make responsible policy recommendations. We may tell the society to jump out of the market frying pan, but we have no basis for predicting whether it will land in the fire or a luxurious bed.

We can never do without the state; nor can we escape from the issue of 'who monitors the monitors?' Only careful and prudent consumers can have good suppliers and good products, and only prudent patients have good doctors. So I prefer a Japanese proverb: 'Rather than scold your cat for eating your goldfish, hide the fish instead' to 'It is like trusting a wolf to watch over sheep.' Therefore, I conclude this book with the following passage from Adam Smith (1776: pp.605–6).

I mean not, however, by any thing which I have here said, to throw any odious imputation upon the general character of the servants of the East India Company, and much less upon that of any particular persons. It is the system of government, the situation in which they are placed, that I mean to censure; not the character of those who have acted in it. They acted as their situation naturally directed, and they who have clamoured the loudest against them would, probably, not have acted better themselves. ... The members of those councils [of Madras and Calcutta], however, had been bred to professions very different from war and politics. But their situation alone, without education, experience, or even example, seems to have formed in them all at once the great qualities which it required, and to have inspired them with both abilities and virtues which they themselves could not well know that they possessed. If upon some occasions, therefore, it has animated them to actions of magnanimity which could not well have been expected from them, we should not wonder if upon others it has prompted them to exploits of somewhat a different nature.

Notes

Chapter 1

1 A consensus from which there has been some dissent (e.g., Ramseyer and Rosenbluth 1993) – a dissent with which I largely agree.

2 However, this figure counts only those from plants with over twenty employees. See Miwa (1998c: p.80, note 7).

3 Mishina (1958: pp.100, 104). For a detailed account of the industry during this time, see MITI (1956, 1957), Kato (1960), and the Industrial Rationalization Investigation Group of MITI 1962.

4 Products vary greatly, with each product changing radically in performance and quality over time. Therefore, I adopt these figures as scale indices, following the industry custom.

5 The three largest manufacturers in 1960, Toshiba Machines, Hitachi Seiki, and Toyoda Machine Works, all fall into this category.

6 The steel industry and the petroleum-refining industry in postwar Japan are the examples where the government faced relatively easy issues (see Miwa 1996a: Part III). In the financial sector until now, the government simplified the issues it faced by limiting new entry and imposing large costs on the national economy. On this point, see Miwa (1993a) and Miwa and Ramseyer (2003b, 2003e).

7 The table is the subject of discussion below, making reference to Nakamura (1989: pp.12–13, table 1–2) and JMTBA (1962). For an outline of wartime control, see Nakamura (1974, 1977) and Hara (1976).

8 See JMTBA (1962: pp.134, 136; see also the pig iron rationing flowchart for machine tool manufacturing on p.135). For details of the overall system of control for machinery production, including machine tools, see Hashii (1940b: p.31 and after for the rationing flowcharts).

9 The issue is much simpler if only the quantity constraint (and not the price) of materials is binding.

10 To readers who reply that firms will not follow instructions and will pad production costs, and accordingly direct production control is indispensable, I would like to add that under these assumptions, not following the instructions would be against a firm's interest. It is impossible not to follow instructions as to cost when the government knows the cost.

11 Ikegai Metalworks (*Tekkojo*), Ohkuma Metalworks, Karatsu Metalworks, Tokyo Gas–Electricity Industries, Niigata Metalworks.

12 Sawai (1984: p.162). The plant census shows that the number of machine tool factories with over five operatives was 4,759 in 1939 and 3,213 in 1942, when the PTCA was established.

13 Here the Shipbuilders Control Association was an exception.

14 They manufactured 34 and 33 percent, respectively, of aircraft engines in 1943, and 38 and 30 percent in 1944. See Murakami (1994: p.166, table 5).

15 Apart from Toyota, this same difficulty was experienced by all automobile manufacturers, including Japanese ones. No other car maker could match Toyota's success, particularly in the second half of the 1950s and the 1960s. See Miwa (1996a: ch. 4).

16 Ikegai was one of the Five Majors machine tool makers. The company was not particularly large, however, with a workforce of 731 in 1937. The other four of the Five Majors were all of a similar size, with workforces ranging from 561 to 828. See Sawai (1993: p.106).

17 However, this group was characterized as 'sectors contributing little to diverting labor force … to more urgent need.'

18 The company history of the Industrial Bank of Japan (Industrial Bank of Japan 1957: p.555) lists such orders as to dismiss the entire directorate of both Tokyo Tanko-sho (Tokyo Forge) and Tokyo Aircraft, to dismiss with penalty a production supervisor of Toyo Soda, to consign the management of Tokyo Forge to Nissan Motors, and to establish cooperative relationships between Kobe Steel and Nichia Steel. Assuming that these cases were representative of the norm of government interventions of this type, it seems to have had no remarkable impact.

19 Note that the terms 'government' and 'executive' are used interchangeably throughout this book. The Japanese parliament is distinguished from the executive/government by using the term 'Diet.'

20 Despite such government efforts, Karatsu Metalworks, for instance, did not accept requests to expand capacity, which some criticized as 'an act of a traitor' (Hayasaka 1964: p.492).

21 See the statement of Okinori Kaya, finance minister of the time (Ando 1966: p.191).

22 The prelude to the so-called period of free armaments without treaty restrictions was notification of the abrogation of the Washington Treaty in December 1934. The London Conference in 1936 failed to reach any agreement due to Japan's withdrawal, so the 'no armament restriction treaty' period began in January 1937. It was in April 1937 that Japan began the construction of seventy vessels, including battleships like the *Yamato* and the *Musashi* and aircraft carriers like the *Shokaku* and the *Zuikaku* as part of the third armaments supplement plan. See MITI (1979: p.430).

23 'Subsidies were proposed for equipment costs, production costs, patent right purchasing costs, costs of developing skilled workers, and so forth … tax exemptions, expansion of government–private research institutions, inducements for mergers, and other forms of coordination among corporations' (MITI 1979: p.357).

24 Proposed to the 73rd Diet on 17 March and promulgated on 29 March as Law No. 40. By Imperial Order No. 499 of 8 July, it was decided that the Act would take effect on 11 July. See Kawasaki (1943: pp.26–7).

25 See Mori (1943: pp.392–5). For the text of the Act, see Hashii (1940a: pp.79–86) and JMTBA (1962: pp.188–93). For details of the Act, see Hashii (1940a), Mori (1943: pp.392–5), JMTBA (1962), MITI (1976), and Sawai (1984).

26 MITI (1976: pp.456–60). Most of the items listed in the text were only added with the March 1941 revision.

27 However, the figures in Figure 1.2 are taken from the plant census, in which the industry classification category was the 'machine tools and tools manufacturing industry.' This corresponds to 'metal-working machinery' in the postwar manufacturing census. Therefore, those figures include not only the number of 'machine tool' factories, the object of study in Part I and Sections 2.1–2.4 of Part II, but also plants for 'metal-working machinery other than machine tools,' 'accessories for metal-working machinery,' and 'tools.' The plant census studied the state of factories on the final day of each year. Accordingly, the number of plants in 1938 was deemed to be the number of plants on 31 December 1938. At this moment, the number of licensed producers was eleven.

28 See Kawasaki (1943: pp.110–11), JMTBA (1962: p.118), and Sawai (1984: p.167). For details of the rules, see Hashii (1940a: pp.106–21). The Rules Concerning Machine Tool Supply Controls of July 1938 were limited in application to machine tools produced by factories equipped with more than thirty machine tools. These rules placed subject factories under a product rationing system, which required them to request the approval of the commerce minister for the supply of every product to a user other than manufacturers of arms and related products. Supply to arms and related manufacturers remained unregulated (for details, see Hashii 1940a: pp.128–38). The new rule regarding supply was subsequently also applied to producers of machine tools equipped with less than thirty machine tools, which was intended

to restrict the demand for products of smaller producers (see Kawasaki 1943: p.53; Sawai 1984, pp.165–7).

29 The term 'control association' is used here to refer to associations designated specifically for the purpose of issuing steel rationing certificates and not to refer to associations established for wider industry control as described above.

30 Hayasaka (1964) includes many references to cases where machine tool makers engaged in trial production, designing, and manufacturing on request from the military. For instance, on pp.472–5 Hayasaka mentions a case where precision boring machines were being produced at the request of the Navy for torpedo boat production. It is important for readers to note that those particular requests or orders for trial production or manufacturing are excluded from the object of study here.

31 The following description of the industry totally depends on the Japan Bearing Industry Association (1965: pp.17–27).

32 For other myths about prewar Japan, see Miwa and Ramseyer (2000a, 2000b, 2002b, 2002c, 2004b).

Chapter 2

33 See also, for example: 'In short, the contribution of the MIPA and policy loans based on it was that they facilitated the modernization and expansion of the machinery industry to cope with the new open system, realized with the trade liberalization since 1961. This enabled manufacturers to participate in international competition, and otherwise they would have been decisively inferior in both cost and quality and unable to survive in internationally competitive markets' (Yonekura 1965a: p.41). 'The MIPA had played a great role in raising the level of Japan's machinery industry, later becoming an excellent model of industrial policy for underdeveloped countries' (Kuroda Seiko 1995: p.129).

34 See Miwa and Ramseyer (2003d). Readers who can read Japanese should see Miwa and Ramseyer (2002e), which discusses the misunderstandings surrounding Japan's industrial policy in much greater detail.

35 This part depends heavily on Miwa and Ramseyer (2003d). For more details, see Miwa and Ramseyer (2002e: part I).

36 From Miwa and Ramseyer (2003d). I gratefully acknowledge the permission of both the co-author and the publisher. Copyright © 2003, Federal Legal Publications, Inc.

37 Given that elite bureaucrats came from elite universities like the University of Tokyo, they may simply have regurgitated the Marxist theories that they learned at school. These scholars then adopted the claims of their former students, now working as government bureaucrats, as fact – a self-referential loop if ever there was one. The process resembles the perhaps apocryphal story of the Yale law professor who, when told by a law journal that he needed to support his assertion with a footnote, asked a friend at the *New York Times* to make the point in an article and then cited that article in his manuscript. For an elaborate inquiry tying the Marxist theory of the bureaucrats to the scholars (albeit an inquiry that treats the theory as truth), see Gao (1997).

38 Dore (2002: pp.19, 23–4; see also, for example, Dore 1986: p.25 – 'control over the long-term growth and structure of the economy has been highly concentrated in a single ministry, MITI').

39 The idea that bureaucrats controlled the allocation of credit in 1960s and 1970s Japan is another legend, also untrue. See Miwa and Ramseyer (2004a).

40 On this, see Miwa and Ramseyer (2000b) (in brief, Miwa and Ramseyer 2003c); and on prewar Japan in general see Miwa and Ramseyer (2002b).

41 I gratefully acknowledge the permission to quote this from the publisher, Oxford University Press.

42 This discussion draws heavily upon official documents of the government and the government's councils and papers by persons directly involved in the policies. Most of these documents use terms in fashion since the prewar period. As popular as the terms are, their importance is hard

to clarify: 'modernization' (*kindai-ka*), 'rationalization' (*gori-ka*), 'upgrading' (*kodo-ka*), 'international competitiveness' (*kokusai kyoso-ryoku*), 'excessive competition' (*kato kyoso*), 'industrial order (restructuring)' (*sangyo taisei (seibi)*), 'industrial structure' (*sangyo kozo*), 'promotion' (*shinko*). Most of these terms were created and adopted as political slogans. Some, such as 'excessive competition,' are downright incoherent.

43 See chapter 8 of Miwa (1996a), entitled 'Industrial Policy of Japan: A Beginner's Guide,' for an introduction to industrial policy in general and a brief description of the role of councils (*shingikai*), advisory committees (*iinkai*), and study groups (*kenkyu-kai*). See also Chapter 4 of this book and Miwa and Ramseyer (2002e, ch. 3).

44 For this, argues Sugiyama (1966a: p.19), a supplementary rule concerning the validity of the Act was altered from stating that the Act would be abolished to that the Act would expire. The author was then chief of the Promotion Subsection of the Heavy Industries Section in the Heavy Industries Bureau of MITI. In 1970, however, following the report of the Industrial Structure Investigation Group entitled 'Policies for the Machinery Industry in the Future,' the government established the Act on Temporary Measures for the Promotion of Specific Electronics and Specific Machinery Industries, the so-called *Kiden-ho*, as a successor to both the MIPA and the Act on Temporary Measures for the Promotion of Electronics Industry, which was to expire at the same moment (MITI annual report for FY1970: p.119, hereafter, simply annual report). Nowhere in the relevant parts of this annual report do we find such phrases as 'industry reorganization' or 'system restructuring,' which played such a key role in 'industrial policy' in the 1950s and 1960s.

45 Sugiyama (1966b: p.11). Figures by MITI. As Yonekura (1965a: p.38) points out, the volume of loans allocated in part reflected the size of particular industries and hence is not necessarily a good indicator of policy priority.

46 See Miwa (1996a: part III) for an outline, the background, and the implications of those incidents, and also Miwa and Ramseyer (2003d) for the Sumitomo Metals incident. See generally Miwa and Ramseyer (2002e).

47 Annual report for FY1955: p.115.

48 *Ibid.*: pp.4–5. Hidaka (1956: p.8), which is a work by the chief of the Heavy Industries Section of the Heavy Industries Bureau, who was an official in charge of planning the Act, reveals that in industries expected to be designated, about 90 percent of firms had paid-up capital of less than ¥10 million and that only 5 percent had a capitalization of more than ¥100 million. Indeed, most firms with more than ¥100 million in paid-up capital were not specialist producers but showed active diversification into other areas.

49 In 1957, the Transportation Ministry, requesting the designation of the shipbuilding industry and the railway vehicle parts industry, proposed that the Act be placed under the joint jurisdiction of MITI and the Transportation Ministry. These two Ministries reached an agreement whereby these two industries, which were at the time under the jurisdiction of the Transportation Ministry, would be designated and that the preparation of the basic rationalization plan for these industries would require cooperation between the two ministries. It was through this process that the railway vehicle parts industry became designated under the Act. See MITI (1990: p.572).

50 For details, see relevant articles in each issue of the *Monthly Bulletin of the Federation of Japanese Machinery Producers* (*Nikki-ren kaiho*) in 1956 and 1957. Regarding the machine tool industry, for instance, see the article by the Heavy Industries Section of MITI in the April 1957 issue, pp.21–31.

51 Recognizing that 'though the machinery industries play a key role in Japan's economic growth at present many of them are quite inferior in international competition,' the General Principles for the Trade and Foreign Exchange Liberalization Plan of 24 June 1960 declared the adoption of various measures to facilitate liberalization and specified detailed measures for individual major machinery industries. The MITI annual reports for both FY1960 and FY1961 include only a short description of the extension of the MIPA. At the beginning of the section on 'industrial policy' in the 'general introduction,' the annual report for FY1961 simply states: 'Concerning the domestic industries, for adopting trade liberalization ahead of schedule, the focus of policy was placed primarily upon the improvement of international competitiveness of

industries by drastic reform of its structures' (pp.1–2). This appears in almost the same manner later in 'major policy measures' in the section on 'the heavy industries.'

52 For more details of this plan, see Section 2.3.8.

53 See MITI (1990: pp.564–70). An official associated with the administration of the First Act made the following comment: 'Compared with the corporate plan intended to actively promote equipment modernization on an enormous scale through leasing equipment machines, nobody can deny that measures under the MIPA will be of lesser effect and of much less urgency as policies for equipment modernization' (Hidaka 1956: p.8).

54 Sugiyama (1966b: p.12) includes lists in his table 7 of the rationalization cartels implemented under the MIPA. For instance, the sector coordination cartel in the forging press industry, the first cartel established, was joined by 117 producers or 70 percent of industry members. In terms of the activities of this cartel, 'mechanical press machines and hydraulic press machines were classified into a hierarchy of nine categories by size, and each producer could enter a maximum of only three consecutive categories within that hierarchy.' The machine tool industry, the industry of our primary concern, is nowhere to be found in Sugiyama's list. Furthermore, Yonekura (1965a: p.39) comments as follows: 'Having seen in detail the reality of these cartels, cooperative actions are by far the most thoroughgoing and effective in the textile machinery industry. However, in other industries, merely enforcing measures of the greatest common benefit, therefore cartels seem to have had no effect at present.' The 1961 revision newly stipulated that the government could issue orders to enforce joint operations for the restriction of standards of even unrelated enterprises under certain conditions. However, such authority was never exercised (Sugiyama 1966a: p.9).

55 'In addition, new preferential tax treatments such as tax exemptions both for scrapping machine equipment and for mergers were newly introduced in FY1966, which were intended to contribute much to policies during the Third MIPA' (Sugiyama 1966b: p.19). These are discussed further below.

56 See Miwa (1996a: pp.148–9) on the *kanmin* system. The 'New Industrial Order Controversy' was fiercely debated within this conceptual framework. For the details of this controversy and the reasons why the draft bill was not approved, see Tsuruta (1982, 1988) and Miwa (1996a: ch. 8). For more details of the bill, see Miwa and Ramseyer (2002e: ch. 5).

57 During the period of the Third Act, the powerful policy of this type that was debated at the Act's beginning was never adopted. We find no sign of such a policy in the machine tool industry either.

58 As shown in Part I (Section 1.3.5), Japan could not overcome this very same constraint even under wartime control.

59 Rather than enter the morass of trying to define 'industrial policy,' I follow Kaizuka (1973), which states that 'the industrial policy refers to the policies that MITI adopts.'

60 As Sugiyama (1966a) points out, there were also 'movements toward industrial order restructuring' in other industries. The examples of the merger between Toyobo and Kurehabo in the textile industry, that of Kawasaki Heavy Industries and Yokoyama Industries in the machinery industry, and a grouping in the machine tool industry provide good illustrations of this. In November 1965, the Machine Tool Builders Association stated that 'a fundamental restructuring of the industrial order was necessary to aid recovery from the machine tool industry depression. Such restructuring should start with business cooperation or the forming of enterprise groups, and then be expected to proceed to mergers in the future.' Beginning with the formation of the First Group of Japanese Machine Tool Builders by Hitachi Seiki, Toyoda Machine Works, Ikegai Metalworks, Kashifuji Metalworks, and Hamai Industries in December 1965, ten groups had been formed by the following year. These ten groups consisted of forty-five companies out of the total of 105 members of the association. However, according to the Japan Long-Term Credit Bank (1966: pp.59, 81):

> Behind the recent formation of industry groups can be seen a change in the conditions of competition which accompanied the collapse in demand and the deepening depression. Groups have been formed among companies engaged in different sectors of the industry

and so accordingly there is little problem with conflicts of interest. ... Thus, the benefits evident from group formation are fewer than if groups had been formed among firms in the same sector. ... In addition, the basic motive behind group formation, that is as a tactic for surviving the recession, is by itself a weak point, which carries with it the distinct possibility that group ties may weaken with any economic recovery.

In fact, at the present (2000), all five of the companies that participated in the first group remain independent.

61 For instance, corporate income tax was to be reduced by 5 percent in the case of a merger between companies, one of which had a paid-up capital of ¥300 million and the other of ¥100 million. In the case of a merger between two companies, each with ¥100 million in paid-up capital, corporate income tax was to be reduced by 10 percent. These reductions were valid for three years following a merger (Sugiyama 1966a: p.10).

62 The Loan System for Financing Heavy Machinery Development was established in FY1964 in an effort to upgrade Japan's industrial structure, to protect the domestic market by slowing imports of machines produced abroad, and to improve the international balance of payments. The JDB lent at the special rate of 7.5 percent 80 percent of the money needed for the manufacture of heavy machinery whose production domestically was considered necessary and whose price was more than ¥100 million. There was strong criticism of the ¥100 million threshold of this loan scheme, which was argued to be excessively severe, particularly for machine tools and metalworking machines. Accordingly, this threshold was reduced to ¥50 million for those two categories in FY1966 and thereafter. The maximum upper limit of loans in FY1966 was ¥2.5 billion, ¥1 billion more than in the previous year (Sugiyama 1966a: p.8).

63 This link system was adopted in mid-1953 to promote exports. Under the system, the allocation of foreign currency for importing production materials including raw sugar was linked to the exports that the applicant was able to realize. 'Because of troubles both at home and abroad the system was abolished in April 1955' (Shoko gyosei 1955: III, p.541).

64 As shown in Part I, this was also consistently a serious problem during wartime control.

65 For a brief description of this transitional decade, see Miwa (1999).

66 This point was clearly revealed in sections 3.1 and 3.2 of the Act, which stipulated the duty of MITI. Section 3.1 concerned the promotion and coordination of international trade, and the management of accompanying foreign exchange. Section 3.2 concerned the promotion of production for export, and the expansion, improvement, coordination, and inspection of production, distribution, and consumption of other mining and industrial products.

67 'Before this Japan's administrative organs had been based upon imperial orders called *kansei*. On the contrary, however, with the Act for Organizing State Administrative Organs established in July 1948, MITI was established upon a legal foundation' (MITI 1985b: p.110).

68 MITI (*ibid.*: p.125) explains the point as follows:

> It was a natural consequence that MITI, born along the Dodge Line, placed the promotion of international trade as a trade policy and industrial rationalization as an industrial policy at the core of their policy mix. This policy emphasis was also reflected in the administrative organization of MITI, particularly in the International Trade Bureau and the International Trade Promotion Bureau, which dealt with international trade, and in the International Trade Enterprise Bureau for industrial policy.

69 'Rules concerning the Fixed Numbers of Personnel' revised in response to the organizational reform in 1952. The Heavy Industries Bureau was the fifth-largest in size, following the International Trade Bureau with a staff of 428, the Public Utilities Bureau with 302, the Enterprise Bureau with 282, and the Light Industries Bureau with 253 (MITI 1965: p.655).

70 The 'dual structure' in the Economic White Paper is a phrase that was attached to the following situation: 'Japan's employment structure is polarized, with large-scale modern enterprises on the one hand, and small enterprises based on pre-modern labor–capital relationships, ultra-small enterprises operated by family management, and agriculture on the other. The ratio of

medium enterprises is very small' (p.35). The phrase became famous with the statement that 'in other words, we have in one country a dual structure exhibiting features of an advanced country on the one hand and an undeveloped one on the other' (p.36). The concept has no basis in modern economic theory, and for that reason the many studies based on it have no substance.

71 For the industrial rationalization movement and industrial rationalization policy, see MITI (1961, or 1985a: pp.128–42).

72 With the beginning of the MITI, the Resource Agency took charge of coal and electricity, while the textile industry, the steel industry, and the chemical industry were under the jurisdiction of the International Trade Textile Bureau, the International Trade Steel Bureau, and the International Trade Chemicals Bureau, respectively. Thus the structure of the MITI's organization directly reflected policy emphasis.

73 However, the former remained in effect for more than six months 'in order to avoid disorder due to the elimination of control.' The latter was also retained for six months more 'for the maintenance of public welfare and stability' (Shoko gyosei 1955: II, p.517).

74 That designation dramatically limited a firm's flexibility. 'Operation not being prohibited, each plant continued production. We were strongly ordered to maintain the status quo of the factory equipment, and sometimes received an official inspection by the US Army.' That is, 'factories designated to reparation were nominally in an individual company's possession. The management of their properties were, however, under the supervision of the Far East Committee, and were not allowed to officially abandon the existing equipment or to drastically modify them' (Japan Bearing Industry Association 1965: pp.29, 32).

75 This is most likely the Commerce Ministry. The Munitions Ministry was established in November 1943.

76 See Section 2.4.2 for a detailed comparison of the Japan Machine Tool Builders Union and the PTCA under wartime control, and the Japan Machine Tool Builders Association during the period of the TMPMI Act. Also see note 20 below for a comparison of the PTCA and the Japan Bearing Industry Association.

77 This part has been extracted from 'The Direction of Machinery Industries Promotion' 1956: p.62, which is a publication of the MITI's Heavy Industries Bureau.

78 The Japanese word includes not just scholars but also ex-bureaucrats, journalists, and public intellectuals more generally.

79 See Japan Gear Industry Association (1990), and *Monthly Bulletin of Japan Machinery Producers Federation*, November 1956.

80 *Monthly Bulletin of Japan Machinery Producers Federation*, p.7 of September 1956 issue and p.9 of February 1957 issue.

81 The two leading principles were 'cooperation, that is, the denial of free competition, and cost reduction. Industrial rationalization served as a general term which referred to policies of this nature' (MITI 1961: p.8).

82 Japan Bearing Industry Association (1965: pp.40–1). Consequently, loans for special machines allocated to the bearing industry amounted to zero until FY1959. Finally, ¥275 million in funding was allocated in FY1960 (JDB 1963: p.297).

83 The total budget for machine funding for FY1956 and FY1957 was ¥3.5 billion, while the total amount of funding recommended was a huge ¥7.9 billion. In the end, the JDB made loans for 142 projects to the total value of ¥4.8 billion. The JDB rejected thirty-seven recommended projects, or 20 percent of the total number of projects recommended. 'Some companies recommended proposed projects of an enormous size, well beyond their capacity, and we also have to consider the matter of the limited funding budget' (*ibid.*: p.296).

84 The Machinery Industries Promotion Corporation plan, which preceded the MIPA, included an innovative new concept, divorced from former traditions based on social policy and intended to adopt a policy of focusing upon selected excellent plants. However, even this plan had to declare that 'in selecting excellent plants the Corporation would adopt a policy of "selecting plants compatible with objective standards," emphasizing notions of fairness by reducing the scope for discretion and arbitrariness' (MITI 1990: pp.563–4). I can find no reason to think that the MIPA and related policies were different. This point is consistent with our observation

that the most remarkable peculiarity of small business policies extensively pursued particularly during the same period was the notion of 'indiscriminate' treatment of enterprises. See Yokokura (1988: pp.531–4) and Miwa (1995, 1996a: pp.52–5). For a brief description, see Chapter 3 of this book.

85 Section 18.2 of the JDB Act and section 15.4 of the bank constitution. See JDB (1963: Materials, pp.4, 12).

86 As shown in Table 2.2, the average ratio of funding granted to funding recommended rose to 100 percent in FY1963. This observation is consistent with the description of the bank's partic- ipation in the interviews 'to maintain better mutual understanding with ministries concerned.' Obviously, a vast excess demand remains under such an advantageous special loan rate.

87 JDB (1958: p.34) comments as follows upon section 18.2 of the JDB Act, which provided for this point. This section 'declares that JDB loans are neither subsidies nor bounties, and that the Bank is not permitted to make loans extremely policy-oriented in nature. Obviously, even if not equally matching private financial institutions in the area of strict finance-based discipline, the Bank must be fundamentally managed as a financial institution.'

88 See JDB (1976: p.452, table 1-119) for a list of designated industries for FY1956–FY1970.

89 Some machine tools, called mother machines, are indispensable for producing high-precision machine tools. 'Horizontal boring machines for finishing axial gradients in the main spindle box, grinding machines for grinding main spindles, surface grinding machines for finishing beds, and machine tools for lead feed screw cutting and finishing power transmission gears' (Iida *et al.* 1960: p.146) are examples of these mother machines.

90 The share of funding allocated to the machine tool industry was even greater during the period of the First Act, that is until FY1960. During this period, of the total of JDB designated machinery loans of ¥10.6 billion, the machine tool industry was allocated the largest share, 24.8 percent. This was followed by the auto parts industry with 13.1 percent, and then by the cutting tools industry with 10.6 percent (JDB 1963: materials, p.42).

91 At the last stage of the war, the military suggested that Japanese people (not only soldiers) fight with bamboo spears against modern weapons.

92 Because of the contribution that the machine tool industry had made to military production, the Allied Powers designated the industry as one to be destroyed. The details of the reparations policy were as follows: 'The fact is that Japan's industrial equipment was overwhelmingly designed for war. Despite all the destruction, Japan still retains, in workable condition, more plant and equipment than its rulers ever allowed to be used for civilian supply and consumption even in peaceful years. That surplus must be taken out. ... In steel, and in machine tools and other machinery made from steel, Japan's own figures show that it still has, in workable condi- tion, more than twice the facilities that it had when it invaded Manchuria in 1931.' The Pauley Report recommended that the following machine tools be designated for interim removal: (1) half of capacity for the manufacture of machine tools; (2) all equipment in all Japanese Army and Navy arsenals (except for equipment useful solely for making arms, ammunition, and implements of war, which will be destroyed), in the entire aircraft industry, in all plants making ball bearings and roller bearings, and in all plants making aircraft engines (Ministry of Finance 1982: p.442). For details regarding circumstances, see Ministry of Finance (1984) and MITI (1992). In August 1946, the Far Eastern Commission designated ninety machine tool factories in the private sector as objects of reparations, and these plants were assigned the duty of main- taining their machinery in good condition. After several revisions, finally in May 1949, with the McCoy statement at the then-meeting of the Far Eastern Commission, the attempt to impose reparation payments upon Japan in accordance with the Pauley Report failed. In 1951, with the Dodge Plan, plants previously designated as objects of reparations payments recovered consid- erable autonomy over the use and management of machinery. However, the freedom to transfer and dispose of this equipment was not regained until the Far Eastern Commission was abol- ished when the USA–Japan Peace Treaty came into effect in April 1952 (JMTBA 1962: pp.159–63).

93 '223,000 machine tools, primarily in arsenals and munitions plants, were designated as objects of reparations. Most of them, however, were not removed from Japan and were later sold in Japan' (Japan Long-Term Credit Bank, Research Division 1966: p.7).

94 In the 1980s, the value of exports in this industry was six to ten times larger than that of imports. Therefore some have listed this industry as one of the 'three major sources' of trade conflict, along with cars and semiconductors (JMTBA 1992: pp.20, 158–9).

95 Note that remarkable continuity exists between the period following the second half of the 1930s and the period following the second half of the 1950s in the following areas. First, the growth in the second half of the 1950s was a consequence of the explosive prewar growth. The postwar growth in the late 1950s started and expanded upon the technological accumulation and machines produced during the prior period of growth. Second, major machine tool producers in the postwar growth period had their grounding during the prewar growth period. Examples include Toshiba Machines, Hitachi Seiki, and Toyoda Machine Works.

96 As shown in Part I (Section 1.3.6), we observe almost the same phenomenon during the prewar period of explosive growth. Figures 1.2 and 1.3 for 1931–42 correspond to Figures 2.2 and 2.3. It is important to note two points, however. First, since the prewar plant censuses do not provide figures for metal machine tools, I use instead the figures for the metal machine tool manufacturing industry, including the metal machine tool industry (then called 'the machine tools and tools manufacturing industry'). Second, the smallest workforce size category was five to twenty-nine rather than ten to nineteen.

97 Growth continued in terms of product value, and, as previously mentioned, Japan became the world largest producer of machine tools in the 1980s. The production levels attained in 1991 represented historical records. If we assign 1970 production levels a base value of 100, 1991 output was 76.4 in terms of number of machines produced and 145.6 in terms of aggregate weight, but a massive 417.3 in terms of product value. In monetary terms, product value increased from ¥3.1 billion in 1970 to ¥13.0 billion in 1991.

98 Of 114 projects recommended to the JDB for funding under the Act in FY1963, fourteen projects (12.3 percent) were for the machine tool industry. In addition, fifteen (6.5 percent) of the 232 Small Business Finance Corporation loans were for this industry (Industrial Structure Investigation Group 1964: pp.8–9).

99 This is a statement by Tetsuo Sahase, an advisor to the Machinery Division of Nichimen Jitsugyo Co. quoted in Hayasaka (1964: p.12). Details of the process remain unclear to the present author.

100 Japan Long-Term Credit Bank, Research Division (1966: p.31). Many small producers, numbering, say, between 200 and 400 and often called 'outsiders,' did not join the association. These outsiders actively produced primarily small-scale cheap lathes and drilling machines. New entrants to the industry can be classified roughly into three groups. (1) Re-manufacturers, formerly engaged in the repair and sale of used machines. The number of these entrants was the largest. A typical such enterprise was Yamazaki Metalworks (later, Yamazaki Mazak) which entered in 1960. (2) Parts suppliers, machining firms, and foundries in the sewing machine and textile machine industries. Examples of these enterprises were Han'nya Metalworks (engine lathes), Kitamura Metalworks (surface grinders), and Yamato Heavy Industries (surface grinders). (3) Other machinery producers. Those producers from the textile machinery industry were the largest group, and examples include Enshu, O-M, and Ishikawa Seisakujo (*ibid.*).

101 Between 1935 and 1944, 450,000 machine tools were produced domestically, and 30,000 were imported (Toyo Keizai Shimpo-sha 1950: p.309).

102 Here 'obsolete' does not necessarily mean 'out of use.' For instance, Fukao (1979: p.91), a managing director of Mitsubishi Heavy Industries and the first head of the Nagoya engine factory during the war, states:

> *Hakusho* [White Paper] published by the government after the war argued that because of hard use during the war equipment remaining in this country needed to be improved in the areas of efficiency and precision. This issue was too abstract and general, and could not be applied to our industry but only to such industries as the steel industry, where production totally depended on equipment. In my view, no equipment could have been used so excessively during the war as to be out of use now. … Many argue that in the USA old model machine tools are decommissioned swiftly and replaced by new ones, but I do not believe this. By changing attachments and partial improvement even an old machine tool works effectively.

The second volume of the Japan Machinery Producers Federation Report of the Study Group on Foreign Machinery Producers, entitled *The Machine Tool Industry in West Germany* (June 1963), quotes from *The Financial Times*, 29 December 1961, as follows: 'the share of machine tools less than 10 years old is reported to be 40 percent in the USA, 41 percent in both the UK and France, 44 percent in Italy, and 45 percent in West Germany.' However, the Research Division of the Japan Long-Term Credit Bank (1966: p.22), which was cited in support of the Basic Promotion Plan for the Metal Machine Tool Manufacturing Industry, reports these same figures to have been 17 percent in the USA in 1963 and 36 percent in the UK in 1960.

103 The following description relies upon MITI Heavy Industries Section (1957).

104 The list was comprehensive in that it included almost all types of machine tool, including lathes, drilling machines, boring machines, milling machines, surface grinders, broaching machines, grinding machines, gear cutters, and toothed wheel finishing machines, each of which had a detailed and comprehensive description of targeted machines. Concerning lathes, for instance, the list included nineteen types of lathe, beginning with engine lathes, for each of which the list included detailed performance requirements expressed as a combination of swing and the main spindle's rotational frequency.

105 This figure is based on the recognition that 'the prices of first-grade domestic machine tools are 10–20 percent higher than German counterparts although 20–30 percent lower than American ones' (MITI Heavy Industries Section 1957: p.29).

106 Okazaki and Okuno-Fujiwara (1999: p.25) comment on the organization and function of control associations, taking the Steel Control Association as an example. As already mentioned in Section 2.3.7, this focus on the Steel Control Association is a source of misunderstanding and results in gross overestimates of the role and effectiveness of government plans. This is because of the association's peculiarities, such as the particular importance of steel rationing during this period, the key position the association occupied in the overall system of wartime control, and the product characteristics of steel as a raw material, which make it well suited to rationing.

107 In comparison with advanced producers in Europe and the USA, the specialization evident among Japanese producers is relatively weak, and Japanese producers still maintain a Jack-of-all-trades character to some extent.

108 I have constructed the list from a survey of the JMTBA of sixty-three members in 1958. The number was judged 'large' when it was more than ten and 'small' when less than two. The figures are taken from table 6.4 in Iida *et al.* (1960: p.145).

109 With the following explanation, the Research Division of Japan Long-Term Credit Bank (1966: pp.33–5) concludes that:

> Each group of producers, large, medium-sized, and small, forms their own respective market, and maintains differences in production models, prices, and quality with other groups. This has meant that there has been almost no competition between producers across groups. Both during the prewar period and during the first postwar decade Japan's machine tool builders copied foreign machines. Likewise, producers in lower classes have copied the products of major Japanese producers. Their technology levels, however, have been completely different, and their products have been substantially inferior in precision and performance to the majors. Consequently entries of small producers have been totally neglected by major producers. ... In fact, large firms in such industries as automobiles, electronics and electrical products, industrial machinery, and steel have purchased machine tools for their equipment investment only from major producers.

110 With the five steps of liberalization implemented by August 1963, the liberalization ratio in the machine tool industry had reached 90 percent. The remaining non-liberalized products were scheduled to be totally liberalized by October 1964. The liberalization program was prepared and implemented, allegedly taking into consideration 'the international competitiveness of each product.' At the first stage of the program in December 1961, 'in addition to the five most competitive products such as medium-sized engine lathes and knee-type milling machines, the list of products targeted for liberalization included eleven products that were

considered as "give-up" products. That is, products well beyond the capability of domestic production, and examples included multi-spindle hobbing machines and thread grinding machines.' This illustrates that the promotion of domestic production was not a policy of the highest priority (JDB 1964: pp.40–3).

111 For more details on industrial policy in 1960s Japan, see Miwa and Ramseyer (2002e), chapter 3 of which provides an extensive critical review of the conventional wisdom. Part II draws heavily on this chapter.

Chapter 3

112 In Japan, people prefer to use 'policies for medium and small-sized enterprises' to this expression. As is usual in Japan, I do not distinguish here medium-sized enterprises from smaller ones and therefore do not adopt this 'idiosyncratically Japanese' expression.

113 Worldwide interest in small businesses rose particularly after the 1970s, and in Japanese small businesses in relation to the country's economic development in the 1980s. See Miwa (1996a, ch. 2). Interest in Japanese small businesses and policies stems from a search for 'lessons' for the marketization of former socialist economies. On this point, see Miwa (1999).

114 I thank Ken'ichi Imai of the Asian Research Institute for this information. Many scholars suggest that 'Japan's main bank system' would be a useful reference for developing economies, of whom which Aoki and Patrick (1994) are representative. On Japan's main bank system, see Miwa (1996a: ch. 6) and Miwa and Ramseyer (2001c: chs 5 and 6, 2002d).

115 Likewise, a society where everybody can enjoy the highest level of medical care everywhere and at any time is impossible to achieve. Nobody can 'support' and 'promote' every small business in Japan, where the overwhelming majority of firms are small. In the same way, nobody can implement a policy to improve the 'international competitiveness' of every industry.

116 The definition of 'small business' (in common parlance in Japan, medium-sized and small enterprises) depends on the type of industry. In manufacturing and mining, 'small business' means an enterprise with less than ¥100 million in paid-up capital or fewer than 300 employees. These figures are originally from *Jigyosho tokei chosa* ('census of establishments') and therefore are establishment-based, not company-based (e.g., a company with a head office and five factories is counted as six in establishment-based statistics but as one in company-based statistics).

117 For example, see Komiya *et al.* (1988), Miwa (1996a), and Miwa and Ramseyer (2002e, 2003d). Chapter 9 of Miwa (1996a) identifies the effects of a government policy in the steel industry called the 'investment coordination policy.' Originally published in 1977, this paper was one of the pioneering works to identify the effects of 'industrial policy.'

118 Concerning this, see Chapter 4 of this book.

119 The conventional wisdom, that a series of deconcentration policies, as part of a 'democratization' policy in Japan, contributed much to Japan's economic growth, is also based on overvaluation of policy effects. Although there are famous examples such as Mitsui, Mitsubishi, and Sumitomo, there are various definitions of *zaibatsu*. *Zaibatsu* dissolution policy, for instance, was implemented by the post-surrender military government in Japan for the democratization of Japanese economic institutions, which used the term *zaibatsu* 'to include any private enterprise conducted for profit, or combination of such enterprises, which, by reason of relative size in any line or the cumulative power or its position in many lines, restricts competition or impairs the opportunity for others to engage in business independently, in any important segment of businesses, and any individual, family, allied group, or judicial person owning or controlling such an enterprise or combination.' The total number of *zaibatsu* on the designation list was eighty-three. See Miwa (1993b). For prewar *zaibatsu*, see also Miwa and Ramseyer (2002b); for *zaibatsu* dissolution programs, see Miwa and Ramseyer (2003a); for *keiretsu* and 'main bank,' see Miwa and Ramseyer (2001c, 2002a, 2002d, 2004b).

120 Because of conflicts of interest between small firms and their huge cost to the national economy, such restriction of competition is hardly easy to realize. Consequently, elimination of 'excessive competition,' particularly in the small business sector, has been an 'eternal' policy issue.

121 See Section 1.3.5.

122 The standard definition of small businesses, mentioned above, derives from article 2 of this Act.

123 The same applies to the image of the subcontracting system, which has also been criticized as embodying a 'dual structure.' For the details, see Miwa (1996a: ch. 2). Readers may comment that profit rates in small business are higher than in large firms simply because the hazard rate of the former is much higher and the profits include a big risk premium. However, note that the issue here is whether small business profit rates were much lower than expected due to the dual structure disadvantage, and I am arguing that on the contrary the profit rate was rather higher than expected. In addition, the hazard rate, at least in Japan, was not as high as is usually understood. So far as I know, no systematic data is available for small business hazard rates. In Japan, as a by-product of the *Basic Survey on the Reality of Manufacturing* (*Kigyo jittai kihon chosa hokoku-sho*; Statistics Bureau, MITI), we have two years of data on survival rates. The fourth edition, in 1971, covers the period 1969–71, towards the end of Japan's high-growth era, while the seventh edition, in 1987, covers the period 1985–7. The former states that the two-year hazard rate (= 1 − [survival rate]) for all manufacturing firms was 6.6 percent, for firms with one to three employees was 10.2 percent, for firms with four to nine employees was 5.4 percent, and for firms with ten to nineteen employees was 3.7 percent. The figures for 1985–7 were much lower than the corresponding figures for 1969–71.

124 It is a view also expressed as the 'financial dual structure,' 'the financial difficulty of small business,' or ' burden shifting to small business.' For the details of this view, see Miwa (1996a: ch. 5) and Miwa and Ramseyer (2001c: ch. 4). Closely connected with this view is the conventional wisdom that in Japan before the 1970s the allocation of credit was strictly controlled by the government. However, as has been shown in Miwa and Ramseyer (2004a), this wisdom is untrue.

125 Note that the above discussion, the second and the third points in particular, do not depend on the definition of small businesses. Accordingly, criticism that emphasizes the difference between firms with fewer than twenty-nine employees and those with 100–299 employees is ineffective. For the details, see Miwa (1996a: chs 2, 3).

126 As discussed in Part II (Section 2.3.12), a similar assumption underlies common views peculiar to the Japanese economy, emphasizing the singularity of the Japanese economy and the Japanese firm. See Miwa (*ibid.*) for critical comments on those views. Most of these views simply 'interpret' and 'theoretically explain' the phenomena, assuming both that those arguments are obvious and firmly proved, without careful examination, and that the policy or the system worked effectively.

127 *Nihon Keizai Shimbun* (*Japan Economic Journal*), 12 January 1975, cited in Miwa (1996a: p.53). For the details, see Miwa (*ibid.*: ch. 3).

128 See Miwa (*ibid.*: ch. 8) for a brief description of the industrial policy-formation process, and for more details see Miwa and Ramseyer (2002e: Part I).

129 I do not argue that even the amount of funds allocated to each region is 'indiscriminate,' for instance, proportional to its population. 'Regional development' policies as a whole had a strong income-redistributing effect between regions, but they were 'indiscriminate' in the sense that they treated equally developed regions 'equally.'

130 For example, the 14 March 1997 issue of *Nikkei Construction*. As a member of the Deregulation Subcommittee of the Administrative Reform Committee, I took charge of the review of the public facilities construction system and had many opportunities to confirm the facts. See Administrative Reform Committee (1998: pp.318–29, 548–64). See also Chapter 4 of this book for this organization.

131 See *ibid.* I will refer to the Administrative Reform Committee in the next chapter.

132 Calder (1988: pp.312–13), for example, observed that:

> While the Reagan administration in the mid-1980s was attempting to disband the U.S. Small Business Administration and end its meager and declining volume of subsidized loans, the small business-oriented People's Finance Corporation in Japan disbursed nearly the volume of subsidized loans annually of the vaunted Japan Export–Import Bank.

However, attentive readers will find almost the same policy menu in the Small Business Administration in the USA. See Parris (1968: ch. III), for instance.

Chapter 4

133 As is well known, at least in theory RPM can either promote or retard economic efficiency, depending on the circumstances. I table that issue for the purposes of this book. See, generally, Posner (1976: pp. 67–8, 146–66).

134 See *Decisions of the Fair Trade Commission*, vol. 29, pp.31–50. Note that this is an outline of the case rather than an economic analysis. For the latter, see Miwa (1991: ch. 7).

135 Neither discussion concerning the appropriateness of the policy in this case nor that concerning the 'regulation of abuses of positions of authority and responsibility' is the issue here. For the latter, see Miwa (1982: ch. 4; 1991: ch. 7).

136 The Japanese Diet consists of two Houses, the House of Representatives and the House of Councilors. The enactment of a new law usually requires the completion of the last two steps in both Houses.

137 This point applies not only to regulations but also to government policy in general, including industrial policy. See Miwa (1996a: ch. 8).

138 In some cases, interest groups other than those within the relevant industry will dominate the process. The Central Council for Job Stability of the Ministry of Labor has strongly opposed any deregulation and liberalization of the (charged) employment agency field, representing the interests of labor unions. On this matter, see ARC (1996: pp.242–9, 456–60).

139 See note 26 in Miwa (1998c: p.293) for an illustrative example of the Japan Medical Association's position under the Act on Central Conference for Social Security Medical Care enacted in 1950.

140 *Yomiuri Shimbun* is the biggest newspaper in Japan. Its circulation was nearly 10 million copies of the morning edition and 4.5 million copies of the evening edition during 1991–3. The evening editions are predominantly sold in packs together with morning editions. *Asahi Shimbun* is the second-largest paper, with circulations of 8 million and 4.5 million, respectively. The circulation of *Mainchi Shimbun*, the third-largest, is 4 million and 2 million, respectively. The so-called five nationwide newspapers, which include these three titles and the *Nihon Keizai Shimbun* (Japan Economic Journal) and *Sankei Shimbun*, account for 60 percent of national sales of daily papers and 66 percent of sales of evening papers. Tsuneo Watanabe is both president of the biggest newspaper company, Yomiuri, and writer-in-chief of this newspaper.

141 The other six industries are newspaper transportation, publishing, movie production, newspaper advertising agencies, textbook publishing, and broadcasting.

142 I deeply thank Naohiko Jinno for his cooperation in this research.

143 Before being elected to the Diet, Tagawa and Fujio worked for *Asahi Shimbun* and *Yomiuri Shimbun*, respectively. 'We strongly hoped to maintain the authority of newspapers, and commenced the project with an indomitable resolve' (Tagawa 1995: p.149). I deeply thank Seiichi Tagawa for his cooperation in this research.

144 Part of the process of these concerted actions of the JNCA is said to have involved the JNCA making a blacklist of persons opposing the interests of the industry, whose opinions JNCA members will not publish. There is no way to confirm this rumor, although several people in the industry have hinted that I am on the list.

145 As discussed elsewhere (notes 49 and 50 of Miwa 1997b), the JNCA strongly demanded that their representatives and supporters be accepted as members of the FTC's study groups. It finally achieved this.

146 During the period 1994–7, although they rarely surfaced, many took part in activities concerning this issue on various fronts, predominantly initiated by the JNCA. The activities usually focused on preventing the subcommittee of the FTC from reaching the direct conclusion that RPM exemptions be abolished. For instance, first the FTC was pressured to add many industry-friendly members to the subcommittee, but these efforts failed. After this, the

JNCA agreed with the FTC that a new committee be organized, with which the JNCA intended to have the conclusion of any report altered from a direct abolition to merely presenting arguments for and against the abolition. For the details of these activities, see Miwa (1997b: notes 49–51). In addition to the DS of the ARC, I was also a member of both the subcommittee and the parent committee of the FTC. Consequently, I was privy to much relevant information.

147 Although the name is similar, this body differs from the Government Headquarters for Promoting Administration Reform, which is the body that approved the Three-Year Program to Promote Administration Reform on 31 March 1998. All cabinet members and also other key figures, like the chairman of the FTC, belong to the latter, and the prime minister chairs this body. The former is an organization internal to the LDP.

148 For the final opinion and relevant detailed information, see ARC (1998). Miwa (1998a) extracts the relevant parts of the opinion and provides commentary.

149 Each member of the subcommittee and the ARC was subjected to immense pressure from many sides, some of which might be classed as blackmail. The campaign placed publishers under great pressure, which saw some of them abandon the publication of books or newspapers that advocated the re-evaluation, even though these works had been fully prepared for publication. See Miwa (1997b: p.41, note 1 and p.48, note 53).

150 The JNCA side placed strict limits on the circulation of the draft opinion. The interests of each newspaper company differed, and further opinions regarding the matter differed within the industry to a great extent. As a result, the JNCA always sent a big delegation to meetings with the DS.

151 During the same period, many Anti-monopoly Act exemptions were created either by revising or newly enacting laws, and the MIPA discussed in Part II (Sections 2.2.2 and 2.2.3 in particular) is a perfect example of this.

152 He repeated this same statement to this committee on 3 July.

153 The 1953 amendment of the Anti-monopoly Act covered many important issues, some of which I refer to in the text above. For the details of this amendment, see FTC (1997: pp.69–75). Consequently, the time spent at the meeting on the RPM exemption was limited.

154 As explained above, the creation of this study group was a political compromise. Obviously, the proposals are also compromising.

Conclusion

155 See the preface to the Japanese edition of Stigler (1975: p.i).

References

Administrative Reform Committee (Gyosei kaikaku iinkai, ARC) (1996) *Hikari kagayaku kuni wo mezashite – Kisei kanwa no suishin ni kansuru iken (1)* (Toward a Shining Country: Opinion to Promote Deregulation (1)). Tokyo: Gyosei kanri kenkyu senta (Administrative Management Research Center).

—— (1998) *Souri heno zen-teigen* (All Opinions to the Prime Minister). Tokyo: Gyosei kanri kenkyu senta.

Administrative Reform Conference (Gyosei kaikaku kaigi) (1997) *Chukan hokoku* (Interim Report), 3 September.

Aisan kogyo K.K. (1973) *Aisan kogyo 35 nen-shi* (35 Years of Aisan Industries Co.). Aisan kogyo K.K.

Ando, Yoshio (ed.) (1966) *Showa keizai-shi heno shogen, 2* (Testimonies to the Economic History of Showa, 2). Tokyo: Mainichi shimbun-sha.

Aoki, Masahiko and H. Patrick (1994) *The Japanese Main Bank System: Its Relevance for Developing and Transforming Economies*. Oxford: Clarendon Press.

Armstrong, M., S. Cowan, and J. Vickers (1994) *Regulatory Reform: Economic Analysis and British Experience*. Cambridge, Mass.: MIT Press.

Calder, K.E. (1988) *Crisis and Competition: Public Policy and Political Stability in Japan. 1949–1986*. Princeton, NJ: Princeton University Press.

Carliner, G. (1986) 'Industrial policy for emerging industries,' in P.R. Krugman (ed.), *Strategic Trade Policy and New International Economics*. Cambridge, Mass.: MIT Press.

Clark, R. (1985) 'Agency costs versus fiduciary duties,' in Pratt and Zeckhauser (eds), *Principals and Agents: The Structure of Business*. Cambridge, Mass.: Harvard Business School Press.

Coase, R.H. (1964) 'Comment,' *American Economic Review*, May.

Demsetz, H. and K. Lehn (1985) 'The structure of corporate ownership: causes and consequences,' *Journal of Political Economy*, 93 (6).

Dore, R. (1986) *Flexible Rigidities: Industrial Policy and Structural Adjustment in the Japanese Economy, 1970–80*. Stanford, Calif.: Stanford University Press.

—— (2002) 'Setting agendas,' in *Anglo-Japanese Academy Proceedings*, International Center for Comparative Law and Politics, University of Tokyo, Publication No. 7.

Economic Planning Agency (Keizai kikaku-cho), *Keizai hakusho* (Economic White Paper), annual publication.

Fair Trade Commission (1995) *Saihan tekiyo jogai ga mitomerareru chosakubutsu no toriatsukai nituuite (chukan houkoku)* (Concerning the Scope of Resale Price Maintenance Exemptions for Publications under the Antimonopoly Act (Interim Report)), July.

—— (1997) *Dokusen kinshi seisaku 50 nenshi (jo, ge)* (Fifty Years of Antimonopoly Policies (I, II)). Tokyo: Kosei torihiki kyokai.

Fukao, Junji (1956) *Kaiso-roku* (Recollections), mimeo.

—— (1979) *Gijutsu kaiso 70 nen* (70 Years of Recollections on Technology). Tokyo: Fukao Junji gijutsu kaiso 70 nen kanko-kai.

Gao, Bai (1997) *Economic Ideology and Japanese Industrial Policy*. Cambridge: Cambridge University Press.

Hara, Akira (1976) *Senji tosei keizai no kaishi* (Commencement of the Wartime Control Economy), in *Nihon rekishi 20: Kindai*, 7 (Japanese History, 20: Modern, 7). Tokyo: Iwanami shoten.

—— (1989) *Senji tosei* (Wartime Control), in Takafusa Nakamura (ed.) *'Keikaku-ka' to 'minshu-ka'* ('Planning' and 'Democratization'). Tokyo: Iwanami shoten.

Hashii, Makoto (1940a) *Kosakukikai to jidosha tosei* (Control on Machine Tools and Automobiles). Tokyo: Shoko gyosei-sha.

—— (1940b) *Kikai no jukyu-chosei* (Demand–Supply Coordination of Machines). Tokyo: Shoko gyosei-sha.

Hashimoto, Juro (1993) *Kikai kogyo shinko rinji sochi-ho ni kansuru minkan kigyo no hyoka – 'Kaisha-shi' wo mochiita bunseki* (Evaluation by Private Companies of the Act on Temporary Measures for the Promotion of the Machinery Industries: Study Based on 'Company Histories'). *Gunosis of Sangyo joho senta in Hosei University*, Vol. 2, March.

Hattori, Takushiro (1965) *Daitoa senso zenshi* (Total History of the Great East Asian War). Tokyo: Hara-shobo.

Hayasaka, Tsutomu (1964) *Kosakukikai to bunmei – zenshu* (Machine Tool and Civilization: The Complete Works). Tokyo: Hayasaka tsutomu zenshu kanko iinkai.

Hayashi, Shintaro (1953) *Kikai yushutsu shinko taisaku taikei shiken* (My View of the Export Promotion Policies for Machines), *Sangyo kikai* (Industrial Machinery), August–November.

—— (1961) *Nihon kikai yutshutsu ron* (On Japan's Machinery Exports). Tokyo: Toyo keizai shimpo-sha.

Heckman, J.J. (2000) 'Causal parameters and policy analysis in economics: a twentieth century retrospective,' *QJE*, February.

Hidaka, Junnosuke (1956) *Kikai kogyo shinko rinji sochi-hoan nitsuite* (Concerning the Draft Bill of the Act on Temporary Measures for the Promotion of the Machinery Industries), *Nikkiren kaiho*, May.

Hitachi Seiki K.K. (1963) *Hitachi seiki 25 nen no ayumi* (25 Years of Hitachi Seiki). Tokyo: Hitachi seiki shashi henshu iinkai.

Iida, Hikoshiro, Shoichi Hashimoto, and Hiroo Kato (1960) *Kikai kogyo* (The Machinery Industry). Tokyo: Keizai ohrai-sha.

Industrial Bank of Japan (Nihon kogyo ginko, IBJ) (1957) *Nihon kogyo ginko 50 nen-shi* (50 Years of the Industrial Bank of Japan). Tokyo: Nihon kogyo ginko, shiryo-shitsu.

Industrial Rationalization Investigation Group (Sangyo gorika chosakai) (1962) *Chukan hokoku-sho (jukogyo-bukai kosakukikai sho-iinkai)* (Interim Report (Machine Tool Subcommittee of the Heavy Industries Division). MITI.

Industrial Structure Investigation Group (Sangyo kozo chosakai), (1964) *Sangyo kozo chosakai jukogyo-bukai hokokusho: Fuzoku shiryo* (Report of the Industrial Structure Investigation Group, Heavy Industries Division: Materials). MITI.

—— (1965) *Nihon no sangyo kozo, dai 2 kan* (Industrial Structure in Japan, Volume II). Tokyo: Tsusho sangyo kenkyu-sha.

Ito, Takatoshi (1992) *The Japanese Economy*. Cambridge, Mass.: MIT Press.

Itoda, Shogo (1995) *Jirei: Dokusen kinshi-ho (shin-pan)* (Cases: The Antimonopoly Act (new edition)). Tokyo: Seirin shoin.

Japan Bearing Industry Association (1965) *Nihon no jikuuke kogyo no hatten katei* (Development Process of the Bearing Industry in Japan). Tokyo: Kikai shinko kyokai.

Japan Development Bank (Nihon kaihatsu ginko, JDB) (1958) *Nihon kaihatsu ginko to sono ayumi* (Japan Development Bank and its History). Tokyo: Nihon kaihatsu ginko.

—— (1963) *Nihon kaihatsu ginko 10 nen-shi* (Ten Years of Japan Development Bank). Tokyo: Nihon kaihatsu ginko.

—— (1976) *Nihon kaihatsu ginko 25 nen-shi* (25 Years of Japan Development Bank). Tokyo: Nihon kaihatsu ginko.

Japan Gear Industry Association (1990) *50 nen no ayumi* (Progress over 50 Years). Tokyo: Nihon haguruma kogyo-kai.

Japan Long-Term Credit Bank, Research Division (Nihon choki shinyo ginko, chosa-bu) (1966) *Kosakukikai kogyo no genjo to mondai-ten* (The Present State and the Problems of the Machine Tool Industry), *Chosa geppo* (Monthly Research Reports), December.

Japan Machine Tool Builders Association (Nihon kosakukikai kogyo-kai, JMTBA) (1962) *Nihon no kosakukikai kogyo hattatsu no katei* (Development Process of the Machine Tool Industry in Japan). Tokyo: Kikai kogyo shinko kyokai.

—— (1969) *Kosakukikai tokei yoran 1969* (Machine Tool Statistics Handbook 1969). Tokyo: Nihon kosakukiaki kogyo-kai.

—— (1992) *Seicho, henkaku – 10 nen no kiroku* (Growth and Change: Record of 10 Years). Tokyo: Nihon kosakukiaki kogyo-kai.

Johnson, C. (1982), *MITI and the Japanese Miracle: The Growth of Industrial Policy, 1925–1975*. Stanford, Calif.: Stanford University Press.

Kaizuka, Keimei (1973) *Keizai seisaku no kadai* (Issues on Economic Policy). Tokyo: University of Tokyo Press.

Kato, Hiroo (1960) *Kosakukikai kogyo no kozo to kadai* (Structure and Problems of the Machine Tool Industry), in Hiromi Arisawa (ed.) *Gendai sangyo koza IV: Kikai kogyo 2* (Modern Industries Series IV: The Machinery Industry 2). Tokyo: Iwanami shoten.

Kawasaki, Shigenori (1943) *Senji kikai gyosei* (Wartime Administration Concerning the Machinery). Tokyo: Dohbunkan shuppan.

Kim, Hyung-Ki, Michio Muramatsu, T.J. Pempel, and Kozo Yamamura (eds) (1995) *The Japanese Civil Service and Economic Development: Catalysts of Change*. Oxford: Clarendon Press.

Kitano, Shigeo (1944) *Gunju-sho oyobi Gunju kaisha-ho (kaitei-ban)* (The Munitions Ministry and the Munitions Company Act (revised edition)). Tokyo: Shoko gyosei-sha.

Komiya, Ryutaro (1990) *The Japanese Economy: Trade, Industry, and Government*. Tokyo: University of Tokyo Press.

Komiya, Ryutaro, Masahiro Okuno, and Kotaro Suzumura (eds) (1988) *Industrial Policy of Japan*. Tokyo: Academic Press.

Krugman, P. (1997) *The Age of Diminishing Expectations: U.S. Economic Policy in the 1990s*, 3rd edition. Cambridge, Mass.: MIT Press.

Kuroda Seiko K.K. (1995) *Kuroda seiko 70 nen-shi* (70 Years of Kuroda Seiko). Kuroda seiko K.K.

Kyogoku, Jun'ichi (1983) *Nihon no seiji* (Politics in Japan). Tokyo: University of Tokyo Press.

Laffont, J.-J. and J. Tirole (1993) *A Theory of Incentives in Procurement and Regulation*. Cambridge, Mass.: MIT Press.

Maekawa, Masao (1996) *Nakajima hikoki monogatari* (Story of Nakajima Aircraft Co.). Tokyo: Kojin-sha.

Magaziner, I.C. and T.M. Hout (1981) *Japanese Industrial Policy*. Berkeley, California. Institute of International Studies, University of California.

Magaziner, I.C. and R.B. Reich (1982) *Minding America's Business: The Decline and Rise of the American Economy*. New York: Harcourt Brace Jovanovich.

Milhaupt, C.J. and M.D. West (2002) 'Law's dominion and the market for legal elites in Japan,' University of Michigan, Olin Center for Legal and Economics Studies, 02-006, and Columbia Law School Center for Legal and Economics Studies, 206.

Ministry of Finance (Ookura-sho, MoF), Zaisei-shitsu (ed.) (1982) *Showa zaisei-shi* (Fiscal History of Showa), Vol. 20: Materials in English. Tokyo: Toyo keizai shimpo-sha.

—— (ed.) (1984) *Showa zaisei-shi* (Fiscal History of Showa), Vol. 1: *Sohsetsu, baisho, sengo-shori* (General Remarks, Reparations, and Postwar Management). Tokyo: Toyo keizai shimpo-sha.

Ministry of Finance, Showa zaisei-shi shiryo-shitsu (ed.) (1957) *Showa zaisei-shi, XI: Kin'yu, II* (Fiscal History of Showa, Vol. VI: Finance, II). Tokyo: Toyo keizai shimpo-sha.

Ministry of International Trade and Industry (Tsusho sangyo-sho or Tsusan-sho, MITI) *Tsusho sangyo-sho nenpo* (Annual Report of MITI), annual publication.

—— (1956) *Gijutsu hakusho* (White Paper on Technology). Tokyo: Kogyo gijutsu shuppan-sha.

—— (1957) *Sangyo gorika hakusho* (White Paper on Industrial Rationalization). Tokyo: Nikkan kogyo shimbun-sha.

—— (1961) *Shoko seisaku-shi, dai 9-kan, sangyo gorika (jo), senzen-hen* (History of Commerce Policies, Vol. 9, Industrial Rationalization (I), The Prewar Period). Tokyo: Shoko seisaku-shi kankokai.

—— (1962) *Shoko seisaku-shi, dai 3-kan, gyosei kiko* (History of Commerce Policies, Vol. 3, Administrative Machinery). Tokyo: Shoko seisaku-shi kankokai.

—— (1964) *Shoko seisaku-shi, dai 11-kan, sangyo tosei* (History of Commerce Policies, Vol. 11, Industry Control). Tokyo: Shoko seisaku-shi kankokai.

—— (1965) *Tsusho sangyo-sho 40 nen-shi* (40 Years of MITI). Tokyo: Tsusho shiryo chosa-kai.

—— (1972) *Shoko seisaku-shi, dai 10-kan, sangyo gorika (ge), sengo-hen* (History of Commerce Policies, Vol. 10, Industrial Rationalization (II), The Postwar Period). Tokyo: Shoko seisaku-shi kankokai.

—— (1976) *Shoko seisaku-shi, dai 18-kan, kikai kogyo (jo), senzen-hen* (History of Commerce Policies, Vol. 18, The Machinery Industry (I), The Prewar Period). Tokyo: Shoko seisaku-shi kankokai.

—— (1979) *Shoko seisaku-shi, dai 13-kan, kogyo gijutsu* (History of Commerce Policies, Vol. 13, Industrial Technology). Tokyo: Shoko seisaku-shi kankokai.

—— (1985a) *Shoko seisaku-shi, dai 1-kan, sosetsu (jo)* (History of Commerce Policies, Vol. 1, General Remarks (I)). Tokyo: Shoko seisaku-shi kankokai.

—— (1985b) *Shoko seisaku-shi, dai 2-kan, sosetsu (ge)* (History of Commerce Policies, Vol. 2, General Remarks (II)). Tokyo: Shoko seisaku-shi kankokai.

—— (1990) *Tsusyo sangyo seisaku-shi, dai 6-kan: Dai 2-ki, jiritsu kiban kakuritsu-ki (2)* (History of Trade and Industry Policies, Vol. 6: The Second Stage, The Establishment of the Foundation for Independence (2)). Tokyo: Tsusho sangyo chosakai.

—— (1992) *Tsusyo sangyo seisaku-shi, dai 3-kan: Dai 1-ki, keizai fukko-ki (2)* (History of Trade and Industry Policies, Vol. 3: The First Stage, Postwar Recovery (2)). Tokyo: Tsusho sangyo chosakai.

Ministry of International Trade and Industry, Heavy Industries Section (Jukogyo-ka) (1957) 7 *gyoshu no gorika kihon keikaku naru (2) – kinzoku kosakukikai* (Now Finalized the Rationalization Basic Plans in Seven Industries (2): The Machine Tool Industry,' *Nikkiren kaiho* (Monthly Bulletin of Japan Machinery Producers Federation), April.

Mishina, Yoritada (1958) *Nihon no kosakukikai* (Machine Tools in Japan). Tokyo: Nihon hyoron shin-sha.

Mitsubishi Heavy Industries (Mitsubishi jukogyo K.K.) (1964) *Hiroki 25 nen* (25 Years of Hiroshima Seiki). Hiroshima: Mitsubishi jukogyo K.K., Hiroshima seiki seisakujo.

Mitsubishi Heavy Industries (Moriya Sodan-yaku) (1988) *Meiko kosaku-bu no senzen-sengo-shi: Watashi to koh7uki seisan* (Prewar and Postwar Days in Nagoya Aircraft Manufacturing Plant: Aircraft Manufacturing and Myself). Nagoya: Mitsubishi jukogyo K.K. Nagoya Aircraft Manufacturing Plant (private circulation).

Miwa, Yoshiro (1982) *Dokkin-ho no keizaigaku* (Economics of the Anti-monopoly Act). Tokyo: Nihon keizai shimbun-sha.

—— (1990) *Nihon no kigyo to sangyo soshiki* (Firms and Industrial Organization in Japan). Tokyo: University of Tokyo Press.

—— (1991) *Nihon no torihiki kanko* (Japanese Trade Customs). Tokyo: Yuhi-kaku.

—— (1993a) *Kin'yu gyosei kaikaku* (Financial Administration Reform). Tokyo: Nihon keizai shimbun-sha.

—— (1993b) 'Economic effects of the anti-monopoly and other deconcentration policies in postwar Japan,' in Juro Teranishi and Yutaka Kosai (eds), *The Japanese Experience of Economic Reforms*. London: Macmillan.

—— (1995) 'Policies for small business in Japan,' in Kim, Hyung-Ki *et al.* (eds).

—— (1996a) *Firms and Industrial Organization in Japan*. London: Macmillan.

—— (1996b) *Seifu no noryoku, kodo to kino: (1) Senji tosei-ka no kosakukikai sangyo* (The competence, behavior, and function of the state: (1) the machine tool industry under wartime control), *Keizaigaku ronshu* (Economic Review), 61 (4) and 62 (1).

—— (1997a) *Seifu no noryoku, kodo to kino: (2) Kikai kogyo shinko rinji sochi-ho kano kikai kogyo* (The Competence, Behavior, and Function of the State: (2) The machinery industries under the Act on Temporary Measures for the Promotion of the Machinery Industry), *Keizaigaku ronshu*, 63 (1, 3).

—— (1997b) 'Shakaiteki kisei' no seiji keizaigaku (Political economy of 'social regulation'), *Keizaigaku ronshu*: 63 (2).

—— (1997c) *Naze chosakubutsu saihan seido wo mondai ni surunoka* (Why we re-evaluate the present RPM exemptions for publications under the Anti-monopoly Act), *Keizai semina*, September.

—— (1997d) *Chosakubutsu saihan-sei mondai ga shitekishita mono?* (What has the battle over the RPM exemptions for publications provoked?), *Keizai semina*, November.

—— (1997e) *Kiseikanwa ha akumu desuka?* (Is Deregulation a Nightmare?). Tokyo: Toyo keizai shimpo-sha.

—— (1998a) *Chosakubutsu saihan wo meguru kobo* (The battle over the RPM exemptions for publications), *Ronso toyo keizai*, November.

—— (1998b) *Seizogyo deha taikenzumi – Kisei kanwa gyosei kaikaku ga hiraku keizai shakai* (The matter has already been settled in the manufacturing sector: our economic society finds a way through deregulation and administrative reform), *Ekonomisuto*, 2 February.

—— (1998c) *Seifu no noryoku* (The Competence of the State). Tokyo: Yuhi-kaku.

—— (1999) ' "Market" and "marketization": from the Japanese experience,' *Finansharu rebyu* (Financial Review), No. 50, March.

Miwa, Yoshiro and J.M. Ramseyer (2000a) 'Corporate governance in transitional economies: lessons from the pre-war Japanese cotton textile industry,' *Journal of Legal Studies*, January.

—— (2000b) 'Seisaku kin'yu to keizai hatten: Senzenki Nihon kogyo ginko no keesu' (Policy finance and economic growth: the case of the prewar Industrial Bank of Japan), *Keizaigaku ronshu*, 66 (3).

—— (2000c) 'Rethinking relationship-specific investments: subcontracting in the Japanese automobile industry,' *Michigan Law Review*, August.

—— (2001a) '*Nihon no keizai seisaku to seisaku kenkyu*' (Japanese economic policy and policy research),' *Keizai kenkyu*, 52 (3).

—— (2001b) '"Keiretsu no kenkyu"no keiretsu no kenkyu' (Research on the keiretsu in 'Research on the Keiretsu'), *Keizaigaku ronshu*, 67 (2, 3).

—— (2001c) *Nihon keizai ron no gokai: 'Keiretsu' no jubaku kara no kaiho* (Misunderstandings in the Theory of the Japanese Economy: Liberation from the Spell of the 'keiretsu'). Tokyo: Toyo keizai shimpo-sha.

—— (2002a) 'The fable of the keiretsu,' *Journal of Economics and Management Strategy*, summer.

—— (2002b) 'Banks and economic growth: implications from Japanese history,' *Journal of Law and Economics*, April.

—— (2002c) 'The value of prominent directors: corporate governance and bank access in transitional Japan,' *Journal of Legal Studies*, June.

—— (2002d) 'The myth of the main bank: Japan and comparative corporate governance,' *Law and Social Inquiry*, spring.

—— (2002e) *Sangyo seisaku ron no gokai: kodo seicho no shinjitsu* (Misunderstandings about Industrial Policy: The Truth about High Growth). Tokyo: Toyo keizai shimpo-sha.

—— (2002f) 'Who appoints them, what do they do? Evidence on outside directors from Japan,' Harvard Law School, Olin Center for Law, Economics and Business, 374.

—— (2003a) 'Does ownership matter? Evidence from the zaibatsu dissolution program,' *Journal of Economics and Management Strategy*, spring.

—— (2003b) '*Kin'yu kisei no seiji keizai gaku: Shusshi ho 2 jo 3 ko ni yoru nonbanku kin'yu gaisha CP no hakko seigen*' (The political economy of financial regulation: commercial paper issues by nonbank intermediaries), *Keizaigaku ronshu*, 68 (4).

—— (2003c) 'Property rights and indigenous tradition among early twentieth-century Japanese firms,' in A. Rosett and L. Cheng (eds), *Asian Law and Development: Universal Norms and Local Practices*. New York: RoutledgeCurzon.

—— (2003d) 'Capitalist politicians, socialist bureaucrats? Legends of government planning from Japan,' *Antitrust Bull*, fall.

—— (2003e) 'The legislative dynamic: evidence from the deregulation of the financial services industry in Japan,' in D. Foote (ed.), *Law in Japan: A Turning Point?* University of Washington Press (forthcoming).

—— (2003f) 'Financial malaise and the myth of the misgoverned bank,' in C.J. Milhaupt (ed.), *Global Markets, Domestic Institutions: Corporate Law and Governance in a New Era of Cross-Border Deals*. New York: Columbia University Press, Spring.

—— (2004a) 'Directed credit? The loan market in high-growth Japan,' *Journal of Economics and Management Strategy*.

—— (2004b) *Fable of the Keiretsu and Other Tales from Japan We Wish Were True*. Chicago, Ill.: University of Chicago Press.

Mori, Chikao (1943) *Kikai tosei* (Control of the Machinery). Tokyo: Shoko gyosei-sha.

Morozumi, Yoshihiko (1966) *Sangyo seisaku no riron* (Theory of Industrial Policy). Tokyo: Nihon keizai shimbun-sha.

Murakami, Katsuhiko (1994) '*Gunju sangyo*' (The munitions industry), in Ohishi (ed.), *Nihon teikoku-shugi-shi, 3: dai 2-ji taisen-ki* (History of Imperialism in Japan, 3: Period of World War II). Tokyo: University of Tokyo Press.

Nakahara, Shigetoshi (1981) *Daitoa hokyu-sen* (The Great East Asian Supply War). Tokyo: Hara-shobo.

Nakamura, Takafusa (1974) *Nihon no keizai tosei – Senji-sengo no keiken to kyokun* (Economic Control in Japan: Experiences and Lessons from the Wartime and Postwar Period). Tokyo: Nihon keizai shimbun-sha.

—— (1977) '*Senso keizai to sono hokai*' (War economy and its collapse), in *Nihon rekishi, 21: Kindai, 8* (Japanese History, 21: Modern, 8). Tokyo: Iwanami shoten.

—— (1983) *Economic Growth in Prewar Japan*. New Haven, Conn.: Yale University Press.

—— (1989) '*Gaisetsu: 1937–54 nen*' (Summary: 1937–54), in Takafusa Nakamura (ed.), '*Keikaku-ka*' to '*minshu-ka*' ('Planning' and 'Democratization'). Tokyo: Iwanami shoten.

—— (1995) *The Postwar Japanese Economy: Its Development and Structure, 1937–1994*, 2nd edition. Tokyo: University of Tokyo Press.

Nakamura, Takafusa and Akira Hara (1972) '*Keizai shin-taisei*' (New economic order), in Nihon seiji gakkai (Japan Political Sciences Association) (ed.), '*Konoe shin taisei*' *no kenkyu* (Studies of 'Konoe New Order'). Tokyo: Iwanami shoten.

Niigata Metalworks K.K. (1968) *Niigata tekkojo 75 nen-shi* (75 Years of Niigata Metalworks). Niitata tekkojo shiryo hensan iinkai.

Noguchi, Yukio (1995) *1940-nen taisei: Saraba 'senji keizai'* (The Year 1940 Regime: Farewell to 'Wartime Economy'). Tokyo: Toyo keizai shimpo-sha.

Ohkawa, Kazushi and Henry Rosovsky (1973) *Japanese Economic Growth: Trend Accumulation in the Twentieth Century*. Stanford, Calif.: Stanford University Press.

Okazaki, Tetsuji (1988) '*Dainiji sekai taisen-ki no Nihon ni okeru senji keikaku keizai no kozo to unko – Tekko bumon wo chushin toshite*' (Structure and enforcement of wartime planned economy in Japan during the World War II period: focusing upon the steel sector), *Shakai kagaku kenkyu* (Social Science Studies) 40 (4).

—— (1999) 'Corporate governance,' in Okazaki and Okuno-Fujiwara (eds).

Okazaki, Tetsuji and Masahiro Okuno-Fujiwara (eds) (1999) *The Japanese Economic System and Its History* (translated by Susan Herbert). Oxford: Oxford University Press.

Okumura, Shoji (1977) *Gijutsu-shi wo miru me* (A Look at the History of Technology). Tokyo: Gijutsu to ningen.

Onozuka, Ichiro (1962) *Sengo zosen-shi – Taiheiyo senso to keikaku zosen* (Postwar History of Ship-building: Pacific War and Planned Shipbuilding). Tokyo: Nihon kaiji shinko-kai.

Parris, A.W. (1968) *The Small Business Administration*. New York: Frederick A. Praeger.

Posner, R.A. (1976) *Antitrust Law: An Economic Perspective*. Chicago, Ill.: University of Chicago Press.

Ramseyer, J.M. (1996) *Odd Markets in Japanese History: Law and Economic Growth*. Cambridge: Cambridge University Press.

Ramseyer, J.M. and F.M. Rosenbluth (1993) *Japan's Political Market Place*. Cambridge, Mass.: Harvard University Press.

Reich, R.B. (1987) *Tales of a New America*. New York: Times Books.

Rosovsky, H. (1972) 'What are the lessons of Japanese economic history?' in A.J. Youngson (ed.), *Economic Development in the Long Run*. London: Allen & Unwin.

Saga, Shintaro (1953) '*Yushutsu shinko taisaku no hansei – Hayashi jimukan no kikai yushutsu shinko taisaku taikei shiken ni yosete*' (Reconsideration of export promotion policies: response to Official Hayashi's view on the measures to promote machinery exports), *Sangyo kikai*, November.

Sawai, Minoru (1984) '*Senji keizai tosei no tenkai to nihon kosakukikai kogyo – Nicchu senso-ki wo chushin to shite*' (Development of wartime control and the machine tool industry: focusing upon the Sino-Japanese War period), *Shakai kagaku kenkyu* (Social Science Studies), 36 (1).

—— (1993) '*Senzen-senchu-ki Nihon ni okeru kosakukikai kigyo no gijutsu to keiei*' (Technology and management of machine tool makers in prewar and wartime Japan), in Takeoka, Takahashi, and Nakaoka (eds), *Shin-gijutsu no dounyu* (Introducing New Technology). Dobunkan shuppan.

Scherer, F.M. and D. Ross (1990) *Industrial Market Structure and Economic Performance*, 3rd edition. Boston: Houghton Mifflin.

Shoko gyosei-shi kankokai (1955) *Shoko gyosei-shi* (History of Commerce Administration), II and III. Tokyo: Shoko gyosei-shi kankokai.

Small and Medium-sized Enterprise Agency (Chusho kigyo-cho, SMEA) (1992) *Chusho kigyo shisaku no aramashi* (Outline of Small Business Policies). Tokyo: Chusho kigyo-cho.

Smith, A. (1776) *An Inquiry into the Nature and Causes of the Wealth of Nations* (London). Modern Library edition, 1937, New York: Random House.

Spulber, D.F. (ed.) (2002) *Famous Fables of Economics: Myths of Market Failure*. Malden: Basil Blackwell.

Stigler, G.J. (1965) 'The economist and the state,' *American Economic Review*, March [reproduced as chapter 4 of Stigler 1975].

—— (1975) *The Citizen and the State*. Chicago: University of Chicago Press.

—— (1988) *Memories of an Unregulated Economist*. New York: Basic Books.

—— (1992) 'Law and economics?' *Journal of Law and Economics*, October.

Stigler, G.J. and C. Friedland (1962) 'What can regulators regulate? The case of electricity,' *Journal of Law and Economics*, October.

Sugiyama, Hiroshi (1966a) '*Showa 41 nendo jukogyo-kyoku kankei yosan, zaiseitoyuushi, zeiseikaisei ni tsuite*' (The budget, fiscal investment and loan program, and tax reforms, in relation to the Heavy Industries Bureau, for fiscal year 41 of Showa), *Nikkiren kaiho*, March.

—— (1966b) '*Kikai kogyo shinko rinji sochi-ho no kaisei: Sono seika to kongo no unyo*' (Revision of the Act on Temporary Measures for the Promotion of the Machinery Industries: past performance and future enforcement), *Nikkiren kaiho*, May.

Tagawa, Seiichi (1995) *Yareba dekiru yase-gaman no michi* (Never Admit Defeat before Accomplishing the Purpose). Tokyo: Gyoken-sha.

Teratani, Takeaki (1993) *Zosengyo no fukko to hatten* (Recovery and Development of the Shipbuilding Industry). Tokyo: Nihon keizai hyoron-sha.

Tokyo Chamber of Commerce (1941) *Zenkoku ni okeru chusho kigyo godo no tenbo* (Future of Small Business Mergers across the Country). Tokyo: Tokyo shoko kaigi-sho.

Toshiba (Tokyo shibaura denki) K.K. (1963) *Tokyo shibaura denki K.K. 85 nen-shi* (85 Years of Toshiba). Tokyo: Tokyo shibaura denki K.K.

Toyoda, Eiji (1985) *Ketsudan* (Resolution). Tokyo: Nihon keizai shimbun-sha.

Toyoda Machine Works K.K. (1991) *Waza ni gijutsu wo motomete – Toyoda koki K.K. 50 nen-shi* (In Search for Technology in Skills: 50 Years of Toyoda Koki K.K.). Toyoda Koki K.K., henshu iinkai.

Toyoda, Masataka (1942) *Kigyo seibi ha doushite suruka?* (How We Promote Enterprise Reorganization?). Tokyo: Shoko gyosei-sha.

Toyo Keizai Shimpo-sha (1950) *Showa sangyo-shi* (Industrial History of Showa), Vol. 1. Tokyo: Toyo keizai shimpo-sha.

Trezise, P.H. and Yukio Suzuki (1976) 'Social and cultural factors in Japanese economic growth,' in H. Patrick and H. Rosovsky (eds), *Asia's New Giant: How the Japanese Economy Works*. Washington, DC: Brookings Institution.

Tsuruta, Toshimasa (1982) *Sengo Nihon no sangyo seisaku* (Industrial Policy in Postwar Japan). Tokyo: Nihon keizai shimbun-sha.

—— (1988) 'The rapid growth era,' in Komiya *et al.* (eds).

Tyson, L. D'Andrea and J. Zysman (1989) 'Preface: the argument outlined,' in C. Johnson, L. D'Andrea Tyson and J. Zysman (eds), *Politics and Productivity: The Real Story of Why Japan Works*. New York: Ballinger.

Ueda, Kazuo (1999) 'The financial system and its regulations,' in Okazaki and Okuno-Fujiwara (eds).

US Strategic Bombing Survey (1946) *The Effects of Strategic Bombing on Japan's War Economy*. Overall Economic Effects Division.

Vogel, E. (1979) *Japan as Number One: Lessons for America*. Cambridge, Mass.: Harvard University Press.

von Hayek, F. (1945) 'The use of knowledge in society,' *American Economic Review*, September.

Woodall, B. (1996) *Japan Under Construction: Corruption, Politics, and Public Works*. Berkeley Calif.: University of California Press.

World Bank (1992) *The East Asian Miracle: Economic Growth and Public Policy*. Oxford: Oxford University Press.

Yokokura, Takashi (1988) 'Small and medium enterprises,' in Komiya *et al.* (eds).

Yonekura, Atsushi (1965a) '*Kikai kogyo shinko rinji sochi-ho no igi to zaisei shikin tokubetsu yuushi no motarashita koka* (The Significance of the Act on Temporary Measures for the Promotion of the Machinery Industries and the Effect of Fiscal Fund Special Loans), *Nikkiren kaiho*, January.

—— (1965b) '*Kikai kogyo shinko rinji sochi-ho ha ikani kaizen sarerubekika: sono hihan to kaizen no hoko*' (How the Act on Temporary Measures for the Promotion of the Machinery Industries should be improved: critical review and the direction of improvement), *Nikkiren kaiho*, April.

Yonekura, Seiichiro (1993) '*Seifu to kigyo no dainamizumu: Sangyo seisaku no sofuto na sokumen — kikaik-ogyo shinko rinji sochi-ho no kanagata-kogyo ni ataeta eikyo kara*' (Dynamism in the relationship between the government and enterprises: 'soft' side of industrial policy – from the impact of the Act on Temporary Measures for the Promotion of the Machinery Industries on the Metal Mold Manufacturing Industry), *Hitotsubashi daigaku kenkyu nenpo, shogaku kenkyu*, August.

Index

Index of Names

For Product Safety Concerns and Information please contact our EU
representative GPSR@taylorandfrancis.com
Taylor & Francis Verlag GmbH, Kaufingerstraße 24, 80331 München, Germany

www.ingramcontent.com/pod-product-compliance
Ingram Content Group UK Ltd.
Pitfield, Milton Keynes, MK11 3LW, UK
UKHW021836240425
457818UK00006B/205